Street by Stree

BLACK...
PRESTON

CHORLEY, CLEVELEYS, FLEETWOOD, LEYLAND, LYTHAM ST ANNE'S, POULTON-LE-FYLDE

Bamber Bridge, Clayton-le-Woods, Coppull, Eccleston, Freckleton, Kirkham, Knott End-on-Sea, Longton, Preesall, Thornton, Warton

3rd edition August 2005
© Automobile Association Developments Limited 2005

Original edition printed May 2001

Ordnance Survey® This product includes map data licensed from Ordnance Survey® with the permission of the Controller of Her Majesty's Stationery Office. © Crown copyright 2005. All rights reserved. Licence number 399221.

Published by AA Publishing (a trading name of Automobile Association Developments Limited, whose registered office (from 1st October 2005) will be Fanum House, Basing View, Basingstoke, Hampshire RG21 4EA. Registered number 1878835).

Mapping produced by the Cartography Department of The Automobile Association. (A02417)

A CIP Catalogue record for this book is available from the British Library.

Printed by Oriental Press in Dubai.

Ref: ML075y

Key to map pages	ii-iii
Key to map symbols	iv-1
Enlarged map pages	2-7
Main map pages	8-97
Index – towns & villages	98
Index – streets	98-113
Index – featured places	113-115
Acknowledgements	115

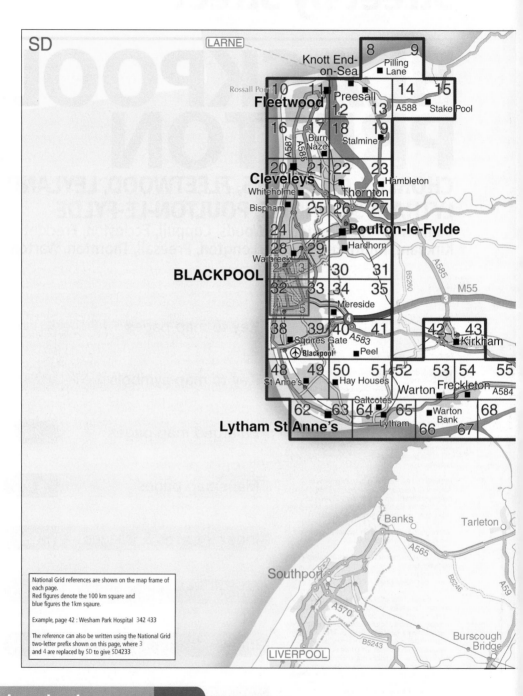

SD

LARNE

8　9

Knott End-on-Sea
Pilling Lane

Rossall Point　10　11
Fleetwood　Preesall　14　15
12　13　A588　Stake Pool

16　17　18　19
Burn Naze　Stalmine
A587　A585

20　21　22　23
Cleveleys　Hambleton
Whiteholme　Thornton

Bisphan　25　26　27

24　Poulton-le-Fylde

28　29　Hardhorn

Warbreck　3

BLACKPOOL　30　31

32　33　34　35
Mereside

B5260　M55

38　39　40　41　42　43
Squires Gate　A583　Kirkham
Blackpool　Peel

48　49　50　51　52　53　54　55
St Anne's　Hay Houses　Warton　Freckleton　A584
Saltcotes
62　63　64　65　Warton Bank　68
Lytham St Anne's　Lytham　66　67

Banks　Tarleton

A565

Southport

A570　B5246　A59

B5243　Burscough Bridge

LIVERPOOL

National Grid references are shown on the map frame of each page.
Red figures denote the 100 km square and blue figures the 1km sqaure.

Example, page 42 : Wesham Park Hospital 342 433

The reference can also be written using the National Grid two-letter prefix shown on this page, where 3 and 4 are replaced by SD to give SD4233

Enlarged scale pages 1:10,000 6.3 inches to I mile

0　1/4　miles　1/2

0　1/4　1/2　kilometres　3/4　I

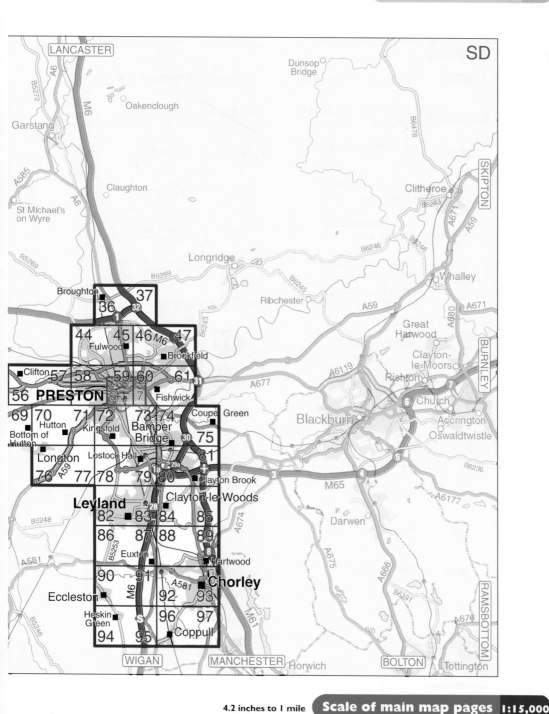

SD

LANCASTER
Dunsop Bridge
Oakenclough
Garstang
Claughton
St Michael's on Wyre
Clitheroe
SKIPTON
Longridge
Ribchester
Whalley
Broughton
37
36 **32**
44 **45** **46** M6 **47**
Fulwood
Brookfield
Great Harwood
Clayton-le-Moors
Clifton
57 **58** **59** **60** **61** **31**
56 PRESTON
Fishwick
Rishton
Church
BURNLEY
7
6
69 **70** **71** **72** **73** **74**
Hutton
Kingsfold
Bamber Bridge
Coupe Green
Blackburn
Accrington
Oswaldtwistle
Bottom of Hutton
30
75
81
Longton
Lostock Hall
5
76 **77** **78** **79** **80**
Clayton Brook
Clayton-le-Woods
3
M65
4
Leyland
82 **83** **84** **85**
Darwen
86 **87** **88** **89**
Euxton
8
Hartwood
90 **91**
M6
A581
Chorley
Eccleston
92 **93**
Heskin Green
96 **97**
94 **95**
Coppull
RAMSBOTTOM
WIGAN
MANCHESTER Horwich
BOLTON
Tottington

4.2 inches to 1 mile   Scale of main map pages 1:15,000

0   1/4   miles   1/2   3/4
0   1/4   1/2   kilometres 3/4   1   1 1/4   1 1/2

iv

Junction 9	Motorway & junction
Services	Motorway service area
	Primary road single/dual carriageway
Services	Primary road service area
	A road single/dual carriageway
	B road single/dual carriageway
	Other road single/dual carriageway
	Minor/private road, access may be restricted
← ←	One-way street
	Pedestrian area
	Track or footpath
	Road under construction
	Road tunnel
P	Parking
P+	Park & Ride
	Bus/coach station
	Railway & main railway station
	Railway & minor railway station
⊖	Underground station

⊖	Light railway & station
+++++++++	Preserved private railway
LC	Level crossing
•—•—•—•	Tramway
-----------	Ferry route
....	Airport runway
— · — · — · —	County, administrative boundary
ᵛᵛᵛᵛᵛᵛᵛᵛᵛᵛᵛ	Mounds
17	Page continuation 1:15,000
3	Page continuation to enlarged scale 1:10,000
	River/canal, lake, pier
	Aqueduct, lock, weir
465 ▲ Winter Hill	Peak (with height in metres)
	Beach
	Woodland
	Park
	Cemetery
	Built-up area
	Featured building

⌐⌐⌐⌐⌐⌐	City wall	♟	Castle
A&E	Hospital with 24-hour A&E department	🏛	Historic house or building
PO	Post Office	Wakehurst Place NT	National Trust property
📖	Public library	Ⓜ	Museum or art gallery
𝑖	Tourist Information Centre	🐓	Roman antiquity
𝑖	Seasonal Tourist Information Centre	⚲	Ancient site, battlefield or monument
■ ■	Petrol station, 24 hour Major suppliers only	▬▬	Industrial interest
†	Church/chapel	❋	Garden
🚺	Public toilets	◉	Garden Centre Garden Centre Association Member
♿	Toilet with disabled facilities	🌳	Garden Centre Wyevale Garden Centre
PH	Public house AA recommended	🌲	Arboretum
🍴	Restaurant AA inspected	🐄	Farm or animal centre
Madeira Hotel ▬	Hotel AA inspected	🦌	Zoological or wildlife collection
🎭	Theatre or performing arts centre	🦜	Bird collection
🎥	Cinema	🦆	Nature reserve
⚑	Golf course	🐟	Aquarium
▲	Camping AA inspected	Ⅴ	Visitor or heritage centre
🚐	Caravan site AA inspected	⚐	Country park
▲🚐	Camping & caravan site AA inspected	◑	Cave
🎡	Theme park	🗼	Windmill
🏛	Abbey, cathedral or priory	🛢	Distillery, brewery or vineyard

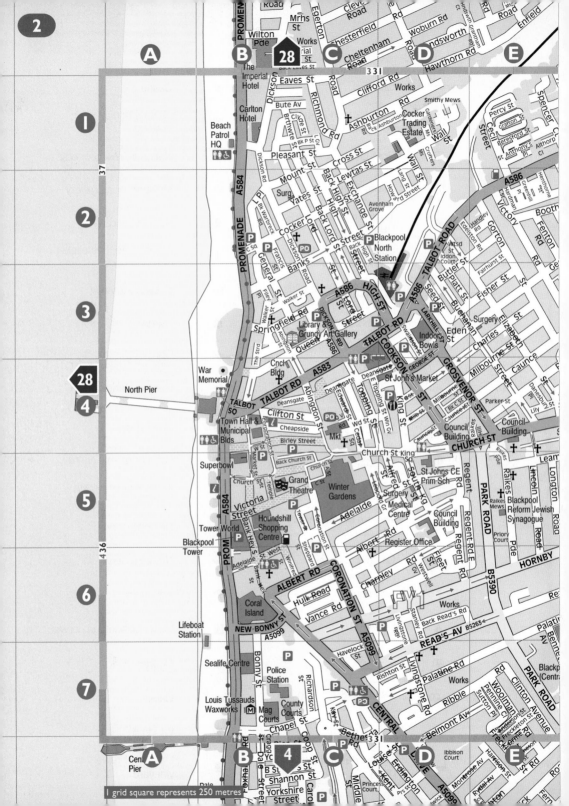

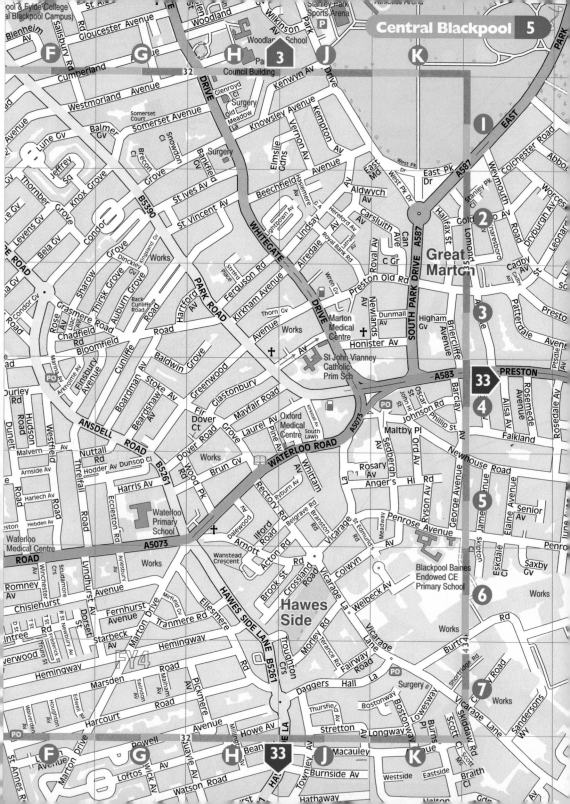

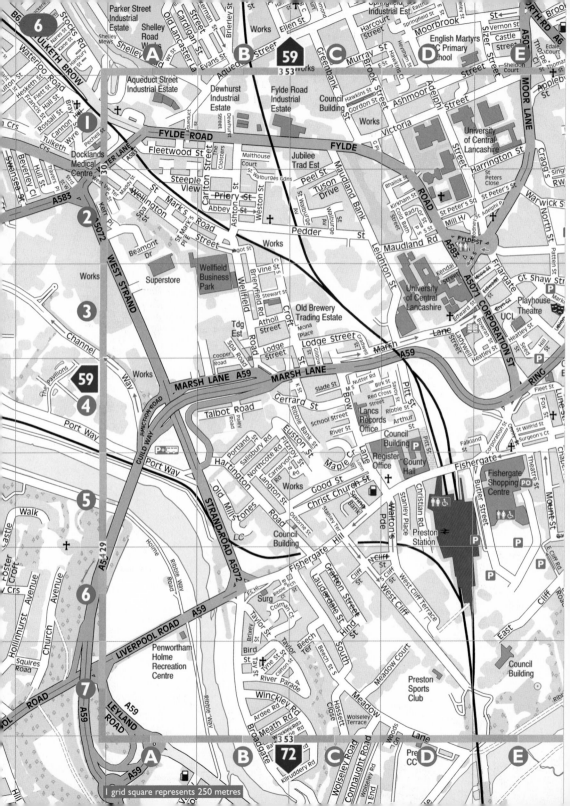

I grid square represents 250 metres

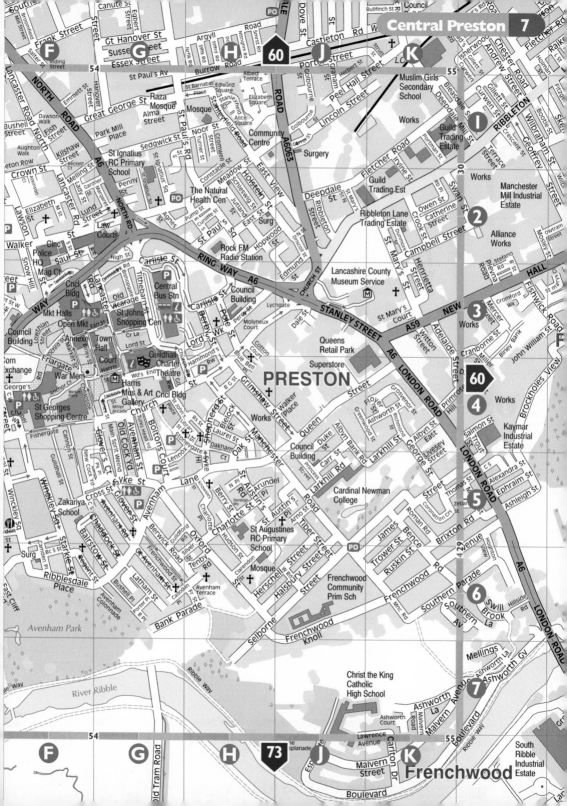

PRESTON

Frenchwood

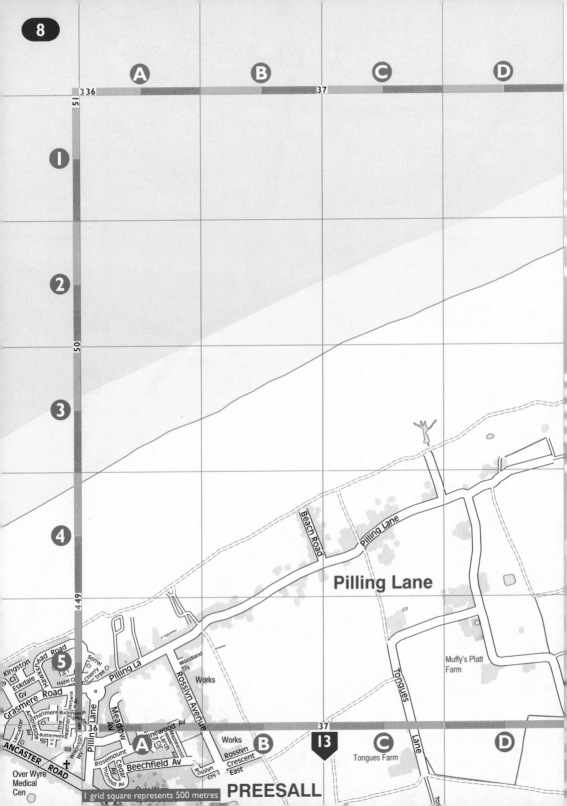

8

A   B   C   D

336   37

51

1

2

50

3

449

4

Beach Road

Pilling Lane

Pilling Lane

Muffy's Platt Farm

5

Kingston Cl
Eskdale Gv
Grasmere Road
Hawkswead Road
The Heathers
Lancaster
Ambleside
Buttermere Cl
Windermere

Sorrel Cl
Cherry Tree Cl
Hazel Cl
Buckthorn Pl
Lavender
Verbena
KC

Pilling La
Pilling Lane

Woodland Crs

Works

Rosslyn Avenue

Tongues Lane

Pilling Lane

Meadow AV

Winson

Pinewood Av
Larch Cl
Cedar Av
Thornhill Rd
Maplewood Rd
Rosemount
Beechfield Av
Rosslyn Crs

336   37

A   Works   B   **13**   C   D

ANCASTER ROAD

Over Wyre Medical Cen

Rosslyn Crescent East

Tongues Farm

PREESALL

1 grid square represents 500 metres

E   F   39   G   H   40   51

I

2

50

3

Cocker's Dyke
Houses

Fluke Hall Lane

Fluke
Hall

Fluke Hall Lane

Sandfield
Cottage

4   Fluke   Hall

Carr House
Farm

Beech House

Duck Street

449

Libby
Lane

Pilling St Johns
CE School

5

Wheel Lane

Townson
Hill

38   E   39   F   14   G   H   40

Smithson's

Hooles Farm

**Smallwood
Hey**

St Johns
Avenue

Pasture House
Farm

Lane   Smallwood   Hey   Road

A B C D

330 31

1

48

2

Rossall Point

Sea Wall

Outer

Cemetery

Princes Way

West Gate
Knowsley
Lancaster
Gate
High Gate
The Ridgeway
Leighton Av
St Ca
Rossall Grange Lan

Golf Course

Fleetwood
Golf Club

Teviot Av
Ettrick Av

3

47

Fleetwood
Charles Saer
Community
Prim Sch

Saer
Douglas
H Ct
Calder
Lothian
Avenue
Grange
Leven Ct
Creta
Esk N
Waverl

Princes Way

Medlock Av
Rothwell Dr

Rede Avenue
Crake Avenue
Burnside Av

Eden Av
St John Av
Frothway
Derwent Av

PO

4

Chatsworth

Avenue

Eamont Pl

Tr Av
S Ct
Wansbeck Av
To
B Pl

Hodder Avenue

Navena Av

Lazenby Av
Alder Ct
Elf Ct
Kew Ct

Allen W
Tees Ct
Cri deas

Brock Av

Pike Ct

Silverdale

Av
Northway
Beck Ct
B Pl Ct

Duddon Avenue

Fleetwood
High School

Marine Pde

Buttermere Av

Fern Ct

Furness Av

Middleton Av
Caton Av
Mere Ct
Eskdale Av
Tarn Ct

Carlisle Avenue

Parade

5

446

Marine
Parade
Fairway

Tatham
Court
W Ct

Inglewood Ct
Ennerdale Avenue
Cartmel Av

Larkholme
Pde
Bowness

Larkholme Avenue
Newby Ct

Lark Ct
Kirkstone Av

Southway

Parade

330 31

A B 16 C D

Ben
tham
Av

Thirlmere Av

Patterdale

Broadway

Falmouth
Avenue
The
Roundway
Fairway
Hov Av

Sea Wall

Dean Av
Million

Ullsw
Av
Sevenn
Avon
Str

Windermere

Bowland Av
H
Larkholme
Prim Sch

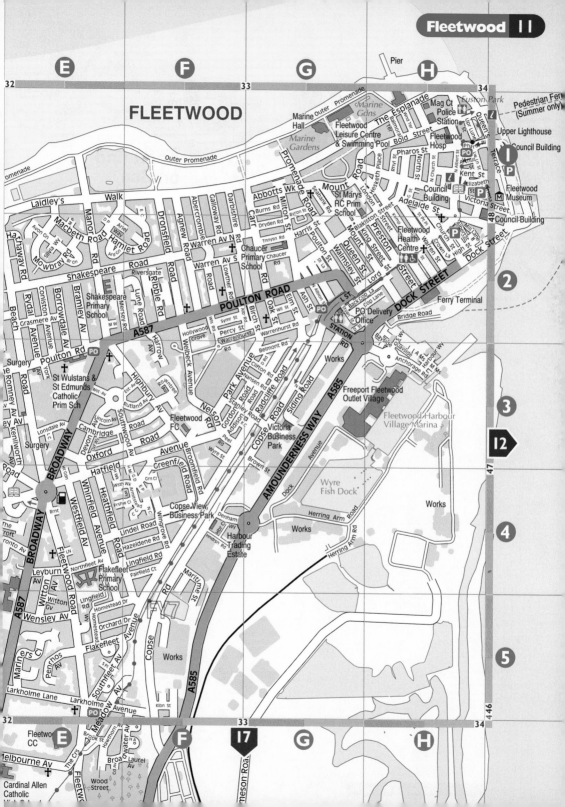

12

A B C D

334
Euston Park
Mag Ct
Police
Station
Upper Lighthouse
Council Building
BOURNE MAY ROAD ESPLANADE
Fleetwood Hosp
Knott End Golf Club
Worsley
Salisbury
BARTON SQ
B5270
Over Wyre Medical Cen
PO
Westbourne Road
Plantation Avenue
Holme Road
Barton Av
Ashton Av
Wayside
Quale
Fairway Gdns
LANCASTER ROAD
Coniston Avenue
Kingston Cl
Eskdale Cl
Grasmere Road
Hawkshead Road
Kent St

1

Council Building
Victoria Street
Council Building
Fleetwood Museum
Parksway
Links
Wyresdale Rd
Bleasdale Rd
Holmefield Rd
Lilac Av
Knott End-on-Sea

2
STREET
Dock Street
Ferry Terminal
The Glen
Hackensall Road
Golf Course
Meadow
Lane

Harbour Wy
Garage Rd

3
Works
Hackensall Hall
Whinny Lane
whinny Lane
New Heys Farm
Brine Wells
Clods Carr Lane

11

47

4
Coat Walls Farm

446

5
Brine Wells
Agglebys

334
35
A B **18** C D

I grid square represents 500 metres

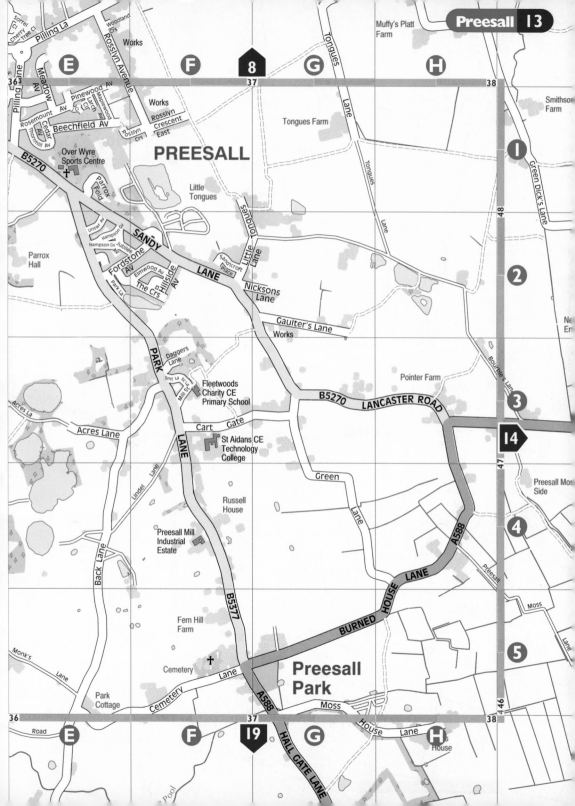

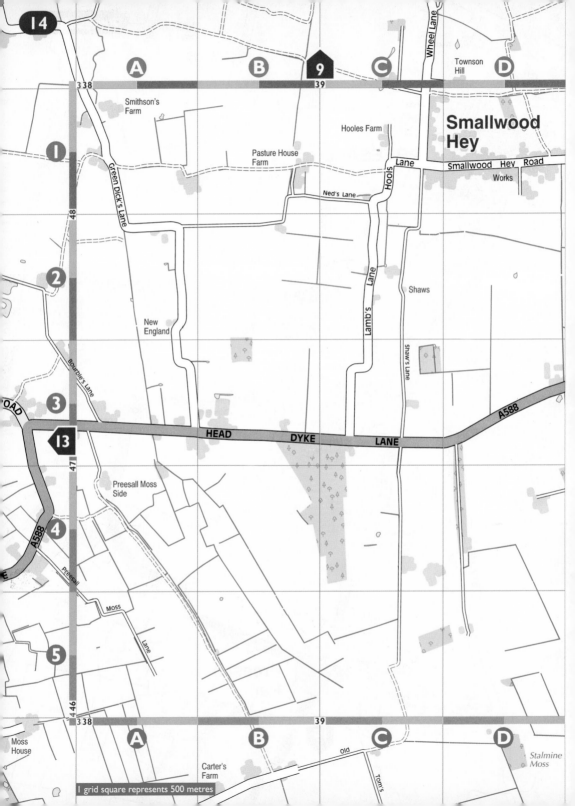

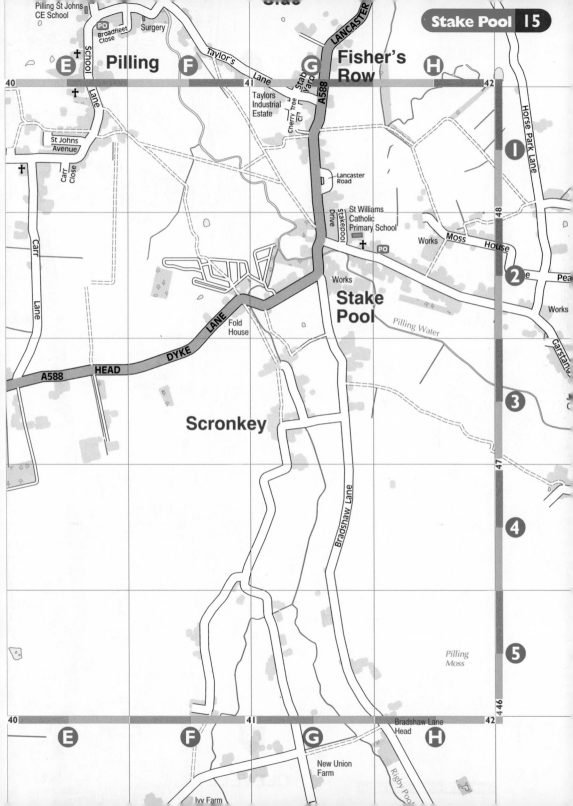

16

A   B   **10**   C   D

3 30   31

46

1

Tatham Court
W Ct
Larkholme
Parade
Newby
Clark
Larkholme Avenue
Bowness
Kirks
Southway
Pde Pl
Dean
Milton
Thirlmere Av
Patterdale Avenue
Ullswater
Windermere
BROADWAY
Falmouth Avenue
The
Roundway
Severn
Avon
Holme
Strand
Bowland Av
Larkholme Prim Sch
Sea Wall
Fairway
Hove Av
Plymouth Av
Rossall Gate
Southgate
Rossall Cl
Rossall Way
Rossall Hospital
Bristol
West

45

2

Ainsdale Av
Wentworth
Formby
Sunningdale Av
Sandy Lane
Rossall La
A587
B5409

3

Rossall School
Rossall Junior School
BROADWAY

4

College Ca
Osborne Gv
Osborne Rd
Westbourne Road
Shaftesbury Av
King's Walk
Garden Walk
Egremont Avenue
Promenade
The Bay Drive
Marlborough Av
North Square
Green
West
The Sq
East Ct
South Sq
The Wy Ga
Milnthorpe
Penrith Av
Tebay Av
Alston Av
Cleveleys
Oxenho
Kendal Av
Westmorland Av

444

5

North
The Corners
The Cove
Cross Way
Queens Gate
Rossall Gdns
Dorset Av
Works
Carr Gate
Thornton
South Av
Lanefield
The Cl
Drive
Rossall
Cumber
Westmorland Av

3 30   31

A   B   **20**   C   D

Jubilee Dr
The Links
Palatine Road
Promenade
Manor Beach Primary School
Manor Drive
Beach Rd
Leicester
Gloucester
Bedford Av
ROAD
Beach Av
Weeton
Ocean
Bchcm Dr
West Dr
Stockdo
Ryden
Cambridge
Oxford
Ward

CLEVELEYS

I grid square represents 500 metres

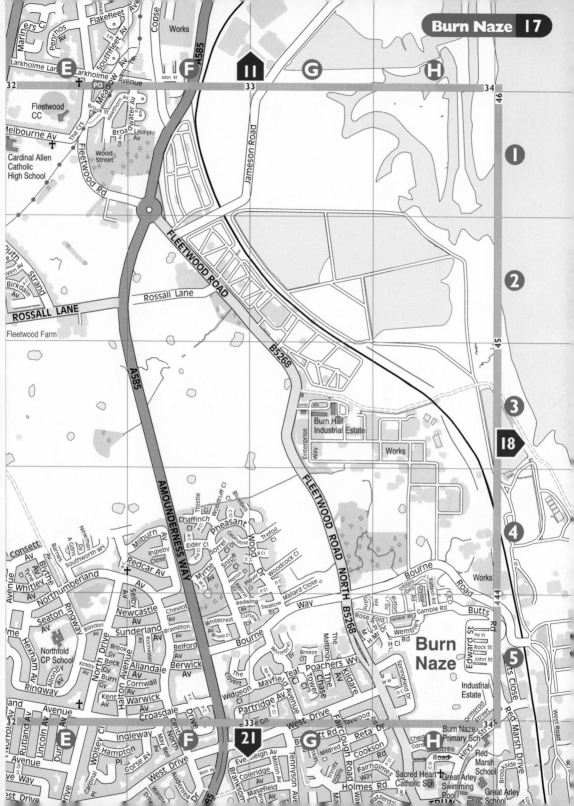

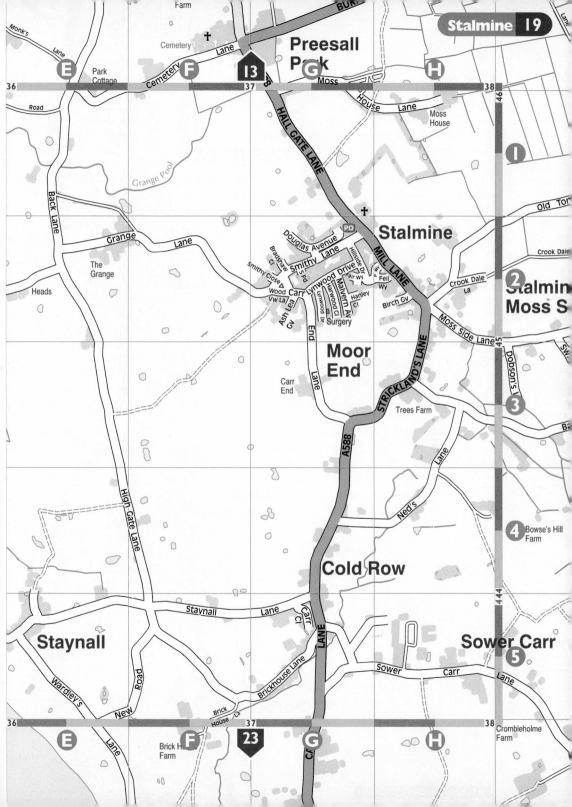

Preesall Park

Stalmine

Moss House

Moss House Lane

Old Tor

Crook Dale

Stalmin Moss S

Crook Dale La

Douglas Avenue

PO

Smithy Lane

Hillside Dr

Bradshaw Cl

Lynwood Drive

Fair Wy

P Wy

Fell Wy

St's Rd

Malvern Av

Harwood Cl

Hanley Cl

Birch Gv

Smithy Close

Wood Vw La

Carr

Harwood Dr

Lynwood Dr

Surgery

Ash Lea Gv

MILL LANE

Moor End

Carr End

STRICKLAND'S LANE

Trees Farm

Moss Side Lane

Dobson's

Bowse's Hill Farm

A588

Ned's Lane

Cold Row

Staynall

Staynall Lane

High Gate Lane

Brickhouse Lane

New Road

Wardley's Lane

Brick House

Brick H. Farm

Sower Carr

Sower Carr Lane

Crombleholme Farm

Monk's Lane

Cemetery

Cemetery Lane

Park Cottage

Road

BUR

Moss

Back Lane

Grange Lane

Grange pool

The Grange

Heads

HALL GATE LANE

E   F   13   G   H   I

36   37   38   46

2

3

45

4

444

5

E   F   23   G   H

36   37   38

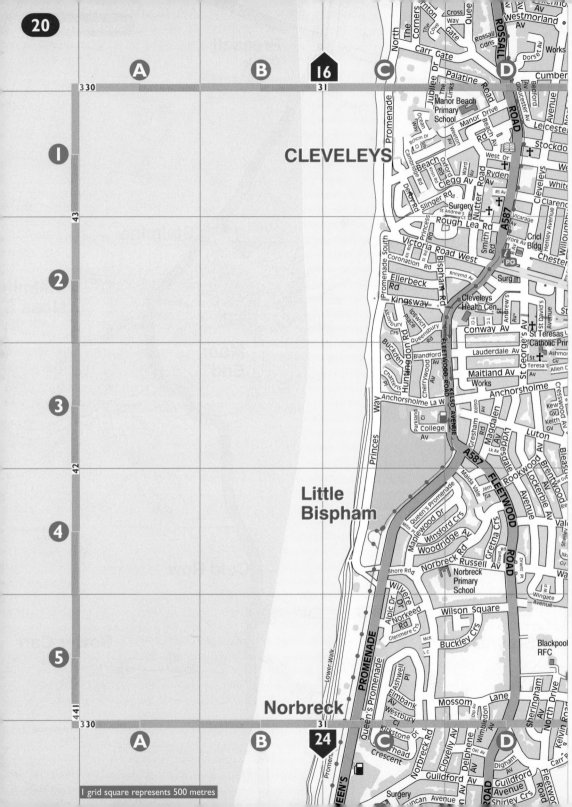

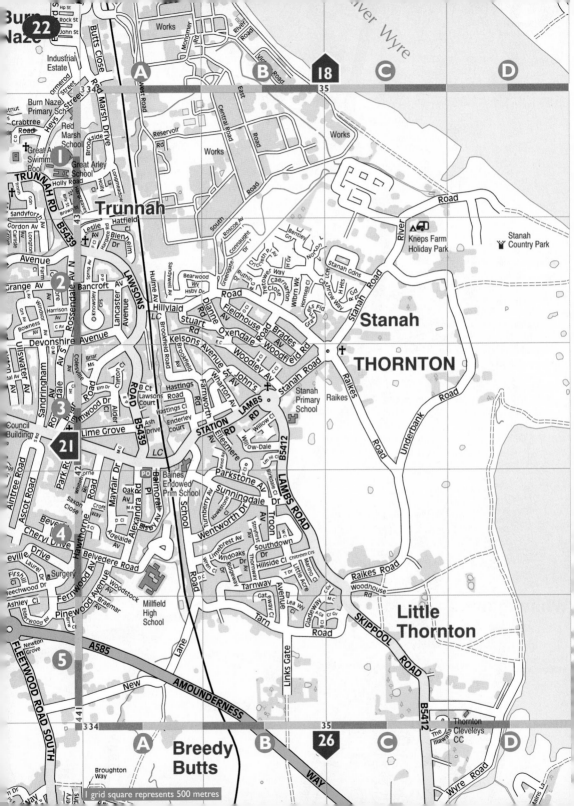

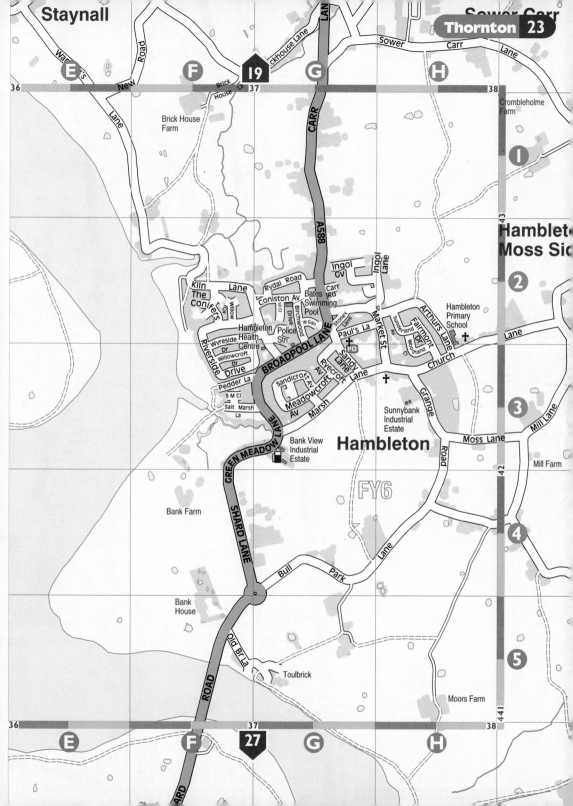

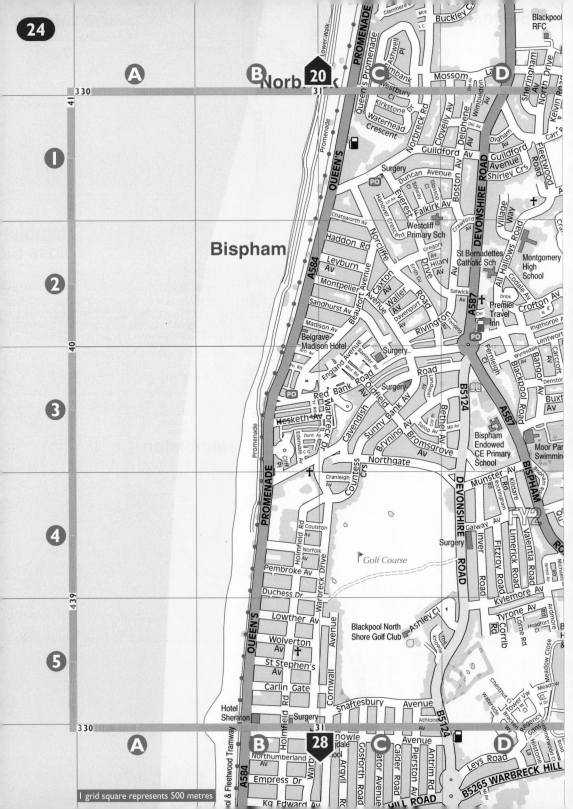

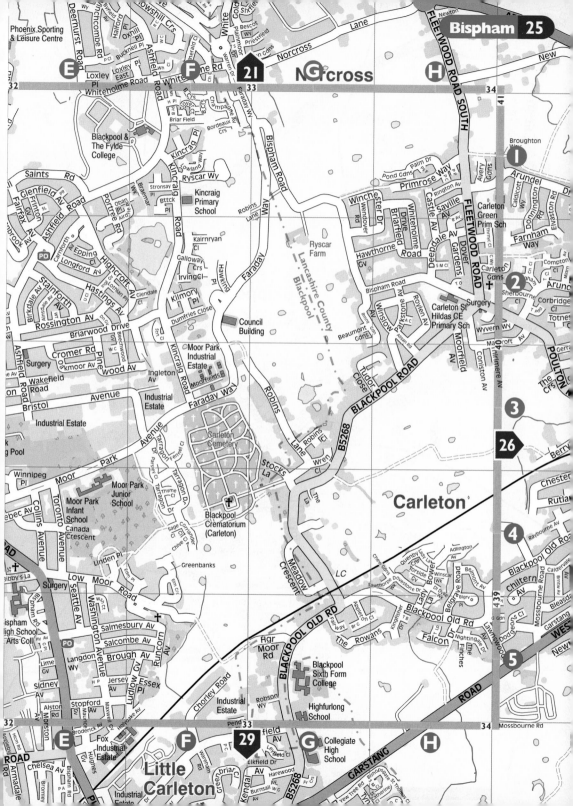

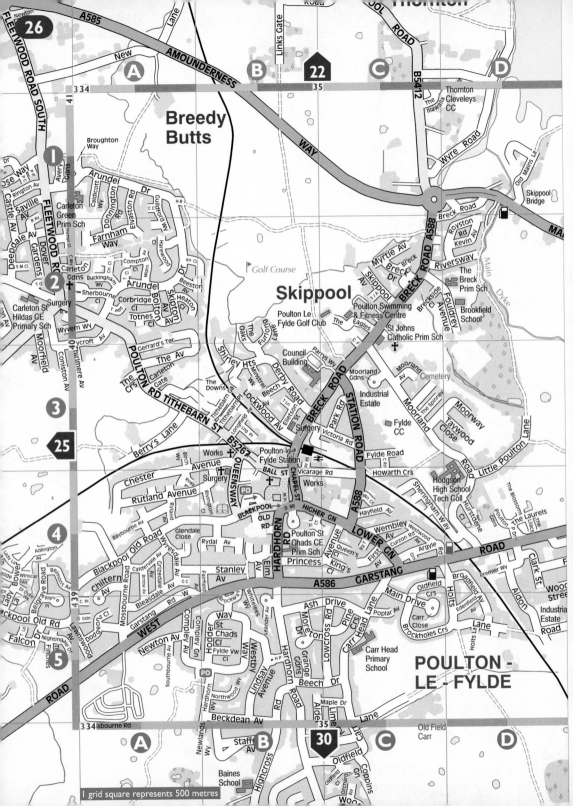

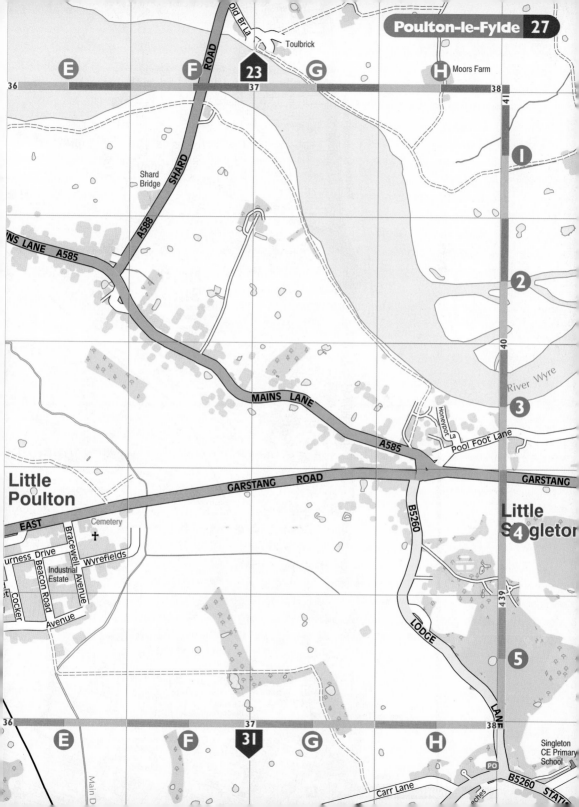

Toulbrick

Moors Farm

E **F** **G** **23** **H**

36 37 38 41

I

Shard
Bridge

SHARD ROAD

Old Br La

A588

NS LANE A585

2

River Wyre

3

MAINS LANE

Honeypot La

A585

Pool Foot Lane

GARSTANG ROAD GARSTANG

**Little
Poulton**

EAST

Cemetery

B5260

**Little
S gleton**

4

439

Bracewell Avenue

urness Drive

Wyrefields

Industrial
Estate

Beacon Road

Cocker

Avenue

LODGE LANE

5

E **F** **31** **G** **H**

36 37 38

Singleton
CE Primary
School

PO

Main D

Carr Lane

B5260 STATI

eches

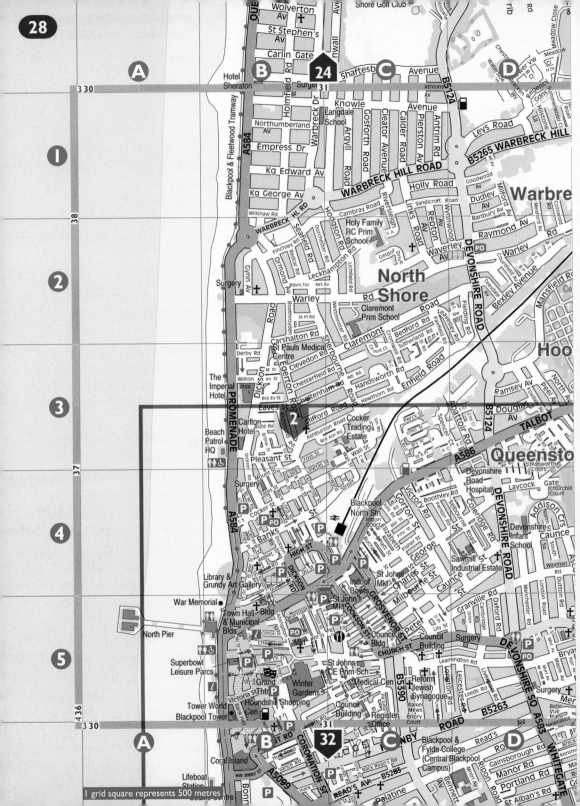

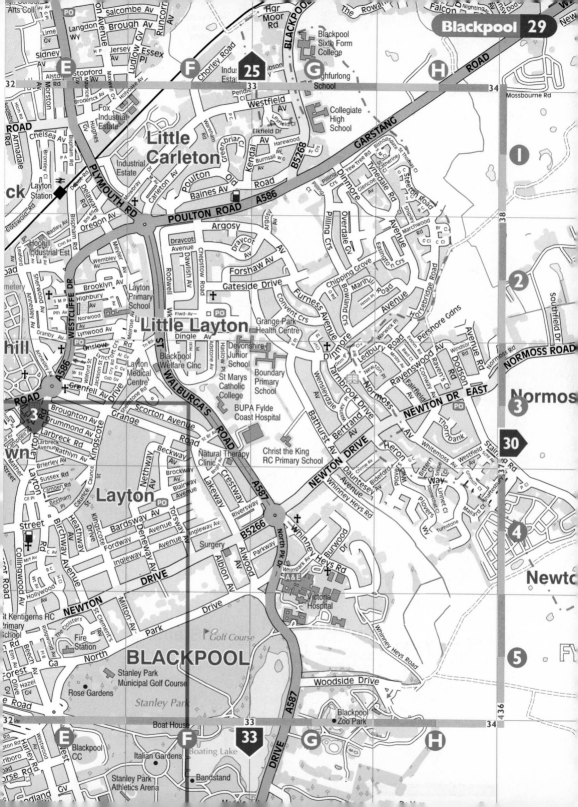

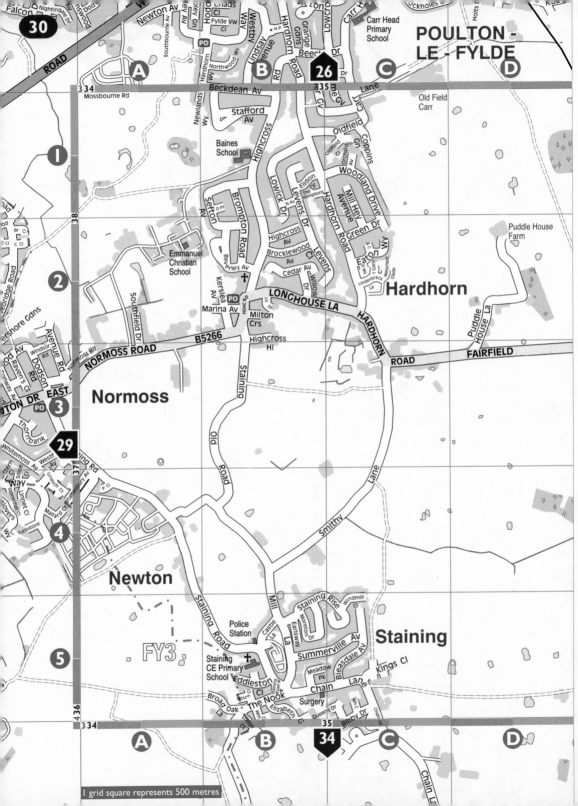

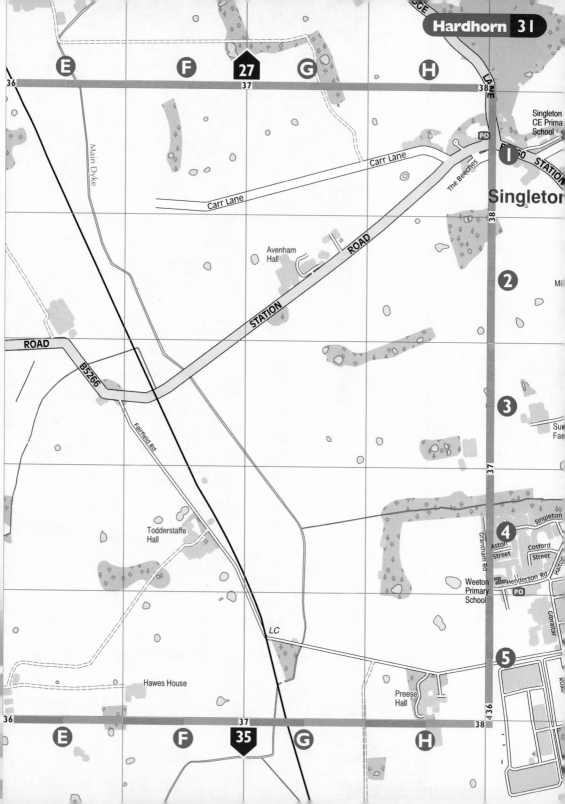

E F 27 G H

36 37 38

Main Dyke

Singleton
CE Prima
School

PO

I

STATION

Carr Lane

Carr Lane

Carr Lane

The Beeches

Singleton

38

2

Mi

Avenham
Hall

STATION

ROAD

ROAD

B5266

3

Su
Fa

Fairfield Rd

37

Singleton

4

Aston
Street

Cosford
Street

Grantham Rd

Halton

Todderstaffe
Hall

Weeton
Primary
School

Henderson Rd

PO

Gibraltar

5

LC

436

Hawes House

Preese
Hall

Road

36 37 38

E F 35 G H

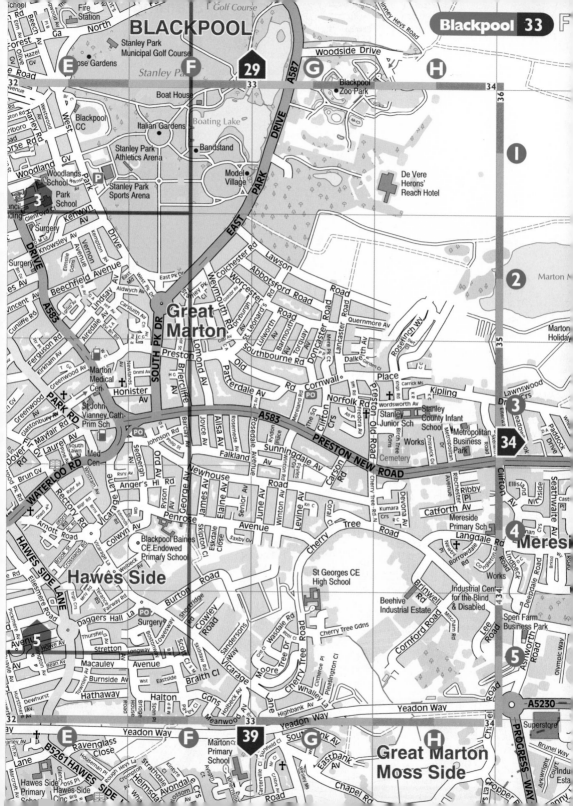

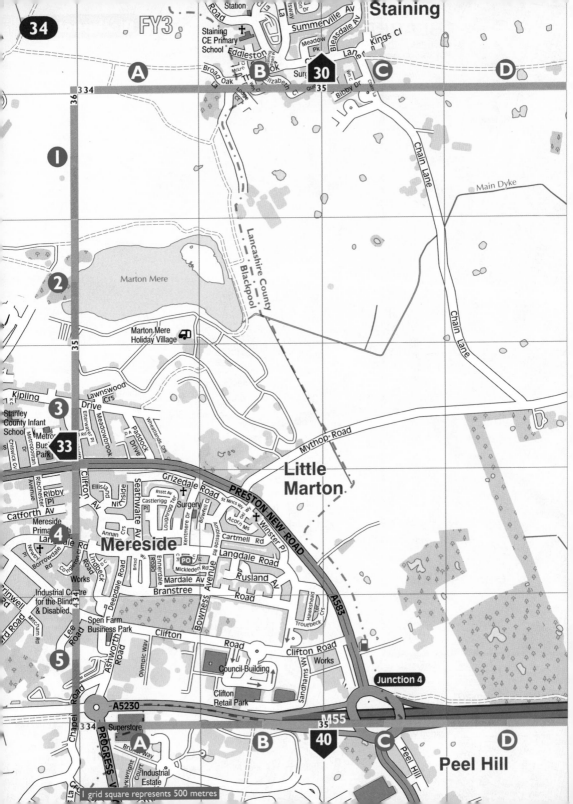

E
F
31
G
H

Hawes House

Preese Hall

36
37
38
36

Mythop

Mythop Road

Mythop Road

Knowsley

St Mic
Prima

M55

36
37
38

E
F
41
G
H

Moss House F

Moss House Lane
Moss House Lane
Plu

House

1

2

35

3

4

434

5

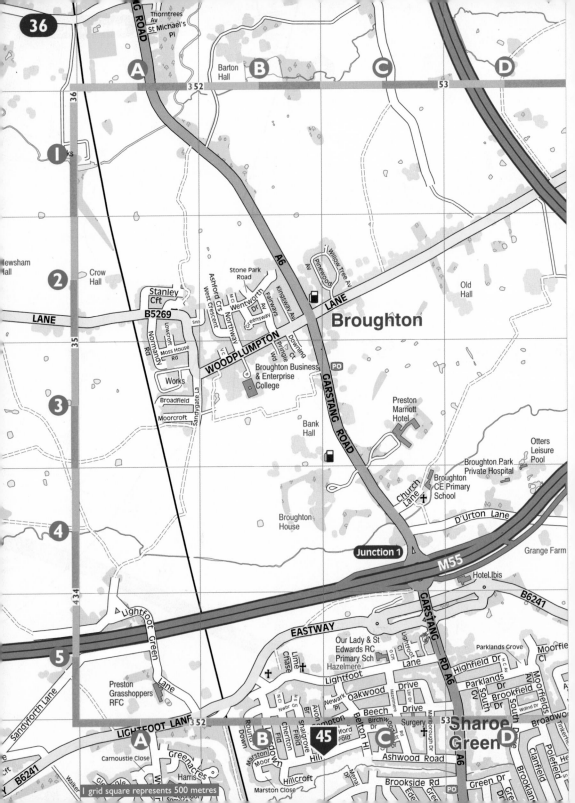

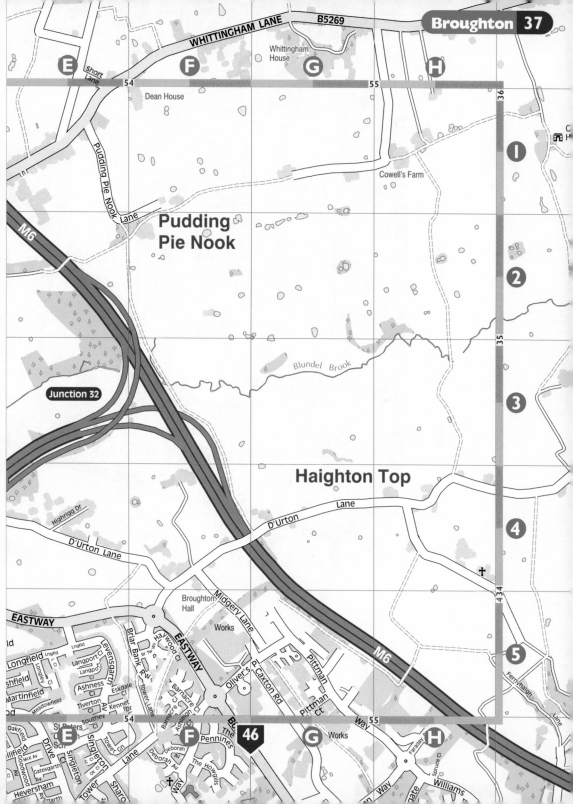

WHITTINGHAM LANE   B5269

E   Short Lane   F   Whittingham House   G   H

54   55   36

Dean House

Pudding Pie Nook Lane

M6

Pudding Pie Nook

Cowell's Farm

I

2

Junction 32

Blundel Brook

35

3

Haighton Top

D'Urton   Lane

Highrigg Dr

D'Urton Lane

4

Broughton Hall

Midgery Lane

Works

EASTWAY

Longfield   Lngfld   Lngfld

Levensgarth   Briar Bank   Haywood Cl   EASTWAY   Oliver's Pl   Caxton Rd   Pittman   M6   434

Langport Cl   Langpo Cl

Ashness Cl   Eskdale Cl   Kennet   Tower Lane   Barnacre Cl

Tiverton Av   Southey   Cl

5   Fernyhalgh Lane

St Peters   Singleton   Southey   Barnacre Cl   Ashleigh   Pittman Way   Works   Way

54   55

E   F   **46**   G   Works   H

Longfield   Drive   Singleton Lane   Deborah Av   The Pennines   The Howgills   Faraday Cl   Spruce Cl   Williams

Heversham   Tower

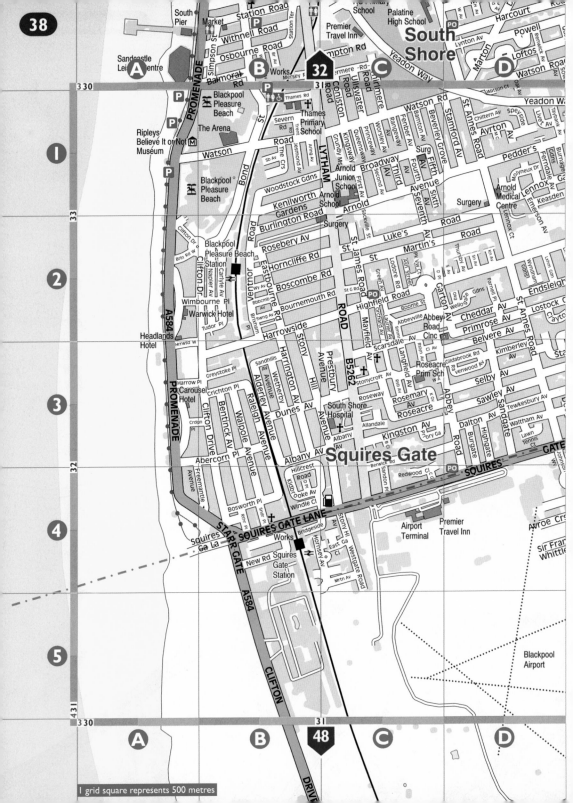

South Pier

Market

Station Road

Sandcastle Leisure Centre

South Shore

Palatine High School

Harcourt

Powell

Lynton Av

Loftos

Watson Rd

Withnell Road

Osbourne Road

Simpson St

Balmoral Rd

Station Ter

B

Works

Mersey E

Yeadon Way

Marton

A

32

31

C

D

330

Watson Ct

Yeadon Wa

PROMENADE

Blackpool Pleasure Beach

Thames Rd

Coniston Road

Ulswater Road

Kinmere Rd

Beverley Grove

St Annes Road

Stamford Av

Ayrton Av

Chiltern Av

Speyside

Live

Taybank

33

Ripleys Believe It or Not Museum

The Arena

M

Watson

Bond St

Severn Rd

Trent Rd

Jesmond Rd

The Crs

Sd Av

LYTHAM

Thames Primary School

Worsley Av

Rangeway

Fember Av

Bamton Av

Princeway

Queensway

Grundy Ms

Arnold Junior School

Arnold

Road

Surg

Fifth

Fourth

Third

Second Av

First Av

Broadway

Fifth

Sixth

Seventh

Avenue

Sackville St

Surgery

Arnold Medical Centre

Kensden

Lennox

Pedder's

Ferndale

Molyneux Dr

Emerson Rd

Gdns

Lennox Ct

1

Woodstock Gdns

Kenilworth Gardens

Burlington Road

Arnold School

Surgery

St Luke's

St

James

Road

Martin's

Road

Road

St G Rd

Green Rd

D Pl

Carton

Thursby

Endsleigh

St Annes Road

Lostock

Wyndham

Cayto

Clifton Dr

Brin Rd W

Napier Av

Carlyle Av

ROAD

Rosebery Av

Horncliffe Rd

Boscombe Rd

Bournemouth Rd

Eastbourne Road

Wy C Av

Bbbcmb

A584

Swng Av

Brixham

Tudor Rd

Highfield Road

Boome St

Abbeville Road

Mayfield Rd

Lodore Road

Orchard Rd

Smth

Rd W

Wello

Abbey Clnc

Cheddar Av

Primrose Av

Belvere Av

Kimberley Av

St Annes Road

2

Wimbourne Pl

Warwick Hotel

Harrowside

Harrowside W

Headlands Hotel

Harrow Pl

Greystoke Pl

Harrington Avenue

Sandhills Avenue

Wetherby Avenue

Stony Hill

Prestbury Avenue

B5262

Scarsdale

Langfield Av

Roseacre Prim Sch

Gildabrook Rd

Wenwood Rd

Roseacre

Selby Av

Sawley Av

Tewkesbury Av

3

PROMENADE

Clifton Drive

Crdgn Pl

Bentinck Av

Alderley Avenue

Raleigh Avenue

Dunes Av

Roseway

Stonycroft Av

South Shore Hospital

Rosemary Av

Roseacre

Allandale

Rsn Rd

St K Av

Abbey

Road

Dalton Av

Burgate

Highgate

Waltham Av

GATE

Crichton Pl

Walpole Avenue

Albany Av

Kingston Av

Albany

Prv Ga

32

Carousel Hotel

Abercorn

Freemantle Avenue

Bosworth Pl

Berwick Rd

Squires Gate

Sndon Ct

Redwood

PO

SQUIRES

Lawn Tennis Ct

4

STARR GATE

A584

Squires Ga La

SQUIRES GATE LANE

New Rd

Hillcrest Road

Kidd Cl

Rothr Pl

Sndr Pl

Cooke Av

Windle Cl

Works

Bridgeside

Hornsey Av

Stony Hl

East Ga Cl

Westgate Av

Mrtn Av

PO

Airport Terminal

Premier Travel Inn

Squires Gate Station

Awroe Crs

Sir Fran Whittle

5

CLIFTON

Blackpool Airport

330

431

A

B

48

C

D

DRIVE

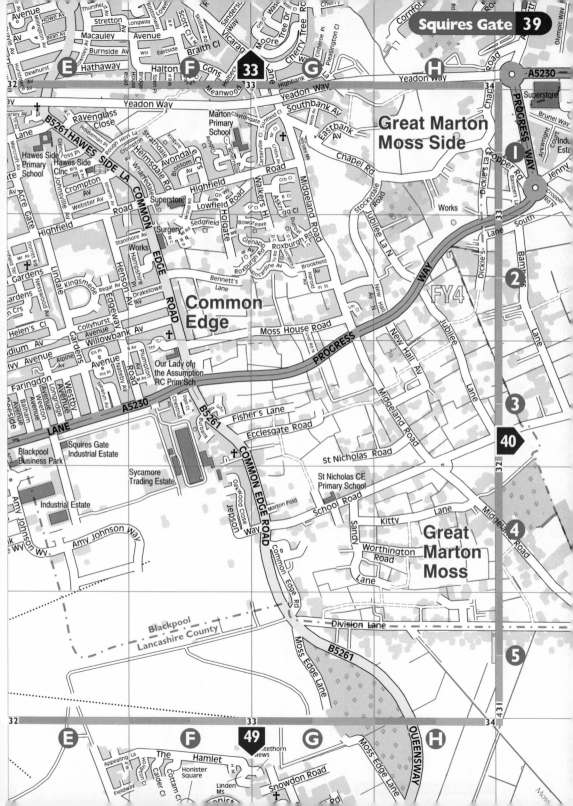

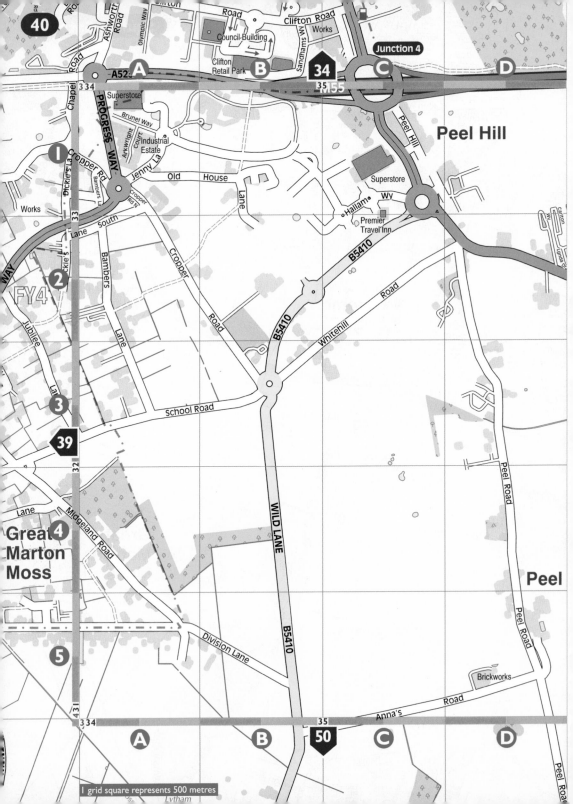

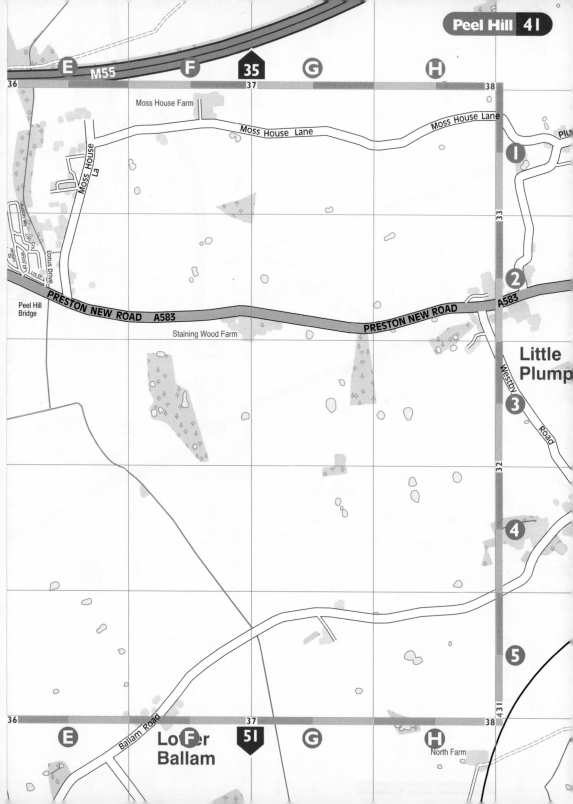

E M55 **F** **35** **G** **H**

36 37 38

Moss House Farm

Moss House Lane Moss House Lane

Plu

Moss House La **1**

33

Austin Wy

Cl Crs

Henry Dr

Lts Dr

Lotus Drive

PRESTON NEW ROAD A583 PRESTON NEW ROAD A583

2

Peel Hill
Bridge

Staining Wood Farm

PRESTON NEW ROAD

**Little
Plump**

Westby Road

3

32

4

5

431

36 37 38

E Ballam Road **Lower
Ballam** **51** **G** **H**

North Farm

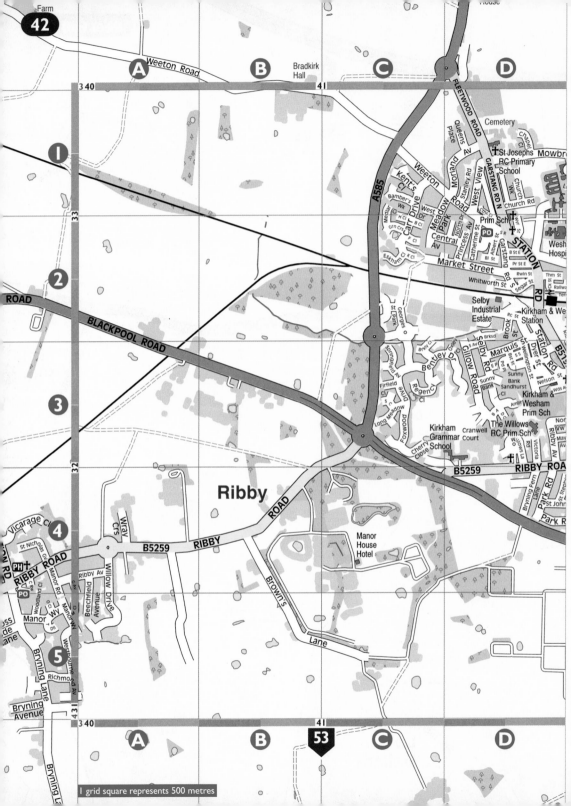

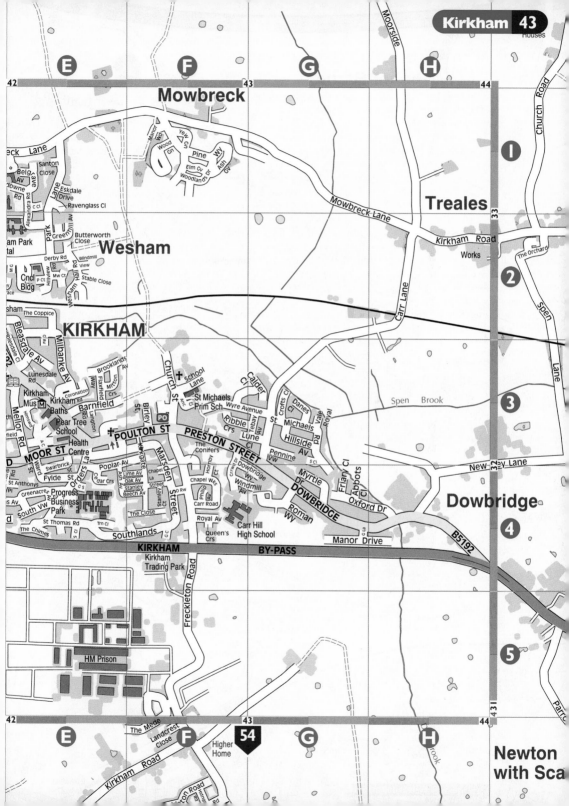

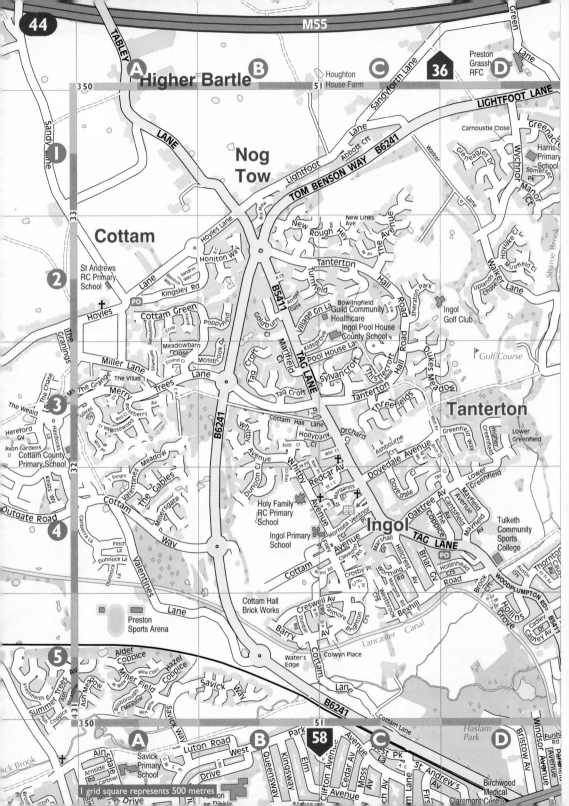

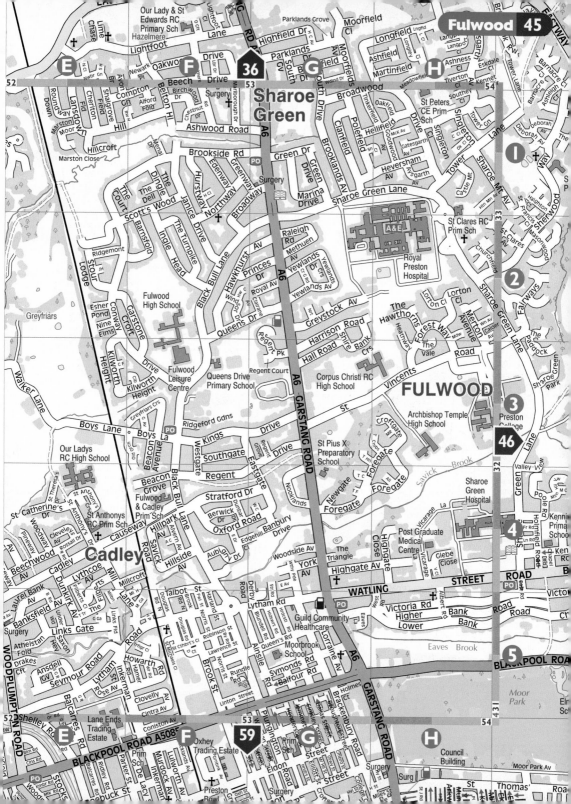

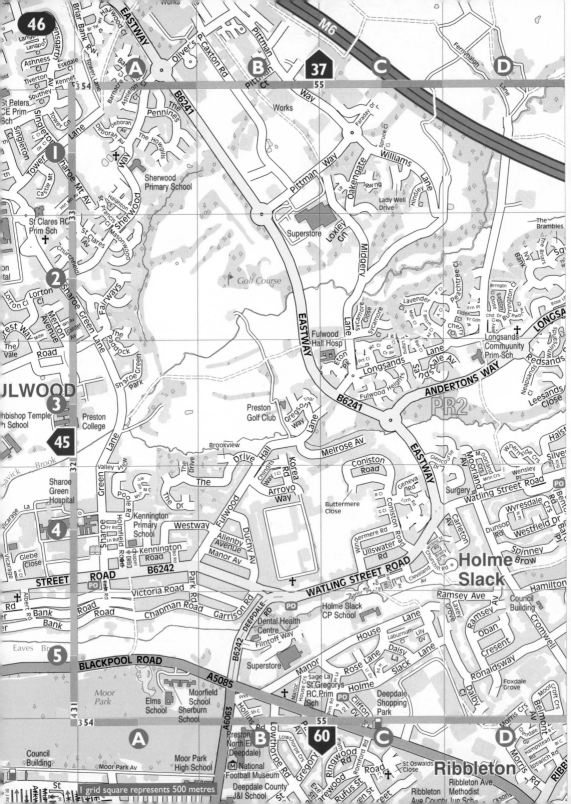

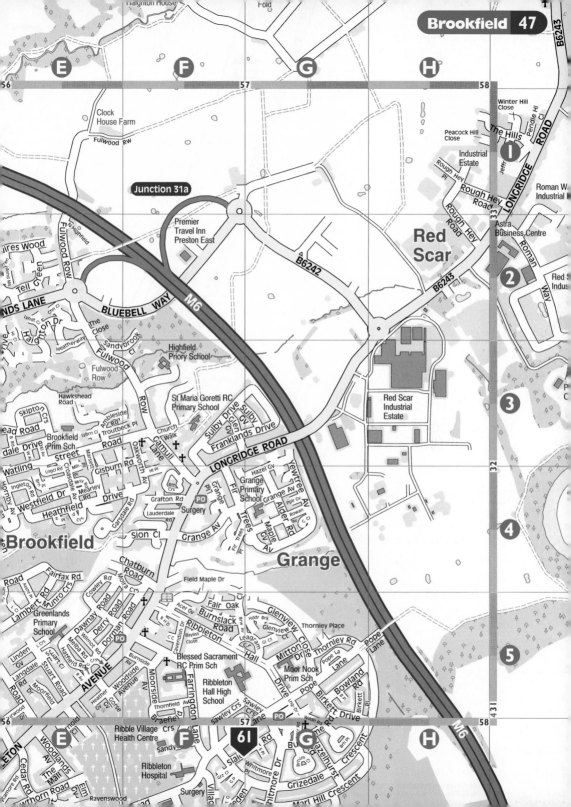

B6243

E   F   G   H

56   57   58

Haighton House

Fold

Clock House Farm

Fulwood Rw

Winter Hill Close

Peacock Hill Close

Pendle Hi Cl

The Hills

LONGRIDGE ROAD

Jeff

Industrial Estate

Roman W. Industrial

Junction 31a

Premier Travel Inn Preston East

Rough Hey Pl

Rough Hey Road

Rough Hey Road

Astra Business Centre

Roman Way

Red Scar

B6242

B6243

Red Indus

2

Fulwood Row

Ft Highfield

Haighton Dr

Lynd

Chn Cl

NDS LANE

BLUEBELL WAY

M6

The Close

Sandybrook

Heatherway

Fulwood Row

Fulwood Row

Highfield Priory School

Red Scar Industrial Estate

3

32

Hawkshead Road

Skipton Crs

lead Road

dale Drive

Brookfield Prim Sch

Street

Watling

Hornby AV

Ingle

Brn

Ambleside Rd

Troutbeck Pl

Lybrn Cl

Mln

ROW

Crosdale Rd

Oakworth Av

Church Walk

Camull Lane

St Maria Goretti RC Primary School

Sulby Drive

Sulby

Glen CV

Glen

Franklands Drive

LONGRIDGE ROAD

431

Brookfield

Gisburn Rd

Westfield Dr

Mearley Drive

Heathfield

Garsdale Rd

HI Pl

Grafton Rd

Lauderdale Rd

PO

Surgery

Sion Cl

Grange PI

Grange AV

Fir

Fir Trees

Hazel Gv

Grange Primary School

Grange AV

Pplr Gv

Alder Rd

Rowan

C Cl

Maple CV

Yewtree AV

4

Grange

Chatburn Road

Fairfax Rd

Munro Crs

Lambert Rd

Cowley Rd

Mora Crs

Derry Road

Dorman Road

Field Maple Dr

Acer Gv

Fair Oak

Burnslack Road

Ribbleton Hall

Glenview Close

Glenview

Thornley Place

Thornley Rd

Pope Lane

5

Greenlands Primary School

Linden Gv

Langdale Rd

Dawnay Road

Melba Rd

Wilmot Rd

Hatfield Rd

Stuart Road

Moorfield

PO

Burnside AV

Blessed Sacrament RC Prim Sch

Ribbleton Hall High School

Mitton Drive

Moor Nook Prim Sch

Pope Lane

Pope

Bowland Road

Birkett Drive

Birkett

M6

AVENUE

Woodside Avenue

Farringdon

Thornfield Av

Gorse

Sawley Crs

Sawley Crs

Wadh Rd

Heather Gv

Baxdale Crs

E   F   61   G   H

56   57   58

Ribble Village Health Centre

Ribbleton Hospital

Surgery

Whitmore Dr

Village

Eeden

Whitmore

Hazelhurst Crescent

Grizedale Rd

Marl Hill Crescent

Woodlands

The Mall

Cedar Rd

Elm

Thorn Rd

Ravenswood

48

A   B   **38**   C   D

330   31

31

Blackpool Airport

I

Duncan Cl

Anson Cl

Benbow Wk

Ramsey Cl

Golf Course

2

St Anne's Old Links Golf Club

Highbury Road West

Heele'

30

Sidmouth Rd

Salcombe Road

Kilgrimol Gdns

Seaton Crs

Tudor Road

St David's Road

Barton Road

Kendal Rd

Myerscough Avenue

Dalton St

Forshaw Avenue

Lamdale Rd

Trtb

3

CLIFTON

NORTH

DRIVE

A584

Summerfields

Todmorden Road

Norwood Road

Wyredale Rd

Avndl Rd

Caryl Road

Lime Grove

Road

St David's Cl

North Cross Grove

Cross Street

Council Building

PO

West

Bentinck Rd

Cavendish

St Hilda's Rd

Lime Grove

St Leonard's

St Andrew's Road

Fleet St

Road

4

Sandgate

CLIFTON DRIVE

North

Rowsley Rd

Dvnsort Rd

Chatsworth Road

Road

Road

Toy & Teddy Bear Museum

S

NORTH

Beach Road

Promenade

Beach

429

The Best Western Glendower Hotel

The Red Rose School

Dyslexia North West

Ribble

St D R

St Geo

Dove St

St

Coun Build

5

Salters Bank

St Anne's Pier

St Anne' Swimmir Pool

330   31

A   B   C   **62**   D

I grid square represents 500 metres

E   F   39   G   H

32   33   34   31

Lancashire County

B5261

Moss Edge Lane

Moss Edge Lane

Queensway

Moss Sluice

1

2

Wilding's La

30

3

50

Hay
Hou

B5261

HEYHOUSES

4

Grassation Rd

5

Whitethorn Mews

The Hamlet

Appealing La

Cottam Cl

Honister Square

Linden Ms

Snowdon Road

Scafell Rd

Everest Road

Walter Av

Coniston Av

Hoyle Av

Bowness Av

Queensway Industrial Estate

Everest Cl

Leach

Blackpool Road

Birkdale Av

Crosby

Cudworth Road

Kilnhouse

Road

North Eaves Rd

Hesketh Road

Melling's La

Clover Av

Derwent Rd

Spring Gdn

Rodney Avenue

Frobisher Drive

Drake Cl

Collingwood Avenue

Dawson

Blundell Road

Clive Avenue

Chatham Av

Grenville Av

Cramere

St Anne's CC Surgery

Highbury Road E

Highbury Road

Crosland Road N

Cromer Rd

Harwich Rd

Scarborough Rd

Ashley Road

Filey Rd

Whitby Rd

Sharman Road

Kingsmere Av

Keswick Road

Rydal Av

Road East

Dorset Road

Headroomgate Road

Folkestone Road

Margate

Dover Road

Walmer Rd

Ramsgate Road

Scarborough Road

The Croft

EAST B5233

Lowton Road

Beverley Rd

Crosland Road

Weeton Avenue

Mayfield Primary School

Gretdale Av

Clarendon Road North

Council Building

Heyhouse Endowed CE Junior Sch

Westby Rd

ST ANNE'S ROAD

Clarendon Road

Shepherd Rd N

Salwick

Heaton Road

Poulton Avenue

Newton Road

Singleton Avenue

Elmhurst Road

Tudor Av

Thornton Av

Rossendale Rd

Hope St

Shepherd Road

Inskip Place

Elswick Place

Oxford Road

Church Road

Surgery

Heyhouse Endowed CE Infant School

Alexandra Rd

Holmefield Road

Curzon Road

Albert Road

Church Road

Parkside Rd

Fairview Av

Moorland Rd

Otley Road

Boston Road

St Anne's Station

North Crs

St Alban's Road

Don St

B5233

Trafalgar St

Brighton Avenue

Edward Street

Hove

Warwick Road

Patrick St

Kenilworth Road

Leamington Road

Thomas St South

Links Gate

Banbury Road

Lima Rd

Beauclerk

Stratford Road

Winston Av

Ripley Drive

Church Road

Skipton Av

Clifton Primary School

Clitheroe Rd

Sawley

Hampton Rd

The Mall

Arnside Av

Ulve

HEYHOUSES

Clifton Gdns

Smithy

Hilton Avenue

Brook

St George's Av

W Crs

St Anne's Rd W

Wood St

Surgery

Orchard Rd

Park Road

All Saints' Road

Bromley Road

Andrew's Road

Eaton Ct

Lawrence Avenue

Lindsay Av

Haymarket

Greenways

Lomond Avenue

Roseway

Clifton

Bedford Hotel

St Annes College Grammar School

St Thomas CE Primary School

Royal Lytham & St Anne's Golf Club

Golf Course

Lytham St Annes High Tech College

E   F   63   G   H

33   34

Lindum Hotel

The Grand Hotel

Pleasure Island

DRIVE

SOUTH

York Road

Queen's Road

Osborne Rd

Victoria Road

King's Road

Links Road

Balmoral Road

Surgery

E   F   **41**   G   H

36   37   31   38

Lower
Ballam

North Farm

I

Ballam Road

Brays Road

Ivy Farm

LYTHAM   ROAD

LC

2 Moss
Side

Higher
Ballam

Moss Side
Station

30

Ballam Road

3

Peg's   Lane

52

B5259

Cartmell Lane

4

Birks Farm

Eastham Hall
Caravan
Site

SALTCOTES

A429

Eastham
Hall

5

ROAD

Green   Drive

E   **64**   F   G   H

36   37   38

Laburnum
Avenue

Golf Course

Laurel
Avenue

Cem

Lilac

Wicklow Av

Grampian Av

Cotswold rd

Cheviot

Lytham Green
Drive Golf Club

Saltcotes

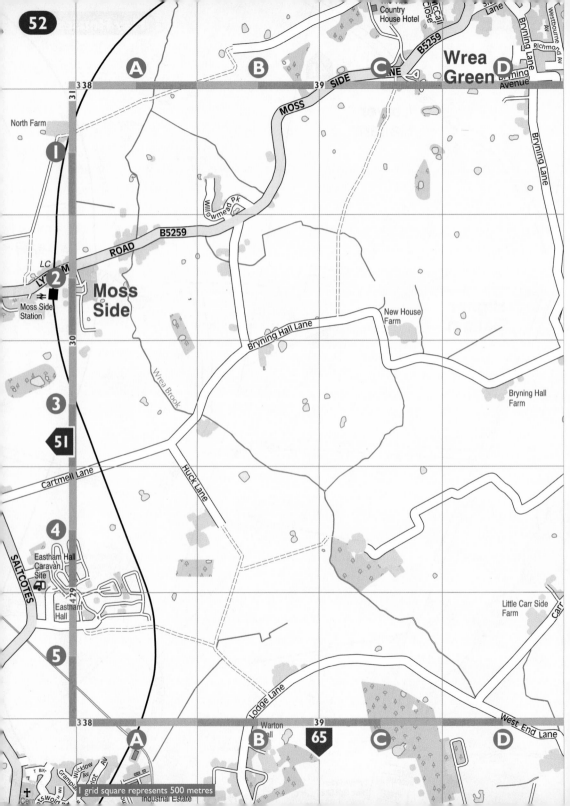

North Farm

A

B

Country
House Hotel

McCall
Close

Lane

B5259

C

SIDE

LANE

**Wrea
Green**

Bryning Lane

AV

Westbourne AV

Richmond

Bryning
Avenue

D

Bryning Lane

338

31

39

MOSS

1

Willowmead Pk

ROAD

B5259

LC

LY

M

2

Moss Side
Station

**Moss
Side**

New House
Farm

Bryning Hall Lane

Wrea Brook

Bryning Hall
Farm

3

Cartmell Lane

Huck Lane

4

SALTCOTES

Eastham Hall
Caravan
Site

A 429

Eastham
Hall

Little Carr Side
Farm

Carr

5

338

Lodge Lane

Warton
Hall

39

West End Lane

A

B

C

D

30

Wicklow

AV

Grampian

Pilot AV

Cem

Cotswold

WY

Biffr

Industrial Estate

1 grid square represents 500 metres

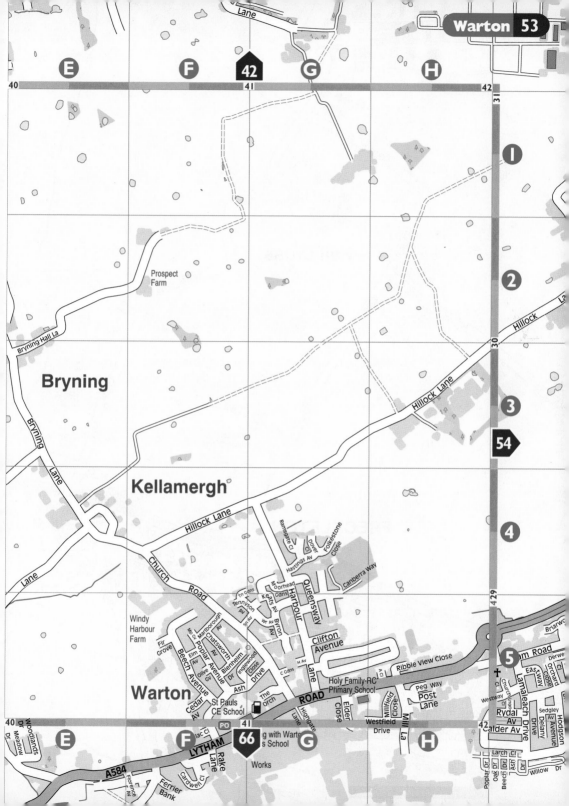

Lane

E F 42 G H

40 41 42
31

I

2

Prospect
Farm

Bryning Hall La

Hillock La

30

Bryning

3

Hillock Lane

54

Kellamergh

4

Hillock Lane

Ramsgate Cl
Dover
Folkestone Close
Hastings Av
Canberra Way

Windy
Harbour
Farm

Church Road

Tn Gdns
Moorhead
Keats Av
Tennyson Av
Sh Av
Wt Av

Harbour

Queensway

5
m Road
Brnarw
Derwe

Fir Grove
Marlborough Av
Chatsworth Av
Elm Cl
Olive Av
Blenheim Dr
Inglewood Close
C Gdns
H Av
Byron Av

Clifton
Avenue

Ribble View Close

A Cl

Eastway
Orchard
Delany

Lane

Beech Avenue
Poplar Avenue
Cedar Av
Ash

St Pauls
CE School

The Orch

Lytham
Lane

Highgate
Lane

Holy Family RC
Primary School

Elder Close

Peg Way

Post
Lane

Lamaleach Drive

Westway
Churchfield
Av
Sedgley
Av
Hodgson
Avenue

Rydal
Av
Calder Av

Warton

ROAD

Millfield Close

Mill La

Westfield
Drive

40 41 66 G H 42

E Woodlands Dr Meadow Dr F LYTHAM

Poplar Dr
Oak Dr
Beech Dr
Larch Cl
Ash Dr
Willow

A584

Mac Cl
Rake Lane
Cardwell Cl
Florence Av
Ferrier
Bank

g with Warto
s School

Works

Rydal
Av

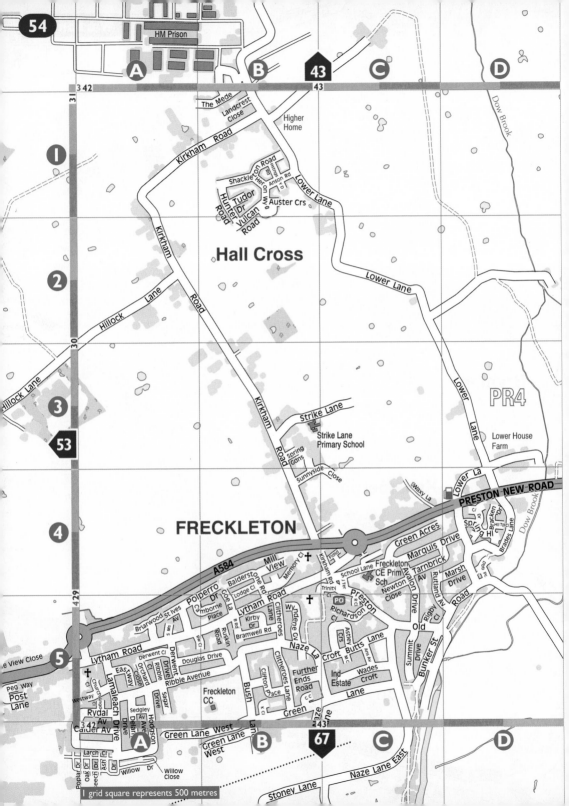

HM Prison

A **B** 43 **C** **D**

3 42
43
31

The Mede
Landcrest Close

Higher Home

1

Kirkham Road

Shackleton Road
Heron Wy
Anson Rd
Hunter Road
Tudor Dr
Vulcan Road
Auster Crs

Lower Lane

Hall Cross

2

Hillock Lane

Kirkham Lane

30

Lower Lane

Hillock Lane

3

Kirkham Road

Strike Lane

Strike Lane Primary School

PR4

53

Spring Gdns
Sunnyside Close

Lower House Farm

Lower Lane

4

FRECKLETON

429

Waxy La

Lower La

PRESTON NEW ROAD

Dow Brook

A584

Mill View
Memory Cl

Green Acres

Marquis Drive

Spring Hl
Bracken Dr
Brades Lane

Polperro Dr
Baldersto
Coe La
Lodge Cl
mborne Place

Lytham Road
Kirby Dr
Bramwell Rd

Clitheroes Lane
School Lane
Freckleton CE Prim Sch
Newton Close

Tarnbrick AV

Marsh Drive

Preston
PO
Richardson Cl

Astley AV
Rutland AV
Rigby Cl

Marsh Road

Briarwood
st Ives AV
St Ives

Ruskin Road

Indene Cl

Naze La
Croft
Butts Lane

Old

Bunker St
Summit Drive

5

Lytham Road

Derwent Cl
Derwent Drive
Ribble
Orchard Cl
Eastway

Douglas Drive

Ribble Avenue

Clitheroes Lane

Clifton Place

Further Ends Road

Ind Estate

Wades Croft

Lane

Lamaleach Drive

Peg Way
Post Lane
e View Close

Rydal AV
Calder Av
Sedgley AV
Hodgson
Delph
Sugar Drive

Freckleton CC

Bush

Green

Naze Lane

3 42

A

Green Lane West

Green Lane West

B

67

C

D

43

Poplar Dr
oak Dr
eech
Ash
Larch Cl
Willow
Willow Close

Stoney Lane

Naze Lane East

1 grid square represents 500 metres

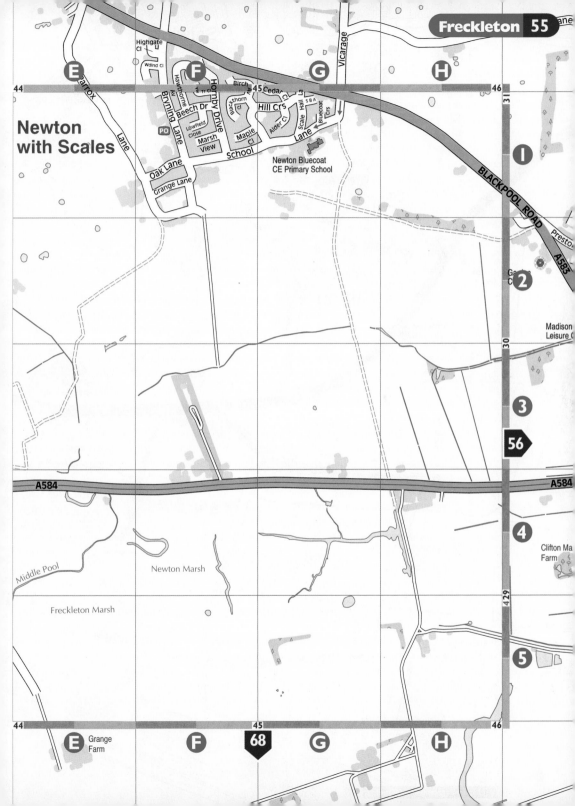

Newton
with Scales

Newton Bluecoat
CE Primary School

Highgate Cl

Wdlnd Cl

Birch

Cedar

Hill Crs

Scale Hill La

Bluecoat Crs

S B A

Hawthorne Av

Beech Dr

Hornby Drive

Bryning Lane

Oak Lane

Grange Lane

PO

Marsh View

Lowfield Close

Maple Cl

Alder Cl

Backthorn Cl

School

arrox Lane

Vicarage

BLACKPOOL ROAD

A583

Preston

Madison Leisure C

Gaston Cl

A584

A584

Middle Pool

Newton Marsh

Freckleton Marsh

Clifton Ma Farm

Grange Farm

E F G H

I

2

3

56

4

29

5

E F 68 G H

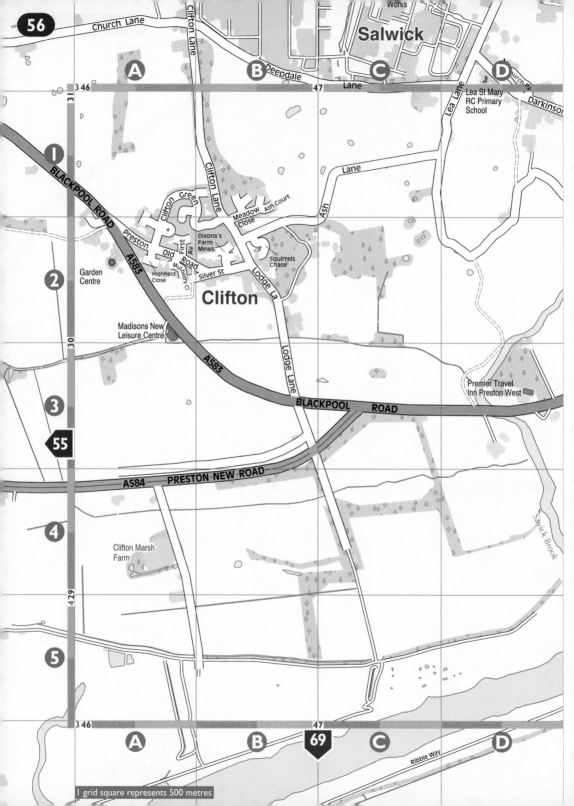

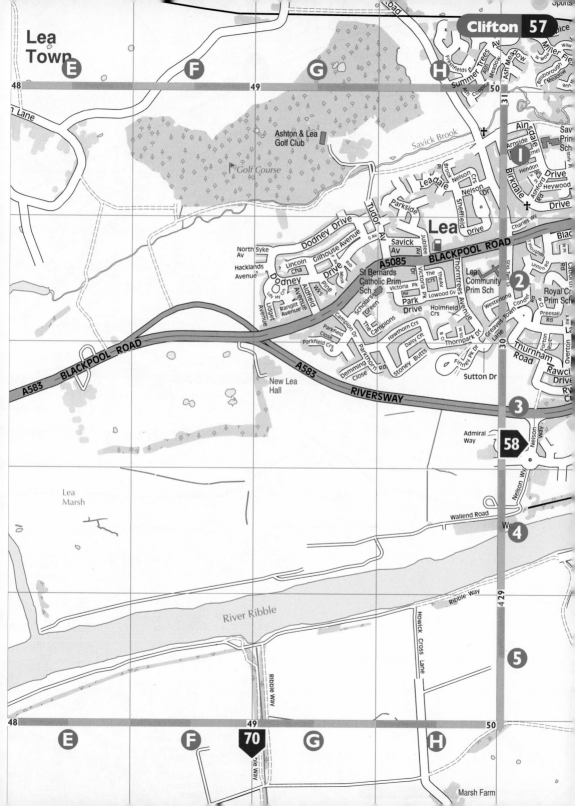

Lea Town

E   F   G   H

48   49   50
31

Lea Lane

Ashton & Lea Golf Club

Golf Course

Savick Brook

I

Ainscale
Arnside
Birkdale
Hendon
Heywood
Drive
Ashford Rd

Sav
Prin
Sch

Leadale
Brock
Nelson Crs
Nelson Dr
Sheffield
Parkside
Tudor Av
Dodney Drive
Gilhouse Avenue
Savick Av
Jubilee
Lincoln Cha
Drive
Pine
Aldfield Avenue
Ludget Avenue
North Syke Av
Hacklands Avenue
Dodney
Ranglit Avenue

Lea

Charles Wy

Blac
W Pl
Layto
Catherin Rd

Blackpool Road

A5085
St Bernards Catholic Prim Sch
Scholars Green
The Campions
Campion Dr
Parkfield Close
Parkfield Crs
Demming Close
Parkthorn Rd
Stoney Butts
Victoria Pk
The Av
Lowood Gv
Park Drive
Holmfield Crs
Hawthorn Crs
Daisy Clt
Thornpark Dr
Finney Pk Dr
Sutton Dr

Lea Community Prim Sch
Thorntrees Avenue
Greaves-Town Lane
Westerlong
Conder
Preesall Rd
Forton Rd
Overton Rd
Thurnham Road
Rawcl Drive

Royal Cr Prim Sch
La

2

30

New Lea Hall

Blackpool Road
A583
Riversway

3

Admiral Way

58

Nelson Wy
Nelson

Lea Marsh

Wallend Road
We

4

River Ribble

Ribble Way

429

Howick Cross Lane

Ribble Way

5

48   49   50

E   F   70   G   H

ble Way

Marsh Farm

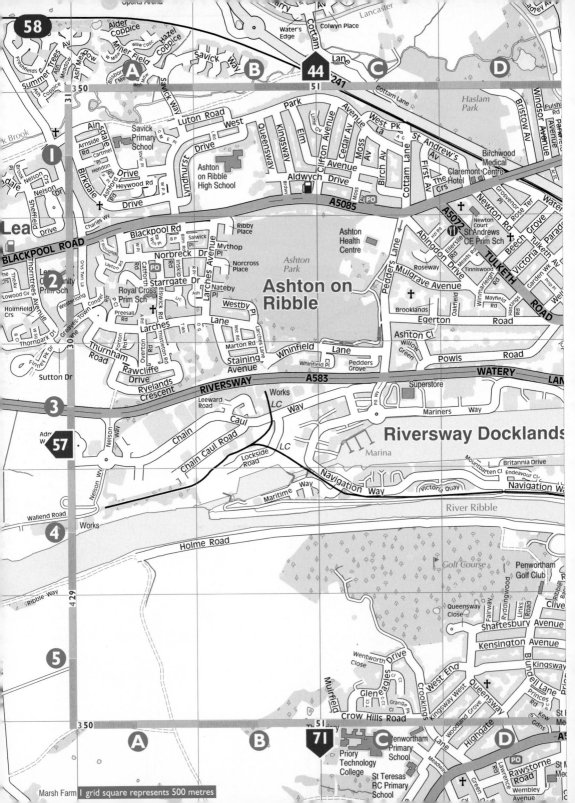

58

44

A **B** **C** **D**

Sports Arena
Lancaster
Colwyn Place
Water's Edge
Cottam

Alder Coppice
Miller Field
Hazel Coppice
Willw Cppc
Savick Way
Cottam Lane
Haslam Park
241
51

Summer Trees
Ash Coppice
Ash Meadow
Freshfields Dr
Bilsbor Me
MsW
Savick Way
241
Windsor Avenue
Fulshaw Av
Bristow Av

k Brook

I

Nelson Crs
Nelson Dr
Sheffield Drive
Charles W
Brook
dale
Birkdale Drive
Arnside Rd
Cartmel
Hendon
Ainscale Rd
Ashford
Heywood Rd
Lyndhurst Drive
Savick Primary School
Luton Road
West Drive
Queensway
Kingsway
Park Avenue
Elm
Lime
Clifton Avenue
Cedar Av
Moss Av
Birch Av
West PK La
St Andrew's
Cottam Lane
First Av
Birchwood Medical Centre
Claremont Centre
The Hotel
A G
Crs
Rose Ter
Grosvenor Rd
Windsor Avenue
Newton Rd

31 **3 50** 50

Ashton on Ribble High School
Aldwych Drive
Brown
PO
A5085
Moss Av
St Andrews CE Prim Sch
A507
Ellerslie Rd
Newton Court
Beech Grove
Tulketh
Victoria
Parade

Lea

2

Lee Comnity Prim Sch
Lowood Gv
Thorntrees Avenue
Holmfield Crs
Westerlong
Greaves Town La
Conece
Royal Cross Prim Sch
Catforth Rd
Eawick Rd
Preesall Rd
Thistleton Rd
Forton Rd
Overton Rd
Larches
Larches
Lane
Blackpool Rd
Norbreck Rd
Starrgate Dr
Inskip Pl
Nateby Pl
Westby Pl
Marton Rd
Staining Avenue
Ribby Place
Mythop Pl
Salwick Pl
Drve
Larches Avenue
Norcross Place
Whinfield
Whinfield Pl
Lane
Pedders Grove
Ashton Health Centre
Ashton Park
Ashton on Ribble
Pedders Lane
Mulgrave Avenue
Brooklands
Egerton Road
Ashton Cl
Willow Green
Powis Road
Roseway
Winmarleigh Rd
Tinniswood Rd
Oakfield
Mayfield Rd
Hastings Rd
Garden Wk
Abingdon Drive
TULKETH ROAD

BLACKPOOL ROAD

3

57

Adm W
Leeward Road
Nelson Way
Chain
Caul
Chain Caul Road
Lockside Road
Works
LC
LC
Riversway Way
Navigation Way
Maritime Way
Navigation Way
Marina
Riversway Docklands
Mariners Way
Superstore
Mountbatten Cl
Britannia Drive
Endeavour Cl
Victoria Quay
Navigation Wa
RIVERSWAY
A583
WATERY LANE
Thurnham Road
Rawcliffe Drive
Ryelands Crescent
Sutton Dr
Finney Pk Dr
Thornpark Dr

30

57

4

Wallend Road
Works
Holme Road
River Ribble
Golf Course
Penwortham Golf Club
Ribble Way

429

5

Wentworth Close
Gleneagles
Grange Pk
Muirfield
Crookings
West End
Kingsway West
Queensway
Kingsway
Blundell Lane
Princes Rd
Kew
Queensway Close
Fairway
Ryddinglowood
Links Road
Shaftesbury Avenue
Kensington Avenue
Crow Hills Road
Clive
St M

71

A **B** **C** **D**

3 50
51
A5

Priory Technology College
St Teresas RC Primary School
enwortham Primary School
Woodland Grove
Highgate
Green
Lawrence Road
Wembley Avenue
Rawstorne Road
PO
St H
Gdns
Medw

Marsh Farm I grid square represents 500 metres

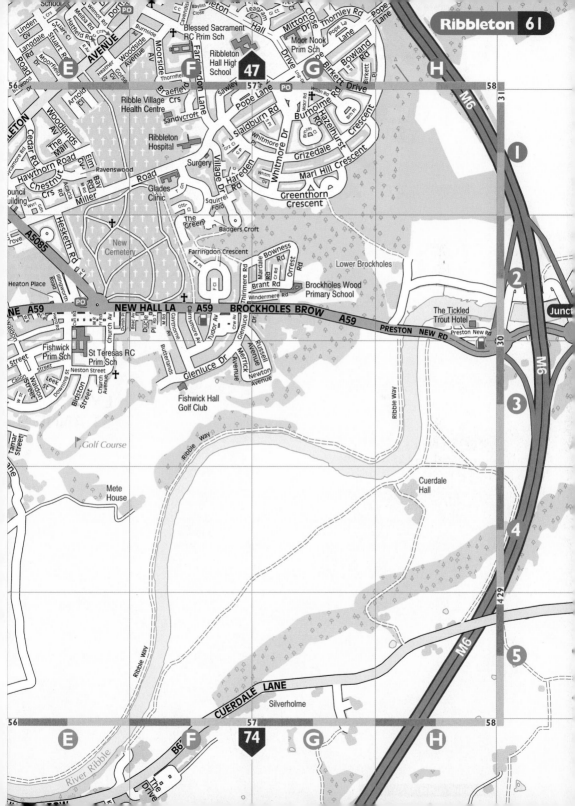

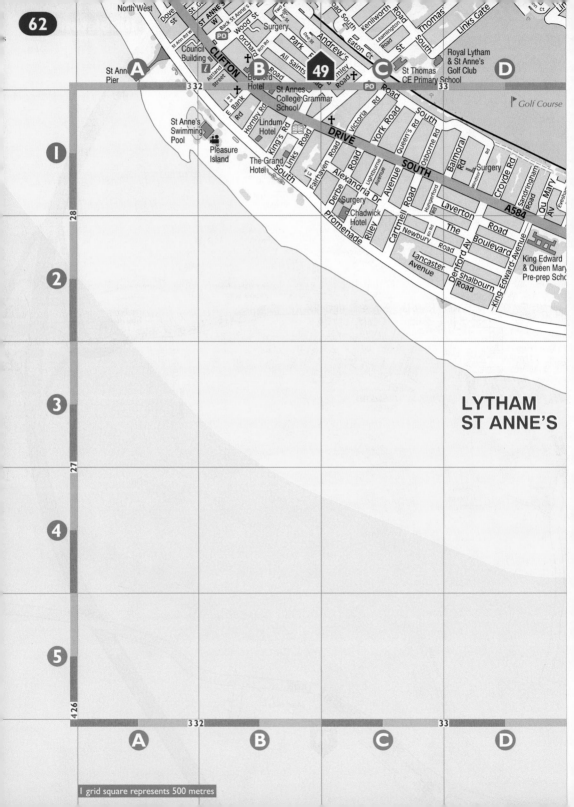

North West

Dove St

ST ANNE'S
W

Wood St

Surgery

Kenilworth Road

St Thomas
South

Links Gate

Council
Building

Orchard

All Saints

Eaton Ct

Road

Leamington
Road

Andrew's

Royal Lytham
& St Anne's
Golf Club

St Ann
Pier

A

i

CLIFTON

B

Bedford
Hotel

St Annes
College Grammar
School

49

Imley
Road

PO

C

St Thomas
CE Primary School

33

D

Golf Course

3 32

St Anne's
Swimming
Pool

Hornby Rd

Lindum
Hotel

King's Rd

Links Road

Victoria Rd

York Road

Queen's Rd

Osborne Rd

Road

South

Balmoral Rd

Surgery

Croyde Rd

Sandringham
Road

Qu Mary
Av

I

28

Pleasure
Island

The Grand
Hotel

South

Fairhaven Road

Alexandria Dr

Derby
Road

Surgery

Lightburne
Avenue

Road

Avenue

Hungerford

Laverton
Road

Windsor Rd

A584

Chadwick
Hotel

Promenade

Riley

Cartmell
Road

Newbury

kn rd

The
Boulevard

King Edward
& Queen Mary
Pre-prep Scho

2

Lancaster
Avenue

Road

Denford Av

shalbourn
Road

King Edward Avenue

King Edward
& Queen Mary
Pre-prep Scho

3

27

**LYTHAM
ST ANNE'S**

4

5

426

3 32

33

A

B

C

D

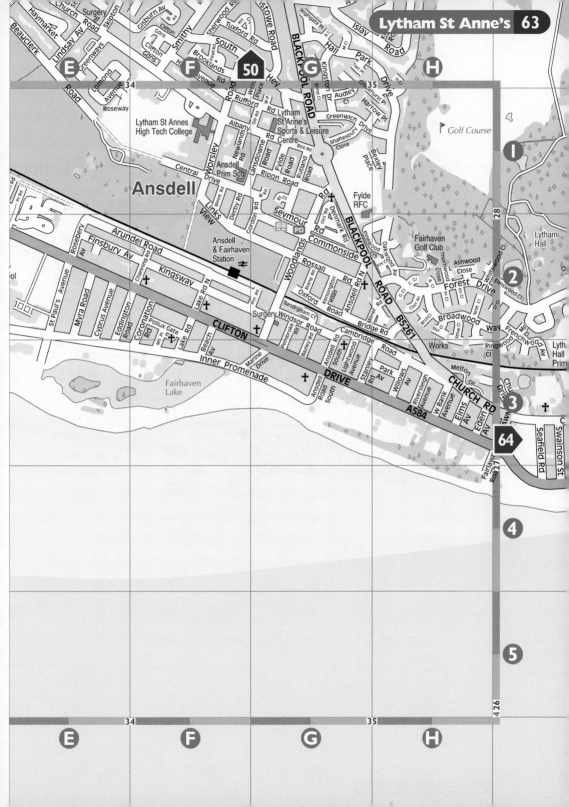

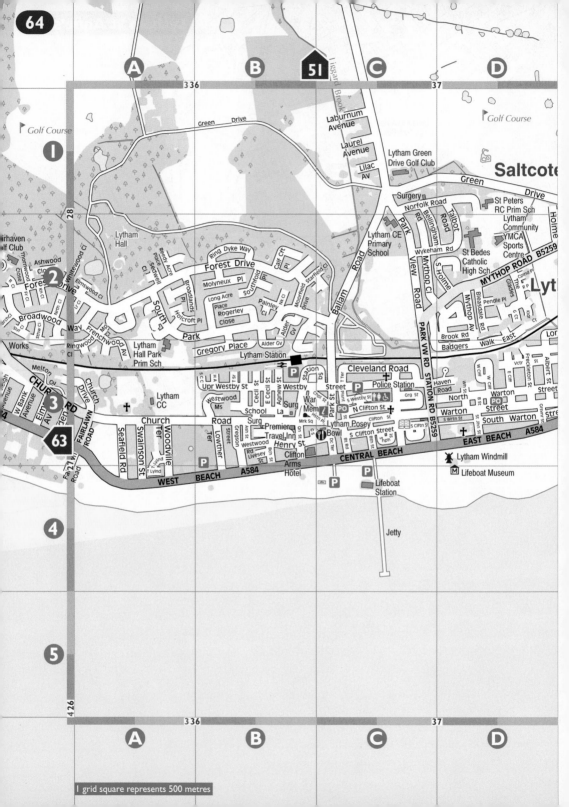

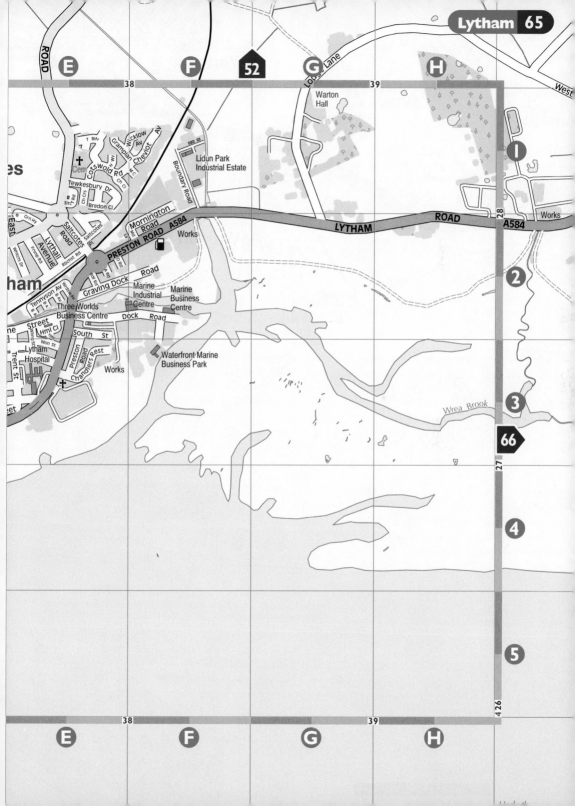

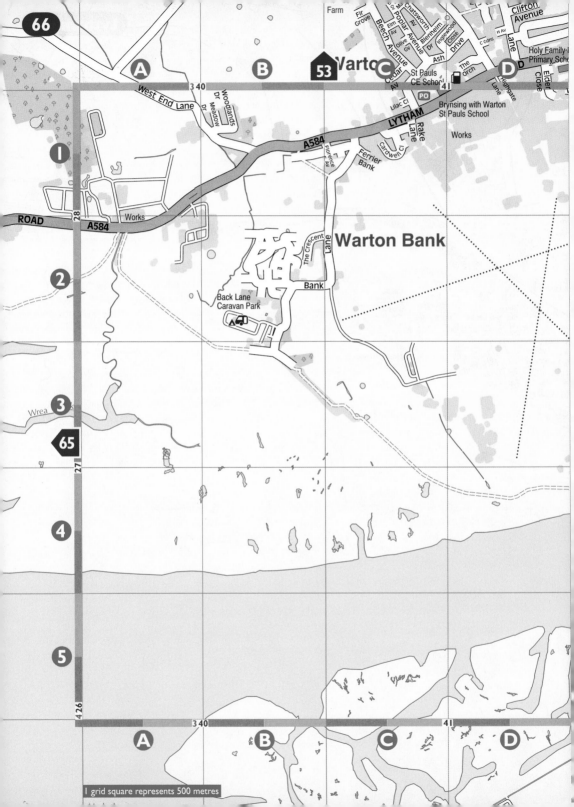

66

A   B   53 **Warto**C   D

West End Lane   3 40

Woodlands Dr
Meadow Dr

1

A584   LYTHAM

Florence Av

Ferrier Bank

Cardwell Cl

Rake Lane

Farm

Fir Grove

Chatsworth Av
Poplar Avenue   Blenheim Dr
Beech Avenue   Elm Av
Olive Gv   Inglewood Close
Ash   C Gdns   H Av

Cedar Av

St Pauls CE School

PO

Clifton Avenue

The Orch

Highgate Lane

Elder Close

Holy Family Primary Sch

Brynsing with Warton St Pauls School

Works

ROAD   28   A584   Works

2

The Crescent

Bank

Lane   **Warton Bank**

Back Lane Caravan Park

Wrea   **3**

27

65

4

26

5

4 26   3 40   4 1

A   B   C   D

1 grid square represents 500 metres

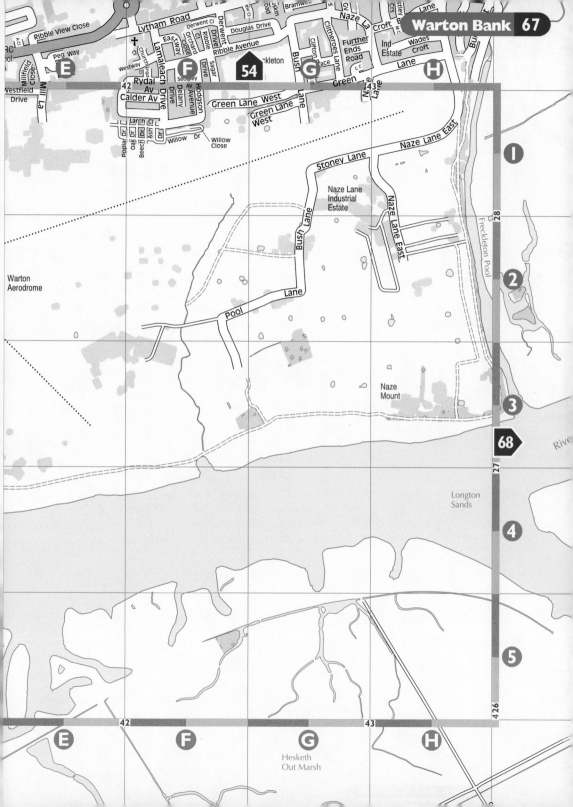

Ribble View Close

Lytham Road

Peg Way

Derwent Cl

Derwent Drive

Douglas Drive

Naze La

Bramwell

Croft

Lane

Ind Estate

Wades Croft

E

Millfield Close

Westfield Drive

Mill La

Westway

Lamaleach Drive

Rydal Av

Calder Av

Churchland

42

Eastway

Sedgley Av

Delany Avenue

Hodgson Drive

Ribble Drive

Sagar Drive

Orchard Drive

Ribble Avenue

Clitheroes Lane

Clifton Place

Bush Green

Further Ends Road

Lane

54

F

G

H

Poplar Dr

Oak Dr

Beech Dr

Larch Cl

Willow Dr

Willow Close

Green Lane West

Green Lane West

Green Lane

Naze Lane

143

Naze Lane East

I

Stoney Lane

Bush Lane

Naze Lane Industrial Estate

Naze Lane East

Freckleton Pool

28

2

Warton Aerodrome

Pool Lane

Naze Mount

3

68

River

27

Longton Sands

4

5

426

E

42

F

G

43

H

Hesketh Out Marsh

68

Bunker St.

Lane East

A

B

55

C

D

3 44

45

Grange
Farm

1

28

Freckleton Pool

2

3

67

27

River Ribble

Hutton
Sands

Hutton
Marsh

Longton
Sands

4

5

Longton
Marsh

426

3 44

45

A

B

C

D

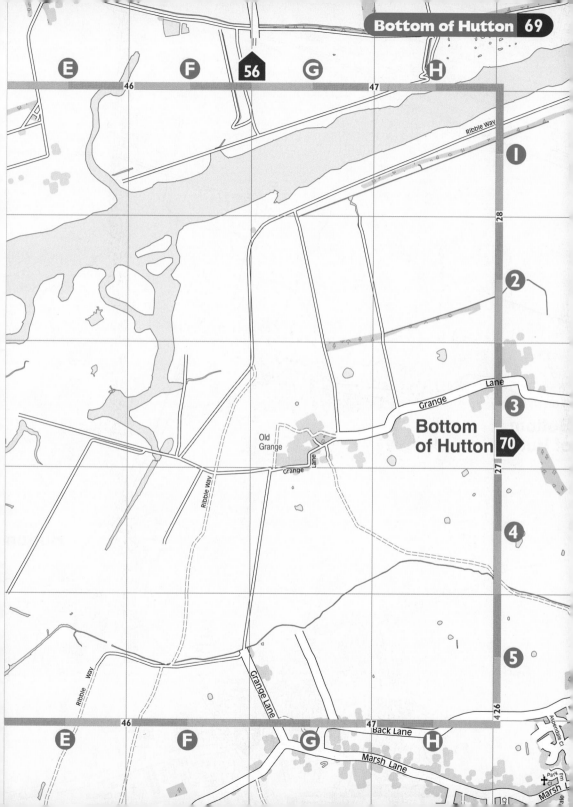

E   F   56   G   H

46   47

Ribble Way

I

28

2

Grange Lane

3

Old Grange

Bottom of Hutton 70

Grange Lane

27

4

Ribble Way

5

426

Ribble Way

Grange Lane

46   47   Back Lane

E   F   G   H

Marsh Lane

✝ Park
Cl

Marsh L

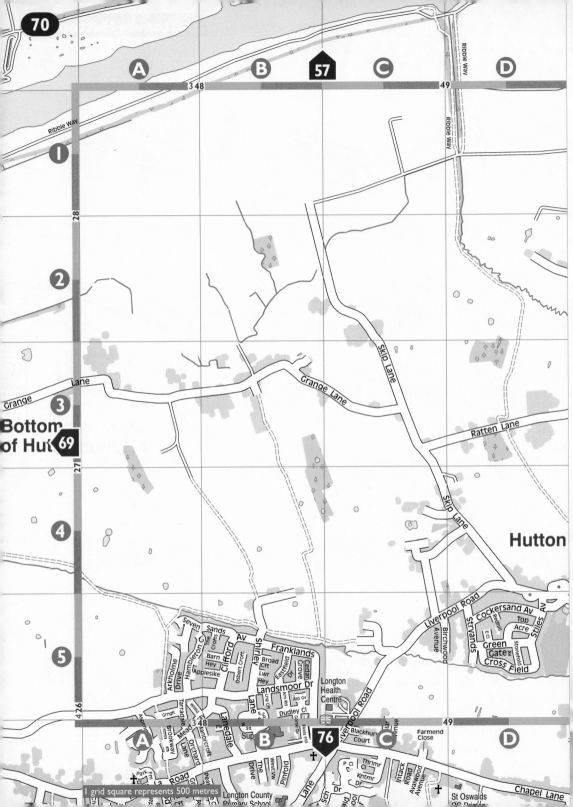

70

A   B   **57**   C   D

Ribble Way

3 48   49

Ribble Way

Ribble Way

1

28

2

Skip Lane

Grange Lane

Grange   Lane

Grange   Lane

3

Bottom of Hut   **69**

Ratten Lane

27

Skip Lane

4

Hutton

5

4 26

Liverpool Road

Cockersand Av

Birchwood Avenue

Stryands

Top Acre

Redhill

Stiles Av

Seven Sands

The Crofts

Clifford Av

Shirley Lane

Franklands

Cedar Grove

Broad Cft

Eastfield Dr

Green Gate

Stonefield

Cross Field

Hambleton Cl

Barn Hey

Osbert Croft

Lwr Hey

Applesike

Arkholme Drive

Landsmoor Dr

Ann Rd

Aid Gv

Corse Fld

Longton Health Centre

Dudley Cl

A   B   **76**   C   D

3 48   49

Lanedale

Manorcroft

Orchard

Brookway

Mead

Grngfl

Wind

W Sq

Sup

Fields Fld

Liverpool Road

Blackhurst Court

Farmend Close

Avalwood Avenue

Intack Road

Chapel Lane

Park Fm

The Drive

Pinfold

West La

Sch Dr

P Cl   L Cl

Thrimr Cl

Kntmr

St Oswalds

I grid square represents 500 metres

Longton County Primary School

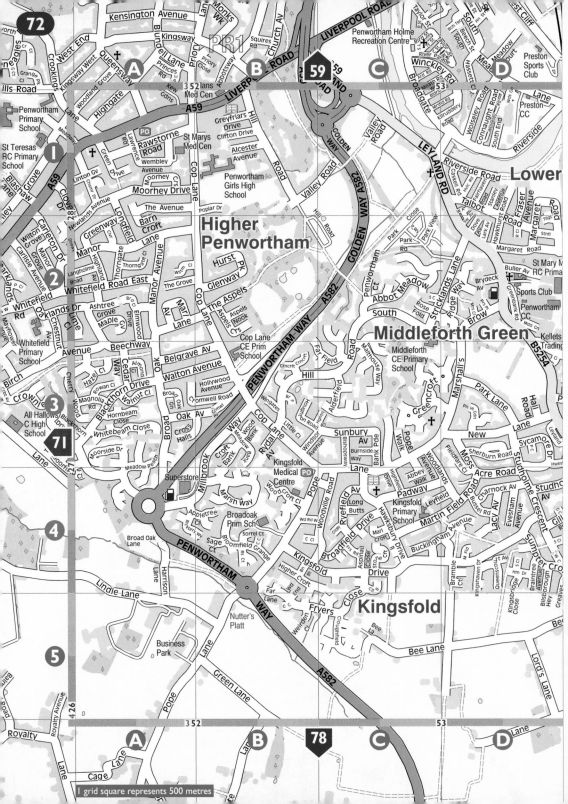

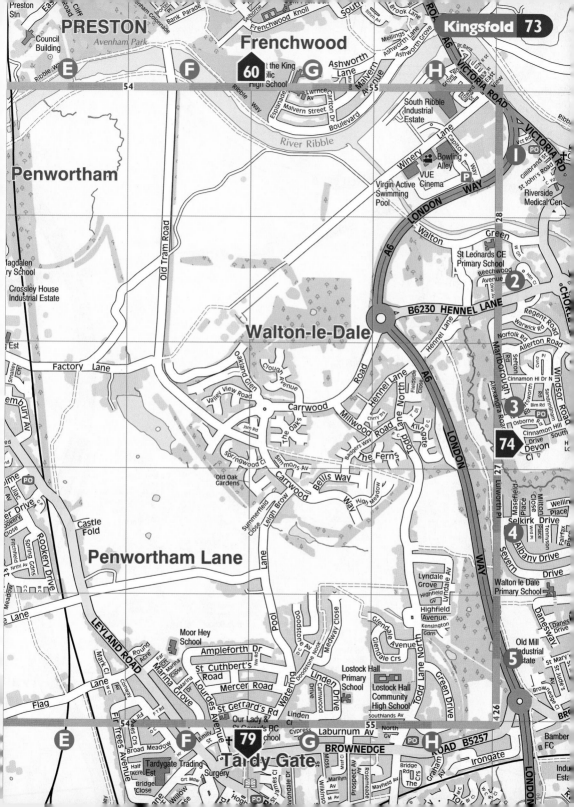

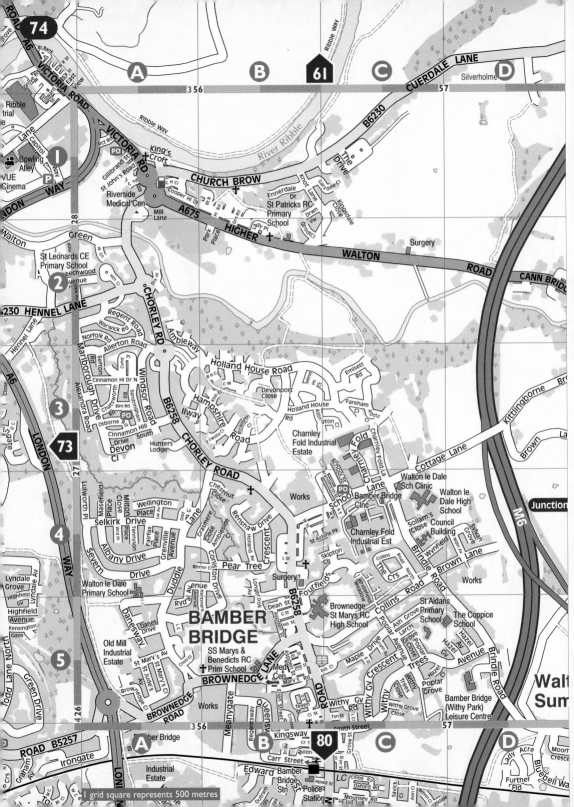

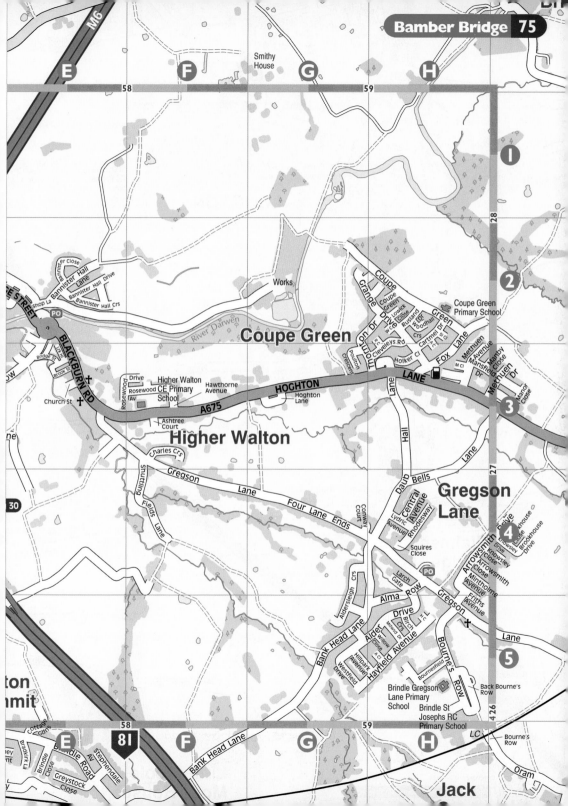

E   F   G   H

58   59

I

28

2

Smithy House

Bannister Hall Lane

er Close

Bannister Hall Drive

Bannister Hall Crs

shop La

PO

STREET

Works

River Darwen

Coupe Green

Coupe Green Primary School

Grange Drive

Thornton Dr

Coupe Green

Lowick Close

Rusland

Woodhall

W Cl

Cartmel Dr

Cleveleys Rd

Poulton Crescent

Holker Cl

Fox Lane

Methuen Avenue

Mansfield Close

Manby Dr

Methuen Dr

M Cl

BLACKBURN RD

Bridge St

Little St

Brook St

Church St

Drive

Rosewood Av

Higher Walton CE Primary School

Hawthorne Avenue

HOGHTON LANE

A675

Hoghton Lane

Lane

Hall

Manor Close

3

27

Ashtree Court

Higher Walton

Charles Crs

Gregson Lane

Shuttling Fields Lane

Four Lane Ends

Daub Bells

Central Avenue

Conway Court

Lydric Avenue

Rhodesway

Gregson Lane

Drive

Knowsley Close

Knowsley Close

Brookhouse Close

Brookhouse Drive

Arrowsmith Close

Arrowsmith

Minthorne Avenue

4

30

Squires Close

Larch Gate

PO

Alma Row

Drive

Friths Avenue

Gregson

Lane

5

Aldersleigh Crs

Willow Close

Birch Cl

Moorca Cl

A Cl

Alder Drive

Bank Head Lane

Lilypark Avenue

Westfield Drive

Hayfield Avenue

L

Bournesfield

Bourne's Row

Back Bourne's Row

426

Brindle Gregson Lane Primary School

Brindle St Josephs RC Primary School

ton mmit

LC

Bourne's Row

Cottage Gdns

Bradkirk La

Brindle Close

Stephendale Av

Greystock Close

BRINDLE Road

E   81   F   G   H

58   59

Oram

Jack

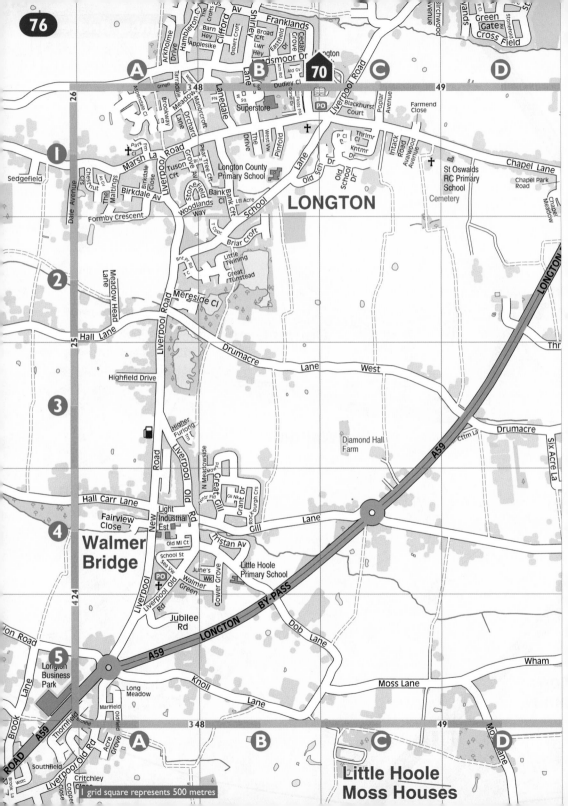

LONGTON

Walmer Bridge

Little Hoole Moss Houses

1 grid square represents 500 metres

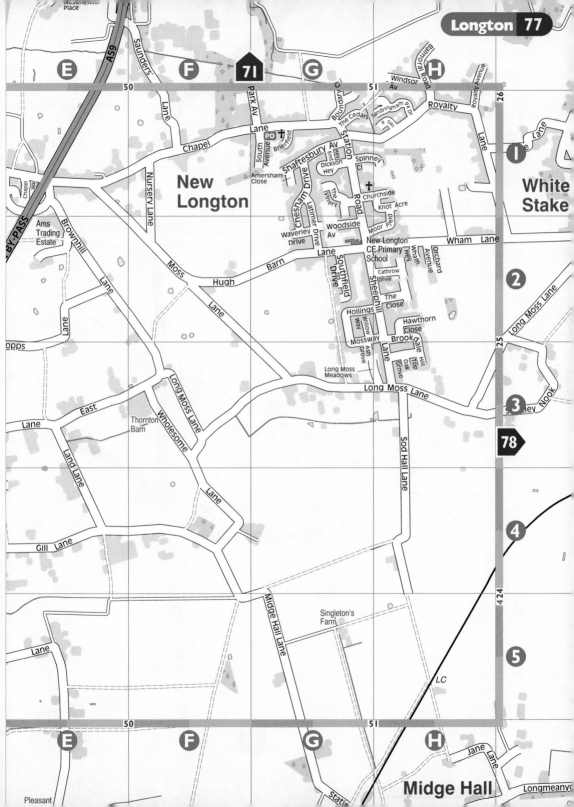

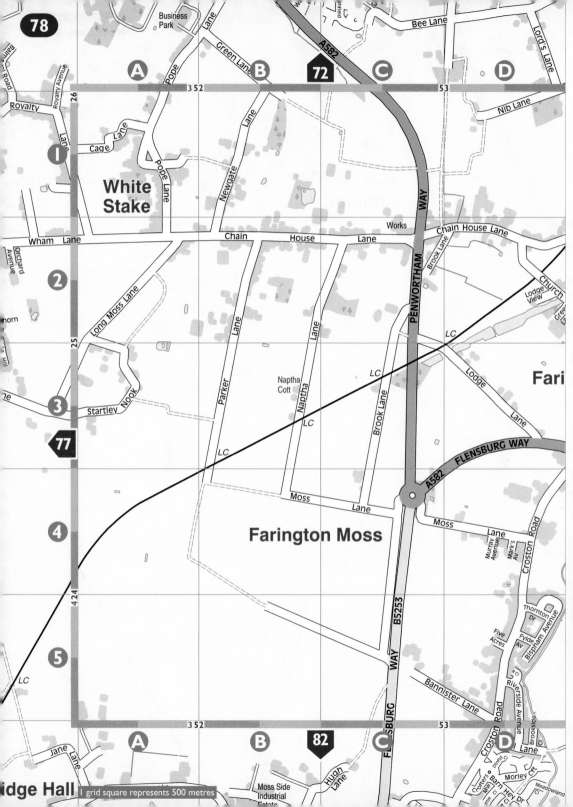

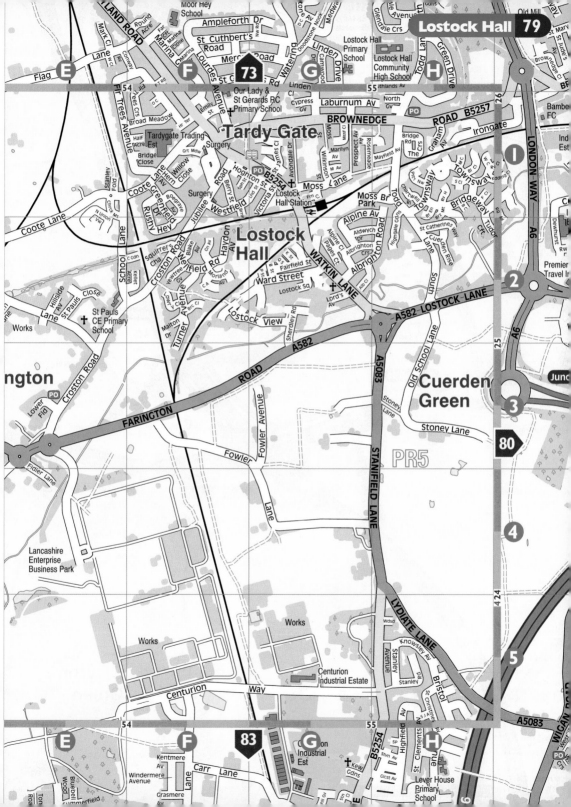

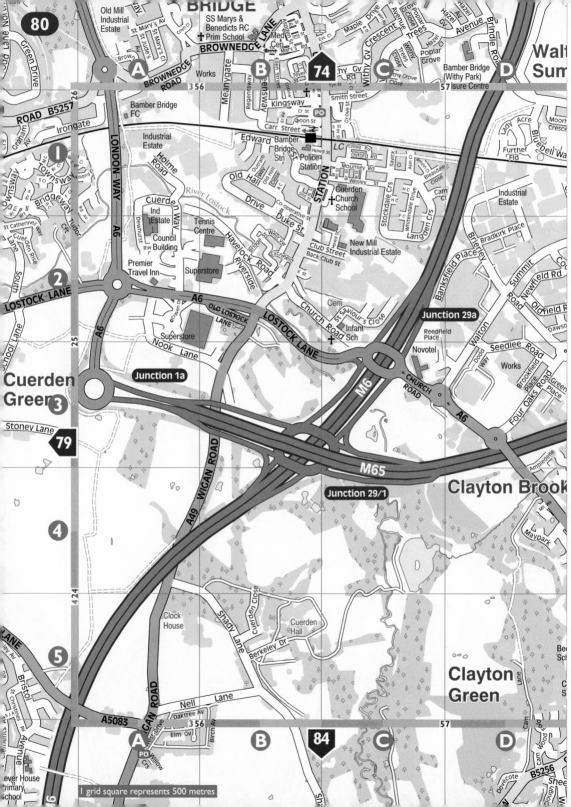

BRIDGE

80

SS Marys & Benedicts RC Prim School

BROWNEDGE LANE

BROWNEDGE ROAD B56

Old Mill Industrial Estate

St Mary's Av
St Jude's

Green Drive

A

Works

B

74

C

Bamber Bridge (Withy Park) Leisure Centre

57

D

Walt
Sum

Maple Drive

Withy Gv Crescent

Trees

Hazel Avenue

Brindle Road

Poplar Grove

Bamber Bridge

ROAD B5257

Graham

Irongate

Townsway

Bridgeway

Bamber Bridge FC

Industrial Estate

Meanygate

LONDON WAY A6

Holme Road

Regentsway

Ellen Street

Kingsway

Carr Street

Edward Bamber Bridge Str

Police Station

STATION

Smith street

LC

Oxford Rd

Mounsey Rd

Wesley

Cuerden Church School

Stockdale Crs

Langden Crs

Bleasdale Close

Whitendale Drive

Cam CI

Lady Acre

Bluebell Wa

Further Fld

Moorh Cresce

Industrial Estate

I

St Catherines Lane

Cuerden Rise

Tudor Av

Cuerden Way

Ind Estate

Dewhurst

Tennis Centre

Council Building

Old Hall

Old Hall Drive

Duke St

West Uw

Club Street

Back Club St

New Mill Industrial Estate

Bankfield Place

Brierley

Bradkirk Place

Summit Road

Newfield Rd

Oldfield Rd

2

LOSTOCK LANE

Premier Travel Inn

A6

Superstore

Havelock Road

Riverside

Church Road

St Saviour's Close

Junction 29a

Walton

Reedfield Place

Novotel

Seedlee Road

Works

Brookfield Place

Four Oaks Road

Cuerden
Green

3

Nook Lane

Superstore

OLD LOSTOCK LANE

LOSTOCK LANE

Infant Sch

Cem

M6

CHURCH ROAD

A6

79

Stoney Lane

WIGAN ROAD A49

Junction 29/1

M65

Clayton Brook

4

5

Bristol

Clock House

Shady Lane

Cuerden Close

Berkeley Dr

Cuerden Hall

Maypark

Clayton
Green

A5083

Nell Lane

Oaktree Av

Elm Gv

Birch Av

356

A

B

84

57

C

D

PO

Willow

B5256

1 grid square represents 500 metres

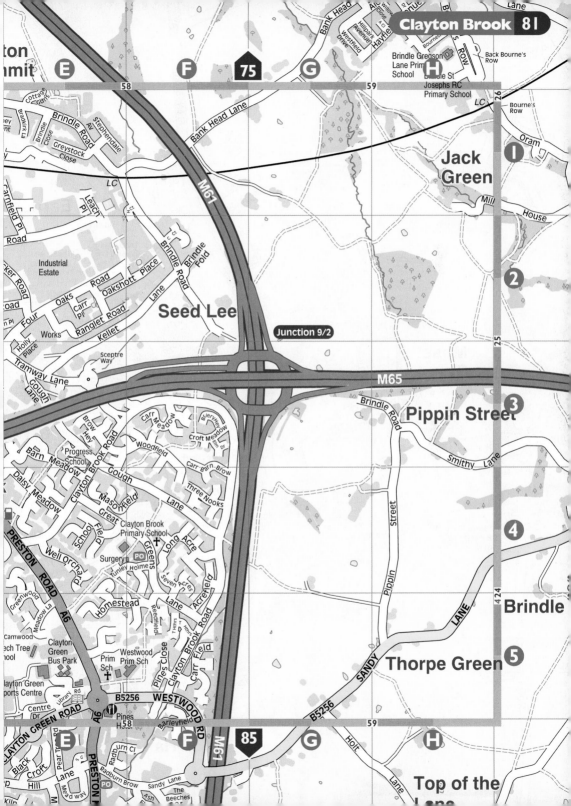

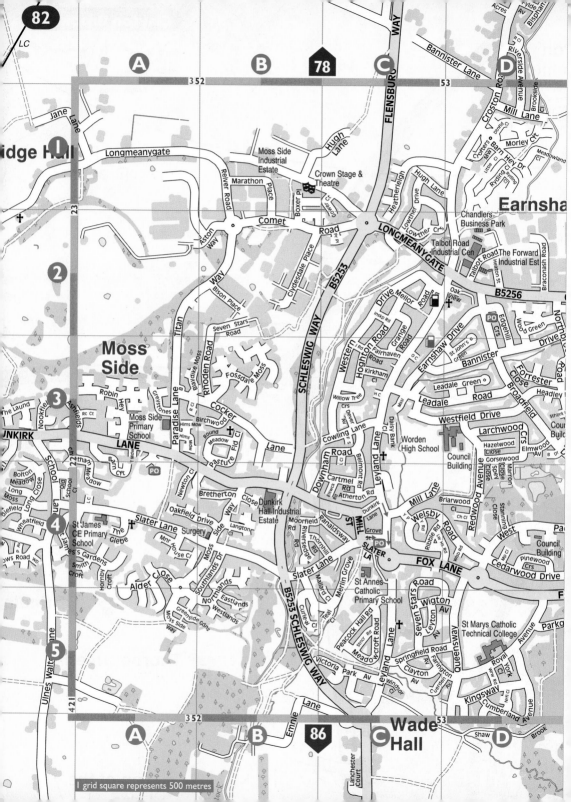

LC

A B 78 C D

352 53

Jane Lane
idge Hall
Longmeanygate

FLENSBURG WAY

Bannister Lane

Croston Road

Mill Lane
Brookside
Riverside Avenue

Acres
Fylde
Bispham

Corners
Barn
Hey Dr
Morley Crt
Meadowland

Ryding
Ryding

Moss Side Industrial Estate

Crown Stage & Theatre

Hugh Lane

Heatherleigh

Hugh Lane

Lowther Drive

Lowther Crs

Chandlers Business Park

Earnsha

Relver Road
Marathon Place
Boxer Pl
Comet
Road

Aston Way
Clydesdale Place

LONGMEANYGATE

Talbot Road Industrial Cen

Oak View

Talbot Road
Heaton St

The Forward Industrial Est

23

2

Titan
Bison Place
Seven Stars Road

Way

SCHLESWIG WAY

B5253

Mellor Road

Drive

Western Road

Houghton Road

Grange Road

Earnshaw Drive

St John's Green

PO
Edgehill Crs

Wood Green

B5256

Northleigh

Drive

Moss Side
Robin Hey
Ashfields
Nookfield
The Laund
RC Ct
Greystones

Rhoden Road

Blaydike Moss

Fossdale Moss

Paradise Lane

Cocker

Birchwood Cl

Lane

Fairhaven Road

Kirkham Cl

Willow Tree Crs

Dewer PNT

Daisy Bank

Bannister

Leadale Green

Leadale Road

Westfield Drive

Forrester Close

Broadfield

Headley

Court Build

3
UNKIRK

Moss Side Primary School

Hims Mdw

Round Meadow Fld

Birchwood Cl

Pasture Fld

LANE

Barn Cft

PO

Cowling Lane

Downham Road

Cartmel Rd

Belmont Rd

Atherton Rd

Leyland Lane

Worden High School

Larchwood Crs

Hazelwood Close

Elmwood Av

Gorsewood

Council Building

Marton Spey

22

Bolton Meadow

Long Moss

Wheatfield

School Road

4

St James CE Primary School
The Glebe
St James's Gardens
Smith Croft

Bretherton Close

Oakfield Drive

Langton Cl

Moorfield

Riversedge

Thornhill Cl

Ranalasway

St MILL

Dunkirk Lane

Grove

Welsby Road

Ribble Rd

Redwood Avenue

Briarwood Close

Stanning Close

West

Council Building

Pinewood Crs

Cedarwood Drive

Parkg

421

Ulnes Walton Lane

Alder Close

Southlands Dr

Mnr House Cl

Northlands

Eastlands

Westlands

Greenside Gdns

Moss Side Way

B5253 SCHLESWIG WAY

Merlin Grove

Mallard Cl

Teal

Curlew Cl

St Annes Catholic Primary School

Peacock Hall Rd

Meadowcroft Road

Leyland Lane

Seven Stars Road

Wigton Av

Leyton

Springfield Road

Clayton Av

Windsor

Queensway

St Marys Catholic Technical College

Royal York

Kingsway

Cumberland Avenue

Farington

5

352

A B 86 C D

Emnie Lane

Victoria Park Av

Shaw

Wade Hall
53

Lanchester Court

Brook

1 grid square represents 500 metres

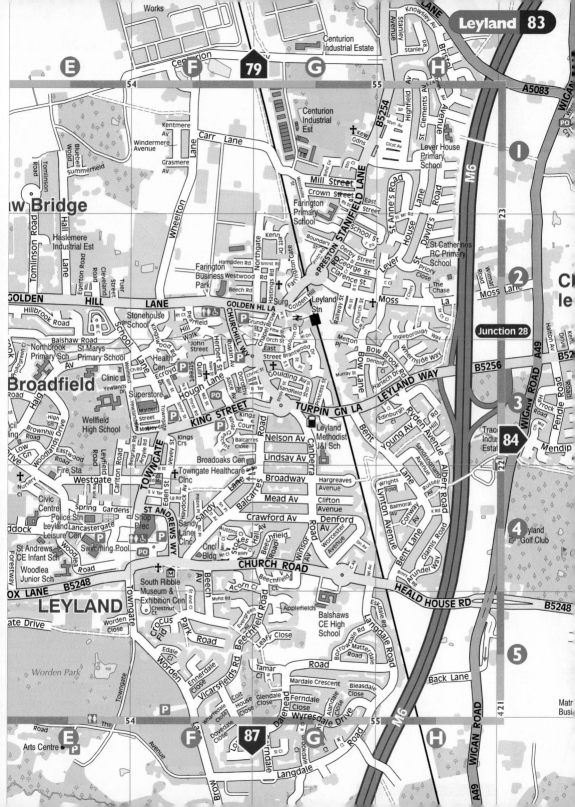

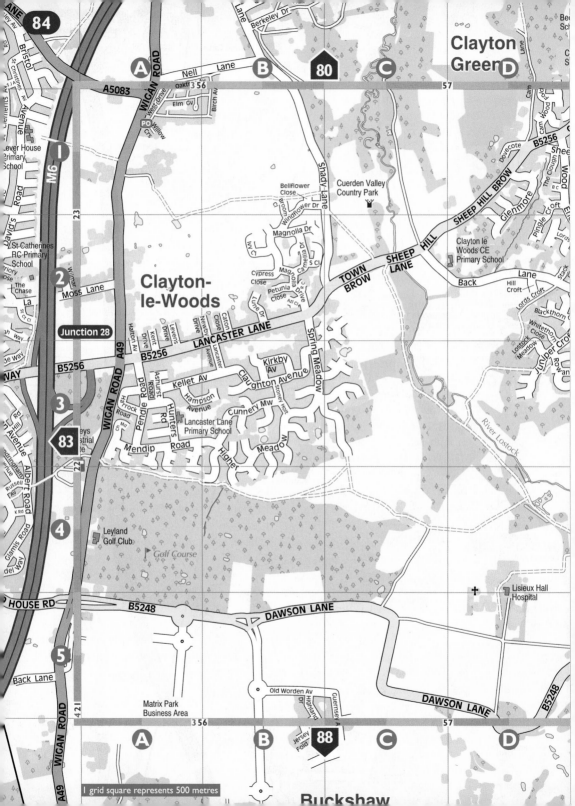

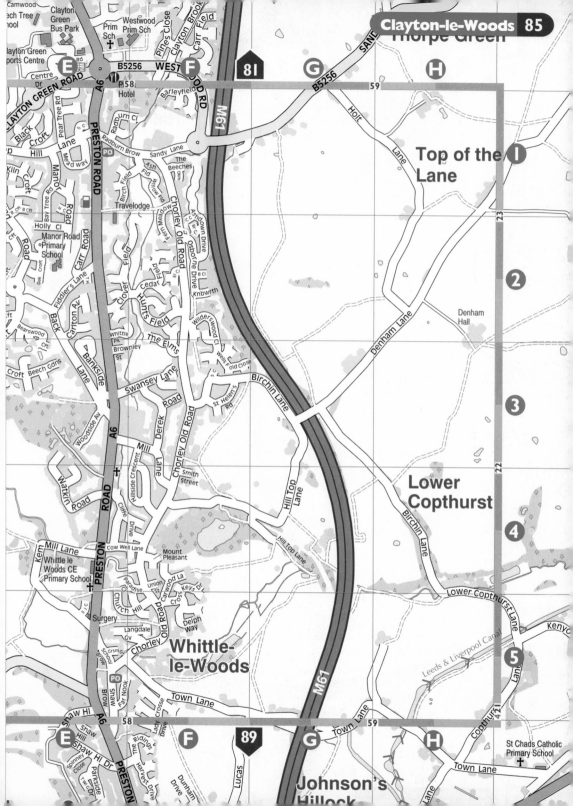

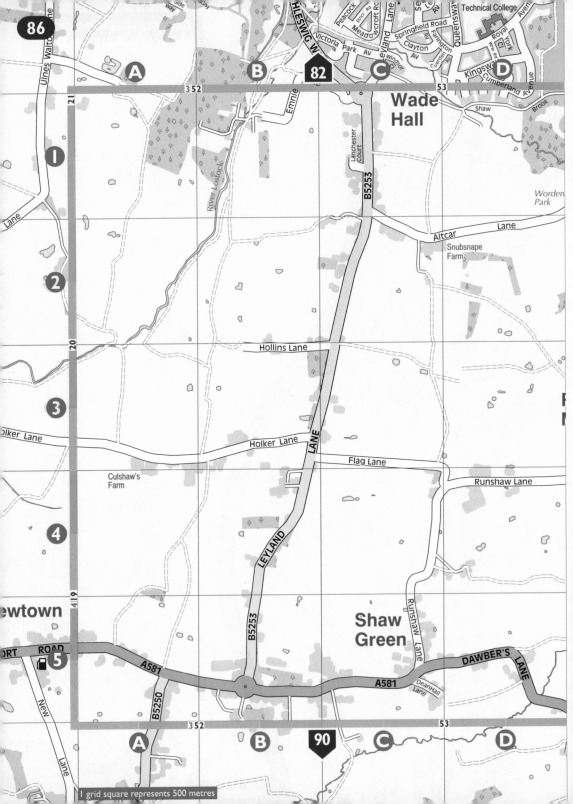

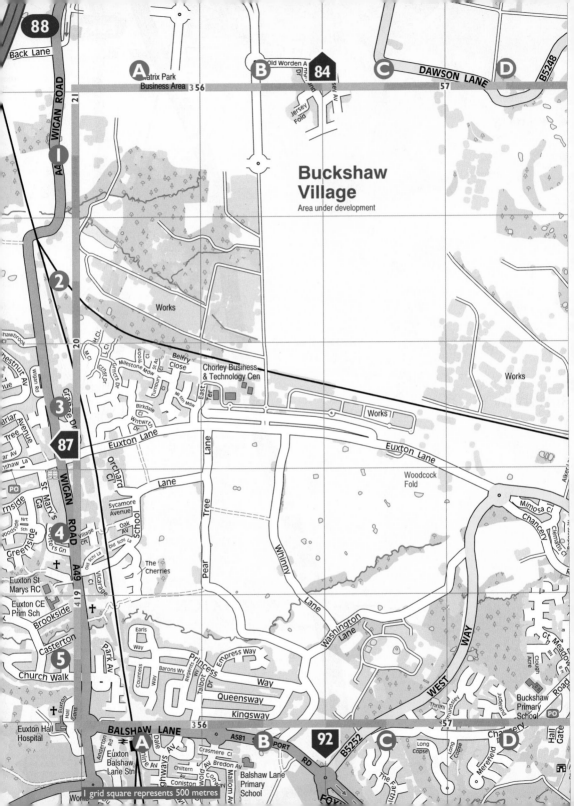

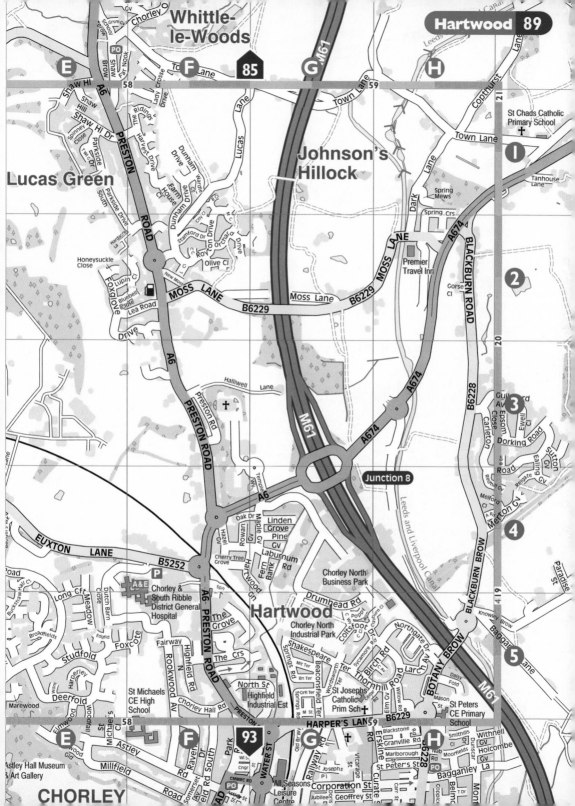

Whittle-le-Woods

Lucas Green

Johnson's Hillock

St Chads Catholic Primary School

Town Lane

Tanhouse Lane

Honeysuckle Close

MOSS LANE
B6229
Moss Lane
B6229

Premier Travel Inn

Gorse Cl

PRESTON ROAD
A6

Halliwell Lane

M61

A674
BLACKBURN ROAD

B6228

Guildford Av
Ewell Cl
Epsom Close
Carleton
Dorking Road
Sutton Gv
Ealing Gv
Regate
Melford
Merton Gv

Junction 8

EUXTON LANE
B5252

Chorley & South Ribble District General Hospital
A&E
P

Linden Grove
Pine Gv
Laburnum Rd

Chorley North Business Park

Hartwood

Chorley North Industrial Park

Drumhead Rd

St Michaels CE High School

North St Highfield Industrial Est

St Josephs Catholic Prim Sch

BLACKBURN BROW
BOTANY BROW
Knowley Brow
Baggan Lane

St Peters CE Primary School

Paradise St

M61

HARPER'S LANE
B6229

Astley Hall Museum & Art Gallery

WATER ST
CMMRC RD
93

All Seasons Leisure Centre

Corporation St

St Peter's St

Bagganley La

PO

CHORLEY

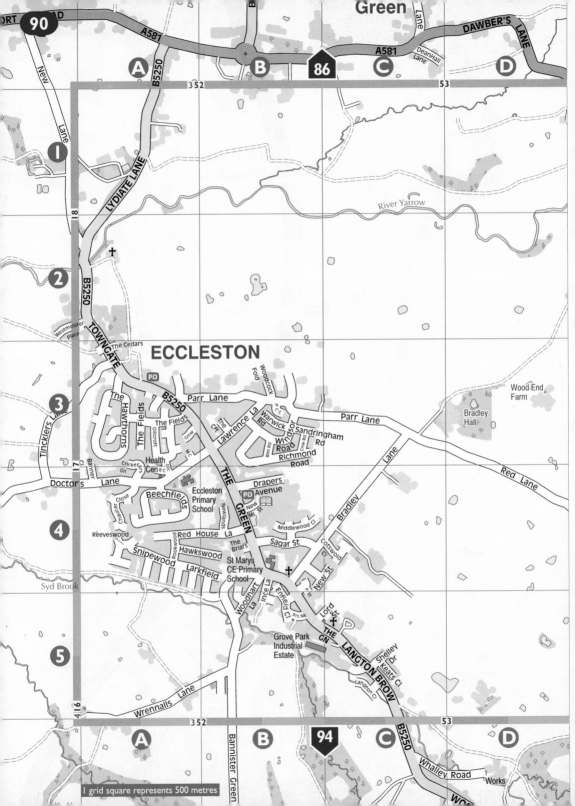

ECCLESTON

Green

90

86

94

A581
DAWBER'S LANE
A581
DeanHall Lane

A B5250 B C D

352 53

New Lane

LYDIATE LANE

River Yarrow

B5250

1

2

Westminster Place

The Cedars

TOWNGATE

B5250

PO

3

Tincklers Lane

The Hawthorns

The Fields

The Fields

Gillcroft

Parr Lane

Woodcock Fold

Woodcock

Lawrence La

Warwick Rd

Windsor Road

Sandringham Rd

Parr Lane

Wood End Farm

Bradley Hall

Red Lane

Health Cen

Cricketers Gn

Banner

Doctor's Lane

Chancel

Close

Beechfields

Eccleston Primary School

Blm Rd

Richmond Road

Chw Rd

THE GREEN

Drapers Avenue

PO

New Ml

Bradley Lane

4

Reeveswood

Red House La

Newlands

Rookwood

Snipewood

Hawkswood

Larkfield

The Briars

Middlewood Cl

Sagar St

Cotswold

St Marys CE Primary School

New St

Woodhart La

Ince La

Enfield Ct

Prs NK

Lord St

THE GN

Shelley Dr

Keats Ct

Syd Brook

5

Grove Park Industrial Estate

THE LANGTON BROW

Langton Cl

416

Wrennalls Lane

Bannister Green

B5250

Whalley Road

WO

Works

A B C D

352 53

E F 87 G H

Church Walk

54

55

BALSHAW

Euxton Hall
Hospital

Euxton
Balshaw
Lane Stn

DAWBER'S LANE

Old Dawber's La

Works

A581

I

Works

Mill Lane

M6

Pincock St

Fieldside Av

A49

Pincock

**Bolton
Green**

Pincock Brow

2

German La

CROSS BROW

Mill Lane

Back Lane

SIBBERING BROW

3

92

**Charnock
Green**

CHARNOCK BROW

Back Lane

M6

4

Delph Lane

Hall Lane

Old Hall

Old

5

Camelot
Theme
Park

Park Hall
Leisure
Centre

54

E F M6 95 G

55 PR7 H

Brook Lane

PRESTON RD

PO Church Lane

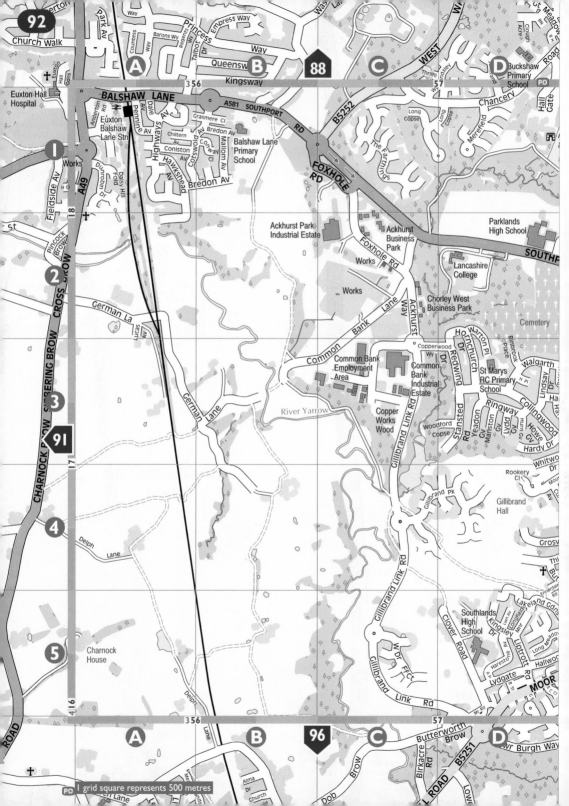

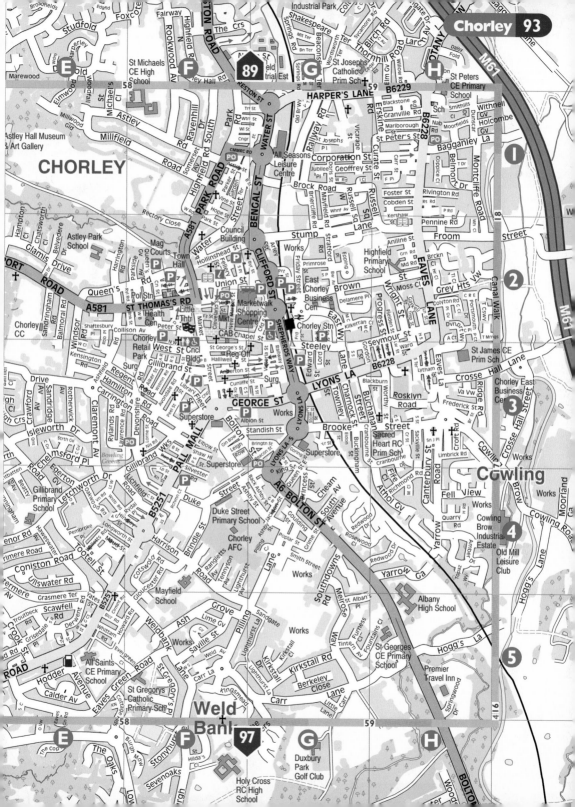

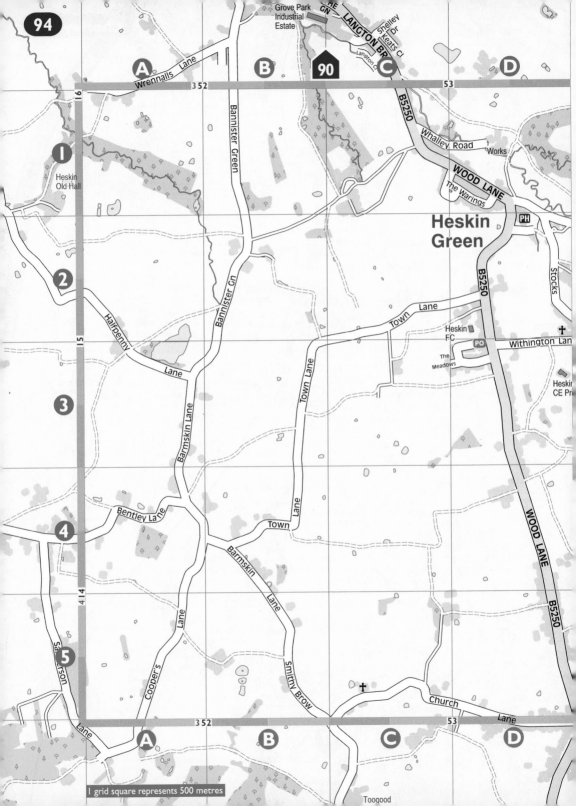

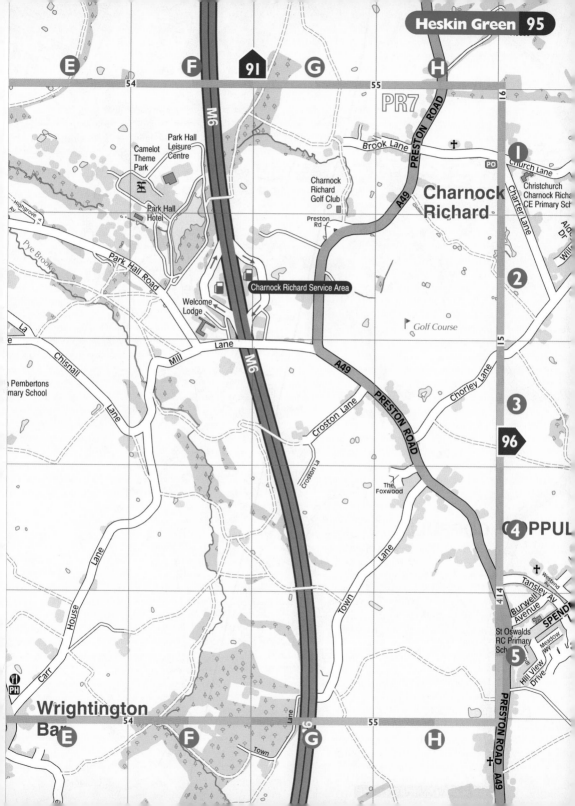

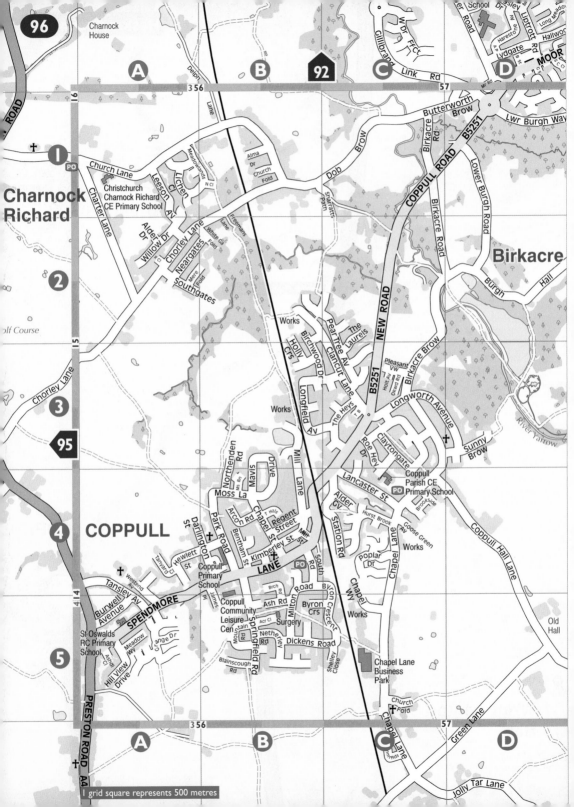

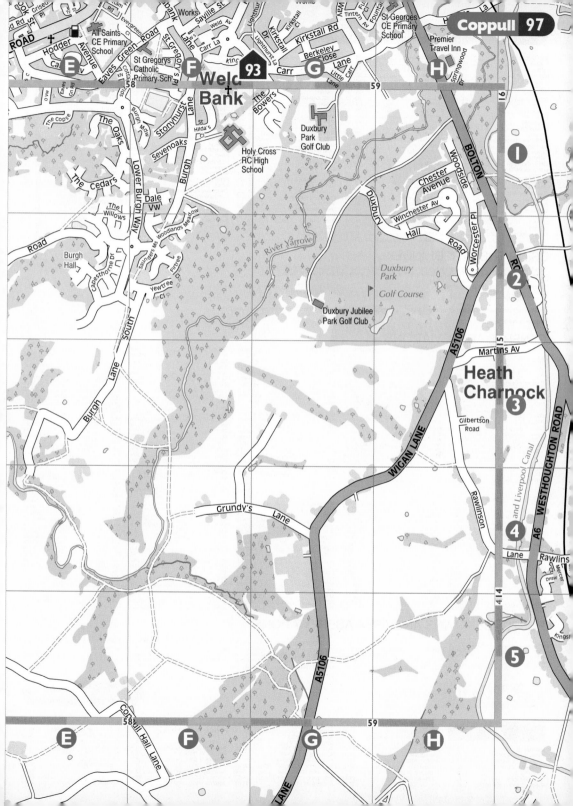

Anchorsholme 21 F3	Hutton 70 D4	New Longton 77 F1	Skippool 26 B2

Anchorsholme 21 F3
Ansdell 63 F1
Ashton on Ribble 58 B2
Bamber Bridge 74 A5
Birkacre 96 D2
Bispham 24 B2
Blackpool 3 J5
Bolton Green 91 H2
Bottom of Hutton 69 H3
Breedy Butts 26 A1
Broadfield 82 D3
Brookfield 47 E4
Broughton 56 C2
Bryning 53 E5
Buckshaw Village 88 B1
Burn Naze 17 H5
Cadley 45 E4
Carleton 25 H4
Charnock Green 91 G4
Charnock Richard 95 H1
Chorley 79 F1
Clayton Brook 80 D4
Clayton Green 80 D5
Clayton-le-Woods 84 A2
Cleveleys 20 B1
Clifton 56 B2
Cold Row 19 G4
Common Edge 39 F2
Coppull 96 A4
Cottam 44 A2
Coupe Green 75 G2
Cowling 93 H4

Cuerden Green 79 H3
Dowbridge 43 H4
Earnshaw Bridge 82 D1
Eccleston 90 A3
Euxton 87 G5
Farington 78 D3
Farington Moss 78 B4
Fishwick 60 C3
Fleetwood 11 F1
Freckleton 54 H4
Fulwood 45 H5
Grange 47 G4
Great Marton 5 K2
Great Marton Moss 39 H4
Great Marton Moss Side 39 H1
Gregson Lane 75 H4
Haighton Top 37 G4
Hall Cross 54 B2
Hambleton 23 G5
Hambleton Moss Side 23 H4
Hardhorn 30 C2
Hartwood 89 G5
Hawes Side 5 J6
Hay Houses 50 A5
Heath Charnock 97 H5
Heskin Green 81 E2
Higher Ballam 51 E2
Higher Penwortham 72 B2
Higher Walton 75 F3
Holme Slack 46 D4
Hoohill 28 D5
Howick Cross 71 G2

Hutton 70 D4
Ingol 44 C4
Jack Green 81 H1
Johnson's Hillock 89 G1
Kellamergh 53 F4
Kingsfold 72 C5
Kirkham 43 F2
Knott End-on-Sea 12 C1
Layton 3 J2
Lea 57 H2
Leyland 83 E5
Little Bispham 8 B4
Little Carleton 51 F1
Little Layton 29 F2
Little Marton 34 B4
Little Poulton 27 E4
Little Thornton 22 C5
Longton 76 B1
Lostock Hall 79 F2
Lower Ballam 51 F1
Lower Copthurst 85 H4
Lower Penwortham 72 D1
Lucas Green 89 E1
Lytham 64 D2
Lytham St Anne's 62 D5
Mereside 34 H4
Middleforth Green 72 C2
Moor End 19 G5
Moss Side 52 A2
Moss Side 82 A3
Mowbreck 43 F1
Mythop 35 E3

New Longton 77 F1
Newton 30 A4
Newton with Scales 55 E1
Nog Tow 44 B1
Norbreck 20 B5
Norcross 21 G5
Normoss 50 A3
North Shore 28 C2
Peel 40 D4
Peel Hill 40 C1
Penwortham Lane 73 E4
Pilling Lane 8 C4
Pincock 91 H1
Pippin Street 81 H5
Poulton-le-Fylde 26 C5
Preesall 13 F1
Preesall Park 13 G5
Preston 7 H4
Pudding Pie Nook 37 F2
Queenstown 3 F1
Red Scar 47 H2
Ribbleton 60 C1
Ribby 42 B4
Riversway Docklands 58 C3
Runshaw Moor 86 D5
St Anne's 49 E5
Saltcotes 64 D1
Scronkey 15 F5
Seed Lee 81 F2
Sharoe Green 45 G1
Shaw Green 86 C5
Singleton 31 H1

Skippool 26 B2
Smallwood Hey 14 D1
South Shore 4 D7
Sower Carr 19 H5
Squires Gate 38 C3
Staining 30 C5
Stake Pool 15 G2
Stalmine 19 H2
Stanah 22 C2
Staynall 19 E5
Tanterton 44 D3
Tardy Gate 79 F1
Thornton 22 C3
Thorpe Green 81 H5
Top o'th' Lane 85 H1
Treales 43 H1
Trunnah 22 A1
Wade Hall 86 C1
Walmer Bridge 76 A4
Walton-le-Dale 73 F2
Walton Summit 74 D5
Warbreck 28 D1
Warton 53 F5
Warton Bank 66 C2
Weld Bank 93 F5
Wesham 43 E2
Whiteholme 21 E5
White Stake 78 A1
Whittle-le-Woods 85 F5
Wrightington Bar 95 E5

USING THE STREET INDEX

Street names are listed alphabetically. Each street name is followed by its postal town or area locality, the Postcode District, the page number, and the reference to the square in which the name is found.

Standard index entries are shown as follows:

Abattoir Rd *BPOOL* FY1 ....2 E1

Street names and selected addresses not shown on the map due to scale restrictions are shown in the index with an asterisk:

Airedale Ct *PLF/KEOS* FY6 * 26 A3

GENERAL ABBREVIATIONS

ACC ....ACCESS	CTYD ....COURTYARD	HLS ....HILLS	MWY ....MOTORWAY	SE ....SOUTH EAST
ALY ....ALLEY	CUTT ....CUTTINGS	HO ....HOUSE	N ....NORTH	SER ....SERVICE AREA
AP ....APPROACH	CV ....COVE	HOL ....HOLLOW	NE ....NORTH EAST	SH ....SHORE
AR ....ARCADE	CYN ....CANYON	HOSP ....HOSPITAL	NW ....NORTH WEST	SHOP ....SHOPPING
ASS ....ASSOCIATION	DEPT ....DEPARTMENT	HRB ....HARBOUR	O/P ....OVERPASS	SKWY ....SKYWAY
AV ....AVENUE	DL ....DALE	HTH ....HEATH	OFF ....OFFICE	SMT ....SUMMIT
BCH ....BEACH	DM ....DAM	HTS ....HEIGHTS	ORCH ....ORCHARD	SOC ....SOCIETY
BLDS ....BUILDINGS	DR ....DRIVE	HVN ....HAVEN	OV ....OVAL	SP ....SPUR
BND ....BEND	DRO ....DROVE	HWY ....HIGHWAY	PAL ....PALACE	SPR ....SPRING
BNK ....BANK	DRY ....DRIVEWAY	IMP ....IMPERIAL	PAS ....PASSAGE	SQ ....SQUARE
BR ....BRIDGE	DWGS ....DWELLINGS	IN ....INLET	PAV ....PAVILION	ST ....STREET
BRK ....BROOK	E ....EAST	IND EST ....INDUSTRIAL ESTATE	PDE ....PARADE	STN ....STATION
BTM ....BOTTOM	EMB ....EMBANKMENT	INF ....INFIRMARY	PH ....PUBLIC HOUSE	STR ....STREAM
BUS ....BUSINESS	EMBY ....EMBASSY	INFO ....INFORMATION	PK ....PARK	STRD ....STRAND
BVD ....BOULEVARD	ESP ....ESPLANADE	INT ....INTERCHANGE	PKWY ....PARKWAY	SW ....SOUTH WEST
BY ....BYPASS	EST ....ESTATE	IS ....ISLAND	PL ....PLACE	TDG ....TRADING
CATH ....CATHEDRAL	EX ....EXCHANGE	JCT ....JUNCTION	PLN ....PLAIN	TER ....TERRACE
CEM ....CEMETERY	EXPY ....EXPRESSWAY	JTY ....JETTY	PLNS ....PLAINS	THWY ....THROUGHWAY
CEN ....CENTRE	EXT ....EXTENSION	KG ....KING	PLZ ....PLAZA	TNL ....TUNNEL
CFT ....CROFT	F/O ....FLYOVER	KNL ....KNOLL	POL ....POLICE STATION	TOLL ....TOLLWAY
CH ....CHURCH	FC ....FOOTBALL CLUB	L ....LAKE	PR ....PRINCE	TPK ....TURNPIKE
CHA ....CHASE	FK ....FORK	LA ....LANE	PREC ....PRECINCT	TR ....TRACK
CHYD ....CHURCHYARD	FLD ....FIELD	LDG ....LODGE	PREP ....PREPARATORY	TRL ....TRAIL
CIR ....CIRCLE	FLDS ....FIELDS	LGT ....LIGHT	PRIM ....PRIMARY	TWR ....TOWER
CIRC ....CIRCUS	FLS ....FALLS	LK ....LOCK	PROM ....PROMENADE	U/P ....UNDERPASS
CL ....CLOSE	FLTS ....FLATS	LKS ....LAKES	PRS ....PRINCESS	UNI ....UNIVERSITY
CLFS ....CLIFFS	FM ....FARM	LNDG ....LANDING	PRT ....PORT	UPR ....UPPER
CMP ....CAMP	FT ....FORT	LTL ....LITTLE	PT ....POINT	VA ....VALE
CNR ....CORNER	FWY ....FREEWAY	LWR ....LOWER	PTH ....PATH	VIAD ....VIADUCT
CO ....COUNTY	FY ....FERRY	MAG ....MAGISTRATE	PZ ....PIAZZA	VIL ....VILLA
COLL ....COLLEGE	GA ....GATE	MAN ....MANSIONS	QD ....QUADRANT	VIS ....VISTA
COMM ....COMMISSION	GAL ....GALLERY	MD ....MEAD	QU ....QUEEN	VLG ....VILLAGE
COMM ....COMMISSION	GDN ....GARDEN	MDW ....MEADOWS	QY ....QUAY	VLS ....VILLAS
CON ....CONVENT	GDNS ....GARDENS	MEM ....MEMORIAL	R ....RIVER	VW ....VIEW
COT ....COTTAGE	GLD ....GLADE	MKT ....MARKET	RBT ....ROUNDABOUT	W ....WEST
COTS ....COTTAGES	GLN ....GLEN	MKTS ....MARKETS	RD ....ROAD	WD ....WOOD
CP ....CAPE	GN ....GREEN	ML ....MALL	RDG ....RIDGE	WHF ....WHARF
CPS ....COPSE	GND ....GROUND	ML ....MILL	REP ....REPUBLIC	WK ....WALK
CR ....CREEK	GRA ....GRANGE	MNR ....MANOR	RES ....RESERVOIR	WKS ....WALKS
CREM ....CREMATORIUM	GRG ....GARAGE	MS ....MEWS	RFC ..RUGBY FOOTBALL CLUB	WLS ....WELLS
CRS ....CRESCENT	GT ....GREAT	MSN ....MISSION	RI ....RISE	WY ....WAY
CSWY ....CAUSEWAY	GTWY ....GATEWAY	MSN ....MISSION	RP ....RAMP	YD ....YARD
CT ....COURT	GV ....GROVE	MT ....MOUNT	RW ....ROW	YHA ....YOUTH HOSTEL
CTRL ....CENTRAL	HGR ....HIGHER	MTN ....MOUNTAIN	S ....SOUTH	
CTS ....COURTS	HL ....HILL	MTS ....MOUNTAINS	SCH ....SCHOOL	
		MUS ....MUSEUM		

POSTCODE TOWNS AND AREA ABBREVIATIONS

BBR ....Bamber Bridge	CHLY/EC ....Chorley/Eccleston	CROS/BRETH ....Croston/Bretherton		PRES ....Preston
BISP ....Bispham	CHLYE ....Chorley east/Adlington/	FTWD ....Fleetwood	Freckleton/Warton	WGNNW/ST ......Wigan northwest/
BPOOL ....Blackpool	....................Whittle-le-Woods	FUL/RIB ....Fulwood/Ribbleton	LEYL ....Leyland	..........................Standish
BPOOLE ....Blackpool east	CHTN/BK ....Churchtown/Banks	GAR/LONG ....Garstang/Longridge	LSTA ....Lytham St Anne's	
BPOOLS ....Blackpool south	CLV/TH ....Cleveleys/Thornton	KIRK/FR/WAR ....Kirkham/	PLF/KEOS ......Poulton-le-Fylde/	
			Knott End-on-Sea	

A

Abattoir Rd *BPOOL* FY1 ....2 E1	Abbotsford Rd *BPOOLE* FY3 ....33 F2	Ackhurst Wy *CHLY/EC* PR7 ....92 C2	Adelaide Av *CLV/TH* FY5 ....22 A4	Adstone Av *BPOOLE* FY3 ....29 F2
Abbey Rd *BPOOL* FY4 ....38 C3	Abbotsway *PRES* PR1 ....59 E5	Acorn Cl *LEYL* PR25 ....83 F4	Adelaide St *BPOOL* FY1 ....11 H1	Agglebys Rd *PLF/KEOS* FY6 ..12 D5
Abbey St *FUL/RIB* PR2 ....6 B2	Abbott Cft *KIRK/FR/WAR* PR4 ....44 C1	Acorn Ms *BPOOLS* FY4 ....54 B4	*FTWD* FY7 ....11 H1	Agnes St *PRES* PR1 ....7 G2
Abbeyville *BPOOLS* FY4 ....38 C2	Abbotts Cl *BBR* PR5 ....74 C5	Acorn St *BPOOLS* FY4 ....81 F5	*FTWD* FY7 ....7 K3	Agnew Rd *FTWD* FY7 ....11 F1
Abbey Wk *PRES* PR1 ....72 C4	Abbotts Wk *FTWD* FY7 ....11 G1	Acre Ga *BPOOLS* FY4 ....39 E1	Adelaide St West *BPOOL* FY1 ....2 B6	Agnew St *LSTA* FY8 ....64 B3
Abbot Meadow *PRES* PR1 ......72 C2	Abercorn Pl *BPOOLS* FY4 ......38 A5	Acregate La *PRES* PR1 ....60 D2	Adelphi Pl *PRES* PR1 ....6 E2	Aiken Ct *KIRK/FR/WAR* PR4 ....43 E5
Abbots Cl *KIRK/FR/WAR* PR4 ....43 G4	Abercrombie Rd *FTWD* FY7 ......11 F1	Acres La *PLF/KEOS* FY6 ....13 E3	Adelphi St *BPOOL* FY1 ....2 C5	Ailsa Av *BPOOLE* FY3 ....33 F3
	Abingdon Dr *FUL/RIB* PR2 ......58 C2	Acreswood Cl *CHLY/EC* PR7 ....96 B5	*PRES* PR1 ....6 D1	Ainsdale Av *BISP* FY2 ....25 E2
	Abingdon St *BPOOL* FY1 ....2 C4	Acton Rd *BPOOLS* FY4 ....5 H6	Adlington Av *PLF/KEOS* FY6 ....26 D4	*CLV/TH* FY5 ....22 B3
	Acacia Rd *FUL/RIB* PR2 ....61 E1	Addison Crs *BPOOLE* FY3 ......3 G2	Admiral Cl *LSTA* FY8 ....49 E2	*FTWD* FY7 ....16 D2
	Acer Gv *FUL/RIB* PR2 ....47 F5	Addison Rd *FTWD* FY7 ....11 G3	Admiral Wy *FUL/RIB* PR2 ....57 H5	Ainsdale Dr *FUL/RIB* PR2 ......58 A1

Ainslie Rd FUL/RIB PR2 .....45 G5
Aintree Rd BPOOLS FY4 .....4 E7
 CLV/TH FY5 .....21 H4
Airdrie Pl BISP FY2 .....25 E2
Airedale Av BPOOLE FY5 .....5 J3
Airedale Ct PLF/KEOS FY6 * 26 A3
Alandale Cl LEYL PR25 .....83 G5
Albany Av BPOOLS FY4 .....38 C5
Albany Ct PLF/KEOS FY6 .....93 H2
Albany Ct CHLYE PR6 .....93 H2
Albany Dr BBR PR5 .....74 A4
Albany Rd FTWD FY7 .....11 F2
 LSTA FY8 .....63 F1
Albatros St PRES PR1 .....60 B1
Albert Rd PRES PR1 .....2 C6
 FUL/RIB PR2 .....45 H4
 LEYL PR25 .....83 H5
 LSTA FY8 .....49 G4
 PRES PR1 .....59 H1
Albert St CHLY/EC PR7 .....93 C5
 FTWD FY7 .....11 F2
 KIRK/FR/WAR PR4 .....42 D2
 LSTA FY8 .....64 D3
Albert Ter PRES PR1 .....7 H1
Albion Av BPOOLE FY3 .....29 F4
Albion St CHLY/EC PR7 .....93 C5
Albrighton Cl BBR PR5 .....79 G2
Albrighton Crs BBR PR5 .....79 G2
Albrighton Rd BBR PR5 .....79 G2
Albyn Bank Rd PRES PR1 .....7 H4
Albyn St East PRES PR1 .....7 F4
Alcester Av FUL/RIB PR2 .....72 B1
Alconbury Crs CLV/TH FY5 .....20 C2
Aldale Gv FUL/RIB PR2 .....58 C1
Aldcliffe Rd FUL/RIB PR2 .....58 A2
Alder Cl CLV/TH FY5 .....22 A3
 CROS/BRETH PR26 .....82 A5
 KIRK/FR/WAR PR4
Alder Coppice FUL/RIB PR2 .....44 A5
Alder Ct FTWD FY7 .....10 C4
Alder Dr BBR PR5 .....79 G2
 CHLY/EC PR7 .....96 A2
Alderfield PRES PR1 .....72 C3
Alder Gv BPOOLE FY3 .....29 E3
 CHLY/EC PR7 .....96 C4
 LSTA FY8 .....64 B3
 PLF/KEOS FY6 .....26 B5
Alderley Av BPOOLS FY4 .....38 B5
Alder Rd FUL/RIB PR2 .....45 J4
Aldersleigh Crs BBR PR5 .....75 G5
Aldersville St KIRK/FR/WAR PR4 .....53 H5
Aldfield Av FUL/RIB PR2 .....57 G2
Aldon Gv KIRK/FR/WAR PR4 .....70 B5
Aldon Rd PLF/KEOS FY6 .....26 D4
Aldwych Av BPOOLS FY3 .....5 J2
Aldwych Dr BBR PR5 .....79 G2
Alert St FUL/RIB PR2 .....59 E2
Alexandra Pavilions PRES PR1 * 7 H1
 BPOOL FY1 .....4 B5
 CLV/TH FY5 .....21 F4
 KIRK/FR/WAR PR4 .....43 E2
 LSTA FY8 .....49 G4
Alexandra St PRES PR1 .....60 C4
Alexandra Dr LSTA FY8 .....62 C1
Alford Fold FUL/RIB PR2 .....45 F1
Alfred St BPOOL FY1 .....2 D5
Alice Av LEYL PR25 .....83 H5
Alice Sq PRES PR1 .....7 H1
Alisan Rd FUL/RIB PR2 .....25 H2
Alker La CHLY/EC PR7 .....88 D4
Alker St CHLY/EC PR7 .....93 F3
Allandale BPOOLS FY4 .....38 C3
Allandale Av CLV/TH FY5 .....17 F5
Allenbury Pl BPOOLE FY3 .....33 G5
Allenby Av FUL/RIB PR2 .....46 B4
Allenby Rd LSTA FY8 .....49 E4
Allen Cl CLV/TH FY5 .....20 D3
Allengate FUL/RIB PR2 .....45 H4
Allen Wy FTWD FY7 .....10 C4
Allerton Rd BBR PR5 .....74 A5
All Hallows Rd BISP FY2 .....24 D2
Allington Cl BBR PR5 .....74 B3
Allonby Av CLV/TH FY5 .....17 E5
All Saints Rd PRES PR1 .....24 D1
 LSTA FY8 .....49 G4
Alma Dr CHLY/EC PR7 .....96 B1
Alma Rw BBR PR5 .....75 H5
Alma St PRES PR1 .....7 G1
Almond Cl FUL/RIB PR2 .....46 C2
 PRES PR1 .....72 A3
Alpic Dr CLV/TH FY5
 BPOOLS FY4
Alpine Av BBR PR5 .....79 G2
Alpine Cl BBR PR5 .....79 G3
Alpine Rd CHLYE PR6 .....89 H4
Alsop St PRES PR1 .....59 G1
Alston Av CLV/TH FY5 .....16 D5
Alston Rd BISP FY2 .....25 E5
Alston St PRES PR1 .....60 D2
Altcar La LEYL PR25 .....86 C2
Althorp Cl FUL/RIB PR2 .....2 E1
Alvern Av FUL/RIB PR2 .....45 F4
Alvern Crs FUL/RIB PR2 .....45 F4
Alwood Av BPOOLE FY3 .....29 F4
Amberbanks Gv BPOOL FY1 .....4 A4
Amber Dr CHLYE PR6 .....93 H4
Amber Ga FUL/RIB PR2 .....44 B2
Amberwood
 KIRK/FR/WAR PR4 .....42 D5
Ambledene BBR PR5 .....80 D4
Ambleside Av CHLY/EC PR7 * 92 A1
Ambleside Cl BBR PR5 .....74 B4
Ambleside Rd BPOOLS FY4 .....34 B4
 FUL/RIB PR2
 LSTA FY8 .....47 E3
Ambrose St LEYL PR25 .....83 G2
Amersham Cl
 KIRK/FR/WAR PR4 .....77 G1
Amounderness Ct
 KIRK/FR/WAR PR4 * 43 F3
Amounderness Wy
 CLV/TH FY5 .....22 A5
 FTWD FY7 .....11 G4

Ampleforth Dr BBR PR5 .....73 F5
Amy Johnson Wy BPOOLS FY4 .....38 D3
Ancenis Ct KIRK/FR/WAR PR4 .....43 F5
Anchorage Ms FTWD FY7 .....11 H5
Anchorage Rd FTWD FY7 .....11 H5
Anchor Ct PRES PR1 .....7 F4
Anchor Dr KIRK/FR/WAR PR4 .....71 E4
Anchorsholme La CLV/TH FY5 .....21 F4
Anchorsholme La East
 CLV/TH FY5 .....20 D3
Anchorsholme La West
 CLV/TH FY5 .....20 C3
Anchor Wy LSTA FY8 .....49 E2
Anderson St BPOOL FY1 * 2 C3
Anderton Rd CHLY/EC PR7 .....92 A1
Anderton St CHLY/EC PR7 .....93 F3
Andertons Wy FUL/RIB PR2 .....46 C3
Andrew St PRES PR1 .....60 C2
Anger's Hill Rd BPOOLS FY4 .....5 J5
Aniline St CHLYE PR6 .....93 H2
Annan Crs BPOOLS FY4 .....34 A4
Annaside Cl BPOOLS FY4 .....39 E1
Anna's Rd BPOOLS FY4 .....50 C1
Annesley Av BPOOLS FY3 .....29 E3
Annis St PRES PR1 .....60 C3
Anstro Av KIRK/FR/WAR PR4 .....54 C5
Ansdel Gv FUL/RIB PR2 .....58 C1
Ansdell Rd BPOOLS FY4 .....5 F4
Ansdell Rd North LSTA FY8 .....63 G2
Ansdell Rd South LSTA FY8 .....63 G3
Ansdell St PRES PR1 * 60 C2
Anson Cl LSTA FY8 .....48 D2
Anson Rd KIRK/FR/WAR PR4 .....54 B1
Antrim Rd BISP FY2 .....28 C1
Appealing La LSTA FY8 .....49 E1
Appleby Cl BBR PR5 .....75 H5
Appleby Rd BISP FY2 .....28 D1
Appleby St PRES PR1 .....6 E1
Applefields LEYL PR25 .....83 G5
Appleside KIRK/FR/WAR PR4 .....70 A5
Appleton Cl PLF/KEOS FY6 .....25 C5
Appletree Cl PRES PR1 .....72 A4
Aqueduct St PRES PR1 .....6 B1
Arcon Rd CHLY/EC PR7 .....96 B4
Ardee Rd PRES PR1 .....6 B7
Arden Cn FTWD FY7 .....11 E2
Ardmore Rd BISP FY2 .....24 D5
Argosy Av BPOOLE FY3 .....29 G2
Argyle Rd LEYL PR25 .....83 F3
 PLF/KEOS FY6
Argyll Rd BISP FY2 .....28 C1
 PRES PR1 .....60 A2
Ariel Wy FTWD FY7 .....11 E2
Arkholme Av BPOOL FY1 .....5 F4
Arkholme Dr
 KIRK/FR/WAR PR4 .....70 A5
Arkwright Ct BPOOLS FY4 .....40 A1
Arkwright Rd PRES PR1 .....59 H1
Arley St CHLY/EC PR7 .....93 G2
Arlington Av BPOOLS FY4 .....38 B1
Armadale Rd BISP FY2 .....29 E1
Armitstead Ct FTWD FY7 * 11 F4
Armitstead Wy FTWD FY7 * 11 F4
Armstrong St FUL/RIB PR2 .....58 D1
Arndale Cl FTWD FY7 .....10 C4
Arnhem Rd PRES PR1 .....60 D3
Arnold Av BPOOLS FY4 .....38 C1
Arnold Cl FUL/RIB PR2 .....61 E1
Arnold Pl CHLY/EC PR7 .....92 D5
Arnold Rd LSTA FY8 .....65 E2
Arno St PRES PR1 .....7 J5
Arnott Rd BPOOLS FY4 .....5 H5
 FUL/RIB PR2
Arnside Av BPOOL FY1 .....5 F5
 LSTA FY8
Arnside Cl BBR PR5 .....75 H2
Arnside Rd FUL/RIB PR2 .....58 A1
Arrowsmith Cl BBR PR5 .....75 H4
Arrowsmith Dr BBR PR5 .....75 H4
Arrowsmith Gdns CLV/TH FY5 .....17 E4
Arroyo Wy FUL/RIB PR2 .....46 B4
Arthurs La PLF/KEOS FY6 .....23 H2
Arthur St FTWD FY7 .....11 H1
 PRES PR1 .....6 D4
Arundel Av BISP FY2 .....24 B3
Arundel Dr PLF/KEOS FY6 .....26 A1
Ascot Rd BPOOLE FY3 .....3 G3
Arundel Pl PRES PR1 .....7 K5
Arundel Rd KIRK/FR/WAR PR4 .....70 B5
 LSTA FY8 .....63 E2
Arundel Wy LEYL PR25 .....83 H4
Ascot Rd BPOOLE FY3 .....3 G3
 CLV/TH FY5 .....21 H4
Ash Av KIRK/FR/WAR PR4 .....53 F5
Ashbourne Crs FUL/RIB PR2 .....44 B5
Ashburton Rd BPOOL FY1 .....2 C1
Ashby St CHLY/EC PR7 .....93 H4
Ashcombe Ga CLV/TH FY5 .....22 B5
Ash Ct KIRK/FR/WAR PR4 .....56 B1
Ashenhurst Ter PRES PR1 * 96 A5
Ashdown Cl PLF/KEOS FY6 .....25 C5
Ashdown Dr CHLYE PR6 .....85 F1
Ashdown Ms FUL/RIB PR2 .....47 E2
Ash Dr CLV/TH FY5 .....22 A3
 KIRK/FR/WAR PR4
 PLF/KEOS FY6
Asheldon St PRES PR1 .....60 D2
Ash Fld CHLYE PR6 .....85 F1
Ashfield FUL/RIB PR2 .....36 D5
Ashfield Ct FUL/RIB PR2 .....44 B2
Ashfield Rd BISP FY2 .....25 E5
 CHLY/EC PR7 .....93 G3
Ashford Crs CAR/LONG PR3 .....36 B2
Ashford Rd FUL/RIB PR2 .....58 A1
Ash Gv BBR PR5 .....74 C5
 KIRK/FR/WAR PR4 .....93 F5
 KIRK/FR/WAR PR4 .....43 F1
 KIRK/FR/WAR PR4 .....77 G3
Ashgrove PRES PR1 .....60 D2
Ash Holme PRES PR1 .....46 C5
Ash La KIRK/FR/WAR PR4 .....56 C2
Ash Lea Gv PLF/KEOS FY6 .....19 G2
Ashleigh Ct FUL/RIB PR2 .....46 A1
Ashleigh Ms BPOOLS FY3 .....3 H7
Ashleigh St PRES PR1 .....60 C4

Ashley Cl BISP FY2 .....24 C5
 CLV/TH FY5 .....21 H5
Ashley Rd LSTA FY8 .....49 F2
Ash Meadow CLV/TH FY5 .....44 A5
Ashmoor St PRES PR1 .....6 D1
Ashmore Gv CLV/TH FY5 .....20 D3
Ashness Cl FUL/RIB PR2 .....37 E5
Ash Rd CHLY/EC PR7 .....96 B5
Ash St BPOOLS FY4 .....38 C2
 FTWD FY7 .....11 G2
Ashton Av PLF/KEOS FY6 .....12 B1
Ashton Cl FUL/RIB PR2 .....58 C2
Ashton Ct LSTA FY8 * 49 E4
Ashtongate FUL/RIB PR2 .....58 B2
Ashton Rd BPOOL FY1 .....4 E1
Ashton St FUL/RIB PR2 .....58 B2
 LSTA FY8 .....64 B3
Ashtree Ct BBR PR5 .....75 F3
Ashtree Gv PRES PR1 .....72 A2
Ashurst Rd LEYL PR25 .....84 A3
Ashwell Pl CLV/TH FY5 .....20 C5
Ashwood Cl LSTA FY8 .....63 H2
Ashwood Rd FUL/RIB PR2 .....45 F1
Ashworth Ct BPOOLS FY3 .....3 G1
Ashworth Gv PRES PR1 .....60 C5
Ashworth La PRES PR1 .....7 K7
Ashworth Rd BPOOLS FY4 .....34 A5
Ashworth St BBR PR5 .....74 C4
 PRES PR1 .....7 K4
Askrigg Cl BPOOLS FY4 .....39 G1
Asland Cl BBR PR5 .....80 C1
Aspden Cl BBR PR5 .....74 B5
Aspels Crs PRES PR1 .....72 B2
Aspels Nook PRES PR1 .....72 B2
The Aspels PRES PR1 .....72 B2
Aspendale Cl
 KIRK/FR/WAR PR4 .....70 A5
Aspinall Cl PRES PR1 .....72 C4
Assheton Pl FUL/RIB PR2 .....37 E4
Astland St LSTA FY8 .....49 E5
Astley Crs KIRK/FR/WAR PR4 .....54 C5
Astley Rd CHLY/EC PR7 .....93 E1
Astley St CHLY/EC PR7 .....93 F1
Aston Av CLV/TH FY5 .....21 G2
Aston Wy CROS/BRETH PR26 .....82 B2
Athelstan Fold FUL/RIB PR2 .....45 E5
Atherton Rd LEYL PR25 .....82 C4
Athlone Av BISP FY2 .....24 C5
Atholl Av CLV/TH FY5 .....93 H4
Atholl Gv CLV/TH FY5 .....21 G5
Athol St PRES PR1 .....6 B3
Atkinson Cl PRES PR1 .....7 F2
Aubigny Dr FUL/RIB PR2 .....45 F4
Auburn Gv BPOOLS FY3 .....3 G3
Audenlea CLV/TH FY5 .....21 F1
Audley Cl LSTA FY8 .....63 G1
Aughton St FTWD FY7 * 11 H1
Aughton Wk PRES PR1 .....7 F1
Auster Crs KIRK/FR/WAR PR4 .....54 B1
Austin Crs FUL/RIB PR2 .....44 D4
Austin Gv BPOOL FY1 .....4 B5
Austin St BPOOLS FY4 .....38 C1
Austin Wy BPOOLS FY4 .....41 E1
Avalon Dr KIRK/FR/WAR PR4 .....54 C4
Avalwood Av
 KIRK/FR/WAR PR4 .....76 C1
Avenham Colonnade PRES PR1 * 7 G6
Avenham La PRES PR1 .....7 G5
Avenham Pl PRES PR1 * 7 H6
Avenham Rd CHLY/EC PR7 .....93 H3
 PRES PR1 .....7 G5
Avenham St PRES PR1 .....7 H6
Avenue Rd BPOOLE FY3 .....29 H2
The Avenue FUL/RIB PR2 .....44 C2
 FUL/RIB PR2
 LEYL PR25 .....87 E1
 PLF/KEOS FY6 .....26 A3
 PRES PR1 .....72 A1
Avery Gdns PLF/KEOS FY6 .....25 C5
Avon Av FTWD FY7 .....16 D1
Avon Br FUL/RIB PR2 .....26 B5
Avondale Crs BPOOLS FY4 .....38 A3
Avondale Dr BBR PR5 .....79 G1
Avondale Rd CHLY/EC PR7 .....93 F3
 LSTA FY8 .....48 C5
Avon Gn FTWD FY7 .....11 E2
Avon Pl BPOOL FY1 .....28 C2
Avonside Av CLV/TH FY5 .....21 H5
Avon St LSTA FY8 .....49 E5
Avroe Crs LSTA FY8 .....38 D4
Aylesbury Av BPOOLS FY4 .....5 G6
Ayr Ct FTWD FY7 .....17 E2
Ayrton Av BPOOLS FY4 .....5 D5
Aysgarth Av FUL/RIB PR2 .....45 H1
Aysgarth Ct BPOOLS FY4 .....39 F1
Azalea Cl FUL/RIB PR2 .....45 J1
 LEYL PR25 .....84 B2

B

Babbacombe Av BPOOLS FY4 .....38 B2
Back Ashburton Rd BPOOL FY1 .....2 C1
Back Ashby St CHLY/EC PR7 .....21 H5
Back Bourne's Rw BBR PR5 .....75 H5
Back Church St PRES PR1 .....2 B5
Back Clarendon Rd BPOOL FY1 .....4 A3
Back Clifton St BPOOL FY1 .....80 B2
Back Cookson St BPOOL FY1 .....2 D4
Back Cop La FTWD FY7 .....11 G2
Back Cunliffe Rd BPOOL FY1 .....5 H5
Back Eaves St BPOOL FY1 .....28 B3
Back Epsom Rd CLV/TH FY5 .....21 H5
Back Glen Eldon Rd LSTA FY8 .....49 F4
Back Grimshaw St PRES PR1 .....7 H4
Back High St BPOOL FY1 .....2 C2
Back La CHLY/EC PR7 .....91 E3
 CHLYE PR6
 LEYL PR25 .....83 H5
 PLF/KEOS FY6 .....19 E1

Back Lord St BPOOL FY1 .....2 C2
Back Moon Av BPOOL FY1 .....4 C4
Back Mt CHLY/EC PR7 * 93 F2
Back Pleasant St CLV/TH FY5 .....49 E5
Back Pleasant St BPOOL FY1
Back Read's Rd BPOOL FY1 .....2 D6
Back St Anne's Rd West
 LSTA FY8 .....49 E5
Back Seed St PRES PR1 .....6 E5
Back Shannon St BPOOL FY1 .....5 E5
Back Springfield Rd North
 LSTA FY8 .....49 E5
Back Starkie St PRES PR1 .....7 F6
Back Warbreck Rd BPOOL FY1 .....2 B2
Back Waterloo Rd BPOOL FY1 .....4 C6
Back West Crs LSTA FY8 * 49 E5
Back Woodfield Rd BPOOL FY1 .....4 C4
Badgers Cft FUL/RIB PR2 .....61 F2
Badgers Wk CHLY/EC PR7 .....89 E4
Badgers Wk East LSTA FY8 .....64 D3
Badgers Wy BBR PR5 .....74 C5
Bagganley La CHLYE PR6 .....89 H5
Bagnold Rd PRES PR1 .....60 C5
Bagot St BPOOL FY1 .....4 C6
Bailey Ct BPOOLE FY3 .....3 H5
Baines Av BPOOLE FY3 .....29 F1
Bairstow St BPOOL FY1 .....4 B1
Bakers Ct LSTA FY8 .....83 G2
Balcarres Cl LEYL PR25 .....83 F5
Balcarres Pl LEYL PR25 .....83 F4
Balcarres Rd CHLY/EC PR7 .....93 F5
 FUL/RIB PR2 .....45 E5
 LEYL PR25 .....83 F4
Balderstone Rd
 KIRK/FR/WAR PR4 .....54 B4
 PRES PR1 .....72 C1
Baldwin Gv BPOOL FY1 .....5 G3
Baldwin St BBR PR5 .....80 B1
Balfour Cl CLV/TH FY5 .....22 B5
Balfour Rd FUL/RIB PR2 .....45 G5
Balfour St LEYL PR25 .....83 F3
Balham Av BPOOLS FY4 .....39 E3
Baliham Rd FUL/RIB PR2 .....58 A2
 LSTA FY8 .....64 C2
Ball St BPOOL FY1 .....4 C5
Balmer Gv BPOOLS FY4 .....5 F1
Balmoral Av LEYL PR25 .....83 H4
Balmoral Pl CLV/TH FY5 .....22 A4
Balmoral Rd BBR PR5 .....74 A3
 BPOOLS FY4 .....32 B5
 CHLY/EC PR7 .....90 B3
 CHLY/EC PR7 .....93 E3
 LSTA FY8 .....62 D1
Balmoral Ter FTWD FY7 .....11 H1
Balniel Cl CHLY/EC PR7 .....93 H4
Balshaw Crs LEYL PR25 .....83 E2
Balshaw La LEYL PR25 .....92 A1
Balshaw Rd LEYL PR25 .....83 E3
Balshaw St BBR PR5 * 74 B4
Balshaw Ter
 KIRK/FR/WAR PR4 .....43 F4
Baltimore Rd LSTA FY8 * 49 E5
Bamber Av BPOOLS FY4 .....24 C3
Bambers La BPOOLS FY4 .....40 A2
Bamber St CHLY/EC PR7 .....93 E5
Bamber's Wk
 KIRK/FR/WAR PR4 .....42 C1
Bamburgh Cl BPOOLS FY4 .....39 G1
Bamton Av BPOOLS FY4 .....38 C1
Banastre Ct CHLY/EC PR7 .....88 D5
Banbury Av BISP FY2 .....28 D2
Banbury Dr FUL/RIB PR2 .....44 B3
Banbury Rd LSTA FY8 .....49 F5
Bancroft Cl CLV/TH FY5 .....21 H2
Bangor Av BISP FY2 .....24 D5
Bank Cl KIRK/FR/WAR PR4 .....76 B1
Bank Cft KIRK/FR/WAR PR4 .....76 B1
Bankfield Gv BPOOLS FY4 .....5 H1
Bank Head La BBR PR5 .....81 F1
Bank Hey St BPOOL FY1 .....2 B6
Bank Pde PRES PR1 .....7 G6
 PRES PR1
Bank Pl FUL/RIB PR2 .....59 E2
Banksfield Av FUL/RIB PR2 .....45 E5
Banksfield Pl BBR PR5 .....80 C2
Bankside CLV/TH FY5 .....85 E5
Banks Rd FUL/RIB PR2 .....45 F5
Bank St CHLY/EC PR7 .....93 F2
Banner Cl CHLY/EC PR7 .....90 A3
Bannerman Ter CHLYE PR6 .....89 G5
Bannister Cl BBR PR5 .....75 E2
Bannister Cl BBR PR5 .....75 E2
Bannister Dr LEYL PR25 .....94 B2
Bannister Hall Crs BBR PR5 .....75 E2
Bannister Hall La BBR PR5 .....75 E2
Bannister La
 CROS/BRETH PR26 .....78 C5
Bannister's Bit PRES PR1 .....72 B4
Bannister St CHLY/EC PR7 .....93 F3
 LSTA FY8 * 64 C3
Bannistre Cl LSTA FY8 .....49 G5
Barclay Av BPOOLE FY3 .....5 K4
Barden Pl FUL/RIB PR2 .....45 F1
Bardsea Pl FUL/RIB PR2 .....44 B5
Bardsway Av BPOOLS FY4 .....21 G1
Bardsway Av BPOOLS FY4 .....3 J3
Barham St BPOOL FY1 .....4 E5
Barker La CHLYE PR6 .....85 F1
Barleyfield CHLYE PR6 .....85 F1
Barlow Crs BPOOLE FY3 .....29 F3
Barlow St PRES PR1 .....59 H1
Barmouth Av BPOOLE FY3 .....33 G5
Barmskin La CHLY/EC PR7 .....94 B4
Barnacre Cl FUL/RIB PR2 .....37 F5
Barn Cft CROS/BRETH PR26 .....82 A5
 PRES PR1 .....72 A2
Barnes Av CLV/TH FY5 .....17 E4

Barnfield BBR PR5 .....79 F1
 KIRK/FR/WAR PR4 .....43 E5
Barnfield Cl CLV/TH FY5
Barnfield Mnr PLF/KEOS FY6 * 27 H4
Barn Hey KIRK/FR/WAR PR4 .....70 B5
Barn Hey Dr
 CROS/BRETH PR26 .....82 D1
Barn Meadow BBR PR5 .....81 E5
Barnsfold FUL/RIB PR2 .....45 F4
Barnside CHLY/EC PR7 .....87 H4
Baron Rd BPOOL FY1 .....4 D5
Barons Great Outdoors
 BPOOL FY1 .....33 H5
Barons Wy CHLY/EC PR7 .....88 A5
Barry Av FUL/RIB PR2 .....44 B5
Bartle Pl FUL/RIB PR2 .....58 A2
Bartle Rd LSTA FY8 .....49 G3
Barton Av BPOOLS FY4 .....4 B5
 PLF/KEOS FY6 .....12 C1
Barton St FUL/RIB PR2 .....48 D5
Barton Sq PLF/KEOS FY6 .....12 C1
Bashall Gv LEYL PR25 .....83 G1
Basil St PRES PR1 .....60 C1
Bassenthwaite Rd
 BPOOLE FY3 .....33 H5
Bath Rd LSTA FY8 .....49 J6
Bath St BPOOLS FY4 .....4 B6
 FUL/RIB PR2 .....6 A1
 LSTA FY8 .....64 C3
Bathurst Av BPOOLE FY3 .....29 G3
Bayliss Cl FUL/RIB PR2 .....47 F5
Bay Rd FUL/RIB PR2 .....61 E1
Bayside FTWD FY7 .....11 H2
Bayswater BISP FY2 .....24 C3
The Bay CLV/TH FY5 .....16 C4
Baytree Cl BBR PR5 .....79 H1
Bay Tree Farm FUL/RIB PR2 .....57 H5
Bay Tree Rd CHLYE PR6 .....85 E2
Bazley Rd LSTA FY8 .....63 G5
Beach Av CLV/TH FY5 .....20 D1
 LSTA FY8 .....63 F3
Beachcomber Dr CLV/TH FY5 .....20 C1
Beach La LSTA FY8 .....64 D3
Beachley Rd FUL/RIB PR2 .....44 B4
 FTWD FY7 .....11 E2
 CAR/LONG PR3 .....8 B4
 LSTA FY8 .....48 D4
Beach St LSTA FY8 .....64 B3
Beacon Av FUL/RIB PR2 .....45 F4
Beacon Gv CLV/TH FY5 .....5 G3
Beacon Rd FUL/RIB PR2 .....27 E4
Beaconsfield Av PRES PR1 .....61 F2
Beaconsfield Ter CHLYE PR6 .....89 G5
Beacon St CHLY/EC PR7 .....93 G3
Beamont Dr PRES PR1 .....4 A1
Bean Av BPOOLS FY4 .....33 E5
Beardshaw Av BPOOL FY1 .....5 G4
Bearswood Cft CHLYE PR6 .....85 E2
Bearwood Wy CLV/TH FY5 .....22 A2
Beattock Pl BISP FY2 .....25 F1
Beatty Av CLV/TH FY5 .....93 E4
Beauclerk Rd LSTA FY8 .....48 D2
Beaufort Av BISP FY2 .....24 C2
Beaumaris Rd BPOOLS FY4 .....83 H4
Beaumont Gdns PLF/KEOS FY6 .....25 G2
Beck Ct FTWD FY7 .....10 D5
Beckdean Av FUL/RIB PR2
Beckett Cl PRES PR1 .....7 F1
Beck Gv CLV/TH FY5 .....17 E5
Beckway Av BPOOLE FY3 .....3 K1
Bedale Pl CLV/TH FY5
Bedford Av FUL/RIB PR2 .....16 D5
Bedford Rd BPOOL FY1 .....28 C2
 FUL/RIB PR2
 LSTA FY8 .....65 E2
Beech Av BPOOLE FY3 .....3 H4
 CHLY/EC PR7 .....87 G4
 KIRK/FR/WAR PR4 .....43 E4
 KIRK/FR/WAR PR4 .....53 F5
 PLF/KEOS FY6 .....26 B5
Beechcroft CLV/TH FY5 * 16 C5
Beech Dr FUL/RIB PR2 .....36 C5
 KIRK/FR/WAR PR4 .....55 F1
 KIRK/FR/WAR PR4 .....67 F1
Beeches Cv CLV/TH FY5 .....22 A5
The Beeches CHLYE PR6 .....31 H1
 PLF/KEOS FY6
Beechfield Av CLV/TH FY5 .....42 A5
Beechfield Cl LEYL PR25 .....13 E1
Beechfield Rd LEYL PR25 .....83 G4
 CHLY/EC PR7 .....90 A4
Beech Gdns CHLYE PR6 .....85 E3
Beech Gv FUL/RIB PR2 .....58 D2
Beech Hill LE BBR PR5 .....74 B5
Beech Rd LEYL PR25 .....83 F2
Beech St PRES PR1 .....6 B6
Beech St South PRES PR1 .....6 C7
Beech Ter PRES PR1 .....6 C7
Beechway FUL/RIB PR2 * 46 A4
 PRES PR1 .....72 A5
Beechwood Av BBR PR5 .....73 H2
 FUL/RIB PR2 .....45 F4
Beechwood CHLY/EC PR7 * 96 C5
Beechwood Cl CHLYE PR6 .....84 D1
Beechwood Dr CLV/TH FY5 .....21 H4
Beechwood Gv BISP FY2 .....25 E5
Bee La PRES PR1 .....72 A2
Beenland St PRES PR1 .....60 D2
Beeston Av PLF/KEOS FY6 .....26 A2
Beetham Pl BPOOLE FY3 .....3 H2
Bela Gv BPOOL FY1 .....4 E5
Belford Av BPOOLE FY3 .....3 K1
Belfry Cl CHLY/EC PR7 .....65 E5
The Belfry LSTA FY8 .....63 E1
Belgrave Av KIRK/FR/WAR PR4 .....43 E1
 PRES PR1 .....72 A3
Belgrave Cl LSTA FY8
Belgrave Pl FUL/RIB PR2 * 46 B1
Belgrave Pl PLF/KEOS FY6 .....25 H5

Belgrave Rd BPOOLS FY4 .....5 J5
LEYL PR25.....83 F4
PLF/KEOS FY6 .....25 H5
Belle Vue Pl BPOOLE FY3 .....3 G5
Bellflower Cl LEYL PR25 .....84 B1
Bellingham Rd LSTA FY8.....64 C1
Bellis Wy BBR PR5 .....73 G4
Bells La BBR PR5 .....75 H4
Belmont Av BPOOL FY1 .....4 D1
FUL/RIB PR2.....46 D5
PLF/KEOS FY6 .....25 H4
Belmont Cl FUL/RIB PR2.....60 D1
Belmont Crs FUL/RIB PR2 .....60 D1
Belmont Dr CHLYE PR6.....93 H1
Belmont Rd FTWD FY7 .....11 G3
FUL/RIB PR2.....59 E1
LEYL PR25.....82 C3
LSTA FY8.....63 F1
Belton Hl FUL/RIB PR2 .....36 C5
Belvedere Dr CHLY/EC PR7 .....93 E2
Belvedere Rd CLV/TH FY5 .....22 A4
LEYL PR25 * 83 G2
Belverdale Gdns BPOOLS FY4 .....39 F3
Belvere Av BPOOLS FY4 .....38 D3
Benbow Cl LSTA FY8 .....48 D2
Bence Rd PRES PR1.....7 K5
Benenden Pl CLV/TH FY5 *.....21 G2
Bengal St CHLY/EC PR7 .....93 G2
Bennett Av BPOOL FY1.....2 E6
Bennett Rd CLV/TH FY5 .....21 G1
Bennett's La BPOOLS FY4.....39 F2
Benson Rd BPOOLE FY3 .....29 E2
Bentham Av FTWD FY7.....10 C5
Bentham St CHLY/EC PR7 .....96 B4
Bentinck Av BPOOLS FY4 .....38 B3
Bentinck Rd LSTA FY8.....48 C3
Bent La LEYL PR25.....83 G3
Bentley Dr BPOOLS FY4 .....41 E2
KIRK/FR/WAR PR4.....42 C3
Bentley Gn CLV/TH FY5.....22 B2
Bentley Mnr FUL/RIB PR2 * 61 F1
Bentley Park Rd
KIRK/FR/WAR PR4.....76 A2
Benton Rd FUL/RIB PR2 .....46 D4
Beresford St BPOOL FY1 .....2 E1
Bergerac Crs BISP FY2 .....25 F1
Berkeley Cl CHLY/EC PR7 .....93 G5
Berkeley Dr BBR PR5 .....80 B5
Berkeley St PRES PR1.....59 G2
Berkley Cl KIRK/FR/WAR PR4.....42 C3
Berry Fld PRES PR1.....72 B3
Berry's La PLF/KEOS FY6 .....26 A3
Berry St BBR PR5.....79 F1
PRES PR1 .....7 H5
Bertrand Av BPOOLE FY3.....29 G3
Berwick Av CLV/TH FY5 .....17 F5
Berwick Dr FUL/RIB PR2.....45 F4
Berwick Rd BPOOLS FY4.....38 C4
LSTA FY8.....49 F4
PRES PR1 .....7 G5
Berwick St PRES PR1 * 61 E2
Beryl Av CLV/TH FY5.....21 E3
Bescot Wy CLV/TH FY5.....21 F5
Best St KIRK/FR/WAR PR4 .....42 D3
Bethel Av BISP FY2 .....24 D3
Bethesda Rd BPOOL FY1 .....2 C7
Beverley Av PLF/KEOS FY6 .....30 B2
Beverley Cl FUL/RIB PR2 .....59 E2
Beverley Gv BPOOLS FY4 .....38 C1
Beverley Rd North LSTA FY8 .....49 G3
Beverley Rd South LSTA FY8.....49 G3
Beverly Cl CLV/TH FY5 .....21 H4
Bexhill Rd FUL/RIB PR2.....44 C5
Bexley Av BPOOLE FY3 .....28 D2
Bexley Pl LSTA FY8 .....63 G1
Bhailok St PRES PR1 .....6 D2
Bibby Dr BPOOLE FY3 .....34 C1
Bibby's La BISP FY2.....24 D4
Bickerstaffe St BPOOL FY1 .....4 B1
Bideford Av BPOOLE FY3 .....29 G4
Bidston St PRES PR1.....61 E3
Billington St KIRK/FR/WAR PR4.....42 D2
Billington St East
KIRK/FR/WAR PR4.....42 D2
Bilsborough Hey PRES PR1 .....72 D5
Bilsborough Meadow
FUL/RIB PR2.....44 A5
Binbrook Pl CHLY/EC PR7 .....92 D2
Bingley Av BPOOLE FY3 .....29 F4
Bingley Cl CHLYE PR6 .....85 F2
Birch Av CHLY/EC PR7.....87 H3
CLV/TH FY5 .....21 E2
FUL/RIB PR2.....58 C1
LEYL PR25.....84 B1
PRES PR1 .....71 H3
Birch Crs BBR PR5 .....75 H5
Birch Fld CHLYE PR6 .....85 E1
Birch Gv PLF/KEOS FY6.....19 H2
Birchin La CHLYE PR6 .....85 G3
Birchover Cl FUL/RIB PR2.....44 C3
Birch Rd CHLY/EC PR7 .....96 B4
CHLYE PR6 .....89 G5
Birch St FTWD FY7.....11 G2
LSTA FY8.....64 D3
Birch Tree Gdns BPOOLE FY3 .....33 H3
Birch Wy PLF/KEOS FY6 .....26 A3
Birchway Av BPOOLE FY3 .....3 H3
Birchwood CROS/BRETH PR26 .....82 A3
Birchwood Av
KIRK/FR/WAR PR4.....70 C5
Birchwood Cl LSTA FY8.....63 H2
Birchwood Dr CHLY/EC PR7 .....96 B2
FUL/RIB PR2.....45 F1
PLF/KEOS FY6 .....23 G2
Bird St PRES PR1 .....6 B7
Birkacre Brow CHLY/EC PR7 .....96 C3
Birkacre Rd CHLY/EC PR7.....96 C1
Birkbeck Pl FTWD FY7.....10 D4
Birkdale Av BISP FY2.....25 E2
FTWD FY7.....17 E2
KIRK/FR/WAR PR4.....76 A1
LSTA FY8.....49 F2
Birkdale Cl CHLY/EC PR7 .....88 A3
CLV/TH FY5 .....22 B3
KIRK/FR/WAR PR4.....76 A1
Birkdale Dr FUL/RIB PR2 .....58 A1
Birkett Dr FUL/RIB PR2.....47 G5
Birkett Pl FUL/RIB PR2 .....47 G5
Birkside Wy BPOOLS FY4 .....34 A4
Birk St PRES PR1 .....6 C4
Birley Bank PRES PR1.....60 C4
Birley St BPOOL FY1 .....2 B4
KIRK/FR/WAR PR4.....43 F3
PRES PR1 .....7 G4
Birnam Gn FTWD FY7 .....11 E2
Birtwistle St BBR PR5.....79 G2
Bishopgate PRES PR1.....7 G3
Bishopsgate BPOOLE FY3 .....29 G1
Bishops Ga LSTA FY8.....50 B5
Bishopsway PRES PR1.....72 C3
Bison Pl CROS/BRETH PR26 .....82 B2
Bispham Av CROS/BRETH PR26.....78 D5
Bispham Rd BISP FY2 .....24 D3
BISP FY2.....25 G1
CLV/TH FY5.....20 C2
Bispham St PRES PR1 * 7 F2
Bittern Cl BPOOLE FY3 .....29 H4
Blackberry Wy PRES PR1.....72 A4
Black Bull La FUL/RIB PR2 .....45 F4
Blackburn Brow CHLYE PR6 .....89 H5
Blackburn Rd BBR PR5.....75 E2
CHLYE PR6 .....89 H2
Blackburn St CHLYE PR6 .....93 G3
Black Cft CHLYE PR6 .....85 E1
Blackfen Pl BISP FY2.....28 D2
Blackfield Rd
KIRK/FR/WAR PR4.....54 B5
Black Horse St CHLY/EC PR7 *.....93 E4
Blackhurst Av
KIRK/FR/WAR PR4.....71 G4
Blackhurst Ct
KIRK/FR/WAR PR4.....76 C1
Blackpool Old Rd BPOOLE FY3 .....25 G5
Blackpool Rd BISP FY2 .....24 D3
FUL/RIB PR2.....57 H2
KIRK/FR/WAR PR4.....42 A2
KIRK/FR/WAR PR4.....56 B3
LSTA FY8.....50 B5
PLF/KEOS FY6 .....25 G3
PRES PR1 .....46 A5
Blackpool Rd North LSTA FY8 .....49 F1
Blacksmiths Rw LSTA FY8 .....50 B4
Blackstone Rd CHLYE PR6 .....93 H1
Blackthorn Cl CLV/TH FY5 .....17 F4
FUL/RIB PR2.....57 H2
KIRK/FR/WAR PR4.....55 F1
Blackthorn Cft CHLYE PR6.....84 D2
Blackthorn Dr PRES PR1 .....71 H3
Blainscough Rd CHLY/EC PR7 .....96 B5
Blairway Av BPOOLE FY3 .....3 K2
Blake Av BBR PR5 .....79 F2
Blakiston St FTWD FY7 .....11 G2
Blanche St FUL/RIB PR2 *.....59 E2
Blandford Av CLV/TH FY5 .....20 C3
Blashaw La PRES PR1 .....71 H1
Blaydike Moss
CROS/BRETH PR26 .....82 A3
Blaydon Av CLV/TH FY5 .....17 E5
Bleachers Dr LEYL PR25 .....82 D3
Bleasdale Av BPOOLE FY3 .....30 C5
CLV/TH FY5 .....20 D3
KIRK/FR/WAR PR4.....43 E2
PLF/KEOS FY6 .....26 A5
Bleasdale Cl BBR PR5 .....80 C1
LEYL PR25.....83 G5
Bleasdale Rd LSTA FY8 .....64 D2
PLF/KEOS FY6 .....12 B1
Bleasdale St East PRES PR1.....7 K1
Blelock St PRES PR1 .....7 H4
Blenheim Av BPOOL FY1 .....3 F7
KIRK/FR/WAR PR4.....42 D3
Blenheim Cl BBR PR5 .....79 H1
Blenheim Dr CLV/TH FY5 .....22 A2
KIRK/FR/WAR PR4.....53 F5
Blenheim Pl LSTA FY8 .....49 E2
Blenheim Wy
KIRK/FR/WAR PR4.....44 A2
Blesma Ct BPOOLS FY4 * 38 C2
Bloomfield Ct PRES PR1.....59 G1
Bloomfield Gra PRES PR1 .....72 B4
Bloomfield Rd BPOOL FY1 .....4 C4
Blossom Av BPOOLS FY4 .....39 F1
The Blossoms FUL/RIB PR2 .....46 C2
PLF/KEOS FY6 .....26 D4
Bluebell Cl BISP FY2 .....24 D5
CHLYE PR6 .....89 E2
CLV/TH FY5 .....17 F4
Blue Bell Pl PRES PR1 .....7 H3
Bluebell Wy BBR PR5 .....80 D1
FUL/RIB PR2.....47 E2
Bluebell Wd LEYL PR25.....83 E1
Bluecoat Crs
KIRK/FR/WAR PR4.....55 G1
Blundell La PRES PR1 .....58 D5
Blundell Rd FUL/RIB PR2 .....45 G5
LSTA FY8.....49 F2
Blundell St BPOOL FY1 .....4 B2
Blythe Av CLV/TH FY5.....17 E4
Boarded Barn CHLY/EC PR7 .....87 H4
Boardman Av BPOOL FY1 .....5 G4
Bodmin St PRES PR1.....60 D2
Boegrave Av BBR PR5 .....79 F1
Bold St FTWD FY7 .....11 H1
PRES PR1 .....59 F1
Bolton Av PLF/KEOS FY6 .....26 A2
Bolton Rd CHLY/EC PR7 .....93 G4
Boltons Ct PRES PR1.....7 G4
Bolton St BPOOL FY1 .....4 B5
CHLY/EC PR7 .....93 G4
Bond St BPOOLS FY4.....4 B7
Bone Cft CHLYE PR6 .....85 E2
Bonney St CLV/TH FY5 .....21 H1
Bonny St BPOOL FY1.....2 B7
Boome St BPOOLS FY4 .....38 C2
Boothley Rd BPOOL FY1.....2 E2
Boothroyden BPOOL FY1.....28 B2
Bootle St PRES PR1 .....60 C2
Borage Cl CLV/TH FY5.....17 G4
Bordeaux Crs BISP FY2.....25 F1
Borrowdale Av FTWD FY7 .....11 E2
Borrowdale Rd BPOOLS FY4 .....33 H4
LEYL PR25.....83 G5
Boscombe Rd BPOOLS FY4 .....38 B2
Bostock St PRES PR1 * 7 G4
Boston Av BISP FY2.....24 D1
Boston Rd LSTA FY8 .....49 H5
Bostonway BPOOLS FY4 .....5 K7
Bosworth Pl BPOOLS FY4.....38 B4
Botany Brow CHLYE PR6 .....89 H5
Boulevard PRES PR1.....73 G1
The Boulevard LSTA FY8.....62 D2
Boundary Cl CHLY/EC PR7 .....90 A4
KIRK/FR/WAR PR4.....77 G1
Boundary Rd FUL/RIB PR2.....45 F5
LSTA FY8.....65 F1
Boundary St LEYL PR25 .....83 G2
Bourble's La GAR/LONG PR3 .....13 H3
Bourne May Rd PLF/KEOS FY6 .....12 B1
Bournemouth Rd BPOOLS FY4 .....38 B2
Bourne Rd CLV/TH FY5.....17 H4
Bournesfield BBR PR5 .....75 H5
Bourne's Rw BBR PR5 .....75 H5
Bourne Wy CLV/TH FY5 .....17 F5
Bovington Av CLV/TH FY5 .....21 F4
Bow Brook Rd LEYL PR25 .....83 G3
The Bowers CHLY/EC PR7.....97 G1
Bowes Lyon Pl LSTA FY8 * 50 A4
Bowfell Cl BPOOLS FY4.....34 B4
Bowgreave Cl BPOOLS FY4 .....39 F2
Bowland Av CHLYE PR6 .....93 G2
FTWD FY7.....16 D1
Bowland Crs BPOOLE FY3 .....29 G2
Bowland Pl FUL/RIB PR2 .....47 G5
LSTA FY8.....50 A5
Bowland Rd FUL/RIB PR2.....47 G5
Bowland View Ct
PLF/KEOS FY6 * 19 H3
Bow La LEYL PR25 .....83 G3
PRES PR1 .....6 C4
Bowlers Cl FUL/RIB PR2 .....46 C3
Bowlingfield FUL/RIB PR2 .....44 C2
Bowness Av BPOOLS FY4 .....34 A5
CLV/TH FY5 .....21 H2
LSTA FY8.....49 F2
Bowness Pl FTWD FY7 .....10 C5
Bowness Rd PRES PR1 .....61 G2
Bowood Ct BPOOLE FY3.....29 H3
Bowran St PRES PR1.....6 E3
Bow St LEYL PR25 .....83 G2
Boxer Pl CROS/BRETH PR26.....82 B2
Boys La FUL/RIB PR2.....45 E3
Bracewell Av PLF/KEOS FY6 .....27 E4
Bracewell Rd FUL/RIB PR2.....47 E3
Brackenbury Cl BBR PR5 .....79 F2
Brackenbury Rd FUL/RIB PR2 .....45 G5
Brackenbury St PRES PR1 .....59 H1
Bracken Cl CHLYE PR6 .....93 H2
Bracken Dr KIRK/FR/WAR PR4.....54 D4
Bracken Wy BISP FY2 .....24 D5
Braconash Rd LEYL PR25 .....82 D2
Braddon St PRES PR1.....60 D3
Brades Av CLV/TH FY5 .....22 B2
Brades La KIRK/FR/WAR PR4 .....54 D4
Bradkirk La BBR PR5.....81 E1
Bradkirk Pl BBR PR5 .....80 D2
Bradley La CHLY/EC PR7.....90 C4
Bradshaw Cl PLF/KEOS FY6 .....19 G2
Bradshaw La GAR/LONG PR3 .....15 G4
Braefield Crs FUL/RIB PR2 .....47 F5
Braemar Av CLV/TH FY5.....22 A5
Braemar Wk BISP FY2.....25 F1
Braintree Av PRES PR1.....72 D4
Braith Cl BPOOLS FY4 .....33 F5
Braithwaite St BPOOL FY1 .....2 B1
Bramble Cl KIRK/FR/WAR PR4 .....42 C2
Bramble Ct CLV/TH FY5 .....21 G2
PRES PR1 .....72 D4
Bramble Gdns PLF/KEOS FY6.....25 G5
The Brambles CHLY/EC PR7.....96 C3
FUL/RIB PR2.....46 D2
The Bramblings PLF/KEOS FY6 .....25 H5
Bramley Av FTWD FY7 .....11 E2
Brampton Av CLV/TH FY5 .....17 F5
Brampton St FUL/RIB PR2 .....59 E2
Bramwell Rd
KIRK/FR/WAR PR4.....54 B5
Brancker St CHLY/EC PR7 .....92 D5
Brandiforth St BBR PR5.....74 B4
Brandwood PRES PR1 .....71 H2
Branksome Av CLV/TH FY5 .....21 F1
Branston Rd BPOOLS FY4.....5 J5
Branstree Rd BPOOLS FY4 .....34 A4
Brant Ct FTWD FY7 .....10 C5
Brant Rd PRES PR1 .....61 G2
Brantwood Dr LEYL PR25.....83 G3
Brathay Pl FTWD FY7 .....10 D4
Braxfield Ct LSTA FY8 *.....48 D5
Brays Heys CLV/TH FY5 * 22 A3
Brays Rd LSTA FY8.....51 F1
Bray St FUL/RIB PR2 .....59 E3
Breck Cl PLF/KEOS FY6.....26 C2
Breck Dr PLF/KEOS FY6 .....26 C2
Breck Rd BPOOLE FY3.....3 G6
PLF/KEOS FY6 .....26 C2
Breckside Cl PLF/KEOS FY6 .....26 C2
Brecon Cl BPOOL FY1 .....5 G1
Bredon Av CHLY/EC PR7.....92 B1
Bredon Cl LSTA FY8 .....65 E1
Breeze Cl CLV/TH FY5 .....17 G5
Breeze Mt BBR PR5.....79 H2
Brennand Cl BBR PR5 .....80 C1
Brentwood FTWD FY7 .....11 E4
Brentwood Av CLV/TH FY5 .....20 D3
PLF/KEOS FY6 .....26 A4
Bretherton Cl
CROS/BRETH PR26 .....82 B4
Bretherton Ter LEYL PR25 .....83 F3
Briar Av CHLY/EC PR7.....87 H3
Briar Bank Rw FUL/RIB PR2.....37 E5
Briar Cft KIRK/FR/WAR PR4 .....76 B2
Briar Fld BISP FY2 .....25 F1
Briarfield Rd PLF/KEOS FY6.....25 H1
Briar Gv FUL/RIB PR2 .....44 C4
Briar Ms CLV/TH FY5 .....22 A3
Briar Rd CLV/TH FY5 .....21 H3
The Briars CHLY/EC PR7 .....90 B4
FUL/RIB PR2.....46 D2
Briarwood KIRK/FR/WAR PR4 .....54 A5
Briarwood Cl LEYL PR25.....82 C4
Briarwood Ct CLV/TH FY5 .....21 H5
Briarwood Dr BISP FY2.....25 E2
Brick House La PLF/KEOS FY6 .....19 F5
Brickhouse La PLF/KEOS FY6.....19 G5
Bridge Bank BBR PR5 .....60 C5
Bridge Cl BBR PR5.....79 F1
Bridge End BBR PR5 .....79 H2
Bridge House Rd BPOOLS FY4.....33 F5
Bridge Rd BBR PR5 .....79 H1
FTWD FY7.....11 H2
FUL/RIB PR2.....59 E1
LSTA FY8.....63 G2
Bridgeside LSTA FY8 .....38 B4
Bridge St BBR PR5.....75 E3
BBR PR5 .....80 B2
Bridge Ter BBR PR5 * 60 C5
Bridgewater Av CLV/TH FY5 .....21 F5
Bridgeway BBR PR5 .....79 H1
Bridleway LSTA FY8.....50 C4
Briercliffe Av BPOOLE FY3 .....5 K3
Briercliffe Rd CHLYE PR6 .....93 G1
Brierfield KIRK/FR/WAR PR4 .....77 G1
Brierley Av BPOOLE FY3 .....3 H2
Brierley Rd BBR PR5 .....80 D2
Brierley St PRES PR1.....59 F2
Briery Cl FUL/RIB PR2 .....46 C4
Brieryfield Rd PRES PR1.....6 B3
Briery Hey BBR PR5 .....81 F3
Briggs Rd FUL/RIB PR2.....59 E1
Brighton Av BPOOLS FY4 .....32 B5
CLV/TH FY5 .....20 D2
LSTA FY8.....49 F4
Brighton Crs FUL/RIB PR2 .....44 C5
Brighton St CHLYE PR6 * 93 H2
Bright St BPOOLS FY4 .....4 B7
Brindle Cl BBR PR5 .....81 E1
Brindle Fold BBR PR5 .....81 F2
Brindle Rd BBR PR5.....74 C4
CHLYE PR6 .....81 G3
Brindle St CHLY/EC PR7 .....93 F4
PRES PR1 .....60 C3
Brinwell Rd BPOOLS FY4 .....33 H4
Brisbane Pl CLV/TH FY5 .....21 E3
Bristol Av BISP FY2 .....25 E3
FTWD FY7.....16 C1
LEYL PR25.....79 H5
Bristow Av FUL/RIB PR2.....58 D1
Britannia Dr FUL/RIB PR2.....58 D3
Britannia Pl BPOOL FY1 .....4 B6
Britannia Wk LSTA FY8 .....50 A3
Brixey St PRES PR1 .....6 B7
Brixham Pl BPOOLS FY4 .....38 B2
Brixton Rd PRES PR1 .....7 K5
Broad Cft KIRK/FR/WAR PR4 .....70 B5
Broadfield
KIRK/FR/WAR PR4.....36 A3
Broadfield Av BPOOLS FY4 .....39 E3
PLF/KEOS FY6 .....26 D4
Broadfield Dr LEYL PR25 .....82 D3
PRES PR1 .....72 C4
Broadfields CHLY/EC PR7.....89 E5
Broadgate PRES PR1 .....6 B7
Broadgreen Cl LEYL PR25.....83 E3
Broadhurst Rd CLV/TH FY5 .....21 E4
Broadlands Pl LSTA FY8 .....64 A2
Broad Meadow BBR PR5 .....79 F1
Broad Oak Gn PRES PR1.....72 A3
Broad Oak La BPOOLE FY3.....30 B5
KIRK/FR/WAR PR4.....72 A4
Broadpool La PLF/KEOS FY6 .....23 G3
Broad Sq LEYL PR25 .....83 F4
Broad St LEYL PR25.....83 F4
Broadwater Av FTWD FY7 .....17 E1
Broadwater Gdns FTWD FY7 * 17 E1
Broadway BPOOLS FY4 .....38 C1
FTWD FY7.....16 D3
FUL/RIB PR2.....45 F2
FUL/RIB PR2.....58 B1
LEYL PR25.....83 G4
Broadwood Cl PRES PR1 .....72 A2
Broadwood Dr FUL/RIB PR2 .....45 G1
Broadwood Wy LSTA FY8.....63 H2
Brock Av FTWD FY7.....10 D4
Brockholes Brow PRES PR1 .....61 F2
Brockholes Crs PLF/KEOS FY6.....26 C5
Brockholes Vw PRES PR1 .....60 C4
Brocklewood Av
PLF/KEOS FY6 .....30 B2
Brock Rd CHLYE PR6 .....93 G1
Brockway PLF/KEOS FY6 .....26 B5
Brockway Av BPOOLE FY3.....3 K2
Broderick Av BISP FY2 .....29 E1
Brodie Cl BPOOLS FY4.....39 F2
Bromley Cl BISP FY2 .....29 E1
Bromley Rd LSTA FY8 .....49 F5
Bromley St PRES PR1 * 6 B2
Brompton Cl LSTA FY8 .....50 B5
Brompton Rd PLF/KEOS FY6 .....30 B1
Bromsgrove Av BISP FY2.....24 C3
Brook Cft FUL/RIB PR2 .....44 D5
Brookdale KIRK/FR/WAR PR4 .....77 H3
Brookdale Av CLV/TH FY5 .....21 E4
Brookdale Cl LEYL PR25 .....87 G1
Brooke St CHLYE PR6 .....93 G3
Brookfield Av BPOOLS FY4 .....39 G2
CLV/TH FY5 .....22 A2
FUL/RIB PR2.....46 C4
Brookfield Dr FUL/RIB PR2 .....36 D5
Brookfield Pl BBR PR5 .....80 D3
Brookfield Rd CLV/TH FY5 .....22 A2
Brookfield St PRES PR1 .....59 H2
Brook Gv CLV/TH FY5 .....17 E5
Brook Hey KIRK/FR/WAR PR4 .....76 A1
Brookhouse St FUL/RIB PR2 .....59 F2
Brooklands FUL/RIB PR2 .....58 C2
Brooklands Av FUL/RIB PR2 .....45 G1
KIRK/FR/WAR PR4.....43 E3
Brooklands Rd LSTA FY8 .....50 A5
Brook La CHLY/EC PR7 .....95 G1
CROS/BRETH PR26 .....78 C3
Brooklyn Av BPOOLE FY3.....29 E2
Brook Meadow
KIRK/FR/WAR PR4.....44 B2
Brook Pl FUL/RIB PR2 .....57 H1
Brook Rd LSTA FY8 .....64 D2
Brook Rd North FUL/RIB PR2 .....45 F5
Brookside CHLY/EC PR7 .....87 H5
CHLY/EC PR7 .....96 C4
CLV/TH FY5 .....22 A1
KIRK/FR/WAR PR4.....42 D2
Brookside Cl
CROS/BRETH PR26 .....82 D1
Brookside Rd FUL/RIB PR2 .....45 F1
Brook St BBR PR5 .....75 E3
BPOOLS FY4 .....5 H6
FTWD FY7.....17 E1
FUL/RIB PR2.....45 F5
KIRK/FR/WAR PR4.....42 D2
Brookview FUL/RIB PR2.....46 B3
Brookway KIRK/FR/WAR PR4 .....76 A1
Broom Cl LEYL PR25 .....84 B1
Broomfield Mill St PRES PR1.....59 H2
Broomfield Rd FTWD FY7.....11 F3
Brough Av BISP FY2 .....25 E5
Broughton Av BPOOLE FY3 .....3 H1
Broughton St PRES PR1 .....45 G5
Broughton Tower Wy
FUL/RIB PR2.....37 F5
Broughton Wy PLF/KEOS FY6 .....26 A1
Brow Hey BBR PR5 .....81 E3
Brownedge Cl BBR PR5 .....74 A5
Brownedge La BBR PR5.....74 B5
Brownedge Rd BBR PR5 .....79 G1
Brownhill La
KIRK/FR/WAR PR4.....77 E2
Brownhill Rd LEYL PR25 .....83 E3
Browning Av CLV/TH FY5.....21 G1
LSTA FY8.....65 E2
Browning Crs PRES PR1 * 60 D1
Browning Rd PRES PR1 .....60 D1
Brown La BBR PR5 .....74 D3
Brownley St CHLYE PR6 .....85 E3
CHLYE PR6 .....93 H3
Browns Hey CHLY/EC PR7 .....88 D5
Brown's La KIRK/FR/WAR PR4.....42 B4
PLF/KEOS FY6 .....18 C2
Brown St BBR PR5.....80 C1
CHLYE PR6 .....93 G2
CLV/TH FY5 .....21 H1
FTWD FY7.....11 G3
Browsholme Av FUL/RIB PR2 .....47 F5
Browsholme Cl BPOOLE FY3 .....29 H2
Brunel Wy BPOOLS FY4 .....40 A1
Brun Gv BPOOL FY1.....5 H5
Brunswick Pl FUL/RIB PR2.....59 E2
Brunswick St CHLY/EC PR7 .....93 G2
Bryan Rd BPOOLE FY3 .....3 G5
Brydeck Av PRES PR1.....72 D2
Bryning Av BISP FY2 .....24 C3
Bryning Fern La
KIRK/FR/WAR PR4.....42 D4
Bryning Hall La
KIRK/FR/WAR PR4.....52 B2
KIRK/FR/WAR PR4.....53 E3
Bryning La KIRK/FR/WAR PR4 .....52 D1
Bryony Cl CLV/TH FY5.....17 F4
Buchanan St BPOOL FY1 .....2 D3
CHLYE PR6 .....93 G3
Buckden Cl CLV/TH FY5 .....20 C2
Buckingham Av PRES PR1.....72 C4
Buckingham Rd LSTA FY8 .....63 G2
Buckingham St CHLYE PR6 .....93 G3
Buckingham Wy
PLF/KEOS FY6 .....26 A2
Bucklands Av FUL/RIB PR2 .....59 F1
Buckley Crs CLV/TH FY5.....20 C5
Bucknell Pl CLV/TH FY5 .....21 E5
Buckshaw Hall Cl CHLY/EC PR7.....89 E5
Buckton Cl CHLYE PR6 .....89 F1
Bude Cl KIRK/FR/WAR PR4 .....44 B2
Buller Av PRES PR1 .....72 D2
Bullfinch St PRES PR1 * 60 B2
Bull Park La PLF/KEOS FY6.....23 G4
Bulmer St FUL/RIB PR2.....59 E1
Bunker St KIRK/FR/WAR PR4.....54 C5
Bunting Pl CLV/TH FY5 .....21 F3
Burbank Cl BPOOLS FY4 .....39 F3
Burford Cl BPOOLE FY3 .....29 G3
Burgate BPOOLS FY4 .....38 D3
Burgess Av BPOOLS FY4.....39 E1
Burgh Hall Rd CHLY/EC PR7.....96 D2
Burgh La CHLY/EC PR7 .....97 F1
Burgh La South CHLY/EC PR7 .....97 E3
Burghley Cl CHLYE PR6.....85 F2
Burghley Ct LEYL PR25 * 83 G3
Burgh Mdw CHLY/EC PR7 .....97 F1
Burgundy Crs BISP FY2 .....21 F5
Burholme Cl FUL/RIB PR2 .....61 G1
Burholme Pl FUL/RIB PR2 .....61 G1
Burholme Rd FUL/RIB PR2.....61 G1
Burleigh Rd PRES PR1 .....6 B5
Burlington Rd BPOOLS FY4 .....38 B2
Burlington Rd West
BPOOLS FY4.....38 A2
Burlington St CHLY/EC PR7 .....93 G3
Burnage Gdns BPOOLS FY4 .....38 D1
Burned House La
PLF/KEOS FY6 .....13 G5
Burn Gv CLV/TH FY5 .....17 E5
Burnsall Av BPOOLE FY3.....29 G1
Burnsall Pl FUL/RIB PR2 .....47 E4
Burns Av CLV/TH FY5 .....21 F2
LSTA FY8.....65 E2
Burnside Av BPOOLS FY4 .....33 E5
FTWD FY7.....10 C4
FUL/RIB PR2.....47 F5
Burnside Wy PRES PR1.....72 C3
Burnslack Rd FUL/RIB PR2.....47 F5
Burns Pl BPOOLS FY4 .....5 K7
Burns Rd FTWD FY7.....11 G1
Burns St PRES PR1 .....60 D1
Burrington Cl FUL/RIB PR2 .....46 D2
Burrow Rd PRES PR1 .....7 H1
Burrow's La PLF/KEOS FY6 .....18 D3
Burton Ct FTWD FY7 .....16 C1
Burton Rd BPOOLS FY4.....5 K7

Burwell Av CHLY/EC PR7 96 A5
Burwood Cl PRES PR1 73 E4
Burwood Dr BPOOLE FY3 29 G4
FUL/RIB PR2 61 E1
Bushell Pl PRES PR1 7 G6
Bushell St PRES PR1 6 E1
Bush La KIRK/FR/WAR PR4 67 G2
Bussel Rd PRES PR1 72 D4
Butcher Brow BBR PR5 74 B1
Bute Av BPOOL FY1 2 B1
Butler Pl PRES PR1 59 H1
Butler Rd BPOOL FY1 4 B2
Butler St BPOOL FY1 2 D3
PRES PR1 6 E5
Butterlands PRES PR1 61 F3
Buttermere Av CHLY/EC PR7 92 D4
FTWD FY7 10 C5
Buttermere Cl BBR PR5 74 A4
FUL/RIB PR2 46 C4
Buttermere Dr PLF/KEOS FY6 12 D1
Butterworth Brow
CHLY/EC PR7 96 C1
Butterworth Cl
KIRK/FR/WAR PR4 43 E2
Butts Cl CLV/TH FY5 18 A5
Butts Rd CLV/TH FY5 17 H5
Buxton Av BISP FY2 24 D3
Byfield Av CLV/TH FY5 21 E5
Byland Cl BPOOLS FY4 38 C3
Bymbrig Cl BBR PR5 80 B1
Byron Av CLV/TH FY5 21 G1
KIRK/FR/WAR PR4 53 G5
LSTA FY8 65 E2
Byron Crs CHLY/EC PR7 96 B5
Byron St BPOOLS FY4 4 C6
CHLY/EC PR7 93 F2
FTWD FY7 11 G2

C

Cadby Av BPOOLE FY3 33 F3
Cadley Av FUL/RIB PR2 44 D5
Cadley Cswy FUL/RIB PR2 45 E4
Cadley Dr FUL/RIB PR2 44 D5
Cadogan Pl PRES PR1 7 G6
Caernarfon Cl CLV/TH FY5 22 B2
Cage La KIRK/FR/WAR PR4 78 A1
Cairndale Dr LEYL PR25 87 G1
Cairn Gv BPOOLS FY4 38 C4
Cairnsmore Av PRES PR1 61 F2
Calder Av CHLY/EC PR7 93 E5
CLV/TH FY5 21 F2
FTWD FY7 10 D4
FUL/RIB PR2 45 H2
KIRK/FR/WAR PR4 67 E1
Calder Cl KIRK/FR/WAR PR4 43 F3
LSTA FY8 49 F1
Calder Rd BISP FY2 28 C1
Calder St FUL/RIB PR2 58 D3
Caldervale Av PLF/KEOS FY6 26 A4
Caldicott Wy PLF/KEOS FY6 26 A1
Caledonian Av BPOOLE FY3 3 G1
Calf Croft Pl LSTA FY8 64 B2
Callon St PRES PR1 61 E3
Calvert Pl BPOOLE FY3 29 G3
Cambell's Ct LSTA FY8 49 E4
Camborne Ct BPOOLE FY3 33 H3
Camborne Pl
KIRK/FR/WAR PR4 54 A5
Cambray Rd BPOOL FY1 28 C2
Cambridge Cl PRES PR1 59 G1
Cambridge Rd BBR PR5 80 C1
BPOOL FY1 3 F4
CLV/TH FY5 20 C1
FTWD FY7 11 F3
LSTA FY8 63 G2
Cambridge St CHLY/EC PR7 93 F3
PRES PR1 59 G1
Cambridge Wk PRES PR1 * 59 G1
Cam Cl BBR PR5 80 C1
Camden Pl PRES PR1 7 F5
Camden Rd BPOOLE FY3 3 H2
Camellia Dr LEYL PR25 84 B2
Cameron Av BPOOLE FY3 3 H1
Cameron Cft CHLYE PR6 * 93 G2
Cam La BBR PR5 84 D1
Camomile Cl CHLY/EC PR7 * 88 D4
Campbell Av BPOOLE FY3 3 H1
Campbell St PRES PR1 7 K2
Campion Cl CLV/TH FY5 17 F4
Campion Dr FUL/RIB PR2 57 G2
The Campions FUL/RIB PR2 57 G2
Cam St PRES PR1 60 C1
Camwood BBR PR5 81 E5
Camwood Dr BBR PR5 73 G5
Cam Wood Fold CHLYE PR6 84 D1
Canada Crs BISP FY2 25 E4
Canal Wk CHLYE PR6 93 H2
Canberra Cl CLV/TH FY5 21 F5
Canberra Ct BPOOLS FY4 * 39 E4
Canberra La KIRK/FR/WAR PR4 44 A4
Canberra Rd LEYL PR25 83 G3
Canberra Wy
KIRK/FR/WAR PR4 53 G4
Cann Bridge St BBR PR5 74 D2
Cannock Av BPOOLE FY3 29 E2
Cannon Hl FUL/RIB PR2 * 59 E2
Cannon St PRES PR1 7 F4
Canterbury Av BPOOLE FY3 5 K2
Canterbury Cl PLF/KEOS FY6 26 A2
Canterbury St CHLYE PR6 93 H4
Cantsfield Av FUL/RIB PR2 44 D4
Canute St PRES PR1 60 A2
Capesthorne Dr CHLY/EC PR7 92 E4
Capitol Wy BBR PR5 73 H1
Capstan Cl LSTA FY8 49 E2
Carcroft Av BISP FY2 24 D3
Cardale KIRK/FR/WAR PR4 71 E4
Cardigan Pl BPOOLS FY4 38 A3
Cardigan St FUL/RIB PR2 59 F2
Cardinal Gdns LSTA FY8 50 B5
Cardinal Pl CLV/TH FY5 21 E1
Cardwell Cl KIRK/FR/WAR PR4 66 C1
Carisbrooke Av BPOOLS FY4 39 G1
Carisbrooke Cl PLF/KEOS FY6 26 A1
Carleton Av BPOOLE FY3 29 F1
FUL/RIB PR2 46 D4
Carleton Dr PRES PR1 71 H2
Carleton Gdns PLF/KEOS FY6 25 H2
Carleton Ga PLF/KEOS FY6 26 A3
Carleton Rd CHLYE PR6 89 H3
Carleton Wy PLF/KEOS FY6 25 H2
Carlin Ga BISP FY2 24 B5
Carlisle Av FTWD FY7 10 D5
PRES PR1 71 H2
Carlisle Gv CLV/TH FY5 21 H2
Carlisle St PRES PR1 7 H3
Carloway Av FUL/RIB PR2 46 C3
Carlton Av CHLYE PR6 85 E2
Carlton Gv BISP FY2 24 B3
Carlton Rd LEYL PR25 83 E4
LSTA FY8 49 F4
Carlton St FUL/RIB PR2 6 B2
Carlton Wy BPOOLS FY4 40 D1
Carlyle Av BPOOLS FY4 38 B2
Carnarvon Rd PRES PR1 6 B5
Carnfield Pl BBR PR5 80 D1
Carnforth Av BISP FY2 25 E2
Carnoustie Dr CHLY/EC PR7 88 A3
Carnoustie Cl FUL/RIB PR2 44 D1
Carnoustie Ct PRES PR1 58 C5
Caroline St BPOOL FY1 4 C1
PRES PR1 60 C2
Carr Barn Brow BBR PR5 81 F3
Carr Cl GAR/LONG PR3 15 E1
PLF/KEOS FY6 19 G5
PLF/KEOS FY6 26 C5
Carr Dr KIRK/FR/WAR PR4 42 C2
Carr End La PLF/KEOS FY6 19 G2
Carr Fld BBR PR5 81 F5
Carr Ga CLV/TH FY5 16 C5
Carr Head La PLF/KEOS FY6 26 C5
Carr Hey CLV/TH FY5 * 21 G2
Carr House La
WGNNW/ST WN6 95 E5
Carrick Ms BPOOLE FY3 33 H3
Carrington Rd CHLY/EC PR7 93 E3
Carr La CHLY/EC PR7 93 G5
GAR/LONG PR3 15 E2
KIRK/FR/WAR PR4 43 H2
KIRK/FR/WAR PR4 52 D5
LEYL PR25 83 F1
PLF/KEOS FY6 23 G1
PLF/KEOS FY6 31 F1
Carr Meadow BBR PR5 81 F3
Carrol St PRES PR1 7 J1
Carr Pl BBR PR5 81 E2
Carr Rd CHLYE PR6 85 E2
CLV/TH FY5 24 D1
FTWD FY7 11 G1
KIRK/FR/WAR PR4 43 F4
PLF/KEOS FY6 23 G2
Carr St BBR PR5 80 B1
CHLYE PR6 93 H1
PRES PR1 7 J5
Carrwood Dr
KIRK/FR/WAR PR4 43 F4
Carrwood Rd BBR PR5 73 G3
Carrwood Wy BBR PR5 73 G4
Carshalton Rd BPOOL FY1 28 B3
Carsluith Av BPOOLE FY3 5 J2
Carson Rd BPOOLS FY4 33 G4
Carter St BPOOL FY1 2 C5
Carterville Cl BPOOLS FY4 39 G1
Cart Ga PLF/KEOS FY6 13 F3
Cartmel Av FTWD FY7 10 C5
Cartmel Dr BBR PR5 75 H3
Cartmell La LSTA FY8 51 H4
Cartmell Rd BPOOLS FY4 34 B4
LSTA FY8 62 C2
Cartmel Pl FUL/RIB PR2 58 A1
Cartmel Rd LEYL PR25 82 C4
Carwood La CHLYE PR6 85 F5
Caryl Rd LSTA FY8 48 C3
Casterton CHLY/EC PR7 87 H5
Castle Av PLF/KEOS FY6 25 H1
Castle Fold PRES PR1 73 E4
Castlegate BPOOL FY1 4 C5
Castle La BPOOLE FY3 30 B5
Castle Mt FUL/RIB PR2 45 E1
Castlerigg Pl BPOOLS FY4 34 A4
Castle St CHLY/EC PR7 93 G3
PRES PR1 59 H2
Castleton Rd PRES PR1 60 B2
Castle Wk PRES PR1 59 E5
Catforth Av BPOOLS FY4 33 H4
Catforth Rd FUL/RIB PR2 58 A2
Catherine Cl KIRK/FR/WAR PR4 42 D1
Catherine St CHLY/EC PR7 * 93 F4
KIRK/FR/WAR PR4 42 D2
PRES PR1 7 K2
Cathrow Dr KIRK/FR/WAR PR4 77 H2
Cathrow Wy CLV/TH FY5 22 B2
Catley Cl CHLYE PR6 89 F2
Caton Av FTWD FY7 10 D5
Caton Cl LEYL PR25 84 B2
Caton Gv BPOOLE FY3 * 29 F3
Catterall Cl BPOOL FY1 3 F1
Caunce St BPOOL FY1 2 E4
BPOOLE FY3 3 G3
Causeway Av FUL/RIB PR2 44 D4
The Causeway CHLYE PR6 93 H2
Cavendish Crs FUL/RIB PR2 47 F5
Cavendish Dr FUL/RIB PR2 47 F5
Cavendish Man CLV/TH FY5 * 20 C1
Cavendish Pl BBR PR5 74 A3
Cavendish Rd BISP FY2 24 C3
LSTA FY8 48 C3
PRES PR1 61 E2
Cavendish St CHLYE PR6 93 H3
Cave St PRES PR1 60 D3
Caxton Av BISP FY2 24 C2
Caxton Rd FUL/RIB PR2 37 G5
Cecilia St PRES PR1 60 D2
Cecil St BPOOL FY1 2 E1
LSTA FY8 64 B3
Cedar Av BBR PR5 * 79 G1
CHLY/EC PR7 87 H3
CLV/TH FY5 21 G3
FTWD FY7 17 E1
FUL/RIB PR2 58 C1
KIRK/FR/WAR PR4 53 F5
PLF/KEOS FY6 13 E1
PLF/KEOS FY6 30 B2
Cedar Crs KIRK/FR/WAR PR4 43 E4
Cedar Fld CHLYE PR6 85 F2
Cedar Gv KIRK/FR/WAR PR4 70 B5
Cedar Rd CHLYE PR6 89 G5
FUL/RIB PR2 61 E1
Cedar Sq BPOOL FY1 2 C4
The Cedars CHLY/EC PR7 90 A3
CHLY/EC PR7 97 E1
KIRK/FR/WAR PR4 77 G1
Cedar Wy PRES PR1 72 A3
Cedarwood Cl LSTA FY8 63 H2
Cedarwood Dr LEYL PR25 82 D4
Cedric Pl BISP FY2 24 C3
Celandine Cl CLV/TH FY5 17 F4
Cemetery La PLF/KEOS FY6 13 F5
Cemetery Rd PRES PR1 60 C2
Central Av BBR PR5 75 H4
KIRK/FR/WAR PR4 42 C2
Central Av North CLV/TH FY5 21 F1
Central Beach LSTA FY8 64 C3
Central Dr BPOOL FY1 2 C7
LSTA FY8 63 F1
PRES PR1 71 H2
Central Rd CLV/TH FY5 22 B1
Centre Dr BBR PR5 81 E5
Centurion Ct FUL/RIB PR2 * 45 H4
Centurion Wy LEYL PR25 79 F5
Chaddock St PRES PR1 7 F5
Chadfield Rd BPOOL FY1 5 F3
Chadwick Gdns BBR PR5 79 F2
Chadwick St BPOOL FY1 4 D1
Chaffinch Cl CLV/TH FY5 17 F4
Chaffinch Ct BPOOLE FY3 * 29 H4
Chain Caul Rd FUL/RIB PR2 58 A4
Chain Caul Wy FUL/RIB PR2 58 A3
Chain House La
KIRK/FR/WAR PR4 78 C2
Chain La BPOOLE FY3 30 C5
BPOOLE FY3 34 C1
Chalfont Fld FUL/RIB PR2 45 E3
Champagne Av BISP FY2 25 F1
Chancery Rd CHLY/EC PR7 92 D1
Chandlers Ford PLF/KEOS FY6 26 C2
Chandlers Rest LSTA FY8 65 E3
Chandler St PRES PR1 * 6 E3
Channel Wy FUL/RIB PR2 59 E3
Channing Rd LSTA FY8 63 F2
Chapel Brow LEYL PR25 83 G3
Chapel Cl KIRK/FR/WAR PR4 42 D1
Chapel La CHLY/EC PR7 96 C5
KIRK/FR/WAR PR4 43 F4
KIRK/FR/WAR PR4 76 D1
Chapel Meadow
KIRK/FR/WAR PR4 76 D1
Chapel Park Rd
KIRK/FR/WAR PR4 76 D1
Chapel Rd BPOOLS FY4 39 G1
FUL/RIB PR2 46 A4
Chapel St BPOOL FY1 2 B7
CHLY/EC PR7 93 F2
CHLY/EC PR7 96 B4
LSTA FY8 64 B3
PLF/KEOS FY6 26 B3
PRES PR1 6 E4
Chapel Wk KIRK/FR/WAR PR4 77 E1
Chapel Wks KIRK/FR/WAR PR4 43 F4
PRES PR1 7 F4
Chapel Wy CHLY/EC PR7 96 C4
Chapel Yd BBR PR5 74 A1
Chapman Rd FUL/RIB PR2 46 A5
Chardonnay Crs BISP FY2 21 F5
Charles Crs BBR PR5 75 F3
Charles St BPOOL FY1 2 E3
Charles Wy FUL/RIB PR2 58 A2
Charlesway Ct FUL/RIB PR2 * 58 A2
Charlotte Pl PRES PR1 7 H5
Charlotte St PRES PR1 7 H5
Charnley Cl PRES PR1 72 B4
Charnley Fold BBR PR5 74 C4
Charnley Fold La BBR PR5 74 C3
Charnley Rd BPOOL FY1 2 C6
Charnley St PRES PR1 6 E4
Charnock Av PRES PR1 72 D4
Charnock Brow Preston Rd
CHLY/EC PR7 91 H4
Charnock Fold PRES PR1 * 60 A1
Charnock Moss
CROS/BRETH PR26 79 E1
Charnock St CHLYE PR6 93 G3
KIRK/FR/WAR PR4 42 D2
LEYL PR25 83 F3
PRES PR1 60 A1
Charnwood Av BPOOLE FY3 29 G4
Charter La CHLY/EC PR7 96 A1
Chartwell Cl CHLYE PR6 85 F2
Chartwell Ri BBR PR5 79 H1
The Chase BPOOLE FY3 * 30 A3
CLV/TH FY5 17 G5
LEYL PR25 83 H2
Chatburn Cl PLF/KEOS FY6 29 H2
Chatburn Rd FUL/RIB PR2 47 E4
Chatham Av LSTA FY8 49 E2
Chatham Pl CHLYE PR6 93 H2
PRES PR1 60 B1
Chatsworth Av BISP FY2 24 C1
FTWD FY7 10 C4
KIRK/FR/WAR PR4 53 F5
Chatsworth Cl CHLY/EC PR7 93 E2
CLV/TH FY5 22 B3
Chatsworth Rd BBR PR5 74 A3
LEYL PR25 83 E3
LSTA FY8 48 D4
Chatsworth St PRES PR1 60 C3
Chatteris Pl CLV/TH FY5 20 C3
Chaucer Av CLV/TH FY5 21 F1
Chaucer Cl CHLY/EC PR7 90 A4
Chaucer Rd FTWD FY7 11 G2
Chaucer St PRES PR1 60 D1
Cheam Av CHLY/EC PR7 93 G4
Cheapside BPOOL FY1 2 B4
CHLY/EC PR7 93 F3
PRES PR1 7 F4
Cheddar Av BPOOLS FY4 38 D2
Cheddar Dr FUL/RIB PR2 46 D2
Chelford Av BPOOLE FY3 29 E2
Chelford Cl PRES PR1 73 E4
Chelmsford Gv CHLY/EC PR7 93 E3
Chelmsford Pl CHLY/EC PR7 93 E4
Chelsea Av BISP FY2 29 E1
Cheltenham Crs CLV/TH FY5 22 B4
LSTA FY8 65 E1
Cheltenham Rd BPOOL FY1 28 B3
Chepstow Rd BPOOLE FY3 29 F2
Cheriton Fld FUL/RIB PR2 45 E1
The Cherries CHLY/EC PR7 88 A4
Cherry Cl FUL/RIB PR2 46 D2
KIRK/FR/WAR PR4 42 C3
Cherrydale BISP FY2 24 D2
Cherry Tree Cl GAR/LONG PR3 15 G1
PLF/KEOS FY6 8 A5
Cherry Tree Ct FTWD FY7 * 11 H1
Cherry Tree Gdns BPOOLS FY4 33 G5
Cherry Tree Gv CHLYE PR6 89 F4
Cherry Tree Rd BPOOLS FY4 33 G5
Cherry Tree Rd North
BPOOLE FY3 33 G4
Cherry Trees BBR PR5 73 G3
Cherry Wd PRES PR1 71 H3
Cherrywood Av CLV/TH FY5 20 C3
LSTA FY8 63 H2
Cherrywood Cl LEYL PR25 82 D4
Cheryl Dr CLV/TH FY5 21 H4
Chesham Dr KIRK/FR/WAR PR4 77 G2
Cheshire House Cl
CROS/BRETH PR26 * 79 E2
Chesmere Cft PRES PR1 * 72 A1
Chesmere Dr PRES PR1 72 A1
Chester Av CHLY/EC PR7 97 H1
CLV/TH FY5 20 D2
PLF/KEOS FY6 26 A4
Chesterfield Rd BPOOL FY1 28 B3
Chester Rd BPOOLE FY3 3 G1
PRES PR1 60 C2
Chestnut Av BPOOLS FY4 39 F3
CHLY/EC PR7 87 H3
CHLYE PR6 89 H5
PRES PR1 71 H2
Chestnut Cl BBR PR5 74 B4
BISP FY2 24 D5
Chestnut Crs FUL/RIB PR2 61 E1
KIRK/FR/WAR PR4 76 A1
Chestnut Ct LEYL PR25 83 F5
Chestnut Dr FUL/RIB PR2 45 F1
Chestnut Gdns CLV/TH FY5 21 H1
Cheviot Av CLV/TH FY5 17 F5
LSTA FY8 65 F1
Cheviot St PRES PR1 59 E3
Chew Gdns PLF/KEOS FY6 25 H4
Chichester Cl CLV/TH FY5 21 G2
Chiltern Av BPOOLS FY4 38 D1
CHLY/EC PR7 92 A1
PLF/KEOS FY6 26 A4
Chiltern Cl LSTA FY8 65 E1
Chiltern Meadow LEYL PR25 84 A3
The Chimes KIRK/FR/WAR PR4 43 E4
Chindits Wy FUL/RIB PR2 46 B4
The Chines FUL/RIB PR2 45 G4
Chingle Cl FUL/RIB PR2 47 E2
Chipping Gv BPOOLE FY3 29 G2
Chirk Dr CLV/TH FY5 * 22 B2
Chislehurst Av BPOOLS FY4 5 F6
Chislehurst Pl LSTA FY8 50 B5
Chisnall La CHLY/EC PR7 95 E3
Chiswell Gv CLV/TH FY5 22 C4
Chiswick Gv BPOOLE FY3 33 H3
Chive Cl BISP FY2 25 F4
Chorley Hall Rd CHLY/EC PR7 89 F5
Chorley La CHLY/EC PR7 95 H3
Chorley Old Rd CHLYE PR6 85 F5
Chorley Rd BBR PR5 74 A3
BPOOLE FY3 25 F5
CHLY/EC PR7 97 G5
Christ Church St PRES PR1 6 C5
Christian Rd PRES PR1 6 D5
Church Av PRES PR1 59 E5
PRES PR1 61 E3
Church Brow BBR PR5 74 A1
Church Cl KIRK/FR/WAR PR4 54 A5
Church Ct PRES PR1 60 C1
Church Dr LSTA FY8 64 A3
Churchfield FUL/RIB PR2 45 H2
Church Fold CHLY/EC PR7 96 B1
CHLY/EC PR7 96 C5
Church Gdns
KIRK/FR/WAR PR4 53 G5
Church Hl CHLYE PR6 85 E5
Churchill Cl CLV/TH FY5 21 H2
Churchill Ct BPOOLE FY3 3 G2
Churchill Dr FUL/RIB PR2 * 46 D4
Churchill Rd FUL/RIB PR2 46 C4
Churchill Wy LEYL PR25 83 F2
Church La CHLY/EC PR7 96 A1
GAR/LONG PR3 36 C4
KIRK/FR/WAR PR4 78 D2
PLF/KEOS FY6 23 H3
WGNNW/ST WN6 94 C5
Church Rd BBR PR5 80 C3
CLV/TH FY5 21 F2
KIRK/FR/WAR PR4 42 D1
KIRK/FR/WAR PR4 53 F4
LEYL PR25 83 F4
LSTA FY8 49 G4
LSTA FY8 63 H3
Church Rw PRES PR1 7 G3
Churchside KIRK/FR/WAR PR4 77 G1
Church St BBR PR5 75 E3
BPOOL FY1 2 B5
CHLY/EC PR7 * 93 F3
FTWD FY7 11 H2
KIRK/FR/WAR PR4 43 F3
LEYL PR25 83 G2
PLF/KEOS FY6 * 26 B4
PRES PR1 7 G4
Church Wk CHLY/EC PR7 87 H5
FUL/RIB PR2 47 F3
KIRK/FR/WAR PR4 42 D1
Chysden Cl CHLYE PR6 89 F2
Cinnamon Ct PRES PR1 72 B4
Cinnamon Hill Dr North
BBR PR5 74 A3
Cinnamon Hill Dr South
BBR PR5 74 A3
Cintra Av FUL/RIB PR2 59 F1
Clairane Av FUL/RIB PR2 45 G2
Clancut La CHLY/EC PR7 96 C3
Clanfield FUL/RIB PR2 45 G1
Clara St PRES PR1 * 60 C4
Claremont Av CHLY/EC PR7 93 E3
Claremont Ct BPOOL FY1 28 C3
Claremont Pl LSTA FY8 49 E3
Claremont Rd BPOOL FY1 28 C3
CHLY/EC PR7 93 E5
Claremount Av LEYL PR25 83 G4
Clarence Av CLV/TH FY5 20 D1
PLF/KEOS FY6 12 C1
Clarence St CHLY/EC PR7 * 93 G3
LEYL PR25 83 G2
Clarendon Rd BPOOL FY1 4 C3
LSTA FY8 49 F3
Clarendon Rd North LSTA FY8 49 F3
Clarendon St CHLYE PR6 93 H3
PRES PR1 7 H6
Clare Rd BPOOL FY1 4 C5
Clark St PLF/KEOS FY6 26 D4
Claughton Av LEYL PR25 84 B3
Clayburn Cl CHLYE PR6 89 H5
Clayton Av LEYL PR25 82 C5
Clayton Brook Rd BBR PR5 81 F5
Clayton Crs BPOOLS FY4 38 D2
Claytongate BPOOLS FY4 39 F1
CHLY/EC PR7 96 C3
Clayton Green Rd CHLYE PR6 85 E1
Clayton's Ga PRES PR1 6 E3
Clayton St BBR PR5 74 B5
Cleator Av BISP FY2 28 C1
Clegg Av CLV/TH FY5 20 C1
Clegg St KIRK/FR/WAR PR4 * 43 E3
Clematis Cl CHLY/EC PR7 88 D4
Clevedon Rd BPOOL FY1 28 B3
FUL/RIB PR2 44 C4
Cleveland Av FUL/RIB PR2 46 C4
Cleveland Rd LEYL PR25 83 E2
LSTA FY8 64 C3
Cleveland St CHLY/EC PR7 93 F2
CHLY/EC PR7 * 96 B4
Cleveleys Av CLV/TH FY5 16 D5
FUL/RIB PR2 45 E4
Cleveleys Rd BBR PR5 75 H3
Cliffe Ct PRES PR1 60 D3
Cliffe Dr CHLYE PR6 85 E4
Clifford Av KIRK/FR/WAR PR4 70 B5
Clifford Rd BPOOL FY1 2 C1
Clifford St CHLY/EC PR7 93 G2
Cliff Pl BISP FY2 24 B3
Cliff St PRES PR1 6 C6
Clifton Av BPOOLE FY3 34 A4
FUL/RIB PR2 58 C1
KIRK/FR/WAR PR4 53 G5
LEYL PR25 83 G4
Clifton Cl CLV/TH FY5 22 A3
Clifton Ct LSTA FY8 * 64 D3
Clifton Crs BPOOLE FY3 33 G3
PRES PR1 60 C1
Clifton Dr BPOOLS FY4 38 B3
LSTA FY8 63 F2
PRES PR1 72 B1
Clifton Dr North LSTA FY8 38 B5
Clifton Dr South LSTA FY8 49 E5
Clifton Flds
KIRK/FR/WAR PR4 * 55 H4
Clifton Gdns LSTA FY8 50 A5
Clifton Gn KIRK/FR/WAR PR4 56 A2
Clifton Gv CHLY/EC PR7 93 E3
PRES PR1 46 C5
Clifton Pl FUL/RIB PR2 * 58 D1
KIRK/FR/WAR PR4 54 B5
Clifton Rd BPOOLS FY4 34 B5
FTWD FY7 11 G3
Clifton St BPOOL FY1 2 B4
LSTA FY8 64 C3
PRES PR1 6 B7
Clinton Av BPOOL FY1 2 E7
Clitheroe Pl BPOOLS FY4 33 G5
Clitheroe Rd LSTA FY8 50 A5
Clitheroes La
KIRK/FR/WAR PR4 54 B5
Clitheroe St PRES PR1 60 C4
Clive Av LSTA FY8 49 E2
Clive Rd PRES PR1 58 D5
Clods Carr La PLF/KEOS FY6 12 D3
The Cloisters BPOOLE FY3 3 H4
FUL/RIB PR2 6 B1
LEYL PR25 83 H2
The Close CLV/TH FY5 16 D5
CLV/TH FY5 20 D2
FUL/RIB PR2 47 E2
KIRK/FR/WAR PR4 43 F4
KIRK/FR/WAR PR4 77 H2
Clough Acre CHLY/EC PR7 88 D5
Clough Av BBR PR5 73 G3
Cloughfield PRES PR1 72 C5
The Clough CHLYE PR6 84 D1
Clovelly Av BISP FY2 24 C1
FUL/RIB PR2 45 F5
Clovelly Dr PRES PR1 71 H1
Clover Av LSTA FY8 49 G2
Clover Ct BISP FY2 25 F1
Clover Dr KIRK/FR/WAR PR4 54 D4
Clover Fld CHLYE PR6 85 E2
Cloverfield PRES PR1 72 A2
Clover Ms BPOOLE FY3 3 H2
Clover Rd CHLY/EC PR7 92 D5
Club St BBR PR5 80 B2
Clydesdale Pl
CROS/BRETH PR26 82 B2
Clyde St BPOOL FY1 2 C1
FUL/RIB PR2 59 E3
Cobden St CHLYE PR6 93 H1

Cocker Av PLF/KEOS FY6 .....27 E5
Cocker La CROS/BRETH PR26 .82 B3
Cocker Rd BBR PR5 .....80 D2
Cockersand Av
  KIRK/FR/WAR PR4 .....70 D5
Cocker Sq BPOOL FY1 .....2 B2
Codale Av BBR PR5 .....24 D2
Colchester Rd BPOOLE FY3 .33 F2
Coldale Ct BPOOLS FY4 * 98 B2
Cold Bath St PRES PR1 .....6 C2
Colebatch FUL/RIB PR2 .....45 F3
Colenso Rd CLV/TH FY5 .....59 E1
Coleridge Av CLV/TH FY5 .....21 F1
Coleridge Rd BPOOL FY1 .....3 F2
Colesville Av CLV/TH FY5 .....21 H5
College Av CLV/TH FY5 .....20 C5
College Ct PRES PR1 .....59 G1
College Ga CLV/TH FY5 .....16 C4
Collingwood Av BPOOLE FY3 .3 H3
  LSTA FY8 .....49 E2
Collingwood Rd CHLY/EC PR7 .92 D5
Collins Av BISP FY2 .....25 E4
Collinson St PRES PR1 .....60 C2
Collins Rd North BBR PR5 .74 C4
Collyhurst Av CLV/TH FY5 .59 E2
Colman Ct PRES PR1 .....6 B6
Colt House Cl LEYL PR25 .....83 F5
Coltsfoot Dr CHLYE PR6 .....89 G5
Columbine Cl PLF/KEOS FY6 * .88 D4
Colville Av BPOOLS FY4 .....3 H5
Colwyn Av BPOOLS FY4 .5 J6
Colwyn Pl FUL/RIB PR2 .....44 C5
Colyton Cl CHLYE PR6 .....93 H2
Colyton Rd East CHLYE PR6 .93 H2
Comet Ct CROS/BRETH PR26 .82 D2
Commercial Rd CHLY/EC PR7 .93 F1
Commercial St BPOOLS FY4 .....2 C1
Common Bank La
  CHLY/EC PR7 .....92 B3
Common Edge Rd
  BPOOLS FY4 .....39 F1
Commonside CLV/TH FY5 .....63 G2
Commonwealth Cl LSTA FY8 .50 A3
Compley Av PLF/KEOS FY6 .26 A5
Compley Gn PLF/KEOS FY6 .26 A5
Compton Cl FUL/RIB PR2 .....26 A2
Compton Gn FUL/RIB PR2 .....45 E1
Conder Av CLV/TH FY5 .....21 H2
Conder Rd FUL/RIB PR2 .....58 A2
Condor Gv BPOOL FY1 .....5 F3
  LSTA FY8 .....48 D3
Congleton Cl BPOOLS FY4 .33 H4
Congress St CHLY/EC PR7 .....93 F1
The Conifers
  KIRK/FR/WAR PR4 .....43 F3
  PLF/KEOS FY6 .....23 F2
Coniston Av CHLY/EC PR7 .92 A1
  CLV/TH FY5 .....21 H5
  FTWD FY7 .....11 E2
  FUL/RIB PR2 .....59 F1
  LSTA FY8 .....49 F1
  PLF/KEOS FY6 .....25 F5
Coniston Dr BBR PR5 .....74 B4
Coniston Rd BPOOLS FY4 .32 C5
  PRES PR1 .....6 A1
  FUL/RIB PR2 .....46 C4
Connaught Dr CLV/TH FY5 .22 B2
Connaught Rd PRES PR1 .72 D1
Consett Av CLV/TH FY5 .....17 E4
Constable Av BBR PR5 .....79 F2
Constable St PRES PR1 .....7 G5
Constant Ct BBR PR5 .....74 A5
  LEYL PR25 .....83 H2
Convent Crs BPOOLE FY3 .29 G2
Conway Av BBR PR5 .....73 E5
  BPOOLE FY3 .....29 G3
  CLV/TH FY5 .....20 D2
  LEYL PR25 .....83 H4
Conway Cl CLV/TH FY5 .....92 B1
Conway Ct BBR PR5 .....75 G4
Conway Dr FUL/RIB PR2 .....45 E2
Conway Rd CHLY/EC PR7 .....90 B5
Cookson Cl KIRK/FR/WAR PR4 54 B5
Cookson Rd CLV/TH FY5 .....21 H4
Cookson St BPOOL FY1 .....2 D3
The Coombes FUL/RIB PR2 .45 H3
Co-operative St BBR PR5 .....80 B1
Cooper Hill Cl BBR PR5 .....74 A1
Cooper Hill Dr BBR PR5 .....74 A1
Cooper Rd PRES PR1 .....6 B4
Cooper's La CHLY/EC PR7 .....94 A5
Coopers Rw LSTA FY8 .....50 B4
Cooper's Wy BPOOL FY1 .....3 F1
Coop St BPOOL FY1 .....2 C7
Coote La KIRK/FR/WAR PR4 .79 E2
Copeland Pl LSTA FY8 .....64 A3
Cop La FTWD FY7 .....11 G2
  PRES PR1 .....72 A1
Copper Beeches PRES PR1 .72 C4
Copperwood Wy CHLY/EC PR7 .92 C5
Coppice Cl CHLYE PR6 .....93 H1
The Coppice FUL/RIB PR2 .44 C4
  KIRK/FR/WAR PR4 .....43 E2
  KIRK/FR/WAR PR4 .....76 B2
Coppins Gn PLF/KEOS FY6 .30 C1
Coppull Hall La CHLY/EC PR7 .96 D4
Coppull Rd CHLY/EC PR7 .....96 C1
Copse Rd FTWD FY7 .....11 E2
The Copse CHLY/EC PR7 .....97 E1
Copthurst La CHLYE PR6 .....89 H1
Coral Cl BPOOLS FY4 .....33 G4
Corbridge Cl BPOOLS FY4 .39 G1
  PLF/KEOS FY6 .....26 A2
Corfe Cl PRES PR1 .....72 B8
The Corners CLV/TH FY5 .....16 C5
Cornfield KIRK/FR/WAR PR4 .44 A2
Cornflower Cl CHLYE PR6 .....89 G5
Cornford Rd BPOOLS FY4 .....33 H5
Cornthwaite Rd FUL/RIB PR2 * .45 G3

Cornwall Av BISP FY2 .....24 C5
  CLV/TH FY5 .....17 E5
Cornwall Ms CLV/TH FY5 * .17 E5
Cornwall Pl BPOOLE FY3 .....33 H5
Coronation Crs PRES PR1 .....7 G5
Coronation Rd CLV/TH FY5 .20 C2
  KIRK/FR/WAR PR4 .....43 E3
  LSTA FY8 .....63 F3
Coronation St BPOOL FY1 .....2 B4
Corporation St BPOOL FY1 .....2 B4
  CHLYE PR6 .....93 G1
  PRES PR1 .....6 E3
Corriander Cl BISP FY2 .....25 F4
Corrib Rd BISP FY2 .....24 D5
Cotswold Av CLV/TH FY5 .....92 A1
Cotswold Cl CHLY/EC PR7 .....90 A2
Cotswold Rd BISP FY2 .....28 D1
  BPOOLE FY3 .....29 E2
  CHLY/EC PR7 .....93 F4
Cottage Flds CHLY/EC PR7 .95 E5
Cottage Gdns BBR PR5 .....81 E1
Cottage La BBR PR5 .....74 C4
Cottage St PRES PR1 * 7 G3
Cottam Av FUL/RIB PR2 .....44 B4
Cottam Cl LSTA FY8 .....49 F1
Cottam Gn KIRK/FR/WAR PR4 .44 B5
Cottam Hall La FUL/RIB PR2 .44 B3
Cottam La FUL/RIB PR2 .....44 C5
  FUL/RIB PR2 .....58 C1
  KIRK/FR/WAR PR4 .....76 D3
Cottam Pl PLF/KEOS FY6 .....26 A5
Cottam St CHLY/EC PR7 .....93 F4
  KIRK/FR/WAR PR4 .....44 A5
Cotton Ct PRES PR1 * 7 G3
Coulston Av BISP FY2 .....24 B4
Counsell Ct CLV/TH FY5 .....21 H2
Countess Cl KIRK/FR/WAR PR4 .43 E1
Countess Crs BISP FY2 .....24 C3
Countesway BBR PR5 .....74 B5
Countess Wy CHLY/EC PR7 .88 A5
Coupe Gn BBR PR5 .....75 J4
Courtfield Av BISP FY2 .....28 D2
The Court FUL/RIB PR2 .....45 E1
  PRES PR1 * 72 B2
The Courtyard
  KIRK/FR/WAR PR4 * 42 D2
Coventry St CHLY/EC PR7 .....93 F4
The Covert CLV/TH FY5 .....17 F5
The Cove CLV/TH FY5 .....16 C5
Coveway Av BPOOLE FY3 .....3 H5
Cowley Rd BPOOLS FY4 .....15 F5
  FUL/RIB PR2 .....47 E5
Cowling Brow CHLYE PR6 .93 H5
Cowling La LEYL PR25 .....82 C3
Cowslip Wy CHLYE PR6 .....89 G5
Cow Well La CHLYE PR6 .....85 E4
Crabtree Av PRES PR1 .....71 H5
Crabtree Orch CLV/TH FY5 .21 H1
Crabtree Rd CLV/TH FY5 .....21 H1
Cragg's Rw PRES PR1 .....6 E1
Cragg St BPOOL FY1 .....2 B7
Craigflower Ct BBR PR5 .....81 F2
Crake Av FTWD FY7 .....11 E2
Cranborne St PRES PR1 * 60 C4
Cranbourne Dr CHLYE PR6 .95 H3
Cranbourne Gv CLV/TH FY5 .22 C5
Cranbourne St BBR PR5 .....80 B1
  CHLYE PR6 .....93 G5
Cranbrook Av BISP FY2 .....24 D2
Cranleigh Av BISP FY2 .....24 C3
Cranwell Cl KIRK/FR/WAR PR4 .42 D3
Craven Cl FUL/RIB PR2 .....45 H1
Craven Dr BBR PR5 .....80 A2
Crawford Av BISP FY2 .....24 C5
  CHLY/EC PR7 .....93 E2
  LEYL PR25 .....83 H3
  PRES PR1 .....6 A1
Crescent Rd CLV/TH FY5 .....26 C3
Crescent St PRES PR1 .....60 C2
The Crescent BBR PR5 .....74 C4
  BBR PR5 .....79 H1
  BPOOLS FY4 .....38 D1
  CHLY/EC PR7 .....89 E5
  FTWD FY7 .....17 E1
  FUL/RIB PR2 .....57 H2
  KIRK/FR/WAR PR4 .....66 B2
  PLF/KEOS FY6 .....13 F2
  PLF/KEOS FY6 .....23 F2
Cresswood Av CLV/TH FY5 .20 D3
Crestway BPOOLE FY3 .....29 F4
Creswell Av FUL/RIB PR2 .....44 B5
Criccieth Place Av CLV/TH FY5 .22 B2
Crichton Pl BPOOLS FY4 .....38 B3
Cricketers Gn CHLY/EC PR7 .90 A3
Croasdale Av FUL/RIB PR2 .22 B3
Croasdale Dr CLV/TH FY5 .....21 F1
Crocus Fld LEYL PR25 .....83 F5
Croft Bank PRES PR1 .....72 B3
Croft Butts La
  KIRK/FR/WAR PR4 .....44 A1
Croft Cl CLV/TH FY5 * 18 A5
  FTWD FY7 .....11 E4
Crofters Gn CHLY/EC PR7 .....87 H4
  PRES PR1 .....59 G1
Crofters Meadow
  CROS/BRETH PR26 .....82 D1
Crofters Ms CHLY/EC PR7 .....89 G2
Crofters Wk LSTA FY8 .....50 C4
Croftgate FUL/RIB PR2 .....45 H3
Croft Meadow BBR PR5 .....81 F3
Crofton Av BISP FY2 .....24 D2
Croft Pk CHLYE PR6 .....93 H5
Crofts Cl KIRK/FR/WAR PR4 .70 B5
The Crofts KIRK/FR/WAR PR4 .70 B5
Croft St PRES PR1 .....6 E5
The Croft CHLY/EC PR7 .....87 G4
  CHLY/EC PR7 .....90 B3
  CLV/TH FY5 .....17 H5
  FTWD FY7 .....10 D4
  LSTA FY8 .....49 H4
  PLF/KEOS FY6 * 26 B5
Croft Wy CLV/TH FY5 .....22 A4

Cromblehome Rd PRES PR1 ..61 E2
Cromer Pl FUL/RIB PR2 .....44 C4
Cromer Rd BISP FY2 .....55 E3
  LSTA FY8 .....49 G2
Cromford Wk PRES PR1 * 60 C3
Crompton Av BPOOLS FY4 .39 E1
Crompton St PRES PR1 .....60 C2
Cromwell Av PRES PR1 .....72 B3
Cromwell Rd BPOOL FY1 .....2 C1
  FUL/RIB PR2 .....46 D5
  PRES PR1 .....72 A3
Cromwell St PRES PR1 .....7 H1
Crookall Cl FTWD FY7 .....11 F4
Crook Dale La PLF/KEOS FY6 .19 H2
Crooked La PRES PR1 .....7 G5
Crookings La PRES PR1 .....58 C5
Crook St CHLY/EC PR7 .....93 E5
  PRES PR1 .....7 K2
Cropper Rd BPOOLS FY4 .....39 H1
Cropper Rd North
  BPOOLS FY4 .....40 A1
Crosby Gv BPOOLE FY3 .....5 K2
Crosby Pl FUL/RIB PR2 .....44 C4
Crosby Rd LSTA FY8 .....49 F2
Crosier Wk KIRK/FR/WAR PR4 .44 A3
Crosland Rd North LSTA FY8 .49 F2
Crosland Rd South LSTA FY8 .49 G3
Cross Brow Preston Rd
  CHLY/EC PR7 .....91 H2
Crosse Hall La CHLY/EC PR7 .93 H5
Cross Fld KIRK/FR/WAR PR4 .70 D5
Cross Green Rd PLF/KEOS FY6 .45 G2
Cross Halls PRES PR1 .....72 A3
Cross Keys Dr CHLYE PR6 .....85 F5
Crossland Rd BPOOLS FY4 .....5 J6
Cross St BPOOL FY1 .....2 C1
  CHLY/EC PR7 * 93 F1
  FTWD FY7 .....11 H1
  LEYL PR25 .....83 F3
  LSTA FY8 .....48 D3
  PRES PR1 .....7 F5
Cross Wy CLV/TH FY5 .....16 D5
Croston La CHLY/EC PR7 .....95 G4
Croston Rd CROS/BRETH PR26 .82 D1
Crowder Av CLV/TH FY5 .....24 B3
Crowell Wy BBR PR5 .....74 B5
Crow Hills Rd PRES PR1 .....58 C5
Crowle St PRES PR1 .....60 D3
Crown La FTWD FY7 .....11 H2
Crownlee PRES PR1 .....71 H3
Crown Rd CHLY/EC PR7 .....93 F2
  PRES PR1 .....7 F2
Croyde St LSTA FY8 .....62 D1
Croydon Rd BPOOLE FY3 .29 E3
Crummock Pl BPOOLS FY4 .34 A4
Crummock Rd PRES PR1 .....61 G2
Crystal Cv LSTA FY8 .....49 E3
Crystal Ms BPOOL FY1 .....4 B1
Crystal Rd BPOOL FY1 .....4 B5
  PRES PR1 .....17 H4
Cudworth Rd LSTA FY8 .....49 F2
Cuerdale La BBR PR5 .....74 C1
Cuerden Av LEYL PR25 .....82 C5
Cuerden Cl BBR PR5 .....80 B5
Cuerden Ri BBR PR5 .....79 H2
Cuerden St CHLYE PR6 .....93 H5
Cuerden Wy BBR PR5 .....80 A1
Culbeck La CHLY/EC PR7 .....87 E4
Culham Cl CLV/TH FY5 .....21 G2
Cumberland Av BPOOL FY1 .....5 H4
  CLV/TH FY5 .....16 D5
  PRES PR1 .....82 D5
Cumbrian Av BPOOLE FY3 .....3 H1
Cunliffe Rd BPOOL FY1 .....5 G4
Cunliffe St CHLY/EC PR7 .....93 F3
  PRES PR1 .....7 H5
Cunnery Meadow LEYL PR25 .84 B3
Cunningham Av CHLY/EC PR7 .92 D4
Curate St CHLY/EC PR7 .....93 H1
Curlew Cl CLV/TH FY5 .....17 F5
Curlew Ms BPOOLE FY3 .....29 H2
Curtis Dr FTWD FY7 .....10 D3
Curwen St PRES PR1 .....60 C2
Curzon Rd LSTA FY8 .....49 G4
  PLF/KEOS FY6 .....26 C2
Custom House La FTWD FY7 .11 H1
Customs Wy FUL/RIB PR2 .....59 E3
Cuthbert Rd FUL/RIB PR2 .....58 A4
Cypress Cl FUL/RIB PR2 .....47 G4
  LEYL PR25 .....84 B2
Cypress Gv BBR PR5 .....79 G1
  BPOOLE FY3 .....3 G1
Cyprus Av LSTA FY8 .....63 E2

D

Daggers Hall La BPOOLS FY4 ..5 J7
Daggers La PLF/KEOS FY6 .....13 F3
Daisy Bank Cl LEYL PR25 .....82 C3
Daisy Clt FUL/RIB PR2 .....57 H3
Daisyfields
  KIRK/FR/WAR PR4 .....44 B1
Daisy Fold CHLYE PR6 .....89 H5
Daisy Hill Fold CHLY/EC PR7 .92 A1
Daisy La PRES PR1 .....60 A1
Daisy Meadow BBR PR5 .....81 E4
Dalby Cl CLV/TH FY5 .....21 F5
  PRES PR1 .....46 D5
Dale Av CHLY/EC PR7 .....97 F1
Dale Dyke Wk PLF/KEOS FY6 .25 H4
Dalegarth Cl BPOOLS FY4 .34 A4
Dalehead Rd LEYL PR25 .....87 G1
Dale Ms BPOOL FY1 .....4 B1
Dalesford Cl CLV/TH FY5 .....22 A4
Dalesford St BPOOL FY1 * 28 A4
Dale Vw CLV/TH FY5 .....17 H4
Dalewood Av BPOOLS FY4 .....5 H5
Dalkeith Av BPOOLS FY4 .....33 G3
Dallam Dell CLV/TH FY5 .....17 H4
Dallas St PRES PR1 .....60 C3

Dalmore Rd FUL/RIB PR2 .....44 C5
Dalton Av BPOOLS FY4 .....38 D3
Dalton St LSTA FY8 .....48 D3
Dane Ms PLF/KEOS FY6 .....30 C2
Danesbury Pl BPOOL FY1 .....2 E4
Danes Cl BBR PR5 .....74 A5
Danes Dr BBR PR5 .....74 A5
Danesway BBR PR5 .....74 A5
  PRES PR1 .....71 H2
Danewerke St PRES PR1 * 7 H2
Danson Gdns BISP FY2 .....24 C3
Darbishire Rd FTWD FY7 .....11 F1
Darkinson La
  KIRK/FR/WAR PR4 .....56 D1
Dark La CHLYE PR6 .....89 H1
Darley Av BPOOLS FY4 .....38 D1
Darlington St CHLY/EC PR7 .96 A4
Dartmouth Cl
  KIRK/FR/WAR PR4 .....42 D5
Dart St FUL/RIB PR2 .....59 E3
Darwen St BBR PR5 .....74 B1
Darwen Vw BBR PR5 .....74 B1
Daub Hall La BBR PR5 .....75 H4
Dauntesey Av PLF/KEOS FY6 .29 G4
Davenport Av BISP FY2 .....24 C2
Daventry Av BISP FY2 .....24 D2
Dawber's La CHLY/EC PR7 .86 D5
Dawlish Av BPOOLS FY4 .....29 F2
Dawlish Pl FUL/RIB PR2 .....44 C5
Dawnay Rd CHLY/EC PR7 .....84 B5
Dawson Pl BBR PR5 .....80 D2
Dawson La BBR PR5 .....84 B5
Dawson Wk PRES PR1 .....7 F1
Dayton Pl BPOOLS FY4 .....5 J6
Deal Pl LSTA FY8 .....49 F2
Dean Ct FTWD FY7 .....16 D1
Deanhall La CHLY/EC PR7 .....93 H2
Deansgate BPOOL FY1 .....2 C4
Dean St BBR PR5 .....74 B5
  BPOOLS FY4 .....4 B7
Deborah Av BBR PR5 .....46 A1
Deepdale Av PLF/KEOS FY6 .25 H2
Deepdale Houses PRES PR1 * .7 J1
Deepdale Mill St PRES PR1 .....7 K1
Deepdale Pk PRES PR1 * 46 D5
Deepdale Rd BPOOLS FY4 .....34 A5
  FTWD FY7 .....11 G3
  PRES PR1 .....60 B1
Deerfold CHLY/EC PR7 .....89 G3
Deerhurst Rd CLV/TH FY5 .....21 E5
Deeside BPOOLS FY4 .....38 D3
Dee St LSTA FY8 .....49 E5
Deighton Av LEYL PR25 .....83 F4
Deighton Rd CHLY/EC PR7 .....95 E4
De Lacy St FUL/RIB PR2 .....58 B2
Delamere Pl CHLYE PR6 .....95 G2
Delany Dr KIRK/FR/WAR PR4 .54 A5
Delaware Rd BPOOLE FY3 .....29 E1
Delaware St PRES PR1 .....60 C2
The Dell FUL/RIB PR2 .....44 C5
The Dellway KIRK/FR/WAR PR4 .71 E5
Delph La CHLY/EC PR7 .....92 A4
Delph Wy CHLYE PR6 .....95 F5
Delta La FTWD FY7 .....11 G2
Demming Cl FUL/RIB PR2 .....57 G5
Denbigh Av CLV/TH FY5 .....21 G3
Denbigh Cl LSTA FY8 .....83 G3
Denbigh Wy PRES PR1 .....7 H5
Denby Rd BBR PR5 .....73 H3
Denebank BISP FY2 .....24 D2
Deneway Av BPOOLE FY3 .....3 K2
Denford Av LEYL PR25 .....83 F5
  LSTA FY8 .....49 F3
Denham La CHLY/EC PR7 .....88 A5
Denham Wy FTWD FY7 .....11 F4
Denholme Gv BISP FY2 .....24 D1
Denmark Rd LSTA FY8 .....63 G1
Denstone Av BISP FY2 .....24 D1
Denville Av CLV/TH FY5 .....21 F4
Denville Rd PRES PR1 .....29 E1
Depot Rd BPOOLS FY4 .....5 H4
Derbe Rd LSTA FY8 .....62 C1
Derby Rd BPOOL FY1 .....28 B5
  FUL/RIB PR2 .....45 G4
  KIRK/FR/WAR PR4 .....43 E2
  LSTA FY8 .....63 E2
  PLF/KEOS FY6 .....23 E1
Derby Sq PRES PR1 .....60 C3
Derby St BBR PR5 .....73 H3
  PRES PR1 .....6 E5
Derek Rd CHLYE PR6 .....85 F3
Derry Rd FUL/RIB PR2 .....58 A4
Derwent Av FTWD FY7 .....10 D4
Derwent Cl KIRK/FR/WAR PR4 .54 A5
Derwent Dr KIRK/FR/WAR PR4 .43 G3
Derwent Pl CLV/TH FY5 .....20 D4
  PLF/KEOS FY6 .....30 D1
Derwent Rd CHLY/EC PR7 .....93 E5
  FUL/RIB PR2 .....45 G1
Derwentwater Pl PRES PR1 * .59 H1
Dever Av LEYL PR25 .....83 F4
Devona Av BPOOLS FY4 .....33 H4
Devon Av FTWD FY7 .....11 E3
Devon Cl BBR PR5 .....74 A3
Devonport Cl BBR PR5 .....74 B3
Devonport Wy CHLYE PR6 .....93 H2
Devonshire Av CLV/TH FY5 .....21 H5
Devonshire Pl PRES PR1 .....61 E2
Devonshire Rd BISP FY2 .....24 D5
  BPOOLE FY3 .....28 D5
  CLV/TH FY5 .....5 F6
  FUL/RIB PR2 .....44 B4
  LSTA FY8 .....48 D4
Devonshire Sq BPOOL FY1 .....3 F6
Devon St BPOOLS FY4 .....5 F6
Dewhurst Av BPOOLS FY4 .....33 G5
Dewhurst Rw BBR PR5 .....80 A2
Dewhurst St PRES PR1 .....6 B1

Dianne Rd CLV/TH FY5 .....22 B2
Dibbs Pocket
  KIRK/FR/WAR PR4 .....54 D4
Dicconson Ter LSTA FY8 .....64 C3
Dickens Rd CHLY/EC PR7 .....96 B5
Dickie's La BPOOLS FY4 .....39 H1
Dickie's La South BPOOLS FY4 .39 H2
Dickinson Rd PRES PR1 .....60 D1
Dickson Hey
  KIRK/FR/WAR PR4 .....77 G1
Dickson Rd BPOOL FY1 .....2 B1
Digham Av BISP FY2 .....24 D1
Dinckley Gv BPOOL FY1 .....5 G2
Dingle Av BPOOLE FY3 .....5 H2
The Dingle FUL/RIB PR2 .....45 F1
Dinmore Av BPOOLE FY3 .....29 G5
Dinmore Pl BPOOLE FY3 .....29 G5
Division La BPOOLS FY4 .....39 G5
Dixon's Farm Ms
  KIRK/FR/WAR PR4 .....56 B2
Dob Brow CHLY/EC PR7 .....96 C1
Dobson Av BBR PR5 .....76 B5
Dobson Av BPOOLS FY4 .....49 E3
Dock Av FTWD FY7 .....11 G4
Dock Rd LSTA FY8 .....65 E2
Dock St FTWD FY7 .....11 H4
Dodd Wy BBR PR5 .....80 D3
Dodgeons Cl PLF/KEOS FY6 .26 A5
Dodgson Pl PRES PR1 .....60 C2
Dodney Dr FUL/RIB PR2 .....57 G2
Dodson Av BPOOLE FY3 .....29 F2
Dole La CHLY/EC PR7 .....93 F4
Doncaster Rd BPOOLE FY3 .....33 G3
Donnington Rd LSTA FY8 .....49 F4
  PLF/KEOS FY6 .....26 A2
Don St LSTA FY8 .....49 E4
Doodstone Av BBR PR5 .....73 G5
Doodstone Cl BBR PR5 .....73 G5
Doodstone Nook BBR PR5 .....73 G5
Dorchester Cl CLV/TH FY5 .....22 A4
Dorchester Rd BPOOL FY1 .....28 B2
Doris St CHLYE PR6 .....93 G1
Dorking Rd FUL/RIB PR2 .....47 E5
Dorothy Av LEYL PR25 .....83 F3
Dorritt Rd BPOOLS FY4 .....39 E2
Dorset Av CLV/TH FY5 .....16 D5
Dorset Rd LSTA FY8 .....49 E3
  PRES PR1 .....60 A2
Dorset St BPOOLS FY4 .....5 F1
Douglas Av BPOOLE FY3 .....29 E2
  PLF/KEOS FY6 .....19 G2
Douglas Cl BBR PR5 .....80 C1
Douglas Dr KIRK/FR/WAR PR4 .43 E2
Douglas Pl FTWD FY7 .....10 D3
Douglas Rd North
  FUL/RIB PR2 .....59 E2
  LSTA FY8 .....48 D5
The Doultons BBR PR5 .....73 H3
Dove Av PRES PR1 .....7 G1
Dove Cl CLV/TH FY5 .....21 F3
Dovecote CHLYE PR6 .....93 H1
Dovedale Av BPOOLE FY3 .....34 A4
Dovedale Cl FUL/RIB PR2 .....44 C4
  PRES PR1 .....87 F1
Dovedale Dr PLF/KEOS FY6 .....25 H2
Dove St LSTA FY8 .....49 E5
  PRES PR1 .....60 B2
Dovetree Cl BBR PR5 .....73 G3
Dowbridge KIRK/FR/WAR PR4 .43 G4
Dowbridge Wy
  KIRK/FR/WAR PR4 .....43 F5
  LSTA FY8 .....50 A5
Downham Rd LEYL PR25 .....82 B4
Downing Ct CAR/LONG PR3 .36 B2
Downing St PRES PR1 .....61 E3
Drake Cl CLV/TH FY5 .....21 F3
Drakelowe Av BPOOLS FY4 .39 F2
Drakes Crt FUL/RIB PR2 .....45 E5
Drakes Hollow BBR PR5 .....80 B5
Draycot Av BPOOLE FY3 .....29 G3
Driscoll St PRES PR1 .....7 J4
The Drive BBR PR5 .....74 C1
  BPOOLE FY3 .....46 A4
  KIRK/FR/WAR PR4 .....76 B1
Dronsfield Rd FTWD FY7 .....11 F1
Drovers Wy LSTA FY8 .....50 C4
Drumacre La East
  KIRK/FR/WAR PR4 .....76 D3
Drumacre La West
  KIRK/FR/WAR PR4 .....76 B3
Drummond Av CHLYE PR6 .....89 G5
Dryburgh Av BPOOLE FY3 .33 F2
Dryden Rd FTWD FY7 .....11 F1
Duchess Dr BISP FY2 .....24 B4
Duchy Av FUL/RIB PR2 .....46 B4
Ducie Pl PRES PR1 .....61 F2
Duckworth St CAR/LONG PR3 .36 D1
Duddle La BBR PR5 .....74 D2
Duddon Av FTWD FY7 .....10 D5
Dudley Av BISP FY2 .....28 B4
Dudley Cl KIRK/FR/WAR PR4 .70 B5
Dukes Meadow FUL/RIB PR2 .44 C3
Duke St BBR PR5 .....80 B2
  BPOOL FY1 .....2 C6
  CHLY/EC PR7 .....93 F4
  PRES PR1 .....6 D5
Dumbarton Cl BPOOLS FY4 .39 G2
Dumfries Cl BISP FY2 .....25 F5

Dunbar Cl *BPOOLS* FY4 ....39 G2
Dunbar Dr *FUL/RIB* PR2 ....45 F4
Dunbar Rd *FUL/RIB* PR2 ....44 B5
Duncan Av *BISP* FY2 ....24 C1
Duncan Cl *LSTA* FY8 ....48 D1
Duncan Pl *FTWD* FY7 ....11 E2
Dundonald St *PRES* PR1 ....60 D5
Dunelt Rd *BPOOL* FY1 ....5 F4
Dunes Av *BPOOLS* FY4 ....38 B3
Dunham Dr *CHLY* PR6 ....89 F2
Dunkirk Av *FUL/RIB* PR2 ....45 E4
Dunkirk La *LEYL* PR25 ....82 C4
Dunlin Cl *CLV/TH* FY5 ....17 G4
Dunlin Dr *LSTA* FY8 ....50 C4
Dunmail Av *BPOOLS* FY3 ....5 K3
Dunmore St *PRES* PR1 ....7 K2
Dunnock La *KIRK/FR/WAR* PR4 ....44 A4
Dunoon Cl *FUL/RIB* PR2 ....44 B4
Dunrobin Dr *CHLY/EC* PR7 ....92 A1
Dunscar Dr *CHLYE* PR6 ....93 H1
Dunsop Cl *BBR* PR5 * 80 D2
 BPOOL FY1 ....5 G5
Dunsop Rd *FUL/RIB* PR2 ....46 D4
Dunvegan Cl *BPOOLS* FY3 ....39 G2
Durham Av *CLV/TH* FY5 ....21 E1
 LSTA FY8 ....49 E4
Durham Rd *BPOOL* FY1 ....3 K4
Durley Rd *BPOOL* FY1 ....4 E4
D'Urton La *FUL/RIB* PR2 ....37 G4
 GAR/LONG PR3 ....37 G4
Dutch Barn Cl *CHLY/EC* PR7 ....89 E4
Duttonfield
 CROS/BRETH PR26 ....82 D1
Dutton Rd *BPOOLE* FY3 ....3 G3
Duxbury Hall Rd *CHLY/EC* PR7 ....97 C1
Dyer St *KIRK/FR/WAR* PR4 ....42 D3
Dymock Rd *PRES* PR1 * 60 D2
Dymock Rd North *PRES* PR1 * 60 D2

E

Eagle Brow Cl *CLV/TH* FY5 ....17 H4
The Eagles *PLF/KEOS* FY6 ....26 C2
Eamont Pl *FTWD* FY7 ....10 D4
Earls Av *BBR* PR5 ....80 B1
Earl St *PRES* PR1 ....7 F3
Earlsway *BPOOLE* FY3 ....30 B5
Earls Wy *CHLY/EC* PR7 ....88 A5
Earnshaw Dr *LEYL* PR25 ....82 C1
Easington Crs *BPOOLE* FY3 ....29 G2
Eastbank Av *BPOOLS* FY4 ....39 G1
East Beach *LSTA* FY8 ....62 B1
East Beach *LSTA* FY8 ....64 D3
East Boothroyden
 BPOOL FY1 ....28 B2
Eastbourne Cl *FUL/RIB* PR2 ....44 B4
Eastbourne Rd *BPOOL* FY1 ....38 B2
East Cecil St *LSTA* FY8 ....64 D3
East Cliff *PRES* PR1 ....6 E6
East Cliff Ct *LSTA* FY8 ....64 D3
East Cliff Rd *PRES* PR1 ....6 E6
East Ct *CLV/TH* FY5 ....16 D4
Eastfield Dr *KIRK/FR/WAR* PR4 ....70 B5
Eastgate *BPOOLE* FY3 ....45 F5
East Gate Cl *LSTA* FY8 ....38 C4
Eastham *PRES* PR1 ....59 G2
East Holme *LSTA* FY8 ....65 E2
Eastlands *CROS/BRETH* PR26 ....82 B3
East Md *BPOOLE* FY5 ....5 J2
Easton Cl *FUL/RIB* PR2 ....46 D2
Eastpines Dr *CLV/TH* FY5 ....21 E4
East Rd *CLV/TH* FY5 ....18 B5
 FUL/RIB PR2 ....46 A4
Eastside *BPOOLS* FY4 ....33 F5
East Sq *KIRK/FR/WAR* PR4 ....70 B5
East St *BBR* PR5 ....80 B2
 LEYL PR25 ....83 G1
East Ter *CHLY/EC* PR7 ....88 B5
East Topping St *BPOOL* FY1 ....2 C4
East Vw *BBR* PR5 ....60 C5
 KIRK/FR/WAR PR4 * 54 C5
 PRES PR1 ....7 H1
East Wy *CHLY* PR6 ....93 G2
Eastway *FUL/RIB* PR2 ....37 F5
 FUL/RIB PR2 ....46 C3
 GAR/LONG PR3 ....36 B5
 KIRK/FR/WAR PR4 ....54 A5
Eastwood Av *BPOOLE* FY3 ....29 E2
 FTWD FY7 ....11 F3
Eastwood Rd *LEYL* PR25 ....83 H5
Eaton Av *BPOOL* FY1 ....4 E5
Eaton Ct *LSTA* FY8 ....49 F5
Eaton Pl *KIRK/FR/WAR* PR4 ....42 C3
Eaton Wy *PLF/KEOS* FY6 ....30 C2
Eaves Green Rd *CHLY/EC* PR7 ....93 E5
Eaves La *CHLYE* PR6 ....93 H4
 FUL/RIB PR2 ....45 G5
Eaves St *BPOOL* FY1 ....2 B1
Eaveswood Cl *BBR* PR5 ....74 B5
Ecclesgate Rd *BPOOLS* FY4 ....39 F3
Eccles St *PRES* PR1 ....60 C4
Eccleston Rd *BPOOL* FY1 ....5 G5
Ecroyd Rd *FUL/RIB* PR2 * 59 F1
Ecroyd St *LEYL* PR25 ....83 F3
Edale Cl *LEYL* PR25 ....83 F5
Edale Ct *PRES* PR1 ....59 H2
Eddington Rd *LSTA* FY8 ....65 E2
Eddleston Cl *BPOOLE* FY3 ....30 B5
Edelston Rd *BPOOL* FY1 ....2 D1
Eden Av *FTWD* FY7 ....10 D4
 LSTA FY8 ....63 H3
Edenvale Av *BISP* FY2 ....24 B3
Edenway *FUL/RIB* PR2 ....45 F1
Edgar St *BPOOL* FY1 ....2 D1
Edge Hill Av *PLF/KEOS* FY6 ....26 D5
Eden St *BPOOL* FY1 ....3 G3
Edgehill Rd *CHLY/EC* PR7 ....89 E5
Edgehill Rd *FUL/RIB* PR2 ....45 F4
Edgehill Crs *LEYL* PR25 ....82 D2

Edgehill Dr *FUL/RIB* PR2 ....45 F4
Edgeway Pl *CLV/TH* FY5 ....22 A3
Edgeway Rd *BPOOLS* FY4 ....39 E2
Edgley Ct *KIRK/FR/WAR* PR4 ....71 F4
Edinburgh Cl *LEYL* PR25 ....83 H3
Edmondsen Pl *FTWD* FY7 ....11 F4
Edmonton Pl *BISP* FY2 ....25 E4
Edmund St *PRES* PR1 ....7 J3
Edward St *PRES* PR1 ....7 H1
Edward St *BBR* PR5 ....73 H1
 BBR PR5 ....80 B1
 BPOOL FY1 ....2 C4
 CHLE PR6 ....93 G3
 CLV/TH FY5 ....17 H5
 LEYL PR25 ....83 F4
 LSTA FY8 ....49 F4
 PRES PR1 ....7 G2
Edward VII Quay
 FUL/RIB PR2 * 58 D3
Edwell Av *BPOOLS* FY4 ....5 F7
Edwinstowe Rd *LSTA* FY8 ....50 A5
Egan St *PRES* PR1 ....7 H2
Egbert St *PRES* PR1 ....60 A2
Egerton Ct *FUL/RIB* PR2 * 58 D2
Egerton Gv *CHLY/EC* PR7 ....93 E4
Egerton Rd *PRES* PR1 ....28 B3
 FUL/RIB PR2 ....58 E2
 LEYL PR25 ....83 G3
Egremont Av *CLV/TH* FY5 ....16 D4
Eider Cl *CLV/TH* FY5 ....17 F4
Eildon Dr *PLF/KEOS* FY6 ....30 B1
Elaine Av *BPOOLS* FY4 ....33 F4
Elbow St *CHLY/EC* PR7 ....93 F3
Elcho St *PRES* PR1 ....7 G3
Elderberry Cl *CLV/TH* FY5 ....17 F4
Elder Cl *CHLYE* PR6 ....85 F2
 FUL/RIB PR2 ....46 D2
 KIRK/FR/WAR PR4 ....53 C5
Elderwood Av *CLV/TH* FY5 ....21 H5
Eldon St *CHLYE* PR6 ....93 F5
 PRES PR1 * 59 G1
Elgin Cl *FUL/RIB* PR2 ....59 G3
Elgin Pl *PRES* PR1 ....60 A1
Elgin St *PRES* PR1 ....60 D3
Elizabeth Cl *BPOOLS* FY3 ....30 B5
Elizabeth St *PLF/KEOS* FY6 ....26 B4
Elizabeth Sq *PRES* PR1 ....7 F1
 FTWD FY7 ....11 H1
 PRES PR1 ....7 F2
Elkfield Dr *BPOOLE* FY3 ....29 G1
Elland Pl *BPOOL* FY1 ....4 B6
Elen Ct *PRES* PR1 ....59 H1
Ellen St *BBR* PR5 ....74 B5
 PRES PR1 ....59 F2
Ellerbeck Av *FUL/RIB* PR2 ....47 E3
Ellerbeck Rd *CLV/TH* FY5 ....20 C2
Ellerslie Rd *FUL/RIB* PR2 ....58 D2
Ellesmere Av *CLV/TH* FY5 ....22 B3
Ellesmere Rd *BPOOLS* FY4 ....5 H6
Elletson St *PLF/KEOS* FY6 ....26 B5
Elliott Cl *PRES* PR1 ....59 G1
Elliott St *PRES* PR1 ....59 G2
Elliott Wk *PRES* PR1 * 59 G2
Elisland *BPOOLS* FY4 ....34 A4
Elm Av *BPOOLE* FY3 ....3 H5
 FUL/RIB PR2 ....58 B1
 KIRK/FR/WAR PR4 ....55 F5
 PLF/KEOS FY6 ....26 B4
Elm Cl *CLV/TH* FY5 ....21 H5
Elm Ct *PLF/KEOS* FY6 * 26 B4
Elm Dr *BBR* PR5 ....74 C5
Elmfield Dr *BBR* PR5 ....81 F3
Elm Gv *CHLYE* PR6 ....89 H5
 PRES PR1 ....61 E1
 FUL/RIB PR2 ....45 F1
 KIRK/FR/WAR PR4 ....53 C5
 LEYL PR25 ....83 A1
Elmhurst Rd *LSTA* FY8 ....49 H3
Elmridge Crs *BISP* FY2 ....25 F4
Elms Av *CLV/TH* FY5 ....21 E2
 LSTA FY8 ....63 H3
Elmslie Dr *CLV/TH* FY5 ....22 B2
Elmsley St *PRES* PR1 ....45 G5
Elmslie Gdns *BPOOLS* FY3 ....5 H2
The Elms *CHLYE* PR6 ....85 F2
Elm St *FTWD* FY7 ....11 G2
Elmswood Cl *LSTA* FY8 ....64 A2
Elmwood Cl *PRES* PR1 ....60 C4
Elmwood Gv *CHLY/EC* PR7 ....93 E1
 PLF/KEOS FY6 ....82 D5
Elmwood Dr *CLV/TH* FY5 ....13 F2
Elsby Av *CLV/TH* FY5 ....21 H5
Elsby Av *CLV/TH* FY5 ....22 A4
Elsinore Cl *FTWD* FY7 ....11 F1
Elston Av *BPOOLE* FY3 * 29 G2
Elswick Pl *BPOOLS* FY4 ....39 E3
 LSTA FY8 ....49 H3
Elswick Rd *FUL/RIB* PR2 ....58 A2
 LEYL PR25 ....83 G2
Elterwater Pl *PLF/KEOS* FY6 ....12 C1
Elterwater Pl *BPOOLE* FY3 ....34 A3
Elton St *FUL/RIB* PR2 ....59 E2
Elvaston Rd *PLF/KEOS* FY6 ....26 A2
Emerald Cl *BBR* PR5 ....21 F5
Emerson Av *BPOOLS* FY4 ....38 D1
Emerson Rd *PRES* PR1 ....60 D1
Emily St *BBR* PR5 ....74 C5
Emisett Rd *BBR* PR5 ....74 C5
Emmanuel St *FUL/RIB* PR2 ....59 F1
Emmett St *PRES* PR1 ....7 F1
Ennie La *CROS/BRETH* PR26 ....86 B1
Empire Gv *BPOOLE* FY3 ....3 F1
Empress Av *FUL/RIB* PR2 ....45 G5
Empress St *BPOOL* FY1 ....28 B1
Empress Wy *CHLY/EC* PR7 ....88 B5
Endeavour Cl *FUL/RIB* PR2 ....58 D4
Enderley Ct *CLV/TH* FY5 ....22 A3
Endsleigh Gdns *BPOOLS* FY4 ....38 D2
Enfield Cl *CHLY/EC* PR7 ....93 F5
Enfield Rd *BPOOL* FY1 ....28 C3
England Av *BISP* FY2 ....24 C3
English Martyrs' Pl *PRES* PR1 ....59 H1
Ennerdale Av *FTWD* FY7 ....10 C5
Ennerdale Cl *FUL/RIB* PR2 ....85 F5
Ennerdale Dr *BBR* PR5 ....74 B1

Ennerdale Rd *BPOOLS* FY4 ....34 A4
 CHLY/EC PR7 ....92 D5
Enterprise Wy *FTWD* FY7 ....17 G3
Ephraim St *PRES* PR1 ....60 C4
Epping Cl *BISP* FY2 ....25 E2
Epping Pl *CHLYE* PR6 ....89 G5
Epsom Rd *CLV/TH* FY5 ....21 F4
Erdington Rd *BPOOL* FY1 ....4 D1
Erith Gv *BISP* FY2 ....24 C2
Erskine Rd *CHLYE* PR6 ....93 H1
Esher Pond *CLV/TH* FY5 * 10 D4
Esk Av *FTWD* FY7 ....10 D4
Eskdale Av *FTWD* FY7 ....10 D5
Eskdale Cl *BPOOLS* FY4 ....33 F4
Eskdale Dr *KIRK/FR/WAR* PR4 ....43 E1
Eskdale Rd *LEYL* PR25 ....83 G5
Eskham Cl *KIRK/FR/WAR* PR4 ....42 C2
Esplanade *PLF/KEOS* FY6 ....12 B1
 PRES PR1 ....73 G1
The Esplanade *FTWD* FY7 ....11 E1
 PRES PR1 * 73 G1
Essex Pl *BISP* FY2 ....25 E5
Eton Pk *FUL/RIB* PR2 ....46 C3
Ettrick Av *FTWD* FY7 ....10 D3
Euston St *PRES* PR1 ....6 B4
Euxton Hall Gdns
 CHLY/EC PR7 ....87 H5
Euxton La *CHLY/EC* PR7 ....89 E4
 CHLY/EC PR7 ....88 D5
Evans St *FUL/RIB* PR2 ....59 F2
Everest Cl *LSTA* FY8 ....49 H3
Everest Dr *BISP* FY2 ....24 C1
Everest Rd *LSTA* FY8 ....49 G1
Evergreen Av *LEYL* PR25 ....83 F5
Evergreen Cl *CHLY/EC* PR7 ....93 E5
The Evergreens
 KIRK/FR/WAR PR4 ....44 A4
Eversleigh Av *CLV/TH* FY5 ....21 F1
Eversleigh St *PRES* PR1 ....59 G2
Everton Rd *BPOOLS* FY4 * 38 C2
Evesham Av *LSTA* FY8 ....72 D4
Evesham Cl *CLV/TH* FY5 ....21 E5
 KIRK/FR/WAR PR4 ....70 D5
Evesham Rd *BPOOLS* FY4 ....29 H2
 LSTA FY8 ....72 D4
Exchange St *BPOOL* FY1 ....2 C2
Exe St *PRES* PR1 ....60 B1
Exeter Dr *CLV/TH* FY5 ....21 H2
Exeter Pl *FUL/RIB* PR2 ....58 A1
Exeter St *BPOOLS* FY4 ....4 E6

F

Factory La *PRES* PR1 ....73 E3
Fairclough Rd *CLV/TH* FY5 ....17 G5
Fairfax Av *BISP* FY2 ....25 E1
Fairfax Pl *BBR* PR5 ....74 A4
Fairfax Rd *FUL/RIB* PR2 ....47 E4
Fairfield Av *BPOOLE* FY3 ....29 H3
 PLF/KEOS FY6 ....26 B2
Fairfield Ct *FTWD* FY7 ....11 F4
Fairfield Dr *FUL/RIB* PR2 * 58 D1
 FUL/RIB PR2 ....28 C2
 LEYL PR25 ....83 E4
Fairfield St *BBR* PR5 ....79 G2
Fairham Av *PRES* PR1 * 72 C4
Fairhaven Av *FTWD* FY7 ....16 D2
Fairhaven Cl *CLV/TH* FY5 ....22 B4
Fairhaven La *LSTA* FY8 ....62 B1
Fairhaven Rd *LEYL* PR25 ....82 D3
 LSTA FY8 ....62 B1
 PRES PR1 ....72 D1
Fairholmes Cl *CLV/TH* FY5 ....21 H1
Fairholmes Wy *CLV/TH* FY5 ....21 G1
Fairhurst St *BPOOL* FY1 ....2 E3
Fairlawn Rd *LSTA* FY8 ....65 H4
Fairmont Dr *PLF/KEOS* FY6 ....23 H2
Fair Oak Cl *FUL/RIB* PR2 ....47 E5
Fairsnape Rd *LSTA* FY8 ....49 G4
Fairview Av *LSTA* FY8 ....49 G4
Fairview Cl *KIRK/FR/WAR* PR4 ....76 A4
Fair Wy *PLF/KEOS* FY6 ....23 G5
Fairway *BPOOLS* FY4 ....29 H5
 CHLY/EC PR7 ....89 F5
 FTWD FY7 ....10 C5
 PRES PR1 ....72 A2
Fairway Gdns *PLF/KEOS* FY6 ....12 B1
Fairway Rd *BPOOLS* FY4 ....5 J7
Fairways *FUL/RIB* PR2 ....46 A2
 LSTA FY8 ....49 G5
Fairways Av *GAR/LONG* PR3 ....36 B2
Falcon Dr *PLF/KEOS* FY6 ....25 H5
Falcon St *PRES* PR1 ....7 F3
Falkirk Av *BISP* FY2 ....24 C1
Falkland St *PRES* PR1 ....6 D4
Fallowfield Cl
 KIRK/FR/WAR PR4 ....42 C2
Fallowfield Rd *LSTA* FY8 ....50 A5
Falmouth Av *FTWD* FY7 ....16 C1
Falmouth Rd *BPOOL* FY1 ....4 B6
Faraday Dr *FUL/RIB* PR2 ....46 C1
Faraday Wy *BISP* FY2 ....24 C5
Far Cft *BBR* PR5 ....75 F5
Fareham Cl *BBR* PR5 ....74 C3
Far Fld *PRES* PR1 ....72 B3
Faringdon Av *BPOOLS* FY4 ....39 F5
Farington Av *LEYL* PR25 ....82 C5
Farington Ga *LEYL* PR25 ....83 G2
Farington Rd
 CROS/BRETH PR26 ....79 E3
Far La *PRES* PR1 ....73 H5
Farm Ct *CLV/TH* FY5 ....20 B1
Farmend Cl *KIRK/FR/WAR* PR4 ....76 C1
Farm House Cl *CHLYE* PR6 ....89 H4
Farnell Pl *BPOOLS* FY4 ....38 D2
Farnham Wy *PLF/KEOS* FY6 ....26 A2
Far Nook *CHLYE* PR6 ....85 E5
Farnworth Rd *CLV/TH* FY5 ....22 A3

Farrington Cl *PRES* PR1 ....61 F2
Farringdon Crs *FUL/RIB* PR2 ....61 F2
Farringdon Pl *FUL/RIB* PR2 ....47 F5
Farringdon Pl *FUL/RIB* PR2 ....61 F2
Farrington St *CHLY/EC* PR7 ....93 F2
The Farthings *CHLY/EC* PR7 ....92 C1
Fayles Gv *CHLY* PR6 ....33 G5
Fazackerley St *FUL/RIB* PR2 ....59 E2
Fazakerley St *CHLY/EC* PR7 ....93 F2
Felgate Brow *BPOOLE* FY3 ....5 J5
Fell Cl *BBR* PR5 ....80 C2
Fellery St *CHLY/EC* PR7 ....93 F2
Fell Vw *CHLYE* PR6 ....93 H4
Fell Wy *PLF/KEOS* FY6 ....19 H2
Fellway *BBR* PR5 ....79 H1
Felstead St *PRES* PR1 ....60 D5
Fenber Av *BPOOLS* FY4 ....38 C1
Fengrove *KIRK/FR/WAR* PR4 ....76 B1
Fennel Cl *BISP* FY2 ....24 C4
Fensway *KIRK/FR/WAR* PR4 ....71 E4
Fenton Rd *BPOOL* FY1 ....4 C1
 FUL/RIB PR2 ....46 C4
Ferguson Rd *BPOOL* FY1 ....5 H5
Fermor Rd *PRES* PR1 ....61 E2
Fern Bank *CHLYE* PR6 ....89 G4
Fern Cl *BBR* PR5 ....79 G1
Fern Ct *FTWD* FY7 ....10 C5
Ferndale Av *BPOOLS* FY4 ....5 G6
Ferndale Ct *CLV/TH* FY5 ....22 A2
 PRES PR1 ....83 G5
Fern Gv *BPOOL* FY1 ....4 E1
Fernhurst Av *BPOOLS* FY4 ....5 G6
Fernleigh Cl *BISP* FY2 ....24 C4
Fern Meadow *CHLYE* PR6 ....85 F2
The Ferns *BBR* PR5 ....73 G3
 FUL/RIB PR2 ....59 E1
Fernwood Av *CLV/TH* FY5 ....21 H5
Fernwood Cl *LSTA* FY8 ....63 H2
Fernyhalgh Ct *FUL/RIB* PR2 * 46 D2
Fernyhalgh Gdns *FUL/RIB* PR2 ....46 D2
Fernyhalgh Pl *FUL/RIB* PR2 ....46 D2
Ferrier Bank
 KIRK/FR/WAR PR4 ....66 C1
Fiddler's La *CROS/BRETH* PR26 ....85 E2
Fidler La *CROS/BRETH* PR26 ....79 E3
Fielden St *CHLYE* PR6 ....93 H2
 FUL/RIB PR2 ....82 C3
Fieldfare Cl *CLV/TH* FY5 ....17 G4
 PRES PR1 ....72 D3
Fieldfare Ct *CHLY/EC* PR7 ....92 C5
Fieldhouse Av *CLV/TH* FY5 ....22 B2
Fielding Rd *BISP* FY2 ....24 C5
Field Maple Dr *FUL/RIB* PR2 ....47 F4
Fieldside Av *CHLY/EC* PR7 ....91 H2
Fieldside Cl *BBR* PR5 ....73 H3
The Fields *CHLY/EC* PR7 ....90 A3
 FUL/RIB PR2 ....4 D5
Fieldway *LSTA* FY8 ....65 E4
Fife Cl *CHLYE* PR6 ....93 H4
Fifth Av *BPOOLS* FY4 ....38 C1
Filberts Cl *FUL/RIB* PR2 ....45 E4
The Filberts *FUL/RIB* PR2 ....45 E5
File St *CHLY/EC* PR7 ....93 F5
Filey Pl *BPOOL* FY1 ....2 B5
 FUL/RIB PR2 ....44 C4
Filey Rd *LSTA* FY8 ....49 G2
The Finches *PLF/KEOS* FY6 ....25 H5
Finch La *KIRK/FR/WAR* PR4 ....44 A4
Finchley Rd *BPOOL* FY1 ....28 B2
Finney Park Dr *FUL/RIB* PR2 ....57 H3
Finsbury Av *BPOOL* FY1 ....5 H4
 LSTA FY8 ....63 E2
Firbank *CHLY/EC* PR7 ....87 H5
Fir Cl *FTWD* FY7 ....10 C4
Firfield Cl *KIRK/FR/WAR* PR4 ....42 C3
Fir Gv *BBR* PR5 ....80 A1
 KIRK/FR/WAR PR4 ....53 F5
Firshill Cl *CLV/TH* FY5 ....21 H4
First Av *BPOOLS* FY4 ....38 C1
 FUL/RIB PR2 ....58 C1
 KIRK/FR/WAR PR4 ....56 A2
 PLF/KEOS FY6 ....13 G5
Firswood Cl *LSTA* FY8 ....63 H2
Fir Tree Av *FUL/RIB* PR2 ....44 D4
Firtree Cl *CHLY/EC* PR7 ....97 F2
Fir Tree Pl *CLV/TH* FY5 ....21 F4
Fir Trees Av *FUL/RIB* PR2 ....47 F4
 PRES PR1 ....59 H5
Fir Trees Crs *BBR* PR5 ....73 F5
Fir Trees Pl *FUL/RIB* PR2 ....47 F4
Fir Trees Rd *BBR* PR5 ....73 F5
Fisher St *PRES* PR1 ....6 D5
Fishergate *PRES* PR1 ....6 C6
Fishergate Ct *PRES* PR1 * 6 C6
Fishergate Hl *PRES* PR1 ....6 B6
Fisher St *BPOOL* FY1 ....2 B2
Fish St *PRES* PR1 ....7 F1
Fishwick Pde *PRES* PR1 ....60 D3
Fishwick Rd *PRES* PR1 ....60 C5
Fishwick Vw *PRES* PR1 ....60 D3
Fitchfield *PRES* PR1 ....73 E4
Fitzgerald St *PRES* PR1 ....60 C2
Fitzroy Rd *BISP* FY2 ....24 D4
Fitzroy St *PRES* PR1 ....6 B4
Five Acres
 CROS/BRETH PR26 ....78 D5
Flag La *CROS/BRETH* PR26 ....86 C5
 PRES PR1 ....73 E5
Flakefleet Av *FTWD* FY7 ....11 E5
Flaxfield Wy
 KIRK/FR/WAR PR4 ....43 E5
Fleet St *BPOOL* FY1 ....2 B3
 CHLY/EC PR7 ....93 F5
 LSTA FY8 ....48 D4
 PRES PR1 ....7 H1
Fleetwood Rd *CLV/TH* FY5 ....20 C2
 FTWD FY7 ....11 E4
 PLF/KEOS FY6 ....25 H1
Fleetwood Rd North
 CLV/TH FY5 ....17 G4
Fleetwood Rd South
 CLV/TH FY5 ....21 H5
Fleetwood St *FUL/RIB* PR2 ....6 A1
 LEYL PR25 ....83 G2

Flensburg Wy
 CROS/BRETH PR26 ....82 C1
Fletcher Rd *PRES* PR1 ....7 J2
Flett St *FUL/RIB* PR2 ....59 E2
Flintoff Wy *PRES* PR1 ....46 B5
Florence Av *KIRK/FR/WAR* PR4 ....66 C1
Florence St *BPOOLS* FY4 ....39 G2
Flowerfield *KIRK/FR/WAR* PR4 ....44 A2
Floyd Rd *FUL/RIB* PR2 * 47 E5
Floyer St *PRES* PR1 ....7 K4
Fluke Hall La *GAR/LONG* PR3 ....9 F5
Foldside *KIRK/FR/WAR* PR4 ....54 C4
Folkestone Rd *CLV/TH* FY5 ....17 F5
 KIRK/FR/WAR PR4 ....53 C4
Folkestone St *LSTA* FY8 ....49 F3
Fordstone Av *PLF/KEOS* FY6 ....15 E2
Fordway Av *BPOOLS* FY3 ....5 J3
Foregate *FUL/RIB* PR2 ....45 H4
Forest Cl *BBR* PR5 ....73 H5
Forest Dr *LSTA* FY8 ....63 H2
Forest Ga *BPOOLE* FY3 ....5 J3
Forest Wy *FUL/RIB* PR2 ....45 H5
Forestway *LEYL* PR25 ....83 E4
Formby Av *FTWD* FY7 ....16 D2
Formby Crs *KIRK/FR/WAR* PR4 ....76 A2
Formby Pl *FUL/RIB* PR2 ....58 A1
Formby Rd *LSTA* FY8 ....49 F2
Forrester Ct *LEYL* PR25 ....83 G2
Forshaw Av *BPOOLE* FY3 ....29 F2
Forshaw Cl *FTWD* FY7 ....11 E4
Forshaw Rd *PRES* PR1 ....72 C4
Forton Rd *FUL/RIB* PR2 ....58 A3
Fossdale Moss
 CROS/BRETH PR26 ....82 B3
Foster Cft *PRES* PR1 ....59 E5
Fosterfield Pl *CHLYE* PR6 ....93 H1
Foster St *CHLYE* PR6 ....93 H1
Fouldrey Av *PLF/KEOS* FY6 ....26 D2
Foundry St *CHLY/EC* PR7 * 93 F2
Fountains Cl *CHLY/EC* PR7 ....93 C5
Fourfields *BBR* PR5 ....74 B5
Four Lane Ends *BBR* PR5 ....75 G4
Four Oaks Rd *BBR* PR5 ....80 D3
Fourth Av *BPOOLS* FY4 ....38 C1
Fowler Av *CROS/BRETH* PR26 ....79 G3
Fowler La *CROS/BRETH* PR26 ....79 F5
Fowler St *FUL/RIB* PR2 ....45 F5
Foxcote *CHLY/EC* PR7 ....89 E5
Foxdale Av *BPOOLE* FY3 ....28 D3
Foxdale Cv *PRES* PR1 ....46 D5
Foxglove Dr *CHLYE* PR6 ....89 E2
Foxhall Rd *BPOOL* FY1 ....4 B1
Foxhall Sq *BPOOL* FY1 ....4 B2
Foxhole Rd *CHLY/EC* PR7 ....92 C2
Fox La *BBR* PR5 ....75 H5
 LEYL PR25 ....82 D5
Foxwood Dr
 KIRK/FR/WAR PR4 ....42 C3
The Foxwood *CHLY/EC* PR7 ....95 H4
Francis St *BPOOL* FY1 ....2 B2
Frank St *BBR* PR5 ....59 E2
Franklands *KIRK/FR/WAR* PR4 ....70 B5
Franklands Dr *FUL/RIB* PR2 ....47 F5
Franklands Fold
 KIRK/FR/WAR PR4 ....76 B1
Frank St *PRES* PR1 ....59 H2
Fraser Av *PRES* PR1 ....72 D2
Frazer Gv *BPOOLS* FY4 ....5 K5
Freckleton Rd
 KIRK/FR/WAR PR4 ....43 F5
Freckleton St *BPOOL* FY1 ....2 E7
 LSTA FY8 ....64 D3
Frederick St *BPOOLS* FY4 ....5 F6
 CHLYE PR6 ....93 H5
Fredora Av *BPOOLE* FY3 ....33 G5
Freemans La *CHLY/EC* PR7 ....96 B1
Freemantle Av *BPOOLS* FY4 ....38 A4
Frenchwood Av *LSTA* FY8 ....64 A2
 PRES PR1 ....7 K6
Frenchwood Knoll *PRES* PR1 ....7 J7
Frenchwood St *PRES* PR1 ....7 H6
Friargate *PRES* PR1 ....6 E2
The Friars *FUL/RIB* PR2 ....45 G4
Friary Cl *KIRK/FR/WAR* PR4 ....43 G4
Friday St *CHLY* PR6 ....93 G2
Frinton Gv *BISP* FY2 ....25 E1
Friths Av *BBR* PR5 ....73 H5
Frobisher Dr *LSTA* FY8 ....49 E2
Frome St *PRES* PR1 ....60 D2
Froom St *CHLYE* PR6 ....93 H2
Fryers Cl *PRES* PR1 ....72 B5
Fulford Av *FUL/RIB* PR2 ....57 G2
The Fulmars *PLF/KEOS* FY6 * 25 H5
Fulshaw Rd *FUL/RIB* PR2 ....58 D1
Fulwood Av *BPOOLE* FY3 ....29 F2
Fulwood Hall La *FUL/RIB* PR2 ....46 B4
Fulwood Hts *FUL/RIB* PR2 ....46 C5
Fulwood Rw *FUL/RIB* PR2 ....47 E1
Furlong Crs *BPOOLE* FY3 ....29 G5
Furlong La *PLF/KEOS* FY6 ....26 B5
Furness Av *BPOOLE* FY3 ....29 G2
 FTWD FY7 ....10 D5
Furness Cl *CHLY/EC* PR7 ....93 G5
Furness Dr *FUL/RIB* PR2 ....58 A1
Further Ends Rd
 KIRK/FR/WAR PR4 ....54 B5
Further Fld *BBR* PR5 ....80 D1
Fylde Av *CROS/BRETH* PR26 ....78 D5
Fylde Rd *LSTA* FY8 ....63 G1
 PLF/KEOS FY6 ....26 C5
 PRES PR1 ....6 D2
Fylde St *KIRK/FR/WAR* PR4 ....43 E4
 PRES PR1 ....6 D2
Fylde View Cl *PLF/KEOS* FY6 ....26 B5

G

The Gables *KIRK/FR/WAR* PR4 ....44 A4
Gadsby St *BPOOL* FY1 ....4 B4

Gainsborough Av BBR PR5 79 F2
Gainsborough Rd BPOOL FY1 3 F6
Galloway Crs BISP FY2 25 F2
Galloway Rd FTWD FY7 11 F1
Galway Av BISP FY2 24 D4
Gamble Rd CLV/TH FY5 17 H5
Gamull La FUL/RIB PR2 47 F3
Ganton Ct PRES PR1 58 C5
Garden Cl BPOOLE FY3 33 G3
Gardeners Ms BPOOL FY1 2 D1
Garden St KIRK/FR/WAR PR4 43 E4
LSTA FY8 * 49 E5
PRES PR1 6 E5
Garden Ter BPOOLS FY4 4 C6
CHLY/EC PR7 93 F1
Garden Wk CLV/TH FY5 16 D4
FUL/RIB PR2 58 D2
Gardner St PRES PR1 7 F2
Garfield St FTWD FY7 11 H1
Garfield Ter CHLYE PR6 89 G5
Garland Gv FTWD FY7 * 10 D3
Garrick Gv BPOOLE FY3 29 E3
Garrison Rd FUL/RIB PR2 46 B5
Garsdale Cl BBR PR5 74 B1
Garsdale Rd FUL/RIB PR2 47 E4
Garstang Cl PLF/KEOS FY6 26 A4
Garstang Rd FUL/RIB PR2 36 C5
FUL/RIB PR2 45 G5
PLF/KEOS FY6 27 F4
Garstang Rd East
PLF/KEOS FY6 26 C4
Garstang Rd North
KIRK/FR/WAR PR4 42 D1
Garstang Rd South
KIRK/FR/WAR PR4 42 D2
Garstang Rd West
BPOOLE FY3 29 G1
PLF/KEOS FY6 26 A5
Garstone Cft FUL/RIB PR2 45 E2
Garton Av BPOOLS FY4 38 C2
Gaskell Crs CLV/TH FY5 21 G2
Gaskell Rd PRES PR1 72 D1
Gaskell St CHLYE PR6 93 H2
Gas Ter LEYL PR25 83 G2
Gatesgarth Av FUL/RIB PR2 45 H1
Gateside Dr BPOOLE FY3 29 F2
Gateway Cl CLV/TH FY5 22 B5
Gathurst Rd FUL/RIB PR2 59 E1
Gaulter's La PLF/KEOS FY6 13 G2
Gaydon Wy CLV/TH FY5 21 E5
Gaythorne Av PRES PR1 61 F2
Geldof Dr BPOOL FY1 28 C2
General St BPOOL FY1 2 B2
Geneva Rd FUL/RIB PR2 46 C4
Geoffrey St CHLYE PR6 93 G1
PRES PR1 60 C2
George Av BPOOLS FY4 5 K5
George's Rd PRES PR1 7 F4
George St BPOOL FY1 2 E3
CHLY/EC PR7 93 F3
LEYL PR25 83 G2
LSTA FY8 64 C3
PRES PR1 7 K4
German La CHLY/EC PR7 92 A2
Gerrard's Ter PLF/KEOS FY6 26 A3
Gerrard St PRES PR1 6 B4
Gilbertson Rd CHLY/EC PR7 97 H3
Gilbert St CHLY/EC PR7 * 93 F4
Gildabrook Rd BPOOLS FY4 38 D3
Gilderdale Ct LSTA FY8 64 D2
Gildow St PRES PR1 6 C3
Gilhouse Av FUL/RIB PR2 57 G2
Gillcroft CHLY/EC PR7 90 A3
Giller Cl PRES PR1 72 D4
Giller Dr PRES PR1 72 D4
Giller Fold PRES PR1 73 E4
Gillett St PRES PR1 60 C2
Gillibrand Cl PRES PR1 72 B5
Gillibrand Link Rd CHLY/EC PR7 92 C5
Gillibrand Pk CHLY/EC PR7 92 C4
Gillibrand St BBR PR5 74 A1
CHLY/EC PR7 93 F3
Gillibrand Wks CHLY/EC PR7 93 F4
Gill La KIRK/FR/WAR PR4 76 B4
Gill Nook KIRK/FR/WAR PR4 76 B4
Gillow Rd KIRK/FR/WAR PR4 42 D3
Gin Bow CHLY/EC PR7 93 G4
Gisburn Av LSTA FY8 50 A5
Gisburn Gv BPOOLE FY3 29 E3
Gisburn Rd FUL/RIB PR2 47 E4
The Glades LSTA FY8 64 D2
Gladeway CLV/TH FY5 22 B5
Gladstone St BPOOLS FY4 4 E6
Gladstone Wy CLV/TH FY5 21 F3
Glamis Dr CHLY/EC PR7 93 E2
Glamis Rd LEYL PR25 83 H4
Glastonbury Av BPOOL FY1 5 J3
Glebe Cl FUL/RIB PR2 45 H4
Glebe La KIRK/FR/WAR PR4 43 G4
The Glebe CROS/BRETH PR26 82 A4
Glenapp Av BPOOLS FY4 39 F2
Glenarden Av CLV/TH FY5 21 E4
Glencoe Av BPOOLE FY3 29 G1
Glencourse Dr FUL/RIB PR2 46 C3
Glencroft CHLY/EC PR7 87 G4
Glencross Pl BPOOLS FY4 39 E1
Glendale Av BBR PR5 73 H5
Glendale Cl BISP FY2 25 F2
LEYL PR25 83 G5
PLF/KEOS FY6 26 A4
Glendale Crs BBR PR5 73 H5
Glendale Gv FUL/RIB PR2 60 D1
Gleneagles Ct
KIRK/FR/WAR PR4 43 F4
Gleneagles Dr FUL/RIB PR2 44 D1
PRES PR1 58 C5
Glen Eldon Rd LSTA FY8 49 E4
Glenfield Av BISP FY2 25 E1
Glen Gv FUL/RIB PR2 47 F3
Glenholme Gdns
PLF/KEOS FY6 25 H5
Glenluce Dr PRES PR1 61 F3
Glenmere Crs CLV/TH FY5 20 C5
Glenmore CHLYE PR6 84 D2
Glenmore Av CLV/TH FY5 21 H2
Glenroyd Cl BPOOLE FY3 5 H1
Glen St BPOOLE FY3 3 H7
The Glen FUL/RIB PR2 61 F1
PLF/KEOS FY6 12 C2
Glenview Cl FUL/RIB PR2 47 G5
Glenview Ct FUL/RIB PR2 47 G5
Glenway PRES PR1 72 B2
Glenwood St BPOOLE FY3 3 G4
Glossop Cl BISP FY2 24 C1
Gloucester Av BPOOL FY1 3 F7
CLV/TH FY5 16 D5
LEYL PR25 83 H1
Gloucester Rd CHLY/EC PR7 93 F5
LSTA FY8 63 G2
Glover's Ct PRES PR1 7 G4
Glover St PRES PR1 7 G5
Godwin Av BPOOLE FY3 5 J2
Goe La KIRK/FR/WAR PR4 54 B4
Golbourne St PRES PR1 7 J1
Goldburn Cl FUL/RIB PR2 44 B2
Golden Hl LEYL PR25 83 G2
Golden Hill La LEYL PR25 83 D2
Golden Wy PRES PR1 72 C2
Goldfinch St PRES PR1 60 B1
Goldsboro Av BPOOLE FY3 5 K2
Goldstone Dr CLV/TH FY5 21 F5
Golf Vw FUL/RIB PR2 44 C2
Good St PRES PR1 6 C5
Goodwood Av BISP FY2 28 D1
FUL/RIB PR2 45 H1
Goose Green Av CHLY/EC PR7 96 C4
Gordale Cl BPOOLS FY4 33 G5
Gordon Av CLV/TH FY5 21 H2
Gordon Rd FTWD FY7 11 F3
LSTA FY8 63 F2
Gordonstoun Pl CLV/TH FY5 21 G2
Gordon St BPOOLS FY4 4 B6
CHLYE PR6 93 G3
PRES PR1 6 C1
Goring St CHLY/EC PR7 93 G3
Gorse Av CLV/TH FY5 21 E1
Gorse Cl CHLYE PR6 89 H2
Gorse Gv FUL/RIB PR2 47 E5
KIRK/FR/WAR PR4 70 B5
Gorse Rd BPOOLE FY3 3 G7
Gorsewood LEYL PR25 82 D3
Gorton St BPOOL FY1 2 E2
Gosforth Rd BISP FY2 28 C1
Gough La BBR PR5 81 E4
Goulding Av LEYL PR25 83 G3
Goulding St CHLY/EC PR7 93 G4
Gower Ct CROS/BRETH PR26 82 A2
Gower Gv KIRK/FR/WAR PR4 76 B5
Goyt St LSTA FY8 49 F4
Gracamy Av
KIRK/FR/WAR PR4 * 66 C1
Gradwell St PRES PR1 6 C3
Grafton Ct CHLY/EC PR7 93 E5
Grafton Rd FUL/RIB PR2 47 F4
Grafton St BPOOL FY1 2 E1
PRES PR1 6 C6
Graham Av BBR PR5 79 H1
Graham St PRES PR1 60 B2
Grampian Wy LSTA FY8 65 E1
Granby Av BPOOLE FY3 29 E2
Grand Manor Dr LSTA FY8 50 B4
Grange Av CLV/TH FY5 21 H2
FUL/RIB PR2 47 G4
Grange Dr BBR PR5 75 G2
CHLY/EC PR7 87 H3
CHLY/EC PR7 96 B5
Grangefield KIRK/FR/WAR PR4 70 A5
Grange Gdns PLF/KEOS FY6 26 B5
Grange La KIRK/FR/WAR PR4 55 F1
KIRK/FR/WAR PR4 69 G5
KIRK/FR/WAR PR4 70 B3
PLF/KEOS FY6 19 E2
Grange Park Cl PRES PR1 58 C5
Grange Pl FUL/RIB PR2 47 F4
Grange Rd FTWD FY7 10 D3
FUL/RIB PR2 45 E5
LEYL PR25 82 C3
LSTA FY8 49 E4
PLF/KEOS FY6 23 H3
The Grange KIRK/FR/WAR PR4 44 A3
Grant Dr KIRK/FR/WAR PR4 76 B4
Grantham Rd BPOOL FY1 * 28 C3
KIRK/FR/WAR PR4 31 H4
Granville Rd BPOOL FY1 3 F4
CHLYE PR6 93 H1
Grasmere Av CLV/TH FY5 21 H2
FTWD FY7 11 E2
LEYL PR25 83 F1
Grasmere Cl BBR PR5 74 A4
CHLY/EC PR7 92 A1
FUL/RIB PR2 46 C4
Grasmere Gv CHLYE PR6 85 E5
Grasmere Rd BPOOL FY1 4 E2
BPOOL FY1 5 F3
LSTA FY8 49 E2
Grasmere Ter CHLY/EC PR7 93 E5
Grassington Pl CLV/TH FY5 21 F4
Grassington Rd LSTA FY8 49 H4
Graving Dock Rd LSTA FY8 65 E2
Gravners Fld CLV/TH FY5 22 B2
Great Avenham St PRES PR1 7 G6
Great George St PRES PR1 7 F1
Great Gill KIRK/FR/WAR PR4 76 B4
Great Greens La BBR PR5 81 E4
Great Hanover St PRES PR1 60 A2
Great Meadow BBR PR5 79 F1
CHLY/EC PR7 88 D5
Great Shaw St PRES PR1 6 E3
Great Townley St PRES PR1 60 D3
Great Tunstead
KIRK/FR/WAR PR4 76 B2
Greaves Meadow PRES PR1 72 D5
Greaves St PRES PR1 * 7 H4
Greaves-Town La FUL/RIB PR2 57 H2
Grebe Cl BPOOLE FY3 29 H3
Greenacres FUL/RIB PR2 44 D1
Green Acres KIRK/FR/WAR PR4 54 C4
Greenacres Av
KIRK/FR/WAR PR4 43 E4
Greenacres Dr CHLY/EC PR7 88 A3
The Greenacres
KIRK/FR/WAR PR4 71 E4
Green Av BPOOLS FY4 38 C2
Greenbank PLF/KEOS FY6 26 C4
Greenbank Av PRES PR1 59 F1
Greenbank Pl PRES PR1 6 C1
Greenbank Rd PRES PR1 72 D2
Greenbanks BISP FY2 25 F4
Greenbank St PRES PR1 59 G2
Greenbriar Cl BPOOLE FY3 29 F1
Greencroft PRES PR1 72 C3
Greendale Cl FTWD FY7 10 C4
Greendale Ms FUL/RIB PR2 58 A1
Green Dick's La GAR/LONG PR3 14 A1
Green Dr BBR PR5 73 H5
CLV/TH FY5 16 C5
FUL/RIB PR2 45 G1
LSTA FY8 64 B1
LSTA FY8 64 D1
PLF/KEOS FY6 30 C2
PRES PR1 72 A1
Greenfield Cl FTWD FY7 11 F4
Greenfield Dr BBR PR5 79 F1
Greenfield Rd CHLYE PR6 93 H2
CLV/TH FY5 21 E4
FTWD FY7 11 F4
Greenfields Crs
KIRK/FR/WAR PR4 42 C2
Greenfield Wy FUL/RIB PR2 44 D3
Greenfinch Ct BPOOLE FY3 29 H4
Greengate CLV/TH FY5 22 B2
Green Ga FUL/RIB PR2 45 E5
KIRK/FR/WAR PR4 70 D5
Green Hey LSTA FY8 65 E2
Greenhill Av KIRK/FR/WAR PR4 43 E2
Greenhill Pl BPOOL FY1 2 E2
Greenlands Crs FUL/RIB PR2 47 E5
Green La CROS/BRETH PR26 78 D2
KIRK/FR/WAR PR4 54 B5
KIRK/FR/WAR PR4 72 B5
PLF/KEOS FY6 13 G4
Green La West
KIRK/FR/WAR PR4 67 G1
Greenmead Cl
KIRK/FR/WAR PR4 44 A3
Green Meadow La
PLF/KEOS FY6 23 F4
Greenmount Av CLV/TH FY5 21 G1
KIRK/FR/WAR PR4 43 E2
Green Oak Pl CLV/TH FY5 21 F4
Green Pl BBR PR5 80 D3
Greenside CHLY/EC PR7 87 H4
Greenside Av FUL/RIB PR2 57 G2
Greenside Gdns
CROS/BRETH PR26 82 A5
Green St CHLY/EC PR7 92 D5
LSTA FY8 64 B3
Greensway GAR/LONG PR3 36 B2
The Green CHLY/EC PR7 90 B5
FUL/RIB PR2 61 F2
Greenthorn Crs FUL/RIB PR2 61 G1
Green Wy BPOOLS FY4 39 F1
Greenway CHLY/EC PR7 90 A3
FUL/RIB PR2 45 F1
PRES PR1 72 A2
Greenways LSTA FY8 49 H5
Greenwich Dr LSTA FY8 63 G1
Greenwood BBR PR5 81 E5
Greenwood Av BPOOL FY1 5 H4
Greenwood Cl LSTA FY8 63 H2
Greenwood St BBR PR5 74 B5
PRES PR1 7 J4
Gregory Av BISP FY2 24 C2
Gregory Pl LSTA FY8 64 B3
Gregson Cl BPOOLS FY4 39 F1
Gregson Dr FTWD FY7 11 F4
Gregson La BBR PR5 75 F4
Gregson St LSTA FY8 64 B3
Gregson Wy FUL/RIB PR2 46 B3
Grenfell Av BPOOLE FY3 29 E3
Grenville Av BBR PR5 74 A4
LSTA FY8 49 E2
Gresham Rd CLV/TH FY5 20 D3
Gresley Pl BISP FY2 25 E5
Greta Pl FTWD FY7 10 D4
Gretdale Av LSTA FY8 49 E3
Gretna Crs CLV/TH FY5 20 D4
Greyfriars Av FUL/RIB PR2 45 F3
Greyfriars Crs FUL/RIB PR2 45 F3
Greyfriars Dr PRES PR1 72 B1
Grey Heights Vw CHLYE PR6 93 H2
Greystock Av FUL/RIB PR2 45 G2
Greystock Cl BBR PR5 81 E1
Greystoke Pl BPOOLS FY4 38 B3
Greystones CROS/BRETH PR26 82 A3
Grime St CHLY/EC PR7 93 G4
Grimsargh St PRES PR1 * 60 D2
Grimshaw St PRES PR1 7 H4
Grindleton Cl BPOOLE FY3 29 H2
Grisedale Pl CHLY/EC PR7 93 E5
Grizedale Av PLF/KEOS FY6 26 A4
Grizedale Cl FUL/RIB PR2 61 F1
Grizedale Ct CLV/TH FY5 * 21 H1
Grizedale Crs FUL/RIB PR2 61 G1
Grizedale Pl FUL/RIB PR2 61 F1
Grizedale Rd BPOOLS FY4 34 A4
Grosvenor Pl FUL/RIB PR2 58 D1
Grosvenor Rd CHLY/EC PR7 92 D4
Grosvenor St BPOOL FY1 2 D4
LSTA FY8 64 D3
PRES PR1 7 K4
Grove Av KIRK/FR/WAR PR4 76 A1
Grove Rd BBR PR5 60 C5
Grove St BBR PR5 80 C1
LEYL PR25 82 C4
LSTA FY8 49 F4
The Grove CHLYE PR6 89 F5
CLV/TH FY5 21 E1
PRES PR1 72 A2
Grundy Ms BPOOLS FY4 38 C1
Grundy's La CHLY/EC PR7 97 F4
Grundy St LEYL PR25 83 F2
Guernsey Av CHLY/EC PR7 84 C5
Guildford Av BISP FY2 24 C1
Guildford Rd PRES PR1 7 G5
Guildford Wy PLF/KEOS FY6 26 A1
Guild Hall Ar PRES PR1 * 7 G4
Guildhall St PRES PR1 7 F5
Guild Rw PRES PR1 7 G4
Guild Wy FUL/RIB PR2 6 A5
Gynn Av BPOOL FY1 28 B2

H

Hackensall Rd PLF/KEOS FY6 12 C2
Hacklands Av FUL/RIB PR2 57 F2
Haddon Pl FUL/RIB PR2 45 F5
Haddon Rd BISP FY2 24 C2
Hadleigh Rd PLF/KEOS FY6 26 A1
Haig Av FUL/RIB PR2 * 59 F1
LEYL PR25 83 E3
Haigh Cl CHLY/EC PR7 92 D3
Haigh Crs CHLY/EC PR7 92 D3
Haighton Ct FUL/RIB PR2 46 A1
Haighton Dr FUL/RIB PR2 47 E2
Haig Rd BPOOL FY1 4 B5
Half Acre BBR PR5 79 F1
Halford Pl CLV/TH FY5 21 E5
Halfpenny La CHLY/EC PR7 94 A2
Halifax St BPOOLE FY3 5 K2
Hallam Wy BPOOLS FY4 40 C2
Hall Av BPOOLS FY4 4 E6
Hall Cft KIRK/FR/WAR PR4 71 E4
Hall Ga CHLY/EC PR7 92 D1
Hall Gate La PLF/KEOS FY6 19 G1
Halliwell Ct CHLY/EC PR7 93 F3
Halliwell La CHLYE PR6 89 F3
Halliwell Pl CHLY/EC PR7 * 93 F3
Halliwell St CHLY/EC PR7 93 F3
Hall La LEYL PR25 83 E2
Hall Park Dr LSTA FY8 50 B5
Hall Rd FUL/RIB PR2 45 G3
PRES PR1 72 D3
Halls Sq CHLYE PR6 * 89 H1
Hall St FUL/RIB PR2 59 E2
Hallwood Rd CHLY/EC PR7 92 D5
Halsbury St PRES PR1 7 J6
Halstead Rd FUL/RIB PR2 46 D3
Halton Av CLV/TH FY5 17 E5
LEYL PR25 84 A2
Halton Gdns BPOOLS FY4 33 F5
Halton Pl FUL/RIB PR2 47 F4
Hambledon Dr PRES PR1 72 D4
Hambleton Cl
KIRK/FR/WAR PR4 70 A5
Hamer Rd FUL/RIB PR2 45 F5
Hamilton LSTA FY8 65 E2
Hamilton Cl LSTA FY8 65 E2
Hamilton Gv FUL/RIB PR2 47 E4
Hamilton Rd CHLY/EC PR7 93 E3
FUL/RIB PR2 46 D5
Hamlet Rd FTWD FY7 11 E2
The Hamlet LSTA FY8 49 F1
Hammerton Pl BPOOLE FY3 29 G2
Hammond Ct PRES PR1 59 G2
Hammond's Rw PRES PR1 7 H4
Hammond St PRES PR1 59 H1
Hampden Rd LEYL PR25 83 F2
Hampshire Pl BPOOLS FY4 39 F2
Hampshire Rd BBR PR5 74 A3
Hampson Av LEYL PR25 84 A3
Hampson Gv PLF/KEOS FY6 13 E2
Hampstead Cl LSTA FY8 50 C5
Hampstead Ms BPOOL FY1 * 28 C3
Hampstead Rd FUL/RIB PR2 60 D1
Hampton Cl CHLY/EC PR7 93 E2
Hampton Ct LSTA FY8 50 A3
Hampton Pl CLV/TH FY5 21 E1
Hampton Rd BPOOLS FY4 32 B5
The Hamptons PLF/KEOS FY6 30 B1
Hampton St FUL/RIB PR2 59 E1
Hanbury St FUL/RIB PR2 * 59 E2
The Handbridge FUL/RIB PR2 45 G3
Handley Rd BPOOL FY1 2 E2
Handsworth Ct BPOOL FY1 28 C3
Handsworth Rd BPOOL FY1 28 C3
Hanley Cl PLF/KEOS FY6 19 G2
Hanover Crs BISP FY2 24 C1
Hanover St PRES PR1 7 F1
Hapton St CLV/TH FY5 17 H5
Harbour Av KIRK/FR/WAR PR4 53 G5
Harbour Cl FTWD FY7 11 F4
Harbour La KIRK/FR/WAR PR4 53 G4
Harbour Wy FTWD FY7 11 H3
Harcourt Rd BPOOLS FY4 5 F7
Harcourt St PRES PR1 59 G2
Hardacre La CHLYE PR6 89 E2
Hardcastle Rd FUL/RIB PR2 45 G5
Hardhorn Rd PLF/KEOS FY6 26 B5
PLF/KEOS FY6 30 C2
Hardhorn Wy PLF/KEOS FY6 26 B5
Hardman St BPOOL FY1 2 E2
Hardwicke St PRES PR1 * 7 G2
Hardy Dr CHLY/EC PR7 92 D3
Hareden Cl BBR PR5 80 C1
Hareden Rd FUL/RIB PR2 61 F1
Harestone Av CHLY/EC PR7 92 D5
Harewood Av BPOOLE FY3 29 G1
Harewood Cl PLF/KEOS FY6 26 A2
Harewood Rd PRES PR1 60 B1
Hargate Rd CLV/TH FY5 22 A2
Hargreaves Av LEYL PR25 83 G4
Hargreaves Ct FUL/RIB PR2 44 B4
Hargreaves St CLV/TH FY5 21 H1
Harland St FUL/RIB PR2 45 F5
Harlech Av BPOOL FY1 5 F5
Harlech Dr LEYL PR25 83 G3
Harlech Gv CLV/TH FY5 22 B2
Harley Rd BPOOLE FY3 3 H6
Harling Rd PRES PR1 60 D2
Harold Av BPOOLS FY4 39 G2
Harold Ter BBR PR5 79 F1
Harperley CHLY/EC PR7 89 E5
Harper's La CHLY/EC PR7 93 G1
Harrington Av BPOOLS FY4 38 B3
Harrington Rd CHLY/EC PR7 93 E2
Harrington St PRES PR1 6 D2
Harris Av BPOOL FY1 5 G5
Harrison Av CLV/TH FY5 21 H2
Harrison La KIRK/FR/WAR PR4 72 A4
Harrison Rd CHLY/EC PR7 93 F4
FUL/RIB PR2 45 G3
Harrison St BPOOL FY1 4 E1
Harris St FTWD FY7 11 G2
PRES PR1 7 G4
Harrock Rd LEYL PR25 84 A3
Harrock Vw CHLY/EC PR7 * 94 B4
Harrogate Rd LSTA FY8 50 A4
Harrop Pl FUL/RIB PR2 47 E4
Harrow Av FTWD FY7 11 F2
Harrow Pl BPOOLS FY4 38 A3
LSTA FY8 63 G1
Harrowside BPOOLS FY4 38 B3
Harrowside West BPOOLS FY4 38 A3
Hartford Av BPOOL FY1 5 G3
Hartington Rd PRES PR1 6 B5
Hartwood Gn CHLYE PR6 89 F4
Harvest Dr CHLYE PR6 89 F1
Harwich Rd LSTA FY8 49 F2
Harwood Av LSTA FY8 49 E3
Harwood Cl PLF/KEOS FY6 19 G2
Hasbury Dr CLV/TH FY5 22 A2
Haslemere Av BPOOLE FY3 5 J2
Haslow Pl BPOOLE FY3 29 F3
Hassett Cl PRES PR1 6 C7
Hastings Av BISP FY2 25 E2
KIRK/FR/WAR PR4 53 G4
Hastings Cl CLV/TH FY5 22 A3
Hastings Pl LSTA FY8 64 B3
Hastings Rd CLV/TH FY5 22 A3
FUL/RIB PR2 58 D2
KIRK/FR/WAR PR4 54 B1
LEYL PR25 83 G2
Hatfield Av FTWD FY7 11 E4
Hatfield Cl CLV/TH FY5 22 A2
Hatfield Gdns FTWD FY7 11 E4
Hatfield Ms FTWD FY7 11 F3
Hatfield Rd FUL/RIB PR2 47 E5
Hatfield Wk FTWD FY7 11 E4
Hathaway BPOOLS FY4 33 E5
Hathaway Rd FTWD FY7 11 E2
Havelock Rd BBR PR5 80 B2
PRES PR1 72 D1
Havelock St BPOOL FY1 2 C7
PRES PR1 59 G1
Haven Rd LSTA FY8 64 C3
Hawarden Rd PRES PR1 61 E2
Hawes Side La BPOOLS FY4 5 H6
Haweswater Av CHLY/EC PR7 93 E4
Hawkhurst Av FUL/RIB PR2 45 F2
Hawkhurst Crs FUL/RIB PR2 45 F2
Hawkhurst Rd PRES PR1 60 B1
PRES PR1 72 D2
Hawking Pl BISP FY2 25 F2
Hawkins Cl PRES PR1 59 G2
Hawkins St PRES PR1 6 C1
Hawksbury Dr PRES PR1 72 C4
Hawkshead PRES PR1 72 D3
Hawkshead Av CHLY/EC PR7 92 A1
Hawkshead Rd FUL/RIB PR2 47 E3
Hawkshead Ter BPOOLS FY4 34 B5
Hawkstone Cl CLV/TH FY5 22 B4
Hawkswood CHLY/EC PR7 90 A4
Hawthorn Av FTWD FY7 17 E1
Hawthorn Cl
KIRK/FR/WAR PR4 42 C2
KIRK/FR/WAR PR4 77 H2
LEYL PR25 * 82 C2
Hawthorn Crs FUL/RIB PR2 57 H2
Hawthorn Rd BPOOL FY1 28 C3
FUL/RIB PR2 61 E1
Hawthorne Av BBR PR5 75 F3
Hawthorne Cl CHLYE PR6 85 E1
Hawthorne Gv PLF/KEOS FY6 25 G2
Hawthorne Rd CLV/TH FY5 21 H4
The Hawthorns CHLY/EC PR7 90 A3
FUL/RIB PR2 45 H2
Haydock Av LEYL PR25 83 F4
Haydock St BBR PR5 * 74 B4
Haydon Av BBR PR5 79 F2
Hayfield Av BBR PR5 75 H5
BISP FY2 25 E5
PLF/KEOS FY6 26 C4
Hayfield Cl BBR PR5 75 H5
Hayling Pl FUL/RIB PR2 44 C4
Haymarket LSTA FY8 49 H5
Haysworth St PRES PR1 59 H1
Haywood Cl FUL/RIB PR2 37 F5
Hazel Av BBR PR5 74 D5
FTWD FY7 17 F1
Hazel Cl BBR PR5 74 C5
PRES PR1 72 A3
Hazel Coppice FUL/RIB PR2 44 A5
Hazeldene Rd FTWD FY7 11 E4
Hazel Gv BBR PR5 74 C5
BPOOLE FY3 3 H5
CHLYE PR6 89 F4
FUL/RIB PR2 47 G4
Hazelhurst Rd FUL/RIB PR2 61 G1
Hazelmere Rd FUL/RIB PR2 36 C5
FUL/RIB PR2 58 C2
The Hazels CHLY/EC PR7 96 B4
Hazelwood Cl LEYL PR25 82 D3
Hazlewood Cl CLV/TH FY5 21 G2
Head Dyke La GAR/LONG PR3 15 E3
PLF/KEOS FY6 14 B3
Headfort Cl BISP FY2 24 D5
Headley Rd LEYL PR25 82 D3
Headroomgate Back Rd
LSTA FY8 * 49 F3
Headroomgate Rd LSTA FY8 49 F3
Heald House Rd LEYL PR25 83 H4
Heald St BPOOLE FY3 3 F2
CHLYE PR6 93 H2
Healey St BPOOLE FY3 3 G1
Heather Cl CHLYE PR6 93 H2
CLV/TH FY5 21 H3
Heather Gv FUL/RIB PR2 47 E5
Heatherleigh
CROS/BRETH PR26 82 C2
The Heathers BBR PR5 81 F5
PLF/KEOS FY6 12 D1

Heatherway *FUL/RIB* PR2 ....47 E3
Heathfield Dr *FUL/RIB* PR2 ....47 E4
Heathfield Rd *FTWD* FY7 ....11 E4
Heathrow Pl *CHLY/EC* PR7 ....92 D3
Heathway *FUL/RIB* PR2 ....45 H2
Heathway Av *BPOOLE* FY3 ....3 J3
Heatley St *PRES* PR1 ....6 E3
Heaton Cl *BBR* PR5 ....74 A2
PLF/KEOS FY6 ....26 A2
Heaton Mount Av
FUL/RIB PR2 ....45 H1
Heaton Pl *PRES* PR1 ....61 E2
Heaton Rd *LSTA* FY8 ....49 G4
Heaton St *LEYL* PR25 ....82 D2
Hebden Av *BPOOL* FY1 ....5 F5
Heeley Rd *LSTA* FY8 ....48 D3
Helen's Cl *BPOOLS* FY4 ....39 E2
Hellifield *FUL/RIB* PR2 ....45 G1
Helmsdale Rd *BPOOLS* FY4 ....39 F1
Helmsley Gn *LEYL* PR25 ....83 G2
Hemingway *BPOOLS* FY4 ....5 F7
Henderson Rd *FTWD* FY7 ....11 F4
Henderson St *PRES* PR1 ....45 G5
Hendon Pl *FUL/RIB* PR2 ....58 A1
Henley Av *CLV/TH* FY5 ....20 D2
Henley Ct *BPOOLE* FY3 * 29 E1
Hennel La *BBR* PR5 ....73 H3
Henrietta St *PRES* PR1 ....7 K2
Henry St *BPOOL* FY1 ....4 D3
LSTA FY8 ....64 B3
Henson Av *BPOOLS* FY4 ....39 E2
Henthorne St *BPOOL* FY1 ....2 E2
Herbert St *LEYL* PR25 ....83 F2
PRES PR1 ....7 J1
Hereford Av *BPOOLE* FY3 ....5 J2
Heriot Cl *CLV/TH* FY5 ....21 F3
Heritage Wy *CLV/TH* FY5 ....21 F3
The Hermitage *CLV/TH* FY5 ....21 F2
Hermitage Wy *LSTA* FY8 ....50 B5
Hermon Rd *CLV/TH* FY5 ....21 E3
Hermon St *PRES* PR1 ....60 C2
Hern Av *BBR* PR5 ....79 F1
Heron Cl *CLV/TH* FY5 ....17 F4
Heron Wy *BPOOLE* FY3 ....29 H3
KIRK/FR/WAR PR4 ....54 B1
Herring Arm Rd *FTWD* FY7 ....11 G4
Herschell St *PRES* PR1 ....7 H6
Hesketh Av *BISP* FY2 ....24 B3
Hesketh Cl *PRES* PR1 ....61 E2
Hesketh Pl *FTWD* FY7 ....11 H1
Hesketh Rd *FUL/RIB* PR2 ....61 E2
LSTA FY8 ....49 G2
Hesketh St *FUL/RIB* PR2 ....59 E2
Hetherington Pl *BISP* FY2 ....25 E5
Heversham Av *FUL/RIB* PR2 ....45 H1
Hewitt St *LEYL* PR25 ....83 G2
Hewlett St *CHLY/EC* PR7 ....96 A4
Hexham Av *CLV/TH* FY5 ....17 E5
Hey End *KIRK/FR/WAR* PR4 ....77 G1
The Heyes *CHLYE* PR6 ....85 E2
Heyhouses La *LSTA* FY8 ....49 H3
Heysham St *PRES* PR1 ....59 G2
Heys St *CLV/TH* FY5 ....21 H1
The Heys *CHLY/EC* PR7 ....96 C3
Heywood Rd *FUL/RIB* PR2 ....58 A1
Higham Gv *BPOOLE* FY3 ....5 K3
Highbank Av *BPOOLS* FY4 ....33 G5
Highbury Av *BPOOLE* FY3 ....29 E2
FTWD FY7 ....11 F3
Highbury Rd *LSTA* FY8 ....48 D2
Highbury Rd East *LSTA* FY8 ....49 E2
Highbury Rd West *LSTA* FY8 ....48 D2
Highcroft Av *BISP* FY2 ....25 E2
Highcross Av *PLF/KEOS* FY6 ....30 B2
Highcross Hl *PLF/KEOS* FY6 ....30 B2
Highcross Rd *PLF/KEOS* FY6 ....30 B2
Higher Bank Rd *FUL/RIB* PR2 ....45 H5
Higher Cft *PRES* PR1 ....72 B4
Higher Furlong
KIRK/FR/WAR PR4 ....76 A3
Higher Gn *PLF/KEOS* FY6 ....26 B4
Higher Greenfield *FUL/RIB* PR2 ....44 D3
Higher Meadow *LEYL* PR25 ....84 B3
Higher Moor Rd *BPOOLE* FY3 ....25 G5
Higher Walton Rd *BBR* PR5 ....74 B2
Highfield Av *BBR* PR5 ....73 H5
FUL/RIB PR2 ....46 C4
LEYL PR25 ....83 H1
Highfield Cl *KIRK/FR/WAR* PR4 ....56 A2
Highfield Dr *FUL/RIB* PR2 ....36 D5
KIRK/FR/WAR PR4 ....76 A3
PRES PR1 ....72 C4
Highfield Gv *BBR* PR5 ....73 H5
Highfield Rd *BPOOLS* FY4 ....38 C2
BPOOLS FY4 ....39 F1
Highfield Rd North
CHLY/EC PR7 ....89 F5
Highfield Rd South
CHLY/EC PR7 ....93 F1
Highgale Gdns *BBR* PR5 ....79 H2
High Ga *FTWD* FY7 ....10 D3
Highgate *BPOOLS* FY4 ....38 D3
PRES PR1 ....72 A1
Highgate Av *FUL/RIB* PR2 ....45 G4
Highgate Cl *FUL/RIB* PR2 ....45 H4
Highgate La *KIRK/FR/WAR* PR4 ....53 G5
High Gate La *PLF/KEOS* FY6 ....19 E4
Highgate Pl *LSTA* FY8 ....50 B5
High Gn *LEYL* PR25 ....83 E3
Highgrove Av *CHLY/EC* PR7 ....95 E1
Highland Av *PRES* PR1 ....72 A2
Highland Dr *CHLY/EC* PR7 ....84 B5
High Meadow *BBR* PR5 ....73 G4
Highrigg Dr *GAR/LONG* PR3 ....37 E4
High St *BPOOL* FY1 ....2 C3
CHLY/EC PR7 ....93 F2
FTWD FY7 ....11 H2
PRES PR1 ....7 G2
Highways Av *CHLY/EC* PR7 ....92 A1
Hilary Av *BISP* FY2 ....24 C2
Hillbrook Rd *LEYL* PR25 ....83 E2
Hill Crs *KIRK/FR/WAR* PR4 ....55 G1
Hill Crest Av *FUL/RIB* PR2 ....36 D5
Hillcrest Av *FUL/RIB* PR2 ....44 C4
Hillcrest Rd *BPOOLS* FY4 ....38 B4
Hill Cft *CHLYE* PR6 ....84 D2
Hillcroft *FUL/RIB* PR2 ....45 E1
Hillock La *KIRK/FR/WAR* PR4 ....53 F4
KIRK/FR/WAR PR4 ....54 A2
Hillpark Av *BBR* PR5 ....75 G5
FUL/RIB PR2 ....45 F4
Hill Rd *LEYL* PR25 ....83 H3
PRES PR1 ....72 B1
Hill Rd South *PRES* PR1 ....72 B3
Hillside Av *CROS/BRETH* PR26 ....79 E2
FUL/RIB PR2 ....45 F4
KIRK/FR/WAR PR4 ....43 G3
PLF/KEOS FY6 ....13 F2
Hillside Cl *BPOOLE* FY3 ....3 H3
CHLY/EC PR7 ....91 H1
CLV/TH FY5 ....22 B4
Hillside Crs *CHLYE* PR6 ....85 F4
Hillside Dr *PLF/KEOS* FY6 ....19 G2
Hillside Rd *PRES* PR1 ....60 C5
The Hills *FUL/RIB* PR2 ....47 H1
Hill St *BPOOLS* FY4 ....4 C6
PRES PR1 ....6 E3
Hill Top *KIRK/FR/WAR* PR4 ....77 H3
Hill Top Cl *KIRK/FR/WAR* PR4 ....54 D4
Hill Top La *CHLYE* PR6 ....85 G4
Hill View Dr *CHLY/EC* PR7 ....96 A5
Hillview Rd *KIRK/FR/WAR* PR4 ....43 E2
Hill Wk *LEYL* PR25 ....83 F2
Hillylaid Rd *CLV/TH* FY5 ....22 A2
Hilstone La *BISP* FY2 ....28 D1
Hilton Av *BPOOLS* FY4 ....4 C6
LSTA FY8 ....50 A5
Hindley Cl *FUL/RIB* PR2 ....46 C1
Hindley St *CHLY/EC* PR7 ....93 E4
Hind St *PRES* PR1 ....6 C6
Hobart Pl *CLV/TH* FY5 ....21 F4
Hockley Pl *BPOOLE* FY3 ....29 F3
Hodder Av *BPOOL* FY1 ....5 F5
CHLY/EC PR7 ....93 E5
FTWD FY7 ....10 D4
Hodder Brook *FUL/RIB* PR2 ....47 G5
Hodder Cl *BBR* PR5 ....80 C1
Hodder Pl *LSTA* FY8 ....49 H4
Hodder Wy *PLF/KEOS* FY6 ....26 B5
Hodgson Av *KIRK/FR/WAR* PR4 ....54 A5
Hodgson Pl *PLF/KEOS* FY6 ....26 B5
Hodgson Rd *BPOOL* FY1 ....28 B1
Hodson St *BBR* PR5 ....74 B5
Hoghton Cl *LSTA* FY8 ....49 F1
Hoghton La *BBR* PR5 ....75 G3
Hoghton Rd *LEYL* PR25 ....82 C3
Hoghton St *BBR* PR5 ....79 F1
Hoghton Vw *PRES* PR1 ....60 C4
Holbeck Av *BPOOLS* FY4 ....33 F5
Holcombe Gv *CHLYE* PR6 ....93 H1
Holcombe Rd *BISP* FY2 ....29 E1
Holcroft Pl *LSTA* FY8 ....64 A2
Holgate *BPOOLS* FY4 ....39 F1
Holker Cl *BBR* PR5 ....75 H3
Holland Av *BBR* PR5 ....74 B4
Holland House Ct *BBR* PR5 ....74 B3
Holland House Rd *BBR* PR5 ....74 B3
Holland Rd *FUL/RIB* PR2 ....59 E2
Hollings *KIRK/FR/WAR* PR4 ....77 G2
Hollinhead Crs *FUL/RIB* PR2 ....44 D4
Hollinhurst Av *PRES* PR1 ....59 E5
Hollins Gv *FUL/RIB* PR2 ....44 D5
Hollinshead St *CHLY/EC* PR7 ....93 F2
Hollins La *CROS/BRETH* PR26 ....86 B3
Hollins Rd *PRES* PR1 ....46 B5
Hollybank Cl *FUL/RIB* PR2 ....44 B3
Holly Cl *CHLYE* PR6 ....85 E2
CLV/TH FY5 ....22 A1
Holly Crs *CHLY/EC* PR7 ....96 B2
Holly Ms *LSTA* FY8 ....49 F1
Holly Pl *BBR* PR5 ....81 E3
Holly Rd *BPOOL* FY1 ....28 C1
CLV/TH FY5 ....21 H1
Hollywood Av *BPOOLE* FY3 ....3 H4
PRES PR1 ....72 B3
Hollywood Gv *FTWD* FY7 ....11 F2
Holman St *PRES* PR1 ....60 C2
Holme Av *FTWD* FY7 ....16 D1
Holmefield Av *CLV/TH* FY5 ....21 E2
Holmefield Cl *CLV/TH* FY5 ....21 E2
Holmefield Rd *LSTA* FY8 ....49 F4
PLF/KEOS FY6 ....12 C1
Holme Rd *BBR* PR5 ....80 A1
PRES PR1 ....6 A5
Holmes Ct *PRES* PR1 ....45 G5
Holme Slack La *PRES* PR1 ....46 C5
Holmes Meadow
CROS/BRETH PR26 ....82 A3
Holmes Rd *CLV/TH* FY5 ....21 G1
Holmeswood
KIRK/FR/WAR PR4 ....43 E3
Holmfield Crs *FUL/RIB* PR2 ....57 H2
Holmfield Rd *BISP* FY2 ....28 B1
FUL/RIB PR2 ....46 A4
Holmrook Rd *PRES* PR1 ....60 B2
Holsands Cl *FUL/RIB* PR2 ....47 E2
Holstein St *PRES* PR1 ....7 H2
Holt Av *CHLY/EC* PR7 ....96 C3
Holt Brow *LEYL* PR25 ....87 F1
Holt La *CHLYE* PR6 ....85 G1
Holts La *PLF/KEOS* FY6 ....26 D5
Holyoake Av *BISP* FY2 ....29 E1
Homestead *BBR* PR5 ....81 E5
Homestead Cl *LEYL* PR25 ....82 C3
Homestead Dr *FTWD* FY7 ....11 E5
The Homestead *LSTA* FY8 * 64 B3
Homestead Wy *FTWD* FY7 ....11 E5
Honey Moor Dr *CLV/TH* FY5 ....17 G5
Honeypot La *PLF/KEOS* FY6 ....27 H3
Honeysuckle Cl *CHLYE* PR6 ....89 E2
Honeysuckle Pl *BISP* FY2 ....25 F1
Honister Av *BPOOLE* FY3 ....5 J3
Honister Cl *FTWD* FY7 ....10 D3
Honister Sq *LSTA* FY8 ....49 F1
Honiton Wy *KIRK/FR/WAR* PR4 ....44 B2
Hools La *GAR/LONG* PR3 ....14 C1
Hope Cl *CLV/TH* FY5 ....17 H5
Hope St *CHLY/EC* PR7 ....93 E4
LSTA FY8 ....49 G4
PRES PR1 ....6 E3
Hopton Rd *BPOOL* FY1 ....4 B3
Hopwood St *BBR* PR5 ....80 C2
PRES PR1 ....7 H2
Hornbeam Cl *PRES* PR1 ....72 A3
Hornby Av *FTWD* FY7 ....16 D1
FUL/RIB PR2 ....47 E4
Hornby Ct *KIRK/FR/WAR* PR4 ....43 F4
Hornby Cft *CROS/BRETH* PR26 ....82 A5
Hornby Rd *BPOOL* FY1 ....2 E6
CHLYE PR6 ....93 H4
LSTA FY8 ....62 B1
Hornchurch Dr *CHLY/EC* PR7 ....92 D2
Horncliffe Rd *BPOOLS* FY4 ....38 B2
Hornsea Cl *CLV/TH* FY5 ....22 B2
FUL/RIB PR2 ....44 C4
Hornsey Av *LSTA* FY8 ....38 B4
Horsebridge Rd *BPOOLE* FY3 ....29 H2
Horsfall Av *LSTA* FY8 ....64 B3
Hough La *LEYL* PR25 ....83 F3
Houghton Av *BPOOLS* FY4 ....5 F7
Houghton Cl *PRES* PR1 ....72 C3
Houghton Rd *PRES* PR1 ....72 B3
Houghton St *CHLYE* PR6 ....93 G2
Houldsworth Rd *FUL/RIB* PR2 ....45 G5
Houseman Pl *BPOOLS* FY4 ....39 E1
Hove Av *FTWD* FY7 ....16 C1
Hove Rd *LSTA* FY8 ....49 F5
Howard Cl *LSTA* FY8 ....49 E2
Howard Rd *CHLY/EC* PR7 ....93 E5
Howard St *BPOOL* FY1 ....2 D2
Howarth Crs *PLF/KEOS* FY6 ....26 C4
Howarth Rd *FUL/RIB* PR2 ....45 E5
Howe Gv *CHLY/EC* PR7 ....92 D3
The Howgills *FUL/RIB* PR2 ....46 A1
Howgill Wy *LSTA* FY8 ....65 E1
Howick Cross La *PRES* PR1 ....57 H5
Howick Moor La *PRES* PR1 ....71 G3
Howick Park Av *PRES* PR1 ....71 G2
Howick Park Cl *PRES* PR1 ....71 G2
Howick Park Dr *PRES* PR1 ....71 G2
Hoylake Cl *FUL/RIB* PR2 ....44 D2
Hoyle Av *LSTA* FY8 ....49 F1
Hoyles La *KIRK/FR/WAR* PR4 ....44 B2
Huck La *LSTA* FY8 ....52 A4
Hudson Ct *BBR* PR5 ....81 F1
Hudson Rd *BPOOL* FY1 ....5 F4
Hudson St *PRES* PR1 ....7 H5
Hugh Barn La
KIRK/FR/WAR PR4 ....77 F2
Hughes Gv *BISP* FY2 ....29 E1
Hugh La *CROS/BRETH* PR26 ....82 C1
Hull Rd *BPOOL* FY1 ....2 C6
Hull St *FUL/RIB* PR2 ....59 E2
Hulme Av *CLV/TH* FY5 ....22 A2
Humber Av *BPOOLE* FY3 * 29 E2
Hungerford Rd *LSTA* FY8 ....62 C1
Hunniball Ct *FUL/RIB* PR2 ....59 E1
Hunstanton Cl *CHLY/EC* PR7 ....88 A2
Hunter Rd *KIRK/FR/WAR* PR4 ....54 B1
Hunters Fold
KIRK/FR/WAR PR4 ....76 B4
Hunters Ldg *BBR* PR5 ....74 A3
Hunters Rd *LEYL* PR25 ....84 A3
Huntingdon Rd *CLV/TH* FY5 ....20 C3
Huntley Av *BPOOLE* FY3 ....29 E3
Hunts Fld *CHLYE* PR6 ....85 F2
Hunt St *PRES* PR1 * 6 B4
Hurn Gv *CHLY/EC* PR7 ....92 D3
Hurst Brook *CHLY/EC* PR7 ....96 C4
Hurstdene Cl *PLF/KEOS* FY6 ....26 D4
Hurstleigh Hts *CLV/TH* FY5 ....22 C2
Hurstmere Av *BPOOLS* FY4 ....33 E5
Hurst Pk *PRES* PR1 ....72 B2
Hurstway *FUL/RIB* PR2 ....45 F1
Hurstway Cl *FUL/RIB* PR2 ....45 F1
Hurstwood Dr *BISP* FY2 ....24 D5
Hutton Hall Av
KIRK/FR/WAR PR4 ....71 F4
Hyde Rd *BPOOL* FY1 ....4 C4

I

Ibbison Ct *BPOOL* FY1 ....4 D1
Iddesleigh Rd *PRES* PR1 * 61 E2
Iddon Ct *BPOOL* FY1 ....2 D2
Idlewood Pl *CLV/TH* FY5 ....21 F4
Ilford Rd *BPOOLS* FY4 ....5 H5
Ilkley Av *LSTA* FY8 ....50 A5
Ilkley Gv *CLV/TH* FY5 ....20 D4
The Illawalla *CLV/TH* FY5 ....26 C1
Illingworth Rd *PRES* PR1 ....61 E2
Ilway *BBR* PR5 ....74 A3
Imperial St *BPOOL* FY1 ....28 B3
Imperial Yd *BPOOL* FY1 * 28 B3
Ince La *CHLY/EC* PR7 ....90 B5
Ingleborough Wy *LEYL* PR25 ....83 H2
Ingleby Cl *CLV/TH* FY5 ....17 F4
Ingle Cl *CHLYE* PR6 ....93 G1
Ingle Head *FUL/RIB* PR2 ....45 F2
Inglenook Cl *CLV/TH* FY5 ....21 F3
Ingleton Av *BISP* FY2 ....25 F3
Ingleton Rd *FUL/RIB* PR2 ....47 E4
Ingleway *CLV/TH* FY5 ....21 E1
Ingleway Av *BPOOLE* FY3 ....3 J3
Inglewood Cl *FTWD* FY7 ....10 C5
KIRK/FR/WAR PR4 ....53 F5
Inglewood Gv *BISP* FY2 ....25 E2
Ingol Gv *PLF/KEOS* FY6 ....23 G2
Ingol La *PLF/KEOS* FY6 ....23 H2
Ingot St *PRES* PR1 ....6 B2
Ingthorpe Av *BISP* FY2 ....24 D2
Inkerman St *FUL/RIB* PR2 ....45 E5
Inner Prom *LSTA* FY8 ....63 F3
Inskip Pl *BPOOLS* FY4 ....39 E3
LSTA FY8 ....49 G3
Inskip Rd *FUL/RIB* PR2 ....58 A2
LEYL PR25 ....82 C2
Intack Rd *KIRK/FR/WAR* PR4 ....76 C1
Inver Rd *BISP* FY2 ....24 D4
Ipswich Pl *CLV/TH* FY5 ....20 C2
Ipswich Rd *FUL/RIB* PR2 ....60 D1
Irongate *BBR* PR5 ....79 H1
Ironside Cl *FUL/RIB* PR2 ....46 B4
Irvine St *PRES* PR1 ....7 K1
Irving Cl *BISP* FY2 ....25 F2
Isherwood St *PRES* PR1 ....60 C2
Islay Rd *LSTA* FY8 ....50 B5
Isleworth Dr *CHLY/EC* PR7 ....93 E3
Ivy Av *BPOOLS* FY4 ....39 E3
Ivy Bank *FUL/RIB* PR2 ....46 D2
Ivy Cl *LEYL* PR25 ....84 B2
Ivy Gdns *CLV/TH* FY5 ....17 H5

J

Jackson Rd *CHLY/EC* PR7 * 92 D5
LEYL PR25 ....82 C3
Jackson St *BBR* PR5 * 80 C1
BPOOLE FY3 ....29 E3
CHLY/EC PR7 ....93 G4
Jacson St *PRES* PR1 ....7 G4
James Av *BPOOLS* FY4 ....33 F4
Jameson Rd *FTWD* FY7 ....17 F1
Jameson St *BPOOL* FY1 ....4 E1
James Pl *CHLY/EC* PR7 ....96 B4
James St *BBR* PR5 ....74 B5
PRES PR1 ....7 K5
Janice Dr *FUL/RIB* PR2 ....45 F1
Jasmine Rd *BBR* PR5 ....73 F3
Jeffrey Sq *BPOOL* FY1 ....5 F2
Jellicoe Cl *LSTA* FY8 ....49 E1
Jem Ga *CLV/TH* FY5 ....20 D4
Jemmett St *PRES* PR1 ....45 G5
Jenny La *BPOOLS* FY4 ....40 A1
Jensen Dr *BPOOLS* FY4 ....41 E2
Jepson Wy *BPOOLS* FY4 ....39 F4
Jersey Av *BISP* FY2 ....25 E5
Jersey Fold *CHLY/EC* PR7 ....88 B2
Jervis Cl *LSTA* FY8 ....48 D2
Jesmond Av *BPOOLS* FY4 ....38 B1
John Hill St *BPOOLE* FY3 ....5 K4
Johnson Rd *BPOOLS* FY4 ....5 K4
Johnspool *FUL/RIB* PR2 ....45 E2
John St *BBR* PR5 ....74 B5
BPOOL FY1 ....4 C4
CHLY/EC PR7 * 96 B4
CLV/TH FY5 ....17 H5
LEYL PR25 ....83 F3
Johnsville Av *BPOOLS* FY4 ....39 E1
John William St *PRES* PR1 * 60 C3
Joyce Av *BPOOLE* FY3 ....33 F3
Jubilee Av *FUL/RIB* PR2 ....57 H2
PLF/KEOS FY6 ....13 E2
Jubilee Dr *CLV/TH* FY5 ....20 C1
Jubilee La *BPOOLS* FY4 ....39 H2
Jubilee La North *BPOOLS* FY4 ....39 G1
Jubilee Pl *CHLYE* PR6 ....93 G1
Jubilee Rd *BBR* PR5 ....79 F2
KIRK/FR/WAR PR4 ....76 A5
Jubilee Ter *KIRK/FR/WAR* PR4 ....54 C4
KIRK/FR/WAR PR4 * 56 A2
Jubilee Wy *LSTA* FY8 ....50 A3
Judeland *CHLY/EC* PR7 ....88 D5
Junction Rd *PRES* PR1 ....6 A4
June Av *BPOOLS* FY4 ....33 G4
June's Wk *KIRK/FR/WAR* PR4 ....76 A4
Juniper Cl *PLF/KEOS* FY6 ....13 E1
Juniper Cft *CHLYE* PR6 ....84 D3
Jutland St *PRES* PR1 ....7 H2

K

Kairnryan Cl *BISP* FY2 ....25 F2
Kane St *FUL/RIB* PR2 ....59 E2
Kay St *BPOOL* FY1 ....2 C7
PRES PR1 * 6 C4
Keasden Av *BPOOLS* FY4 ....38 D1
Keating Ct *FTWD* FY7 ....11 F3
Keats Av *KIRK/FR/WAR* PR4 ....53 G5
Keats Cl *CHLY/EC* PR7 ....90 C5
CLV/TH FY5 ....21 G2
Keele Cl *CLV/TH* FY5 ....21 G2
Keepers Ga *LSTA* FY8 ....50 B4
Keeper's Hey *CLV/TH* FY5 ....17 G5
Keith Gv *CLV/TH* FY5 ....20 D3
Kellet Acre *BBR* PR5 ....79 F2
Kellet Av *LEYL* PR25 ....84 A3
Kellet La *BBR* PR5 ....81 E3
Kellett St *CHLY/EC* PR7 * 93 F2
Kelmarsh Cl *BPOOLE* FY3 ....33 H3
Kelso Av *CLV/TH* FY5 ....20 D3
Kelsons Av *CLV/TH* FY5 ....22 A2
Kelverdale Rd *CLV/TH* FY5 ....21 F4
Kelvin Rd *CLV/TH* FY5 ....24 D1
Kem Mill La *CHLYE* PR6 ....85 E4
Kemp St *FTWD* FY7 ....11 H1
Kempton Av *BPOOLE* FY3 ....5 J1
Kendal Av *BPOOLE* FY3 ....29 F1
CLV/TH FY5 ....16 D5
Kendal Rd *LSTA* FY8 ....48 D2
Kendal St *PRES* PR1 ....6 D3
Kenilworth Av *FTWD* FY7 ....11 E3
Kenilworth Gdns *BPOOLS* FY4 ....38 B1
Kenilworth Rd *LSTA* FY8 ....49 F5
Kenmure Pl *PRES* PR1 ....59 H1
Kennet Dr *FUL/RIB* PR2 ....37 E5
Kennett Dr *LEYL* PR25 ....83 G2
Kennington Rd *FUL/RIB* PR2 ....46 A4
Kensington Av *PRES* PR1 ....58 D5
Kensington Gdns *BBR* PR5 ....73 H5
Kensington Rd *BPOOLE* FY3 ....3 G3
CHLY/EC PR7 ....93 E3
CLV/TH FY5 ....20 C1
LSTA FY8 ....63 G2
Kent Av *BBR* PR5 * 74 A3
CLV/TH FY5 ....17 E5
Kent Dr *LEYL* PR25 ....84 A2
Kentmere Av *BBR* PR5 ....74 A4
LEYL PR25 ....83 F1
Kentmere Dr *BPOOLS* FY4 ....34 A4
KIRK/FR/WAR PR4 ....76 C1
Kent Rd *BPOOL* FY1 ....4 D1
Kent's Cl *KIRK/FR/WAR* PR4 ....42 C1
Kent St *FTWD* FY7 ....11 H1
PRES PR1 ....59 H1
Kenwyn Av *BPOOLE* FY3 ....5 H1
Kershaw St *CHLYE* PR6 ....93 H2
Kerslea Av *PLF/KEOS* FY6 ....30 B2
Keston Gv *BPOOLS* FY4 ....38 C3
Kestrel Cl *CLV/TH* FY5 ....17 F4
Keswick Gv *PLF/KEOS* FY6 ....12 D1
Keswick Rd *BPOOL* FY1 ....4 E1
LSTA FY8 ....49 E3
Kevin Av *PLF/KEOS* FY6 ....26 D2
Kew Gdns *LEYL* PR25 ....83 G1
PRES PR1 ....58 D5
Kew Gv *CLV/TH* FY5 ....20 D3
Kidbrooke Av *BPOOLS* FY4 ....38 B4
Kiddlington Cl *BBR* PR5 ....79 H1
Kidsgrove *FUL/RIB* PR2 ....44 B3
Kielder Ct *LSTA* FY8 ....64 D2
Kilbane St *FTWD* FY7 ....11 F5
Kildare Av *CLV/TH* FY5 ....17 G5
Kildare Rd *BISP* FY2 ....24 D4
Kilgrimol Gdns *LSTA* FY8 ....48 C3
Kilkerran Cl *CHLYE* PR6 ....93 G2
Kilmory Pl *BISP* FY2 ....25 F2
Kilmuir Cl *FUL/RIB* PR2 * 46 C3
Kiln Cft *CHLYE* PR6 ....84 D1
Kilngate *BBR* PR5 ....73 H3
Kilnhouse La *LSTA* FY8 ....49 F2
Kiln La *PLF/KEOS* FY6 ....23 F2
Kilruddery Rd *PRES* PR1 ....72 C1
Kilsby Cl *BBR* PR5 ....74 B3
Kilshaw St *PRES* PR1 ....7 F1
Kilworth Height *FUL/RIB* PR2 ....45 F3
Kimberley Av *BPOOLS* FY4 ....38 D3
Kimberley Rd *FUL/RIB* PR2 ....59 E1
Kimberley St *CHLY/EC* PR7 ....96 B4
Kimberly Cl
KIRK/FR/WAR PR4 ....54 B5
Kincardine Av *BPOOLS* FY4 ....39 F2
Kincrag Pl *BISP* FY2 ....25 F1
Kincraig Rd *BISP* FY2 ....25 F1
King Edward Av *BISP* FY2 ....28 B1
LSTA FY8 ....62 D2
Kingfisher Dr *PLF/KEOS* FY6 ....25 H5
Kingfisher St *PRES* PR1 ....60 B1
King George Av *BISP* FY2 ....28 B1
Kingsbridge Cl *PRES* PR1 ....72 D5
Kings Cl *BPOOLE* FY3 ....30 C5
PLF/KEOS FY6 ....26 C4
Kingscote Dr *BPOOLE* FY3 ....3 J1
Kings Ct *LEYL* PR25 ....83 F3
Kings Crs *LEYL* PR25 ....83 F3
King's Cft *BBR* PR5 ....74 A1
Kingsdale Av *FUL/RIB* PR2 ....46 D3
Kingsdale Cl *BBR* PR5 ....74 C1
LEYL PR25 ....87 G1
Kings Dr *FUL/RIB* PR2 ....45 F3
Kingsfold Dr *PRES* PR1 ....72 B4
Kingshaven Dr *PRES* PR1 ....72 D5
Kingsland Gv *BPOOL* FY1 ....5 G3
Kingsley Cl *CLV/TH* FY5 ....21 G1
Kingsley Dr *CHLY/EC* PR7 ....92 D5
Kingsley Rd *BPOOLE* FY3 ....33 H3
KIRK/FR/WAR PR4 ....44 A2
Kingsmead *CHLY/EC* PR7 ....93 F5
Kingsmede *BPOOLS* FY4 ....39 E2
Kingsmere Av *LSTA* FY8 ....49 F2
Kingsmuir Av *FUL/RIB* PR2 * 46 D4
Kings Rd *CLV/TH* FY5 ....20 C2
LSTA FY8 ....62 B1
King's Sq *BPOOL* FY1 ....2 D5
Kingston Av *BPOOLS* FY4 ....38 C3
Kingston Dr *LSTA* FY8 ....50 B5
King St *BBR* PR5 ....79 G2
BPOOL FY1 ....2 D4
CHLY/EC PR7 ....93 G4
FTWD FY7 ....11 G2
LEYL PR25 ....83 F3
King's Wk *CLV/TH* FY5 ....16 D4
Kingsway *BBR* PR5 ....80 B1
BPOOLS FY4 ....38 C1
CHLY/EC PR7 ....88 B5
CLV/TH FY5 ....20 C2
FUL/RIB PR2 ....58 B1
LEYL PR25 ....82 D5
LSTA FY8 ....63 F2
PRES PR1 ....58 D5
Kingsway Av *GAR/LONG* PR3 ....36 B2
Kingsway West *PRES* PR1 ....71 H1
Kingswood *CHLY/EC* PR7 ....93 E5
Kingswood Cl *LSTA* FY8 ....63 H2
Kingswood Rd *LEYL* PR25 ....83 F2
Kingswood St *PRES* PR1 ....6 C4
Kinnerton Pl *CLV/TH* FY5 ....21 F4
Kinross Crs *BPOOLS* FY4 ....33 G4
Kintbury Rd *LSTA* FY8 ....62 C2
Kintour Rd *LSTA* FY8 ....50 C5
Kintyre Cl *BPOOLS* FY4 ....39 F1
Kipling Dr *BPOOLE* FY3 ....33 H3
Kirby Dr *KIRK/FR/WAR* PR4 ....54 B5
Kirby Rd *BPOOL* FY1 ....4 B3
Kirkby Av *CLV/TH* FY5 ....17 E5
LEYL PR25 ....84 B3
Kirkdale Av *LSTA* FY8 ....49 F4
Kirkgate *KIRK/FR/WAR* PR4 ....43 F3
Kirkham Av *BPOOL* FY1 ....5 H3
Kirkham By-Pass
KIRK/FR/WAR PR4 ....43 F4
Kirkham Cl *LEYL* PR25 ....82 C3
Kirkham Rd *KIRK/FR/WAR* PR4 ....43 H2
KIRK/FR/WAR PR4 ....54 A2
Kirkham St *PRES* PR1 ....6 D2
Kirkstall Av *BPOOL* FY1 ....5 J4
Kirkstall Cl *CHLY/EC* PR7 ....93 G5
Kirkstall Dr *CHLY/EC* PR7 ....93 G5
Kirkstall Rd *CHLY/EC* PR7 ....93 G5
Kirkstone Av *FTWD* FY7 ....10 D5
Kirkstone Dr *CLV/TH* FY5 ....24 C1
Kirkstone Rd *LSTA* FY8 ....48 D2
Kirton Crs *LSTA* FY8 ....50 A5
Kirton Pl *CLV/TH* FY5 ....21 E3
Kittiwake Cl *CLV/TH* FY5 ....21 F3
Kittlingborne Brow *BBR* PR5 ....74 D3

Kitty La *BPOOLS* FY4 ....39 H4
Knaresboro Av *BPOOLE* FY5 * 33 F2
Knaresborough Cl
 PLF/KEOS FY6 ....26 A2
Knebworth Cl *CHLYE* PR6 ....85 F2
Knightsbrdige Cl
 KIRK/FR/WAR PR4 ....42 C2
Knightsbridge Av *BPOOLS* FY6 ...38 D2
Knightsbridge Cl *LSTA* FY8 ....50 D5
Knights Cl *CLV/TH* FY5 ....21 F3
Knoll La *KIRK/FR/WAR* PR4 ....76 A5
Knot Acre *KIRK/FR/WAR* 77 H1
Knot La *BBR* PR5 ....74 B1
Knowle Av *BISP* FY2 ....28 C1
 CLV/TH FY5 ....21 E3
Knowles Rd *LSTA* FY8 ....49 E4
Knowles St *CHLY/EC* PR7 ....93 F4
 PRES PR1 ....60 D3
The Knowle *BISP* FY2 ....24 C5
Knowley Brow *CHLYE* PR6 ....89 H5
Knowsley Av *BPOOLE* FY3 ....5 H1
 LEYL PR25 ....5 H1
Knowsley Brow *CLV/TH* FY5 ....75 H4
Knowsley Crs *CLV/TH* FY5 ....22 C2
Knowsley Ga *FTWD* FY7 ....10 D2
Knowsley Rd *LEYL* PR25 ....83 H4
Knowsley St *PRES* PR1 ....7 H1
Knox Gv *BPOOL* FY1 ....5 F2
Knutsford Rd *BPOOLE* FY5 ....33 H3
Korea Rd *FUL/RIB* PR2 ....46 B3
Kumara Crs *BPOOLS* FY4 ....33 H4
Kylemore Av *BISP* FY2 ....24 D5
Kyston Cl *BPOOL* FY1 ....3 F1

L

Laburnum Av *BBR* PR5 ....79 G1
 LSTA FY8 ....64 C1
Laburnum Cl *PRES* PR1 ....46 C5
Laburnum Dr *FUL/RIB* PR2 ....36 C5
Laburnum Rd *CHLYE* PR6 ....89 G4
Laburnum St *BPOOLE* FY3 ....3 G1
Lacy Av *PRES* PR1 ....72 D4
Lady Acre *BBR* PR5 ....80 D1
Ladybower La *PLF/KEOS* FY6 .....25 H4
Lady Bower La *PLF/KEOS* FY6 .....25 H5
Lady Crosse Dr *CHLYE* PR6 ....89 F1
Lady Green La *FUL/RIB* PR2 ....57 C2
Ladyman St *PRES* PR1 ....6 B3
Lady Pl *BBR* PR5 ....74 B2
Ladysmith Rd *FUL/RIB* PR2 ....9 E2
Lady St *PRES* PR1 ....7 F2
Lady Well Dr *FUL/RIB* PR2 ....46 C1
Ladywell St *PRES* PR1 ....6 A1
Lagonda Dr *BPOOLS* FY4 ....40 D2
Laidley's Wk *FTWD* FY7 ....11 E1
Lakeland Gdns *CHLY/EC* PR7 .....92 D5
Lake Rd *LSTA* FY8 ....63 F3
Lake Rd North *LSTA* FY8 ....63 F2
Lakeside Av *CLV/TH* FY5 ....29 F4
Lakewood Av *CLV/TH* FY5 ....20 D3
Lamaleach Dr
 KIRK/FR/WAR PR4 ....54 A1
Lambert Cl *FUL/RIB* PR2 ....47 E5
Lambert Rd *FUL/RIB* PR2 ....47 E5
Lambs Hill Cl *CLV/TH* FY5 ....22 B3
Lamb's La *GAR/LONG* PR3 ....14 C2
Lambs Rd *CLV/TH* FY5 ....22 A3
Lanark Av *BISP* FY2 ....24 C1
Lancaster Av *CLV/TH* FY5 ....28 C1
 LEYL PR25 ....84 B3
 LSTA FY8 ....62 C2
Lancaster Cl *PLF/KEOS* FY6 ....12 D1
Lancaster Ga *FTWD* FY7 ....10 D5
Lancastergate *LEYL* PR25 ....83 E4
Lancaster La *LEYL* PR25 ....84 A3
Lancaster Rd *BPOOLE* FY5 ....33 G3
 GAR/LONG PR3 ....15 G1
 PLF/KEOS FY6 ....13 G5
 PRES PR1 ....7 F3
Lancaster Rd North *PRES* PR1 .....7 F1
Lancaster St *CHLY/EC* PR7 ....96 A4
Lanchester Ct
 CROS/BRETH PR26 ....86 C1
Lancia Crs *BPOOLS* FY4 ....41 E2
Landcrest Cl *KIRK/FR/WAR* PR4 ...54 B1
Land La *KIRK/FR/WAR* PR4 ....77 E3
Landseer Av *BISP* FY2 ....24 C3
Landseer St *PRES* PR1 ....60 C2
Landsmoor Dr
 KIRK/FR/WAR PR4 ....70 B5
Lanedale *KIRK/FR/WAR* PR4 ......70 B5
Lanefield Dr *CLV/TH* FY5 ....16 D5
The Lane *FUL/RIB* PR2 ....25 G4
Langcliffe Rd *FUL/RIB* PR2 ....47 E4
Langdale Cl *BBR* PR5 ....74 A5
 CLV/TH FY5 ....21 H2
 KIRK/FR/WAR PR4 ....54 A5
Langdale Crs *FUL/RIB* PR2 ....47 E5
Langdale Gv *CHLYE* PR6 ....85 E5
Langdale Pl *BPOOLS* FY4 ....33 H4
 FUL/RIB PR2 ....47 E5
 LSTA FY8 ....48 D5
Langden Crs *BBR* PR5 ....80 C2
Langden Dr *FUL/RIB* PR2 ....47 E5
Langdon Wy *BISP* FY2 ....24 C5
Langfield Av *BPOOLS* FY4 ....38 C3
Langford Rd *FUL/RIB* PR2 ....37 E5
Langholm Cl *LEYL* PR25 ....82 C4
Langholme Rd *PRES* PR1 ....71 H2
Langport Cl *FUL/RIB* PR2 ....37 E5
Lang St *BPOOL* FY1 ....2 D2
Langton Av *CHLY/EC* PR7 ....90 C5
Langton Cl *CHLY/EC* PR7 ....90 C5
 CROS/BRETH PR26 ....82 B4
Langton St *PRES* PR1 ....6 B5
Langwood *FTWD* FY7 ....11 E4
Lansborough Cl
 CROS/BRETH PR26 ....82 A4

Lansdowne Pl *BPOOL* FY1 ....2 B2
Lansdowne Rd
 KIRK/FR/WAR PR4 ....42 D1
 LSTA FY8 ....63 G1
Lansdown Hl *FUL/RIB* PR2 ....45 E1
The Lanterns *FUL/RIB* PR2 ....26 B5
Lappet Gv *KIRK/FR/WAR* PR4 .....44 A3
Lapwing Rw *LSTA* FY8 ....50 C4
The Lapwings *PLF/KEOS* FY6 .....25 H5
Larbreck Rd *BPOOLE* FY3 ....3 H1
Larch Av *CHLYE* PR6 ....89 H5
Larch Cl *KIRK/FR/WAR* PR4 ....67 F1
 PLF/KEOS FY6 ....13 E1
Larch Dr *KIRK/FR/WAR* PR4 * 67 F1
Larches Av *FUL/RIB* PR2 ....58 B2
Larches La *FUL/RIB* PR2 ....58 B2
Larch Ga *BBR* PR5 ....75 H4
Larchgate *FUL/RIB* PR2 ....46 C1
Larch Gv *BBR* PR5 ....74 C5
Larchwood Cl *LSTA* FY8 ....58 A2
Larchwood Crs *LEYL* PR25 ....82 D3
Lark Av *PRES* PR1 ....72 D2
Lark Ct *FTWD* FY7 ....10 D5
Larkfield *CHLY/EC* PR7 ....90 A4
Larkhill *BBR* PR5 ....75 E5
Larkhill Rd *BPOOL* FY1 ....2 D3
 PRES PR1 ....7 K5
Larkholme La *FTWD* FY7 ....11 E5
Larkholme La *FTWD* FY7 ....11 E5
Larkholme Pde *FTWD* FY7 ....10 D5
Latham Av *BPOOLE* FY3 ....5 J2
Latham St *PRES* PR1 ....7 G6
Latimer Dr *KIRK/FR/WAR* PR4 ....77 C1
Lauderdale Av *CLV/TH* FY5 ....20 D3
Lauderdale Rd *FUL/RIB* PR2 ......26 C6
Laundry Rd North *BPOOLS* FY4 ...39 G2
Laurel Av *BPOOL* FY1 ....5 H4
 CHLY/EC PR7 ....87 G4
 FTWD FY7 ....17 F1
 FUL/RIB PR2 ....64 C1
Laurel Bank Av *FUL/RIB* PR2 ....45 E5
Laurel Dr *CLV/TH* FY5 ....21 H4
The Laurels *CHLY/EC* PR7 ....96 C2
 PLF/KEOS FY6 ....26 D4
Laurel St *PRES* PR1 ....7 H4
Laurier Av *BPOOLS* FY4 ....38 C2
Lauriston Cl *BPOOLS* FY4 ....39 G2
Lavender Cl *FUL/RIB* PR2 ....7 J2
Lavender Gv *CHLY/EC* PR7 ....93 F5
Laverton Rd *FUL/RIB* PR2 ....62 C1
Lawnswood Av *PLF/KEOS* FY6 ....25 G5
Lawnswood Crs *BPOOLE* FY3 .....34 A3
Lawn Tennis Cs *BPOOLS* FY4 .....38 D5
Lawnwood Av *CLV/TH* FY5 ....22 B4
Lawrence Av *BBR* PR5 ....74 A4
 PRES PR1 ....49 G4
 PRES PR1 ....73 G1
Lawrence La *CHLY/EC* PR7 ....90 B3
Lawrence Rd *CHLY/EC* PR7 ......93 E5
Lawrence Rw *FTWD* FY7 * 11 G2
Lawrence St *BPOOLS* FY4 ....4 B6
 FUL/RIB PR2 ....45 F5
Lawson Rd *BPOOLS* FY4 ....33 G2
 LSTA FY8 ....49 C1
Lawsons Ct *CLV/TH* FY5 ....22 A3
Lawsons Rd *CLV/TH* FY5 ....22 A3
Lawson St *CHLYE* PR6 ....93 H2
 PRES PR1 ....7 F2
Laxey Gv *PRES* PR1 ....46 D5
Laycock Ga *BPOOLS* FY4 ....3 G2
Layton Rd *BPOOLE* FY3 ....58 A2
 FUL/RIB PR2 ....60 A2
Lazenby Av *FTWD* FY7 ....10 C4
Leach Crs *LSTA* FY8 ....49 F1
Leach La *LSTA* FY8 ....49 E1
Leach Pl *BBR* PR5 ....75 F5
Leadale Cl *FUL/RIB* PR2 ....57 H1
Leadale Gn *LEYL* PR25 ....82 C5
Leadale Rd *LEYL* PR25 ....82 C5
Leaford Av *BPOOLE* FY3 ....29 E2
Leafy Cl *LEYL* PR25 ....83 G5
Leagram Crs *FUL/RIB* PR2 ....47 F5
Lea La *KIRK/FR/WAR* PR4 ....56 D1
Leamington Rd *BPOOL* FY1 ....2 F5
 LSTA FY8 ....49 E5
Leander Av *PLF/KEOS* FY6 ....26 B5
Lea Rd *CHLYE* PR6 ....89 F2
Leavesley Rd *BPOOL* FY1 ....28 C2
Lea Way Cl *CLV/TH* FY5 ....21 G4
Leckhampton Rd *BPOOL* FY1 .....28 B2
Ledbury Rd *BPOOLS* FY4 ....29 G3
Leeds Rd *BPOOL* FY1 ....3 F5
Leehouse Dr *PLF/KEOS* FY6 ......30 B2
Leek St *PRES* PR1 ....61 E3
Lee Rd *BPOOLS* FY4 ....33 H5
Leesands Cl *FUL/RIB* PR2 ....46 B5
Leeson Av *CHLY/EC* PR7 ....96 A1
Leeward Rd *FUL/RIB* PR2 ....58 B3
Leicester Av *CLV/TH* FY5 ....20 D1
Leicester Ga *CLV/TH* FY5 ....21 E1
Leicester Rd *FUL/RIB* PR2 ....59 H2
Leigh Brow *PRES* PR1 ....73 G4
Leigh House Ctyd *BBR* PR5 * 73 H3
Leigh Rw *CHLY/EC* PR7 ....93 F3
Leighton Av *FTWD* FY7 ....10 D3
Leighton St *PRES* PR1 ....6 B4
Leith Av *CLV/TH* FY5 ....20 D2
Lennon St *CHLY/EC* PR7 ....93 F3
Lennox Ct *BPOOLS* FY4 ....38 D1
Lennox Ga *BPOOLS* FY4 ....38 D1
Lennox St *PRES* PR1 ....7 G5
The Lenns *CLV/TH* FY5 ....63 F1
Lennet Av *BISP* FY2 ....29 H4
Linnet La *LSTA* FY8 ....50 C4
Linnet St *PRES* PR1 ....60 B1
Leo Case Ct *PRES* PR1 ....60 D4
Leopold Gv *BPOOL* FY1 ....2 C5
Leslie Av *KIRK/FR/WAR* PR4 ......22 A2
Letchworth Dr *CHLY/EC* PR7 .....93 E4
Letchworth Wks *CHLY/EC* PR7 ...93 E4
Leven Av *FTWD* FY7 ....10 D5
Levens Cl *PLF/KEOS* FY6 ....30 B2

Levens Dr *LEYL* PR25 ....84 A2
 PLF/KEOS FY6 ....30 B1
Levensgarth Av *FUL/RIB* PR2 ....37 E5
Levens Gv *BPOOL* FY1 ....4 B4
Levens St *PRES* PR1 ....60 D2
Lever House La *LEYL* PR25 ....83 H2
Levine Av *BPOOLS* FY4 ....33 G4
Lewtas St *BPOOL* FY1 ....2 C3
Lex St *PRES* PR1 ....60 C3
Leyburn Av *BISP* FY2 ....24 C2
 FTWD FY7 ....11 E4
Leyburn Cl *FUL/RIB* PR2 ....47 E5
Leyfield *PRES* PR1 ....72 C4
Leyfield Cl *BPOOLE* FY3 ....29 C1
Leyfield Rd *LEYL* PR25 ....85 E5
Leyland La *CROS/BRETH* PR26 ...86 B4
 LEYL PR25 ....82 C5
 LEYL PR25 ....86 C1
Leyland Rd *PRES* PR1 ....49 G4
 PRES PR1 ....72 C1
The Leylands *LSTA* FY8 ....64 A4
Leyland Wy *LEYL* PR25 ....83 E5
Leys Rd *BISP* FY2 ....28 D1
Leyton Av *LEYL* PR25 ....82 C5
Library Rd *CHLYE* PR6 ....81 E5
Library St *CHLY/EC* PR7 ....93 F5
 PRES PR1 ....7 G4
Lichen Cl *CHLY/EC* PR7 ....96 A1
Lichfield Rd *BPOOL* FY1 ....28 C2
 CHLY/EC PR7 ....93 F4
Lidget Av *FUL/RIB* PR2 ....57 C2
Liege Rd *LEYL* PR25 ....83 F4
Lightbown Av *BPOOLS* FY3 ......5 H2
Lightburne Av *LSTA* FY8 ....62 C1
Lightfoot Cl *GAR/LONG* PR3 .....36 C5
Lightfoot Green La
 KIRK/FR/WAR PR4 ....36 A5
Lightfoot La *KIRK/FR/WAR* PR4 ..44 B1
Lighthurst Av *CHLY/EC* PR7 .....93 F5
Lighthurst La *CHLY/EC* PR7 ......93 G5
Lightwood Av *CLV/TH* FY5 ....4 E7
 KIRK/FR/WAR PR4 ....36 A5
Lilac Av *BPOOL* FY1 ....5 F5
 LSTA FY8 ....64 C1
 PRES PR1 ....73 G1
Lilac Cl *KIRK/FR/WAR* PR4 ....66 C1
Lilac Gv *PLF/KEOS* FY6 ....12 C1
 PRES PR1 ....60 A1
Lily Gv *PRES* PR1 ....46 C5
Lily St *BPOOL* FY1 ....2 E4
Lima Rd *LSTA* FY8 ....49 G5
Limbrick Rd *CHLYE* PR6 ....93 H5
Lime Av *KIRK/FR/WAR* PR4 ....54 B1
Limebrest Av *CLV/TH* FY5 ....22 B4
Lime Cha *GAR/LONG* PR3 ....36 A5
Limechase Cl *BPOOLS* FY4 ....39 G2
Lime Cl *PRES* PR1 ....71 H2
Lime Gv *BISP* FY2 ....29 F5
 CHLY/EC PR7 ....95 F5
 CLV/TH FY5 ....22 A3
 FUL/RIB PR2 ....58 B1
 LSTA FY8 ....65 F2
 PLF/KEOS FY6 ....26 C5
Limerick Rd *BISP* FY2 ....24 D4
Lime St *CHLY/EC* PR7 ....87 H5
Linadale Av *CLV/TH* FY5 ....21 H2
Lincoln Av *CLV/TH* FY5 ....21 E1
 FTWD FY7 ....11 E3
Lincoln Cha *FUL/RIB* PR2 ....57 C2
 BBR PR5 ....81 E1
Lincoln Cl *BPOOLS* FY4 ....2 E5
Lincoln St *PRES* PR1 ....7 J1
Lincoln Wk *PRES* PR1 * 7 J1
Lindale Gdns *BPOOLS* FY4 ......39 E2
Lindale La *PLF/KEOS* FY6 ....26 A4
Lindbeck Rd *BPOOLS* FY4 ....34 A4
Lindel La *PLF/KEOS* FY6 ....11 E4
Linden Av *FTWD* FY7 ....11 E4
Linden Av *CLV/TH* FY5 ....21 F1
 CLV/TH FY5 ....73 G5
Linden Dr *BBR* PR5 ....21 G5
Linden Gn *CLV/TH* FY5 ....47 E5
Linden Gv *CHLYE* PR6 ....89 G4
 FUL/RIB PR2 ....47 E5
Linden Ms *LSTA* FY8 ....49 F1
Linden Pl *BPOOLS* FY4 ....25 E4
Linderbreck La *PLF/KEOS* FY6 ...30 C2
Lindle Av *KIRK/FR/WAR* PR4 .....71 F4
Lindle Cft *CLV/TH* FY5 ....71 F4
Lindle Crs *KIRK/FR/WAR* PR4 ....71 F4
Lindle La *KIRK/FR/WAR* PR4 .....71 F4
Lindley Cft *CLV/TH* FY5 ....71 G1
Lindley St *BBR* PR5 ....79 G1
Lindsay Av *BPOOLE* FY3 ....5 E2
 LEYL PR25 ....83 G3
 PRES PR1 ....49 H5
 PLF/KEOS FY6 ....25 E4
Lindsay Ct *LSTA* FY8 * 38 B4
Lindsay Dr *CHLY/EC* PR7 ....92 D5
Linfield Ter *BPOOLS* FY4 ....5 E5
Lingfield Rd *FTWD* FY7 * 11 F4
Lingwell Cl *CHLYE* PR6 ....89 F2
Links Fld *FUL/RIB* PR2 ....45 E5
Links Ga *CLV/TH* FY5 ....22 B5
 FUL/RIB PR2 ....45 E5
 LSTA FY8 ....49 G5
Links Rd *BPOOL* FY1 ....5 F5
 LSTA FY8 ....62 B1
 PLF/KEOS FY6 ....12 B1
 PRES PR1 ....46 D5
The Links *CLV/TH* FY5 ....21 E5
Links Vw *CLV/TH* FY5 ....63 F1
Linnet Cl *BPOOLS* FY4 ....29 G1
Linnet Cft *CHLYE* PR6 ....84 D2
Lion La *PRES* PR1 ....72 D5
Liptroft Rd *CHLY/EC* PR7 ....92 D5
Little Acre *CLV/TH* FY5 ....22 B4
Lowcross Rd *PLF/KEOS* FY6 .....26 C5

Little Banks Cl *BBR* PR5 * 81 E5
Little Carr La *CHLY/EC* PR7 ......93 C5
Little Cl *CROS/BRETH* PR26 ......82 D1
 PRES PR1 ....72 B5
Little Poulton La
 PLF/KEOS FY6 ....26 D4
Little Tongues La
 PLF/KEOS FY6 ....13 F2
Little Twining
 KIRK/FR/WAR PR4 ....76 B2
Liverpool New Rd
 KIRK/FR/WAR PR4 ....76 A5
Liverpool Old Rd
 KIRK/FR/WAR PR4 ....76 A3
 KIRK/FR/WAR PR4 ....3 F5
Liverpool Rd *CHLY/EC* PR7 ......3 F5
 KIRK/FR/WAR PR4 ....76 A3
 PRES PR1 ....6 A7
Livesey St *LSTA* FY8 ....64 B5
 PRES PR1 ....7 J4
Livet Av *BPOOLS* FY4 ....38 D1
Livingstone Rd *BPOOL* FY1 ......2 D7
Lochinch Cl *BPOOLS* FY3 ....39 G2
Lockerbie Av *CLV/TH* FY5 ....20 D4
Lockhart Cl *PRES* PR1 ....59 H1
Lockhurst Av *CLV/TH* FY5 ....21 F4
Lockside Rd *FUL/RIB* PR2 ....58 B3
Lockwood Av *FUL/RIB* PR2 ......54 B5
Lodge Cl *BBR* PR5 ....74 C5
 CLV/TH FY5 ....20 C5
 KIRK/FR/WAR PR4 ....54 B5
Lodge Ct *BPOOLE* FY5 ....30 B5
Lodge La *CROS/BRETH* PR26 ....78 D3
 KIRK/FR/WAR PR4 ....54 B4
 KIRK/FR/WAR PR4 ....65 G1
 PLF/KEOS FY6 ....27 H5
Lodge St *PRES* PR1 ....6 C5
Lodore Rd *BPOOLS* FY4 ....38 C2
Lofthos Av *BPOOLS* FY4 ....32 D5
Lomond Av *BPOOLE* FY3 ....33 F3
 LSTA FY8 ....63 E1
Lomond Cl *CHLY/EC* PR7 ....88 A3
London Rd *BPOOLE* FY3 ....5 J1
 PRES PR1 ....7 K4
London St *FTWD* FY7 ....11 G1
London Wy *BBR* PR5 ....73 H5
Long Acre *BBR* PR5 ....81 F4
Long Acre Rd *FUL/RIB* PR2 ......64 B2
Longbrook Av *BBR* PR5 ....74 B4
Long Butts *PRES* PR1 ....72 C4
Long Copse *CHLY/EC* PR7 ....32 C1
Long Cft *KIRK/FR/WAR* PR4 .....70 D5
Long Cft Meadow
 CHLY/EC PR7 ....89 E5
Longfield *FUL/RIB* PR2 ....37 E5
 PRES PR1 ....72 B1
Longfield Av *CHLY/EC* PR7 ......77 C3
 PLF/KEOS FY6 ....26 D5
Longfield Mnr *CHLY/EC* PR7 .....92 D5
Longfield Pl *PLF/KEOS* FY6 ......26 D5
Longford Av *BISP* FY2 ....25 E2
Longhouse La *PLF/KEOS* FY6 ....30 B2
Longley Cl *FUL/RIB* PR2 ....37 E5
Long Meadow *CHLY/EC* PR7 ....92 D5
 KIRK/FR/WAR PR4 ....76 A5
Longmeadow La *CLV/TH* FY5 ....22 B5
Longmeanygate
 CROS/BRETH PR26 ....82 A1
Long Moss La
 KIRK/FR/WAR PR4 ....77 F3
Long Moss Mdw
 KIRK/FR/WAR PR4 ....77 C3
Longridge Av *BPOOLS* FY4 ......39 E3
Longridge Rd *FUL/RIB* PR2 ......47 F4
Longsands La *FUL/RIB* PR2 ......46 D2
Longton Av *CLV/TH* FY5 ....21 H2
Longton By-Pass
 KIRK/FR/WAR PR4 ....71 F4
Longton Rd *BPOOL* FY1 ....76 B5
Longton St *CHLYE* PR6 ....93 H2
Longway *BPOOLS* FY4 ....33 F5
Longworth Av *CHLY/EC* PR7 .....95 E4
Longworth Rd *BBR* PR5 ....74 B4
 CHLY/EC PR7 ....95 E4
 PRES PR1 ....84 B5
Lonsdale Av *FTWD* FY7 ....11 E3
Lonsdale Cha *BBR* PR5 ....79 F1
Lonsdale Cl *LEYL* PR25 ....87 F1
Lonsdale Crs *FTWD* FY7 ....11 E3
Lonsdale Ms *BBR* PR5 * 79 F1
Lonsdale Rd *FUL/RIB* PR2 ....45 G2
Lord's Av *BBR* PR5 ....79 G2
Lords Cft *CHLYE* PR6 ....84 D2
Lord's La *PRES* PR1 ....72 D5
Lord St *BPOOL* FY1 ....2 C5
 CHLY/EC PR7 ....93 G5
 CHLYE PR6 ....93 C5
 FTWD FY7 ....11 H2
 LSTA FY8 ....48 D4
 PRES PR1 ....7 G5
Lord's Wk *PRES* PR1 ....7 H1
Lorne Av *FUL/RIB* PR2 ....45 H2
Lorne Rd *BISP* FY2 ....24 C5
Lorne St *CHLY/EC* PR7 ....93 F5
 LSTA FY8 ....64 C2
Lorton Cl *FUL/RIB* PR2 ....45 H2
Lostock Cft *BBR* PR5 ....79 C2
Lostock Gdns *BPOOLS* FY4 ......38 D2
Lostock La *BBR* PR5 ....79 C2
Lostock Meadow *CHLYE* PR6 ....79 C2
Lostock Rd *BBR* PR5 ....79 C2
Lostock Vw *BBR* PR5 ....79 G2
Lothian Av *FTWD* FY7 ....10 D5
Lothian Pl *BPOOLS* FY4 ....25 E2
Lotus Dr *BPOOLS* FY4 ....46 C2
Loughrigg Ter *BPOOLS* FY4 .....34 A4
Louise St *BPOOL* FY1 ....3 F5
Lourdes Av *BBR* PR5 ....73 F5
Lovat Rd *PRES* PR1 ....59 H1
Lowcroft *KIRK/FR/WAR* PR4 .....36 A2

Lower Bank Rd *FUL/RIB* PR2 ....45 H5
Lower Burgh Rd *CHLY/EC* PR7 ...96 D1
Lower Burgh Wy
 CHLY/EC PR7 ....96 D1
Lower Copthurst
 CHLYE PR6 ....85 H4
Lower Copthurst La
 CHLYE PR6 ....85 H5
Lower Rld *CROS/BRETH* PR26 ...79 E3
Lower Gn *FUL/RIB* PR2 ....26 C4
Lower Greenfield *FUL/RIB* PR2 ..44 D4
Lower Hey *KIRK/FR/WAR* PR4 ....70 B5
Lower House Rd *LEYL* PR25 .....25 G4
Lower Lawson *KIRK/FR/WAR* PR4 .54 B1
Lower Lune St *FTWD* FY7 ....11 H1
Lower Wk *CLV/TH* FY5 ....84 B5
Lowesby Cl *BBR* PR5 ....74 B3
Lowesway *BPOOLS* FY4 ....5 K7
 CLV/TH FY5 ....
Lowfield Cl *KIRK/FR/WAR* PR4 ...55 F1
Lowfield Rd *BPOOLS* FY4 ....39 F1
Low Gn *LEYL* PR25 ....83 E3
Lowick Cl *BBR* PR5 ....75 H2
Lowick Dr *PLF/KEOS* FY6 ....30 B1
Lowland Wy *BISP* FY2 ....25 F1
Low Moor Rd *BISP* FY2 ....25 E4
Lowood Gv *FUL/RIB* PR2 ....57 H2
Lowrey Ter *BPOOL* FY1 ....4 C4
Lowry Cl *BBR* PR5 ....79 F2
Lowther Av *BISP* FY2 ....24 C5
Lowther Crs
 CROS/BRETH PR26 ....82 C2
Lowther Dr *CROS/BRETH* PR26 ..82 C2
Lowther Rd *FTWD* FY7 ....11 F2
Lowther St *PRES* PR1 ....7 F5
Lowthian Ter *LSTA* FY8 ....64 B5
Lowthorpe Crs *PRES* PR1 ....60 B1
Lowthorpe Rd *PRES* PR1 ....60 B1
Lowton Rd *LSTA* FY8 ....49 G3
Loxham Gdns *BPOOLS* FY4 ......38 D2
Loxley Gn *FUL/RIB* PR2 ....46 C2
Loxley Pl *CLV/TH* FY5 ....21 E5
Loxley Pl East *CLV/TH* FY5 ......21 E5
Lucas Av *CHLY/EC* PR7 ....92 A5
Lucas La *CHLYE* PR6 ....89 F1
Lucerne Rd *FUL/RIB* PR2 ....46 C4
Ludlow Gv *BISP* FY2 ....25 F5
Lulworth Av *BPOOLE* FY3 ....33 G3
 FUL/RIB PR2 ....
Lulworth Pl *BBR* PR5 ....74 A4
Lulworth Rd *FUL/RIB* PR2 * 46 A4
Lund St *PRES* PR1 ....7 F2
Lune Cl *KIRK/FR/WAR* PR4 ....43 F3
Lunedale Av *BPOOL* FY1 ....4 E5
Lune Dr *LEYL* PR25 ....84 B2
Lune Gv *BPOOL* FY1 ....5 F1
 BPOOL FY1 ....
Lune Rd *FTWD* FY7 ....11 F2
Lunesdale Ct *LSTA* FY8 ....50 A4
Lunesdale Rd
 KIRK/FR/WAR PR4 ....43 E3
Lune St *PRES* PR1 ....6 E4
Lune Vw *PLF/KEOS* FY6 ....12 C1
Lupin Cl *CHLYE* PR6 ....89 E2
Lupton St *CHLY/EC* PR7 ....93 H4
Luton Rd *CLV/TH* FY5 ....20 D3
Lutwidge Av *PRES* PR1 ....60 C2
Lyceum Av *BPOOLE* FY3 ....3 G6
Lychfield *BBR* PR5 ....80 B2
Lychgate *PRES* PR1 ....7 H3
Lyddesdale Av *CLV/TH* FY5 ......20 D3
Lydd Gv *CLV/TH* FY5 ....21 F5
Lydgate *CHLY/EC* PR7 ....92 D5
Lydiate La *CHLY/EC* PR7 ....90 A1
 LEYL PR25 ....79 H5
Lydric Av *BBR* PR5 ....75 H4
Lyme Gv *PLF/KEOS* FY6 ....12 C1
Lyncroft Crs *BPOOLE* FY3 ....5 J6
Lyndale Av *BBR* PR5 ....73 H5
Lyndale Cl *LEYL* PR25 ....87 G1
Lyndale Gv *BBR* PR5 ....73 H4
Lyndeth Cl *FUL/RIB* PR2 ....47 E2
Lyndhurst Av *BPOOLS* FY4 ......5 F6
Lyndhurst Dr *FUL/RIB* PR2 ......58 A1
Lynn Gv *BPOOL* FY1 ....
Lynn Pl *FUL/RIB* PR2 * 60 D1
Lynton Av *BPOOLS* FY4 ....32 D5
 LEYL PR25 ....83 H4
Lynton Ct *FTWD* FY7 ....16 C1
Lynwood Av *BPOOLE* FY3 ....29 E2
Lynwood Dr *PLF/KEOS* FY6 ......19 G2
Lyons La *CHLY/EC* PR7 ....93 G5
Lyons La South *CHLY/EC* PR7 ...93 G5
Lythall Av *LSTA* FY8 ....65 E2
Lytham Rd *BPOOL* FY1 ....4 C3
 BPOOLS FY4 ....38 B1
 FUL/RIB PR2 ....65 G2
 KIRK/FR/WAR PR4 ....
 LSTA FY8 ....51 H2
Lytham St *CHLYE* PR6 ....93 H3
Lythcoe Av *FUL/RIB* PR2 ....45 E4

Macauley Av *BPOOLS* FY4 ....33 E5
Macbeth Rd *FTWD* FY7 ....11 E2
Mackay Crt *CHLYE* PR6 ....93 G2
Mackenzie Cl *CHLYE* PR6 ....93 G2
Maclaren Cl *BPOOLE* FY3 ....30 B5
Maddy St *PRES* PR1 ....6 A2
Madison Av *BISP* FY2 ....24 B2
Mafeking Rd *FUL/RIB* PR2 ....59 E1
Magdalen Av *CLV/TH* FY5 ....20 D5
Magnolia Cl *FUL/RIB* PR2 ....46 C2
Magnolia Dr *LEYL* PR25 ....84 B2
Magnolia Rd *PRES* PR1 ....72 A3
Maida V *CLV/TH* FY5 ....20 D4
Main Dr *PLF/KEOS* FY6 ....26 C4
Mains La *PLF/KEOS* FY6 ....26 D2
Main Sprit Weind *PRES* PR1 .....7 G4

Mainway Ct *BBR* PR5 * 80 B1
Maitland Av *CLV/TH* FY5 ....20 D5
Maitland Cl *PRES* PR1 ....60 C3
Maitland St *PRES* PR1 ....60 D5
Malcolm Pl *FTWD* FY7 ....11 E2
Malcolm St *PRES* PR1 ....80 D2
Malden St *LEYL* PR25 ....83 F5
Maldern Av *PLF/KEOS* FY6 ....26 A2
Maldon Pl *FUL/RIB* PR2 ....60 D1
Malham Av *BPOOLS* FY4 ....5 G7
Malham Pl *FUL/RIB* PR2 ....47 E3
Mallard Cl *CLV/TH* FY5 ....17 G5
LEYL PR25 ....82 B4
Mallard Ct *BPOOLE* FY3 ....29 H4
Mallards Wk *BBR* PR5 ....80 D4
Mallom Av *PLF/KEOS* FY6 ....92 B1
Mallowdale *CLV/TH* FY5 ....17 G5
The Mall *FUL/RIB* PR2 ....81 E1
LSTA FY8 ....50 A4
Maltby Pl *BPOOLS* FY4 ....5 K4
Malthouse Ct *FUL/RIB* PR2 ....6 B1
Malthouse Wy *PRES* PR1 ....72 C3
The Maitings *CLV/TH* FY5 ....12 C1
KIRK/FR/WAR PR4 ....76 A1
Malton Dr *BBR* PR5 ....79 F2
Malvern Av *BPOOL* FY1 ....5 F5
PLF/KEOS FY6 ....19 G2
Malvern Cl *BBR* PR5 ....79 H1
Malvern Rd *LSTA* FY8 ....63 G1
PRES PR1 ....7 K7
Malvern St *PRES* PR1 ....73 G1
Manchester Rd *BPOOLE* FY3 .....3 G3
PRES PR1 ....7 H4
Manning Rd *PRES* PR1 ....61 G2
Manor Av *FUL/RIB* PR2 ....86 B4
PRES PR1 ....72 A2
Manor Ct *FUL/RIB* PR2 ....44 D1
Manorcroft *KIRK/FR/WAR* PR4 ..76 A1
Manor Dr *CLV/TH* FY5 ....20 D1
KIRK/FR/WAR PR4 ....43 G4
Manor Pk *PRES* PR1 ....71 H2
Manor House Cl
CROS/BRETH PR26 ....82 A4
Manor House Crs *PRES* PR1 ......46 B5
Manor House La *PRES* PR1 ....46 B5
Manor La *PRES* PR1 ....72 A2
Manor Pk *PRES* PR1 ....46 C5
Manor Rd *BPOOL* FY1 ....5 B4
CHLYE PR6 ....85 E1
FTWD FY7 ....11 E1
KIRK/FR/WAR PR4 ....43 F1
Mansfield Dr *BBR* PR5 ....75 H1
Mansfield Rd *BPOOLE* FY3 ....28 D2
Manston Gv *FUL/RIB* PR2 ....92 D3
Maple Av *BPOOLS* FY4 ....3 C5
CLV/TH FY5 ....22 A4
FTWD FY7 * 17 F1
Maplebank *FUL/RIB* PR2 ....57 G2
Maple Cl *KIRK/FR/WAR* PR4 .....55 F1
Maple Ct *LEYL* PR25 * 84 A1
Maple Crs *PRES* PR1 ....72 A2
Maple Dr *BBR* PR5 ....74 C5
PLF/KEOS FY6 ....26 B5
Maple Gv *CHLYE* PR6 ....89 G4
FUL/RIB PR2 ....47 G4
KIRK/FR/WAR PR4 ....53 F5
PRES PR1 ....72 A2
Maplewood Av *PLF/KEOS* FY6 ...13 E1
Maplewood Cl *LEYL* PR25 ....82 D4
LSTA FY8 ....64 A2
Maplewood Dr *CLV/TH* FY5 ....20 C4
Marathon Pl
CROS/BRETH PR26 ....82 B1
Marchwood Rd *BPOOLE* FY3 .....29 H2
Marcroft Av *BPOOLS* FY4 ....39 E1
Mardale Av *BPOOLS* FY4 ....34 A4
Mardale Crs *LEYL* PR25 ....83 G5
Mardale Rd *PRES* PR1 ....61 G2
Maresfield Rd *PRES* PR1 ....72 C1
Marewood *CHLY/EC* PR7 ....89 E5
Margaret Rd *PRES* PR1 ....72 D2
Margaret St *PRES* PR1 ....7 G2
Margate Av *BPOOLS* FY4 ....5 G2
Margate Rd *FUL/RIB* PR2 ....44 C4
LSTA FY8 ....49 F3
Marilyn Av *BBR* PR5 ....79 G1
Marina Av *BPOOL* FY1 ....5 F5
BPOOLS FY4 ....30 B2
Marina Cl *BBR* PR5 ....73 F5
Marina Dr *BBR* PR5 ....73 F5
FUL/RIB PR2 ....45 G1
Marina Gv *BBR* PR5 ....73 F5
Marina Ms *FTWD* FY7 ....11 H5
Marine Dr *LSTA* FY8 ....63 F5
Marine Pde *FTWD* FY7 ....10 C5
Mariners Cl *FTWD* FY7 ....11 E5
Mariners Wy *FUL/RIB* PR2 ....58 C5
Marino Cl *CLV/TH* FY5 ....22 B4
Maritime St *PRES* PR1 ....11 F4
Maritime Wy *FUL/RIB* PR2 ....58 B4
Mark St *PRES* PR1 ....73 G5
Market Buildings *LSTA* FY8 * 49 F5
Market Hall *PRES* PR1 * 7 F3
Market Pl *PLF/KEOS* FY6 ....26 B4
PRES PR1 ....7 F4
Market Sq *LSTA* FY8 ....64 B3
Market St *BPOOL* FY1 ....2 B4
CHLY/EC PR7 ....90 B1
KIRK/FR/WAR PR4 ....42 C2
PLF/KEOS FY6 ....23 G2
PRES PR1 ....7 F3
Market St West *PRES* PR1 ....6 E5
Markham St *FUL/RIB* PR2 ....59 E2
Markland St *PRES* PR1 ....6 C4
Mark's Av *CROS/BRETH* PR26 ...78 D4
Marl Av *PRES* PR1 ....72 A2
Marlboro Av *BPOOLE* FY3 ....3 G6
Marlborough Av *CLV/TH* FY5 .....16 C4
KIRK/FR/WAR PR4 ....43 F5
FUL/RIB PR2 ....36 C5
Marlborough Rd *LSTA* FY8 ....49 E2
Marlborough St *CHLYE* PR6 ......93 H1
Marl Cft *PRES* PR1 ....72 C4

Marlfield *KIRK/FR/WAR* PR4 .....76 A5
Marlfield Cl *FUL/RIB* PR2 ....44 B2
Marl Hill Crs *FUL/RIB* PR2 ....61 G1
Marlhill Rd *BPOOLE* FY3 ....29 G2
Marquis Dr *KIRK/FR/WAR* PR4 ..54 C4
Marquis St *KIRK/FR/WAR* PR4 ..42 D3
Marron Cl *LEYL* PR25 ....82 C6
Marsden Cl *CHLY/EC* PR7 ....5 F7
Marsden Rd *BPOOLS* FY4 ....5 F4
Marsden St *KIRK/FR/WAR* PR4 ..43 F5
Marsett Pl *FUL/RIB* PR2 ....47 E3
Marshall Gv *FUL/RIB* PR2 ....44 C4
Marshall's Brow *PRES* PR1 ....72 D5
Marshall's Cl *PRES* PR1 ....72 D5
Marshdale Rd *FUL/RIB* PR2 ....39 F2
Marsh Dr *KIRK/FR/WAR* PR4 .....54 D4
Marsh La *KIRK/FR/WAR* PR4 .....54 D4
PLF/KEOS FY6 ....23 G5
PRES PR1 ....6 A4
Marsh Rd *CLV/TH* FY5 ....21 G2
Marsh Vw *KIRK/FR/WAR* PR4 ....55 F1
Marsh Wy *PRES* PR1 ....72 B4
Marston Cl *FUL/RIB* PR2 ....45 E1
Marston Moor *FUL/RIB* PR2 ......45 E1
Martin Av *LSTA* FY8 ....38 C4
Martinfield *FUL/RIB* PR2 ....37 E5
Martin Field Rd *PRES* PR1 ....72 D4
Martins Av *CHLY/EC* PR7 ....97 H1
Marton Dr *BPOOLS* FY4 ....32 D5
Marton Fold *BPOOLS* FY4 ....39 G4
Marton Rd *FUL/RIB* PR2 ....58 E3
Marybank Cl *KIRK/FR/WAR* PR4 .46 C2
Maryland *BPOOLS* FY4 * 5 F4
Masefield Av *CLV/TH* FY5 ....21 F1
Masefield Rd *BBR* PR5 ....74 A4
Mason Cl *KIRK/FR/WAR* PR4 .....54 C5
Massnfield *BBR* PR5 ....81 E4
Mason Hill Vw *FUL/RIB* PR2 ......46 A4
Mason House Crs
FUL/RIB PR2 * 44 C3
Mason St *FUL/RIB* PR2 ....89 H5
Mather St *BPOOLE* FY3 * 5 G1
Matlock Pl *FUL/RIB* PR2 ....46 C3
Matterdale Rd *LEYL* PR25 ....45 E5
Matthews Ct *BPOOLS* FY4 ....58 D1
Maudland Bank *PRES* PR1 ....6 C1
Maudland Rd *PRES* PR1 ....6 D2
PRES PR1 ....6 C1
Maud St *CHLY/EC* PR7 ....93 E4
Maureen Av *BBR* PR5 ....79 G1
Maurice Gv *BISP* FY2 ....25 E5
Mavis Dr *CHLY/EC* PR7 ....96 B4
Maxwell Gv *BISP* FY2 ....25 F5
May Bell Av *CLV/TH* FY5 ....21 F1
Maycroft Av *PLF/KEOS* FY6 ....26 A2
Mayfair Cl *LSTA* FY8 ....50 B5
Mayfair Dr *CLV/TH* FY5 ....22 A4
Mayfair Gdns *CLV/TH* FY5 ....22 A3
Mayfair Rd *BPOOL* FY1 ....5 H4
Mayfield Av *BBR* PR5 ....79 H1
BPOOLS FY4 ....5 G2
CLV/TH FY5 ....17 G5
FUL/RIB PR2 ....44 A4
KIRK/FR/WAR PR4 ....42 D3
Mayfield Rd *CHLYE* PR6 ....93 G1
FUL/RIB PR2 ....58 D2
LEYL PR25 ....83 F5
LSTA FY8 ....64 B3
Mayflower Av *PRES* PR1 ....71 H2
Maynard St *FUL/RIB* PR2 ....59 F1
Mayor Av *BPOOL* FY1 ....4 E3
Maypark *BBR* PR5 ....80 D4
McKenzie St *BBR* PR5 ....80 C1
Mead Av *FTWD* FY7 ....11 G3
PLF/KEOS FY6 ....8 C3
Meadow Av *KIRK/FR/WAR* PR4 ..76 A1
Meadow Bank *PRES* PR1 ....72 B3
Meadowbarn Cl
KIRK/FR/WAR PR4 ....76 A1
Meadowbrook *BPOOLE* FY3 .....34 A3
Meadow Cl *BISP* FY2 ....24 D5
KIRK/FR/WAR PR4 ....56 B2
Meadow Ct *PRES* PR1 ....6 C7
Meadow Crs *PLF/KEOS* FY6 ......26 B5
Meadowcroft *CHLY/EC* PR7 ......87 C4
LSTA FY8 ....49 G2
Meadowcroft Av *CLV/TH* FY5 ....21 E2
PRES PR1 ....23 G3
Meadowcroft Rd *LEYL* PR25 ......82 C5
Meadow Dr *KIRK/FR/WAR* PR4 ..66 D1
Meadowfield *FUL/RIB* PR2 ....45 H1
Meadow Fld *PRES* PR1 ....72 B3
Meadow Head La
KIRK/FR/WAR PR4 ....76 A1
Meadowland
CROS/BRETH PR26 ....78 D1
Meadowlands *CHLY/EC* PR7 ......96 A1
Meadow La *BBR* PR5 ....81 E5
LSTA FY8 ....65 F2
Meadow Pk *BPOOLE* FY3 ....30 B5
KIRK/FR/WAR PR4 ....42 D3
Meadow Reach *PRES* PR1 ....72 A4
Meadows *CLV/TH* FY5 ....21 F1
Meadowside
KIRK/FR/WAR PR4 ....76 A4
Meadowside Dr *BBR* PR5 ....75 H5
The Meadows *BBR* PR5 * 74 C4
CHLY/EC PR7 ....94 C5
CLV/TH FY5 ....21 F2
CROS/BRETH PR26 ....82 A4
Meadow St *LEYL* PR25 ....83 F3
PRES PR1 ....7 H2
Meadow Wy *CHLY/EC* PR7 ....96 A5
Meads Rd *FUL/RIB* PR2 ....58 D2
Meadway *BPOOLS* FY4 ....5 K5
CHLYE PR6 ....85 E1
PRES PR1 ....71 H1
Mealhouse La *CHLY/EC* PR7 ......93 G2
Meanwood Av *BPOOLS* FY4 ......33 H5
Meanygate *BBR* PR5 ....80 B1
Mearley Av *FUL/RIB* PR2 ....47 E4
Meath Rd *PRES* PR1 ....72 C1

The Mede *KIRK/FR/WAR* PR4 ....54 B1
Medlar Av *KIRK/FR/WAR* PR4 ....42 C2
Medlar Ct *KIRK/FR/WAR* PR4 * ..43 E5
Medlar La *KIRK/FR/WAR* PR4 ....43 E2
Medlock Av *FTWD* FY7 ....10 C3
Medway Av *FUL/RIB* PR2 ....75 D3
Medway Rd *FUL/RIB* PR2 ....16 D1
Medway St *BBR* PR5 ....75 D5
Melba Rd *FUL/RIB* PR2 ....47 E5
Melbert Av *FUL/RIB* PR2 ....44 D5
Melbourne Av *CLV/TH* FY5 ....21 F5
FTWD FY7 ....16 D1
Melbourne St *PRES* PR1 ....7 F2
Melford Cl *CHLYE* PR6 ....89 H4
Mellings *PRES* PR1 ....60 C5
Mellings Fold *PRES* PR1 * 60 C5
Melling's La *LSTA* FY8 ....49 E5
Melling St *PRES* PR1 ....7 G2
Mellor Av *FUL/RIB* PR2 ....49 G2
Mellor Pl *PRES* PR1 ....7 K5
Mellor Rd *KIRK/FR/WAR* PR4 ....43 E3
LEYL PR25 ....82 C2
Melrose Av *BPOOLS* FY4 ....29 F1
Melrose Av *BPOOLS* FY4 ....29 F1
FUL/RIB PR2 ....46 C3
Melrose Wy *CHLY/EC* PR7 ....93 G4
Melton Av *FUL/RIB* PR2 ....63 H5
Melton Gv *CLV/TH* FY5 ....20 C4
LEYL PR25 ....83 G2
Melville Rd *BISP* FY2 ....24 C5
Memory Cl *KIRK/FR/WAR* PR4 ...54 B4
Menai Dr *FUL/RIB* PR2 ....45 F1
Mendip Cl *FUL/RIB* PR2 ....65 E1
Mendip Rd *LEYL* PR25 ....84 A5
Mercer Rd *BBR* PR5 ....75 F5
Mercer St *PRES* PR1 ....60 D3
Mere Av *FTWD* FY7 ....10 D5
Mere Cl *GAR/LONG* PR3 ....36 B2
Merefold *CHLY/EC* PR7 ....92 D1
Mereland Rd *BPOOLS* FY4 ....33 G5
Merepark La *FUL/RIB* PR2 ....17 E4
Mere Park Ct *BPOOLS* FY4 ....33 G2
Mere Rd *BPOOLS* FY4 ....33 G5
Mereside Cl *KIRK/FR/WAR* PR4 .76 A2
Merlin Gv *LEYL* PR25 ....82 C5
Merlyn Rd *CLV/TH* FY5 ....21 E5
Merrick Av *PRES* PR1 ....61 F3
Merryburn Cl *FUL/RIB* PR2 ....46 A4
Merry Trees La
KIRK/FR/WAR PR4 ....44 A3
FTWD FY7 ....11 E2
Mersey Bk *BPOOLS* FY4 ....32 B5
Mersey St *FUL/RIB* PR2 ....59 E5
Merton Av *FUL/RIB* PR2 ....45 E5
Merton Gv *CHLYE* PR6 ....89 H4
Mete St *PRES* PR1 ....60 D5
Methuen Av *BBR* PR5 ....75 H3
FUL/RIB PR2 ....45 G2
Metheun St *BBR* PR5 ....75 H5
Metropolitan Dr *BPOOLE* FY3 ...33 H3
Mexford Av *BISP* FY2 ....24 D5
Meyler Av *BPOOLE* FY3 ....29 E2
Mickleden Av *FUL/RIB* PR2 ....45 H1
Mickleden Rd *BPOOLS* FY4 ....34 A4
Micklegate *CLV/TH* FY5 ....20 C5
Mickleforth Gv *PRES* PR1 ....72 D2
Middle St *BPOOL* FY1 * 4 A3
Middleton Av *FTWD* FY7 ....10 D5
Middlewood Cl *CHLY/EC* PR7 ....90 B4
Midge Hall La
KIRK/FR/WAR PR4 ....77 G5
Midgeland Rd *BPOOLS* FY4 ....39 G1
Midgeland Ter *BPOOLS* FY4 * ...40 A3
Midgery La *FUL/RIB* PR2 ....37 F5
Milbanke Av *KIRK/FR/WAR* PR4 .44 C4
Milbourne St *BPOOL* FY1 ....2 E4
Milburn Av *CLV/TH* FY5 ....17 F4
Mildred Cl *CLV/TH* FY5 ....21 G5
Miles St *PRES* PR1 ....59 H1
Mile Stone Meadow
CHLY/EC PR7 ....88 A3
Miles Wk *PRES* PR1 ....59 G1
Miletas Pl *LSTA* FY8 ....63 F3
Milford Av *BISP* FY2 ....28 D1
Milford Ter *CLV/TH* FY5 * 21 H1
Millsap Rd *FUL/RIB* PR2 ....41 E5
Millbank Wy *PRES* PR1 ....72 B4
Millcroft *FUL/RIB* PR2 ....45 E4
Milldyke Cl *BPOOLS* FY4 ....39 F2
Millennium Wy *PRES* PR1 ....7 G4
Miller Fld *FUL/RIB* PR2 ....45 F5
Miller La *KIRK/FR/WAR* PR4 .....44 A3
Miller Rd *PRES* PR1 ....61 E1
PRES PR1 ....60 D1
Millers Ct *LSTA* FY8 ....50 B4
Millersdale Cl *CLV/TH* FY5 ....22 C5
Millsgate *KIRK/FR/WAR* PR4 .....44 A4
Miller St *BPOOL* FY1 ....4 B5
PRES PR1 ....60 D1
Millfield Cl *KIRK/FR/WAR* PR4 ..53 H5
Millfield Rd *BPOOLS* FY4 ....39 F2
CHLY/EC PR7 ....93 E1
Mill Ga *FUL/RIB* PR2 ....45 F5
Mill Hvn *FUL/RIB* PR2 ....45 F5
Mill Hey Av *PLF/KEOS* FY6 ....30 C1
Mill Hl *PRES* PR1 ....6 D2
Mill House La *BBR* PR5 ....81 H1
Millington Av *BPOOLS* FY4 ....5 H7
Mill La *BBR* PR5 ....79 G5
BPOOLE FY3 ....30 B5
CHLY/EC PR7 ....91 F2
CHLYE PR6 ....95 F3
CHLYE PR6 ....96 B5
CHLYE PR6 ....85 F3
CROS/BRETH PR26 ....82 D1
FTWD FY7 ....11 F4
FUL/RIB PR2 ....45 E4
KIRK/FR/WAR PR4 ....53 H5
LEYL PR25 ....82 C4
PLF/KEOS FY6 ....19 G2

PLF/KEOS FY6 ....13 F3
PRES PR1 * 6 B3
Mill Vw *KIRK/FR/WAR* PR4 ....54 B4
Millwood Gld *CHLY/EC* PR7 ....93 E1
Millwood Rd *BBR* PR5 ....73 G5
Milner Rd *FUL/RIB* PR2 ....19 F2
Milner St *PRES* PR1 ....59 H1
Milnthorpe Av *CLV/TH* FY5 ....16 D4
Milton Av *BPOOLS* FY4 ....3 J4
CLV/TH FY5 ....21 G1
Milton Cl *PRES* PR1 ....74 A4
Milton Pl *PLF/KEOS* FY6 ....30 B2
Milton Rd *CHLY/EC* PR7 ....96 B5
Milton St *FUL/RIB* PR2 ....11 G1
Milton Ter *CHLYE* PR6 ....89 G5
Mimosa Cl *FUL/RIB* PR2 ....88 D4
Mimosa Rd *FUL/RIB* PR2 ....61 E1
Minster Pk *KIRK/FR/WAR* PR4 ..43 F5
Minstrel Wk *FUL/RIB* PR2 ....26 B5
Mintholme Av *BBR* PR5 ....75 H4
Mirfield Gv *BPOOLS* FY4 ....5 G6
Mitcham Rd *BPOOLS* FY4 ....33 H5
Mitton Crs *KIRK/FR/WAR* PR4 ..43 E5
Mitton Dr *FUL/RIB* PR2 ....47 E4
Moira Crs *FUL/RIB* PR2 ....47 E4
Molyneux Ct *PRES* PR1 ....7 H5
Molyneux Dr *BPOOLS* FY4 ....38 D1
Molyneux Pl *LSTA* FY8 ....64 B2
Mona Pl *PRES* PR1 ....6 C3
Monarch Crs *LSTA* FY8 ....40 B3
Monk's La *FUL/RIB* PR2 ....13 E5
Monks Wk *PRES* PR1 ....59 E5
Monomer Rd *CLV/TH* FY5 ....18 A5
Monroe Dr *FTWD* FY7 ....10 D3
Montague St *BPOOLS* FY4 ....4 B7
Montcliffe Rd *CHLYE* PR6 ....95 H1
Montgomery St *BBR* PR5 ....80 C1
Montjoly St *PRES* PR1 * 60 C4
Montpelier Av *BPOOL* FY1 ....24 C2
Montreal Av *BPOOL* FY1 ....3 F6
Montrose Av *CLV/TH* FY5 ....4 D1
Montrose Cl *CHLYE* PR6 ....93 H4
Moon Av *BPOOL* FY1 ....4 C4
Moon St *BBR* PR5 ....80 B1
Moor Av *PRES* PR1 ....71 G2
Moorbrook St *PRES* PR1 ....59 G2
Moorcroft *KIRK/FR/WAR* PR4 ....36 A3
Moorcroft Crs *FUL/RIB* PR2 ......45 G5
Moore St *BPOOLS* FY4 ....4 C6
PRES PR1 ....60 C4
Moore Tree Dr *BPOOLS* FY4 ......33 G5
Moor Fld *KIRK/FR/WAR* PR4 .....77 G2
Moorfield Cl *FUL/RIB* PR2 ....36 D5
PRES PR1 ....71 H5
Moorfield Dr *FUL/RIB* PR2 ....47 E5
LSTA FY8 ....64 B2
Moorfield Rd *LEYL* PR25 ....82 B4
Moorfields *CHLYE* PR6 ....95 F3
PLF/KEOS FY6 ....25 F3
Moorgate *BPOOLS* FY4 ....39 F2
PLF/KEOS FY6 ....26 C3
Moor Hall St *PRES* PR1 ....59 G1
Moorhead Gdns
KIRK/FR/WAR PR4 ....53 C4
Moorhen Pl *CLV/TH* FY5 ....21 F3
Moorhey Crs *BBR* PR5 ....80 D1
PRES PR1 ....72 A1
Moorhey Dr *PRES* PR1 ....72 A1
Moorhouse St *BPOOL* FY1 ....39 H2
Moorland Av *FUL/RIB* PR2 ....46 D3
PLF/KEOS FY6 ....26 C3
Moorland Ct *PLF/KEOS* FY6 * 26 C3
Moorland Dr *FUL/RIB* PR2 ....46 D4
Moorland Gdns *PLF/KEOS* FY6 .26 C3
Moorland Rd *CLV/TH* FY5 ....16 D5
PLF/KEOS FY6 ....26 C3
Moor La *KIRK/FR/WAR* PR4 ......71 E5
PRES PR1 ....6 E1
Moor Park Av *PRES* PR1 ....60 A1
Moor Park Ct *PRES* PR1 * 59 H1
Moor Rd *CHLY/EC* PR7 ....92 D5
Moorside Av *FUL/RIB* PR2 ....47 F5
Moorside Dr *PRES* PR1 ....72 A3
Moor St *KIRK/FR/WAR* PR4 ......43 E5
Moorview Ct *BPOOLS* FY4 ....39 F1
Moorway *PLF/KEOS* FY6 ....26 B5
Moresby Av *BPOOLE* FY3 ....29 H5
Moreton Dr *BPOOLE* FY3 ....30 B5
PLF/KEOS FY6 ....26 B5
Morland Av *BBR* PR5 ....79 F2
KIRK/FR/WAR PR4 ....42 D1
Morley Rd *BPOOLS* FY4 ....3 H5
Mornington Rd *LSTA* FY8 ....65 F2
PRES PR1 ....61 F2
PRES PR1 ....72 A1
Morris Cl *CHLY/EC* PR7 ....83 F4
Morris Ct *FUL/RIB* PR2 ....60 D1
Morris Crs *FUL/RIB* PR2 ....60 D1
Morrison St *CHLYE* PR6 ....89 G5
Morris Rd *CHLYE* PR6 * 93 H1
FUL/RIB PR2 ....60 D1
Morston Av *BISP* FY2 ....25 E5
Mosley St *LEYL* PR25 ....83 F3
PRES PR1 ....60 C5
Moss Acre Rd *PRES* PR1 ....72 C5
Moss Av *FUL/RIB* PR2 ....58 D4
Moss Bank *CHLY/EC* PR7 ....96 B4
Moss Bank Pl *BPOOLS* FY4 ......33 F5
Mossbourne Rd *PLF/KEOS* FY6 .26 A5
Moss Bridge Pk *BBR* PR5 ....79 G1
Mossbrook Dr
KIRK/FR/WAR PR4 ....44 A3
Moss Cl *CHLYE* PR6 ....96 A4
Moss Edge La *LSTA* FY8 ....39 G5
Mossfield Rd *FUL/RIB* PR2 ....93 H2
Moss Hall La *LSTA* FY8 ....50 C3
Moss House La *BPOOLS* FY4 .....41 E1
GAR/LONG PR3 ....15 H2

Moss House Rd *BPOOLS* FY4 ....39 G2
KIRK/FR/WAR PR4 ....36 A3
Mosslands *LEYL* PR25 ....82 C5
Moss La *BBR* PR5 ....79 G1
CHLY/EC PR7 ....98 B4
CHLYE PR6 ....85 F3
CROS/BRETH PR26 ....78 C4
KIRK/FR/WAR PR4 ....76 C5
KIRK/FR/WAR PR4 ....77 F2
LEYL PR25 ....83 H2
PLF/KEOS FY6 ....23 H5
Mossom La *CLV/TH* FY5 ....17 F4
Moss Side La
KIRK/FR/WAR PR4 ....52 B1
PLF/KEOS FY6 ....19 H2
Moss Side Wy
CROS/BRETH PR26 ....82 B4
Moss St *BBR* PR5 ....79 G1
PRES PR1 * 6 D2
Moss Wy *BPOOLS* FY4 ....39 F1
Mossway *KIRK/FR/WAR* PR4 .....77 G3
Mottram Cl *CLV/TH* FY5 ....20 D4
Mounsey Rd *BBR* PR5 ....80 C1
Mountain Ash *CHLY/EC* PR7 .....96 B5
Mountbatten Cl *FUL/RIB* PR2 ....38 D5
Mount Pleasant *CHLYE* PR6 ......85 F4
Mount Rd *FTWD* FY7 ....11 G1
Mount St *BPOOL* FY1 ....2 B2
FTWD FY7 ....11 G2
PRES PR1 ....6 E5
Mowbray Dr *BPOOLE* FY3 ....29 E1
Mowbray Rd *FTWD* FY7 ....11 E2
Mowbreck
KIRK/FR/WAR PR4 ....43 E2
Mowbreck La
KIRK/FR/WAR PR4 ....43 E2
Muirfield *PRES* PR1 ....58 C5
Muirfield Cl *CHLY/EC* PR7 ....88 A3
FUL/RIB PR2 ....44 D2
Mulberry Av *PRES* PR1 ....71 H5
Mulberry Cl *FUL/RIB* PR2 ....58 C2
Mulberry Ms *BISP* FY2 ....21 F5
Mulgrave Av *FUL/RIB* PR2 ....58 C2
Muncaster Rd *PRES* PR1 ....59 H1
Munro Crs *FUL/RIB* PR2 ....47 E5
Munslow Av *CLV/TH* FY5 ....21 E4
Murchison Gv *CLV/TH* FY5 ....21 G1
Murdock Av *FUL/RIB* PR2 ....59 F1
Murray Av *CROS/BRETH* PR26 ..78 D4
Murray St *LEYL* PR25 ....83 G3
PRES PR1 ....59 G2
Myerscough Av *BPOOLS* FY4 ....39 F3
LSTA FY8 ....48 D3
Myra Rd *LSTA* FY8 ....49 E5
Myrtle Av *BPOOLE* FY3 ....5 F3
CLV/TH FY5 ....17 F4
PLF/KEOS FY6 ....23 H5
Myrtle Dr *KIRK/FR/WAR* PR4 .....45 G4
Mythop Cl *LSTA* FY8 ....64 D2
Mythop Ct *LSTA* FY8 ....64 C2
Mythop Pl *FUL/RIB* PR2 ....58 B2
Mythop Rd *BPOOLE* FY3 ....5 H3
LSTA FY8 ....64 D2

N

Nab Rd *CHLYE* PR6 ....93 H1
Nairn Cl *BPOOLS* FY4 ....39 G1
Nansen Rd *FTWD* FY7 ....17 F2
Napier Av *BPOOLS* FY4 ....38 B2
Napier Ct *LSTA* FY8 ....48 D2
Naptha La *CROS/BRETH* PR26 ...82 B5
Nares St *FUL/RIB* PR2 ....59 E2
Nateby Av *BPOOLS* FY4 ....39 E3
Nateby Cl *LSTA* FY8 ....64 C2
Nateby Pl *FUL/RIB* PR2 ....58 B2
Navena Av *FTWD* FY7 ....10 D4
Navigation Wy *FTWD* FY7 ....11 G3
FUL/RIB PR2 ....58 C4
Naze Av *BBR* PR5 ....54 B5
Naze La East
KIRK/FR/WAR PR4 ....67 H1
Neapsands Cl *FUL/RIB* PR2 ....46 D3
Neargates *CHLY/EC* PR7 ....96 A3
Ned's La *GAR/LONG* PR3 ....14 C1
Nell La *FUL/RIB* PR2 ....19 H4
Nelson Av *LEYL* PR25 ....83 G3
Nelson Crs *FUL/RIB* PR2 ....57 H1
Nelson Rd *BPOOL* FY1 ....4 B4
CLV/TH FY5 ....93 F3
FTWD FY7 ....17 F2
Nelson St *BBR* PR5 ....80 B1
KIRK/FR/WAR PR4 ....42 D3
LSTA FY8 ....65 E3
Nelson Ter *PRES* PR1 * 6 B5
Nelson Wy *FUL/RIB* PR2 ....58 A4
Nene Cl *LEYL* PR25 ....83 H4
Nesswood Av *BPOOLS* FY4 ....39 E2
Neston St *PRES* PR1 ....61 E3
Netherley Rd *CHLY/EC* PR7 ....96 B5
Nethway Av *BPOOLE* FY3 ....3 K2
Nevett St *PRES* PR1 ....60 D5
Neville Av *CLV/TH* FY5 ....21 E4
Neville St *BPOOLS* FY4 ....21 H4
Newark Pl *FUL/RIB* PR2 ....36 C5
New Bonny St *BPOOL* FY1 ....2 B6
Newbury Av *BPOOLS* FY4 ....5 F6
Newbury Cl *FUL/RIB* PR2 ....36 B5
Newbury Rd *FUL/RIB* PR2 ....36 B5
Newbury Wy *BPOOLS* FY4 ....36 A5
Newby Av *FTWD* FY7 ....10 D5
Newby Dr *LEYL* PR25 ....84 A2
Newby Pl *FUL/RIB* PR2 ....33 H4
Newcastle Av *BPOOLE* FY3 ....3 G6
CLV/TH FY5 ....17 G5
New Cock Yd *PRES* PR1 ....7 F5

Newfield Rd BBR PR5 ...80 D2
Newgate FUL/RIB PR2 ...45 G4
Newgate La KIRK/FR/WAR PR4 ...78 B1
New Hall Av BPOOLS FY4 ...39 H2
BPOOLS FY4 ...39 H2
New Hall La PRES PR1 ...37 G5
New Hey La KIRK/FR/WAR PR4 ...43 H4
Newhouse Rd BPOOLS FY4 ...5 K4
Newlands CHLY/EC PR7 ...90 B4
Newlands Av BPOOLE FY3 ...5 J5
PRES PR1 ...71 H2
Newlands Rd LSTA FY8 ...63 F1
Newlands Wy PLF/KEOS FY6 ...10 A1
New La CLV/TH FY5 ...22 A5
PRES PR1 ...72 D3
New Links La FUL/RIB PR2 ...44 C2
Newlyn Av BPOOLS FY4 ...39 E3
Newlyn Pl FUL/RIB PR2 ...44 A5
Newman Gv CLV/TH FY5 ...17 E4
Newman Rd BPOOL FY1 ...28 D2
New Market St CHLY/EC PR7 ...93 F2
New Mill St PRES PR1 ...90 B4
New Moss La CHLYE PR6 ...89 F2
New Preston Ml PRES PR1 * ...7 K3
New Rd BBR PR5 ...73 G5
CHLY/EC PR7 ...96 C2
LSTA FY8 ...38 B4
PLF/KEOS FY6 ...19 E5
New Rough Hey FUL/RIB PR2 ...44 B2
Newsham St FUL/RIB PR2 * ...6 A1
Newsome St LSTA FY8 ...83 F3
New St CHLY/EC PR7 ...90 B4
Newton Av PLF/KEOS FY6 ...26 A5
PRES PR1 ...61 F3
Newton Cl CROS/BRETH PR26 ...82 A4
KIRK/FR/WAR PR4 ...54 C5
Newton Ct FUL/RIB PR2 ...58 B2
Newton Dr BPOOLE FY3 ...29 C4
Newton Dr East BPOOLE FY3 ...29 H5
Newton Pl BPOOLE FY3 ...29 G3
Newton Rd FUL/RIB PR2 ...58 D1
LSTA FY8 ...49 G4
Newton St PRES PR1 ...7 J2
Nib La PRES PR1 ...78 D1
Nichol St CLV/TH FY5 * ...93 F1
Nicksons La PLF/KEOS FY6 ...13 F2
Nightingale Dr FUL/RIB PR2 ...25 H5
Nightingale Wy CHLY/EC PR7 ...93 F3
Nimes St PRES PR1 ...61 F5
Nine Elms FUL/RIB PR2 ...45 E2
Nithside BPOOLS FY4 ...34 A4
Noblett Ct FTWD FY7 ...11 F4
Noel Sq PRES PR1 ...61 E2
Nookfield Cl LSTA FY8 ...64 B2
Nooklands FUL/RIB PR2 ...45 H1
Nook La BBR PR5 ...80 A3
The Nook BPOOLS FY4 ...30 B5
Noor St PRES PR1 ...7 H1
Norbreck Dr FUL/RIB PR2 ...58 A2
Norbreck Rd BISP FY2 ...24 C1
Norcliffe Rd BISP FY2 ...24 C2
Norcross La CLV/TH FY5 ...21 G5
Norcross Pl FUL/RIB PR2 ...58 B2
Norfolk Av BISP FY2 ...24 B4
CLV/TH FY5 ...21 E1
Norfolk Cl LEYL PR25 ...82 D5
Norfolk Rd BBR PR5 ...33 G3
LSTA FY8 ...64 C1
PRES PR1 ...60 A2
Norkeed Rd CLV/TH FY5 ...20 C5
Norman Cl CLV/TH FY5 ...21 F3
Normandie Av BISP FY2 ...24 D4
Normandy Rd
KIRK/FR/WAR PR4 ...36 A2
Normoss Av BPOOLS FY3 ...29 G3
Normoss Rd BPOOLS FY3 ...29 H3
Norris St CHLY/EC PR7 ...93 F4
FUL/RIB PR2 ...59 F5
PRES PR1 ...59 F1
North Albert St FTWD FY7 ...11 H1
North Albion St FTWD FY7 ...11 G2
North Av BPOOLE FY3 ...28 D3
Northbrook Rd LEYL PR25 ...82 D2
North Church St FTWD FY7 ...11 H1
North Cliff St FTWD FY7 ...11 H2
North Clifton St LSTA FY8 ...64 C3
Northcote Rd BPOOL FY1 ...6 B5
Northcote St LEYL PR25 ...83 F3
North Ct CLV/TH FY5 ...16 D4
North Crs LSTA FY8 ...64 C3
North Dr CLV/TH FY5 ...24 D1
KIRK/FR/WAR PR4 ...42 D2
Northenden Rd CHLY/EC PR7 ...96 B4
Northfield Av BPOOL FY1 ...28 B2
Northfleet Av FTWD FY7 ...11 E4
Northgate BISP FY2 ...24 C2
LEYL PR25 ...83 G2
Northgate Dr CHLYE PR6 ...89 H5
North Gv BBR PR5 ...79 H1
North Highfield FUL/RIB PR2 ...47 E2
North Houses La LSTA FY8 ...50 B2
Northlands
CROS/BRETH PR26 ...82 B5
FUL/RIB PR2 ...45 G2
Northleach Av PRES PR1 ...73 E4
North Meadowside
KIRK/FR/WAR PR4 ...76 B4
North Park Dr BPOOLE FY3 ...3 J5
North Prom LSTA FY8 ...64 A1
North Ribble St BBR PR5 ...60 C5
North Rd PRES PR1 ...7 G2
PRES PR1 ...59 H2
Northside CHLY/EC PR7 ...87 H4
North Sq BPOOLE FY3 ...16 C4
CLV/TH FY5 ...16 C4
North St CHLYE PR6 ...90 B4
FTWD FY7 ...11 H1
PRES PR1 ...7 F1
North Syke Av
FUL/RIB PR2 ...57 F2
Northumberland Av BISP FY2 ...28 B1
CLV/TH FY5 ...17 E5

Northumberland St
CLV/TH FY5 ...17 H5
FUL/RIB PR2 ...44 C3
KIRK/FR/WAR PR4 ...54 A5
North Union Vw
CROS/BRETH PR26 ...79 E1
North Vw KIRK/FR/WAR PR4 ...42 D3
North Warton St LSTA FY8 ...64 D3
Northway FTWD FY7 ...10 D5
FUL/RIB PR2 ...45 F2
GAR/LONG PR3 ...36 B2
Northwood Cl LSTA FY8 ...63 H2
Northwood Wy
PLF/KEOS FY6 ...26 B5
Norton V CLV/TH FY5 ...22 B2
Norwich Pl BISP FY2 ...24 C2
PRES PR1 ...7 H5
Norwood Av FUL/RIB PR2 ...44 D3
Norwood Rd LSTA FY8 ...48 C5
Nottingham Rd PRES PR1 ...60 A2
Nursery Cl PRES PR1 ...96 B1
LEYL PR25 ...83 E4
Nursery La KIRK/FR/WAR PR4 ...77 F1
Nuttall Rd BPOOL FY1 ...5 F5
Nutter Rd CLV/TH FY5 ...20 D2
PRES PR1 ...6 C4

O

Oak Av BPOOLS FY4 ...32 D5
CHLY/EC PR7 ...88 A4
CLV/TH FY5 ...22 A4
KIRK/FR/WAR PR4 ...43 E4
PRES PR1 ...72 A3
Oak Cft CHLYE PR6 ...85 E2
Oak Dr CLV/TH FY5 ...88 F4
KIRK/FR/WAR PR4 ...67 F1
Oakengate FUL/RIB PR2 ...46 C1
Oakenhead St PRES PR1 * ...61 E2
Oakfield Ct PRES PR1 ...45 H1
FUL/RIB PR2 ...45 H1
Oakfield Dr CROS/BRETH PR26 ...82 A4
Oakgrove BPOOLS FY4 ...38 D2
Oak Gv KIRK/FR/WAR PR4 ...7 H4
Oakham Ct PRES PR1 ...7 H4
Oakland Av CLV/TH FY5 ...24 D1
Oakland Gln BBR PR5 ...73 F3
Oaklands Dr PRES PR1 ...71 H2
Oaklands Gv FUL/RIB PR2 ...58 B2
Oakland St BBR PR5 ...73 H2
Oak La KIRK/FR/WAR PR4 ...54 C5
Oakleaf Wy BPOOLS FY4 ...34 B4
Oakmere CLV/TH FY5 ...85 F1
Oakmoor Av BISP FY2 ...25 E3
Oakridge Cl FUL/RIB PR2 ...45 H1
Oakshott Pl BBR PR5 ...81 E2
The Oaks BBR PR5 ...73 G3
CHLY/EC PR7 ...97 E1
PLF/KEOS FY6 ...26 B2
Oak St FTWD FY7 ...11 G2
Oaktree Av FUL/RIB PR2 ...44 C4
LEYL PR25 ...80 A5
Oaktree Cl FUL/RIB PR2 ...58 B2
Oak Vw LEYL PR25 ...82 D2
Oakwood Av BBR PR5 ...73 H2
LSTA FY8 ...63 G2
Oakwood Cl BPOOLS FY4 ...59 F4
CLV/TH FY5 ...22 B2
Oakwood Dr FUL/RIB PR2 ...58 B2
Oakwood Rd CHLY/EC PR7 ...93 E4
Oakwood Vw CHLY/EC PR7 ...97 E1
Oakworth Av FUL/RIB PR2 ...58 B2
Oban Crs PRES PR1 ...44 C5
Oban Dr BISP FY2 ...25 E1
Ocean Bvd BPOOLS FY4 * ...38 A1
Ocean Wy CLV/TH FY5 ...20 C1
Old Bridge La FUL/KEOS FY6 ...93 E5
Old Bridge Wy CHLYE PR6 ...93 C1
Oldbury Pl CLV/TH FY5 ...21 F4
Old Cock Yd PRES PR1 ...7 G2
Old Cft FUL/RIB PR2 ...36 C5
Old Dawber's La CHLY/EC PR7 ...91 G1
Oldfield KIRK/FR/WAR PR4 ...76 A5
PRES PR1 ...72 C4
Oldfield Av BBR PR5 ...24 C3
Oldfield Carr La PLF/KEOS FY6 ...30 C1
Oldfield Cl FUL/RIB PR2 ...57 G2
Oldfield Crs PLF/KEOS FY6 ...30 C1
Oldfield Rd BBR PR5 ...80 D2
Old Forge LS FY8 ...50 B4
Old Hall Cl BBR PR5 ...80 B1
Old Hall La CHLY/EC PR7 ...91 G4
Old Hey Cft PRES PR1 * ...72 C4
Old House La BPOOLS FY4 ...40 A1
Old Lancaster La FUL/RIB PR2 ...57 F2
Old Lostock La BBR PR5 ...80 B2
Old Mains La PLF/KEOS FY6 ...26 D1
Old Meadow La BPOOLE FY3 ...16 D5
Old Mill Ct KIRK/FR/WAR PR4 ...76 A4
Old Millstones PRES PR1 ...6 B5
Old Oak Gdns PRES PR1 ...7 F5
Old Orch FUL/RIB PR2 ...45 H1
Old Rw KIRK/FR/WAR PR4 ...43 F4
Old School Dr
KIRK/FR/WAR PR4 ...76 B4
Old School La BBR PR5 ...79 H5
Old St PRES PR1 ...88 A4
Old Tram Rd PRES PR1 ...73 F2
Old Vicarage PRES PR1 ...7 G5
Old Worden Av CHLY/EC PR7 ...84 B5
Olive Cl PRES PR1 ...89 F2
Olive Gv BPOOLE FY3 ...16 B4
Oliver's Pl FUL/RIB PR2 ...44 B3
Ollerton Rd CLV/TH FY5 ...21 F5
Olympic Wy BPOOLS FY4 ...34 A5
Onslow Rd BPOOLS FY3 ...29 G4
Orchard Av BPOOLS FY4 ...38 C2
KIRK/FR/WAR PR4 ...43 F4
PLF/KEOS FY6 ...30 C1
Orchard Cl CHLY/EC PR7 ...88 C1

Orchard Cft BBR PR5 ...79 F1
Orchard Dr CHLYE PR6 ...89 F2
KIRK/FR/WAR PR4 ...11 E5
Orchard Rd BPOOL FY1 ...49 E5
Orchard Rd LSTA FY8 ...76 A1
The Orchards PLF/KEOS FY6 ...25 H2
Orchard St LEYL PR25 ...83 G3
PRES PR1 ...7 F4
The Orchard
KIRK/FR/WAR PR4 ...53 C5
Ord Av BPOOLS FY4 ...5 K4
Orders La KIRK/FR/WAR PR4 ...43 E4
Ord Rd FUL/RIB PR2 ...59 E1
Oregon Av BPOOLS FY4 ...29 E2
Orion Buildings CLV/TH FY5 * ...20 D2
Orkney Rd BPOOL FY1 ...4 E4
Ormerod St CLV/TH FY5 ...17 E5
Orme St BPOOL FY1 ...4 E1
Ormond Av BPOOLS FY4 ...28 B2
Ormond Av CLV/TH FY5 ...21 E2
Ormrod St BBR PR5 ...7 G3
Orrell Cl LEYL PR25 ...81 G2
Orrest Rd PRES PR1 ...61 E2
Osbert Cft KIRK/FR/WAR PR4 ...70 B5
Osborne Av CLV/TH FY5 ...21 E2
Osborne Dr PRES PR1 ...85 F2
Osborne Gv CLV/TH FY5 ...16 D4
Osborne Rd BBR PR5 ...73 H2
CLV/TH FY5 ...16 D4
LSTA FY8 ...62 C1
Osborne St PRES PR1 ...6 C5
Osbourne Rd BPOOLS FY4 ...32 B5
Oscar St BPOOLE FY3 ...5 K4
Oswald Rd FUL/RIB PR2 ...59 E1
FUL/RIB PR2 ...65 E2
Otley Rd LSTA FY8 ...49 H4
Otterburn Cl BPOOLE FY3 ...29 H1
Otters Cl FUL/RIB PR2 ...61 F1
Otway St PRES PR1 ...59 G1
Outer Prom FTWD FY7 ...10 D1
Overton Rd FUL/RIB PR2 ...58 A3
Owens St CHLYE PR6 * ...93 H5
Owen St PRES PR1 ...7 K2
Owtram St PRES PR1 ...60 C3
Oxendale Rd CLV/TH FY5 ...29 H1
Oxenholme Av CLV/TH FY5 ...16 D5
Oxenhurst Rd BPOOLS FY4 ...29 G2
Oxford Av FUL/RIB PR2 ...43 G4
Oxford Rd BBR PR5 ...80 C1
BPOOL FY1 ...3 C1
FTWD FY7 ...11 E5
FUL/RIB PR2 ...45 E4
LSTA FY8 ...49 E4
PRES PR1 ...63 G2
Oxford St CLV/TH FY5 ...93 F3
Oxford Wy FTWD FY7 ...11 E5
Ox Hey Av FUL/RIB PR2 ...57 G2
Oxheys St PRES PR1 ...59 F1
Oxhill Pl CLV/TH FY5 ...21 E5
Oxley Cl KIRK/FR/WAR PR4 ...42 D5
Oxley Rd North PRES PR1 ...60 D3
Oxley Rd South PRES PR1 ...60 D2
Oystercatcher Ga LSTA FY8 ...50 C4
Oystons Ml PRES PR1 ...59 E3

P

Paddock Dr BPOOLE FY3 ...34 A3
The Paddock CLV/TH FY5 ...21 H4
PLF/KEOS FY6 ...26 A2
Padway PRES PR1 ...72 C4
Pages Ct BBR PR5 ...79 G2
Painley Cl LSTA FY8 ...64 B2
Palatine Cl BPOOLS FY4 ...30 A4
Palatine Rd BPOOL FY1 ...2 E6
CLV/TH FY5 ...16 D5
Paley Rd PRES PR1 ...6 B4
Palfrey Cl PLF/KEOS FY6 ...25 H1
Pall Ml CHLY/EC PR7 ...93 F4
Palm Dr PLF/KEOS FY6 ...25 H1
Palmer Av BPOOL FY1 ...28 B1
Paradise Cl CHLYE PR6 ...85 E4
Paradise La CROS/BRETH PR26 ...82 A5
Parbold Cl BPOOLS FY4 ...29 G2
Park Av CHLY/EC PR7 ...88 A5
FTWD FY7 ...11 F5
KIRK/FR/WAR PR4 ...63 H5
PRES PR1 ...60 B1
Park Cl PRES PR1 ...72 C2
Park Dr FUL/RIB PR2 ...57 H2
Parker La KIRK/FR/WAR PR4 ...78 B5
Parker St BPOOL FY1 ...2 E4
PRES PR1 ...93 F1
Park Farm Cl
KIRK/FR/WAR PR4 ...76 A1
Parkfield Cl FUL/RIB PR2 ...58 D1
Parkfield Cl FUL/RIB PR2 ...57 G2
Parkgate Dr LEYL PR25 ...82 D5
Park Hall Rd CHLY/EC PR7 ...95 E2
Parkinson Wy BPOOLS FY4 ...5 H6
Parkland Cl CLV/TH FY5 ...20 C3
Parklands Av PRES PR1 ...71 H2
Parklands Cl PRES PR1 ...71 H2
Parklands Dr FUL/RIB PR2 ...36 D5
Parklands Gv FUL/RIB PR2 ...36 D5
Park La KIRK/FR/WAR PR4 ...43 E2
PLF/KEOS FY6 ...13 H5
PRES PR1 ...72 D3
Park Ml PRES PR1 ...7 G1
Park Pl BBR PR5 ...74 B2
PRES PR1 ...7 G5

Park Rd BPOOL FY1 ...2 E7
CLV/TH FY5 ...17 H5
CHLY/EC PR7 ...93 F2
CHLY/EC PR7 ...96 B4
CLV/TH FY5 ...21 G5
FUL/RIB PR2 ...46 A4
KIRK/FR/WAR PR4 ...49 E5
LEYL PR25 ...83 F5
PRES PR1 ...49 E5
PLF/KEOS FY6 ...25 H2
PRES PR1 ...72 C2
Parkside FUL/RIB PR2 ...57 H1
Parkside Av CHLY/EC PR7 ...92 B5
Parkside Dr CHLYE PR6 ...89 E1
Parkside Dr South CHLYE PR6 ...89 E1
Parkside Rd LSTA FY8 ...49 G4
Parkstone Av CLV/TH FY5 ...22 B4
PLF/KEOS FY6 ...25 H2
Park St CHLY/EC PR7 ...93 F2
CHLY/EC PR7 ...93 F2
LSTA FY8 ...63 G2
Parksway PLF/KEOS FY6 ...12 B1
Parkthorn Rd FUL/RIB PR2 ...58 A3
Park Vw PRES PR1 ...72 C2
Park View Av FUL/RIB PR2 * ...58 D1
Park View Ct BPOOLS FY4 ...58 C2
Park View Rd FUL/RIB PR2 ...58 C2
Parkway BPOOLE FY3 ...29 G4
Park Wy PRES PR1 ...72 C2
Parlick Rd FUL/RIB PR2 ...61 G1
Parr Cottage Cl CHLY/EC PR7 ...90 A3
Parr La CLV/TH FY5 ...20 D2
Parrock Cl PRES PR1 ...72 D4
Parrox Fold PLF/KEOS FY6 ...13 E1
Parrys Wy PLF/KEOS FY6 ...26 B5
Parsley Cl BISP FY2 ...28 F3
Parson's Brow CHLY/EC PR7 ...88 A5
Partridge Av CLV/TH FY5 ...17 F5
Pasture Field Cl
CROS/BRETH PR26 ...82 B4
Pasture Field PLF/KEOS FY6 ...25 H1
Pastures New BBR PR5 ...79 H1
Patten St PRES PR1 ...7 F3
Patterdale Av FUL/RIB PR2 ...53 F3
CLV/TH FY5 ...21 H1
FTWD FY7 ...16 D1
Paul's La FUL/RIB PR2 ...54 B1
Pavey Cl BPOOLS FY4 ...33 F5
The Pavilions FUL/RIB PR2 ...29 F1
Paythorne Cl BPOOLE FY3 ...29 H1
Peace Pl CLV/TH FY5 ...17 G5
Peachtree Cl FUL/RIB PR2 ...46 D2
Peacock Hall Rd LEYL PR25 ...82 C5
Peacock Hill Cl FUL/RIB PR2 ...47 H1
Pearfield LEYL PR25 ...82 C5
Pearl Av BISP FY2 ...29 E1
Pear Tree Av CHLY/EC PR7 ...96 C2
Pear Tree Cl BBR PR5 * ...74 B4
Pear Trees CHLYE PR6 ...74 B4
Pear Tree Cft
KIRK/FR/WAR PR4 ...76 B1
Pear Tree La CHLY/EC PR7 ...88 B4
Pear Tree Rd CHLYE PR6 ...85 E1
Pear Tree St BBR PR5 * ...74 B4
Pechell St FUL/RIB PR2 ...59 E2
Pedder La FUL/RIB PR2 ...23 F3
Pedders Gv FUL/RIB PR2 ...58 C5
Pedder's La BPOOLS FY4 ...5 G5
FUL/RIB PR2 ...58 C2
Pedder St PRES PR1 ...6 C2
Pedders Wy FUL/RIB PR2 ...58 C5
Peel Cl BPOOLE FY3 ...28 D3
Peel Hall St PRES PR1 ...7 J1
Peel Hill BPOOLS FY4 ...40 C1
Peel Hill Hl BPOOLS FY4 ...40 C1
Peel Rd BPOOLS FY4 ...40 D3
FTWD FY7 ...11 F3
Peel St CHLY/EC PR7 ...93 F3
PRES PR1 ...6 C2
Peg's La CLV/TH FY5 ...93 F2
Peg Wy KIRK/FR/WAR PR4 ...53 H5
Pelham Av BPOOLS FY4 ...29 E2
Pemberton Gv BBR PR5 ...24 B4
Pembroke Pl KIRK/FR/WAR PR4 ...93 E4
LEYL PR25 ...83 F4
Pembroke Rd LSTA FY8 ...63 G5
Pembury Av PRES PR1 ...72 D5
Pendlebury Cl
KIRK/FR/WAR PR4 ...76 C1
Pendle Cl BPOOLS FY4 ...29 F1
Pendle Ct KIRK/FR/WAR PR4 ...76 C1
Pendle Pl LSTA FY8 ...64 D2
Pendle Rd LEYL PR25 ...83 A3
Penguin St PRES PR1 ...60 B2
Penhill Cl BISP FY2 ...28 D2
Pennine Av CLV/TH FY5 ...92 H1
Pennine Cl BPOOL FY1 ...7 J3
Pennine Rd CHLYE PR6 ...93 H2
The Pennines FUL/RIB PR2 ...46 A1
Pennine Vw KIRK/FR/WAR PR4 ...43 G3
Pennyfarthing La CLV/TH FY5 ...21 G2
Pennystone Rd BISP FY2 ...24 B5
Penny St PRES PR1 ...7 G2
Penrhos Av FTWD FY7 ...11 E5
Penrose Av BPOOLS FY4 ...5 K5
Penswick Av CLV/TH FY5 ...21 E5
Penwortham Ct PRES PR1 ...72 C2
Penwortham Hall Gdns
PRES PR1 ...72 D3
Penwortham Wy PRES PR1 ...72 B5
Percy St BPOOL FY1 ...2 E1
CHLY/EC PR7 ...93 G5
PRES PR1 ...7 H2
Peregrine Pl
CROS/BRETH PR26 ...82 C2
Pershore Gdns BPOOLE FY3 ...29 H2
Pershore Rd LSTA FY8 ...63 E1
Perth St CLV/TH FY5 ...21 F5
Peterfield Rd PRES PR1 * ...72 D4
Peter St BPOOL FY1 ...2 E3
CHLY/EC PR7 ...93 F2

Petunia Cl LEYL PR25 ...84 B2
Pharos St FTWD FY7 ...11 H1
Pharos St FTWD FY7 ...11 H1
Pheasant Wood Dr
CLV/TH FY5 ...17 F4
Philip Av KIRK/FR/WAR PR4 ...45 F4
Phillip St BPOOLS FY4 ...5 H3
Pickering Cl LSTA FY8 ...49 H4
The Pickerings BBR PR5 * ...79 H1
Pickmere Av BPOOLS FY4 ...5 H7
Pickmere Ct CLV/TH FY5 ...17 G5
Pierston Av BISP FY2 ...28 C1
Pier St BPOOL FY1 ...2 E6
Pike Ct FTWD FY7 ...10 C4
Pikestone Ct CHLYE PR6 ...93 H2
Pilling Av FUL/RIB PR2 * ...47 H4
Pilling Cl CHLY/EC PR7 ...93 G4
Pilling Ct BPOOLE FY3 ...29 C1
Pilling Crs BPOOLE FY3 ...26 C5
Pilling Gv CHLYE PR6 ...89 G4
Pilling La CHLY/EC PR7 ...93 F5
PLF/KEOS FY6
Pincock Brow CHLY/EC PR7 ...91 H2
Pincock St CHLY/EC PR7 ...91 H2
Pine Av BPOOL FY1 * ...5 H6
Pine Cl FUL/RIB PR2 * ...47 H4
Pine Crs FUL/KEOS FY6 ...26 C5
Pine Gv CHLYE PR6 ...89 G4
Pines Cl BBR PR5 ...81 F5
Pine Wks FUL/RIB PR2 ...57 G2
Pineway FUL/RIB PR2 ...45 E4
Pinewood Av CLV/TH FY5 ...22 C3
Pinewood Av BISP FY2 ...25 E3
CLV/TH FY5 ...21 H5
GAR/LONG PR3 ...36 B2
PLF/KEOS FY6 ...13 E1
Pinewood Crs LEYL PR25 ...82 D4
Pinfold BBR PR5 ...63 G2
Pinfold Av KIRK/FR/WAR PR4 ...76 B1
Pinfold Pl KIRK/FR/WAR PR4 ...42 D3
Pinfold St PRES PR1 ...60 D3
Pingle CHLYE PR6 ...84 D2
Pintail Wy LSTA FY8 ...50 C4
Pippin St CHLYE PR6 ...81 H5
Pittman Ct FUL/RIB PR2 ...46 B1
Pittman Wy FUL/RIB PR2 ...37 G5
Pittsdale Av BPOOLS FY4 ...33 G3
Pitt St PRES PR1 ...6 D4
Plainmoor Dr CLV/TH FY5 ...12 C1
Plantation Av PLF/KEOS FY6 ...12 C1
Plant St FUL/RIB PR2 ...59 E2
Pleasant Ct FUL/RIB PR2 ...2 D3
Pleasant Gv CLV/TH FY5 ...21 H2
Pleasant St BPOOL FY1 ...2 B1
LSTA FY8 ...64 C3
Pleasant Vw BPOOLS FY4 ...39 G4
CHLY/EC PR7 ...96 C3
Pleasington Cl BPOOLS FY4 ...33 G5
Pleck Pl PLF/KEOS FY6 ...25 H1
Plevna Rd PRES PR1 ...7 H3
The Ploughlands FUL/RIB PR2 ...58 A2
Plover Cl CLV/TH FY5 ...17 F4
Plover St PRES PR1 ...60 B1
Plovers Wy BPOOLS FY4 ...39 H4
Plumpton Av BPOOLS FY4 ...39 F3
Plumpton Rd FUL/RIB PR2 ...59 E1
Plumtree Cl FUL/RIB PR2 ...46 C2
Plungington Rd FUL/RIB PR2 ...45 G5
PRES PR1 ...59 G1
Plymouth Av FUL/RIB PR2 ...57 G5
Plymouth Gv CHLYE PR6 ...93 H2
Plymouth Rd BPOOLS FY4 ...39 F3
Poachers Wy CLV/TH FY5 ...17 G5
Pochard Pl CLV/TH FY5 ...17 F5
Polefield FUL/RIB PR2 ...45 G1
Pole St PRES PR1 ...7 H3
Pollux Ga LSTA FY8 ...63 F2
Polperro Dr KIRK/FR/WAR PR4 ...54 A5
Pond Gdns PLF/KEOS FY6 ...25 H1
Pool Ct FTWD FY7 ...10 C5
Poole Rd FUL/RIB PR2 ...46 A4
Pool Foot La PLF/KEOS FY6 ...27 H3
Poolhill Cl CLV/TH FY5 ...21 H2
Pool House La FUL/RIB PR2 ...44 B5
Pool La KIRK/FR/WAR PR4 ...42 D5
Pope La FUL/RIB PR2 ...47 G5
FUL/RIB PR2 ...61 F1
PRES PR1 ...72 C3
Pope Wk PRES PR1 ...72 C3
Poplar Av BBR PR5 ...74 C5
BPOOLS FY4 ...5 G4
CHLY/EC PR7 ...87 H3
KIRK/FR/WAR PR4 ...54 F5
KIRK/FR/WAR PR4 ...53 F5
PLF/KEOS FY6 ...26 C1
Poplar Cl BBR PR5 ...74 C5
Poplar Ct CHLY/EC PR7 ...96 C4
Poplar Dr KIRK/FR/WAR PR4 ...67 F1
PRES PR1 ...72 B1
Poplar Gv BBR PR5 ...74 C5
Poplar St CHLY/EC PR7 ...93 G4
Poppyfield KIRK/FR/WAR PR4 ...44 B2
Porter Pl PRES PR1 ...7 G6
Porters Brow PLF/KEOS FY6 * ...19 G2
Porter St East
KIRK/FR/WAR PR4 ...42 D2
Portland Rd BPOOL FY1 ...3 F7
Portland St CHLY/EC PR7 ...93 C2
PRES PR1 ...7 F5
Portman St PRES PR1 ...7 K1
Portree Cl FUL/RIB PR2 ...25 E1
Portree Rd BISP FY2 ...25 E1
Portsmouth Cl CLV/TH FY5 ...17 H2
Portsmouth Dr CHLYE PR6 ...93 H2
Portway BISP FY2 ...25 E1
Port Wy FUL/RIB PR2 ...54 H5
Post La KIRK/FR/WAR PR4 ...53 H5
Poulton Av LSTA FY8 ...49 G3
Poulton Crs BBR PR5 ...75 G3
Poulton Gdns PLF/KEOS FY6 ...26 D4
Poulton Old Rd BPOOLE FY3 ...29 F5

Poulton Rd BPOOLE FY3 29 F2
FTWD FY7 11 F2
PLF/KEOS FY6 26 A3
Poulton St FTWD FY7 11 G2
FUL/RIB PR2 59 E2
KIRK/FR/WAR PR4 43 E3
Powell Av BPOOLS FY4 32 D5
Powis Rd FUL/RIB PR2 58 C3
Poynter St PRES PR1 60 C2
Preesall Cl FUL/RIB PR2 58 A2
LSTA FY8 49 H4
Preesall Moss La
PLF/KEOS FY6 13 H4
Preesall Rd FUL/RIB PR2 58 A2
Prelude Pk
KIRK/FR/WAR PR4 * 76 A5
Premier Wy PLF/KEOS FY6 26 D4
Prenton Gdns CLV/TH FY5 21 F5
Prescot Pl BPOOLE FY3 33 G3
CLV/TH FY5 22 A2
Press Rd LSTA FY8 * 48 D3
Prestbury Av BPOOLS FY4 38 C3
Preston New Rd BPOOLS FY4 41 E2
KIRK/FR/WAR PR4 54 D4
PRES PR1 61 H2
Preston Nook CHLY/EC PR7 90 B5
Preston Old Rd BPOOLE FY3 5 J3
KIRK/FR/WAR PR4 54 C5
KIRK/FR/WAR PR4 56 A2
Preston Rd BBR PR5 80 D3
CHLY/EC PR7 95 G3
CHLYE PR6 89 F3
LEYL PR25 83 G2
LSTA FY8 65 E3
Preston St CHLYE PR6 89 F5
FTWD FY7 11 H2
KIRK/FR/WAR PR4 43 F3
Price St BPOOLS FY4 4 B6
Priestfield CLV/TH FY5 21 F5
Primrose Av BPOOLS FY4 38 D2
Primrose Bank BISP FY2 25 F1
Primrose Gv PRES PR1 46 C5
Primrose Hl PRES PR1 7 K4
Primrose Hill Rd CHLY/EC PR7 87 G3
Primrose La PRES PR1 46 C5
Primrose Rd PRES PR1 46 C5
Primrose St CHLYE PR6 93 G2
Primrose Ter BPOOLS FY4 * 39 G4
Primrose Wy PLF/KEOS FY6 25 H1
Princes Ct PRES PR1 58 D5
Princes Dr FUL/RIB PR2 45 F2
Prince's Rd BBR PR5 74 B1
LSTA FY8 63 G2
PRES PR1 58 D5
Princess Av
KIRK/FR/WAR PR4 42 D2
PLF/KEOS FY6 26 B4
Princess Ct BPOOL FY1 4 C1
Princess Rd CLV/TH FY5 20 C2
Princess St BBR PR5 79 G2
BBR PR5 80 C1
BPOOL FY1 4 B1
CHLY/EC PR7 93 G4
LEYL PR25 83 G3
PRES PR1 7 J5
Princess Wy CHLY/EC PR7 88 A5
Princes Wy CLV/TH FY5 20 C3
FTWD FY7 10 C4
Princeway BPOOLS FY4 38 C1
Pringle Wd GAR/LONG PR3 36 B3
Priory Cl LEYL PR25 83 H2
PRES PR1 59 E5
Priory Ct BPOOL FY1 2 E5
Priory Crs PRES PR1 59 E5
Priory Ga BPOOLS FY4 38 C3
Priory La PRES PR1 59 E5
Priory St FUL/RIB PR2 6 B2
Progress St CHLYE PR6 93 H2
Progress Wy BPOOLS FY4 39 G3
Promenade BISP FY2 24 B3
BPOOL FY1 2 B3
BPOOLS FY4 38 A1
CLV/TH FY5 16 C4
Promenade North
CLV/TH FY5 20 C1
Promenade Rd FTWD FY7 11 G1
Promenade South
CLV/TH FY5 20 C2
Prospect Av BBR PR5 79 G1
Prospect Pl FUL/RIB PR2 58 D2
PRES PR1 72 D2
Prudy Hl PLF/KEOS FY6 26 B3
Pudding Pie Nook La
GAR/LONG PR3 37 E1
Puddle House La
PLF/KEOS FY6 30 D2
Pump St PRES PR1 7 H2

Q

Quaile Holme Rd
PLF/KEOS FY6 12 B1
Quarrybank CLV/TH FY5 21 F4
Quarry Rd CHLYE PR6 93 H4
Quayle Av BPOOLS FY4 32 D5
Quayside FTWD FY7 11 H3
The Quayside FTWD FY7 * 12 A1
Quebec Av BISP FY2 24 D4
Queen Mary Av LSTA FY8 62 D1
Queensbury Rd CLV/TH FY5 20 C3
Queen's Cl PLF/KEOS FY6 26 C4
Queenscourt Av PRES PR1 72 D4
Queen's Crs
KIRK/FR/WAR PR4 43 F4
Queensdale Cl BBR PR5 74 B2
Queens Dr BPOOLE FY3 30 B5
FUL/RIB PR2 45 F2
Queensgate CHLY/EC PR7 93 E3
Queen's Gv CHLY/EC PR7 93 F2
Queens Pl KIRK/FR/WAR PR4 42 D1
Queen's Prom BISP FY2 24 B5
CLV/TH FY5 24 C1
Queen's Rd BBR PR5 74 B2
CHLY/EC PR7 93 E2
FUL/RIB PR2 45 G5
LSTA FY8 62 C1
Queen's Sq PLF/KEOS FY6 26 B4
Queen's Ter FTWD FY7 11 H1
Queen St BBR PR5 79 G2
BPOOL FY1 2 C3
FTWD FY7 11 G2
LSTA FY8 64 B3
PRES PR1 7 J4
Queen St East CHLY/EC PR7 93 G4
Queens Wk CLV/TH FY5 16 D5
Queens Wy PLF/KEOS FY6 26 B3
Queensway BBR PR5 74 B5
BPOOLS FY4 38 C1
CHLY/EC PR7 88 B5
FUL/RIB PR2 58 B1
KIRK/FR/WAR PR4 53 G4
LEYL PR25 82 D5
LSTA FY8 49 H1
PRES PR1 58 D5
Queensway Cl PRES PR1 58 D5
Queen Vera Rd BPOOL FY1 2 C4
Queen Victoria Rd BPOOL FY1 4 E3
Quenby Cnr PLF/KEOS FY6 25 H4
Quernmore Av BPOOLE FY3 33 G2
Quin St LEYL PR25 83 F3

R

Radburn Brow CHLYE PR6 85 E1
Radburn Cl CHLYE PR6 85 E1
Radcliffe Rd FTWD FY7 11 G3
Radley Av BPOOLE FY3 29 E2
Radnor Av CLV/TH FY5 21 F3
Radnor St PRES PR1 6 D2
Radway Cl CLV/TH FY5 21 F5
Radworth Crs BPOOLS FY4 33 H4
Raglan St FUL/RIB PR2 59 F1
Raikes Hl BPOOL FY1 2 E4
Raikes Ms BPOOL FY1 2 E5
Raikes Pde BPOOL FY1 2 E5
Raikes Rd CLV/TH FY5 22 C3
PRES PR1 60 C2
Railway Rd CHLYE PR6 93 G1
Railway St CHLY/EC PR7 93 G3
LEYL PR25 83 G2
Railway Ter KIRK/FR/WAR PR4 42 D2
Rake La KIRK/FR/WAR PR4 66 C1
Raleigh Av BPOOLS FY4 38 B3
Raleigh Cl LSTA FY8 48 D2
Raleigh Rd FUL/RIB PR2 45 G2
Ramper Ga CLV/TH FY5 20 D2
Ramsey Av BPOOLE FY3 28 D3
PRES PR1 46 D5
Ramsey Cl LSTA FY8 48 D2
Ramsgate Cl
KIRK/FR/WAR PR4 53 G4
Ramsgate Rd LSTA FY8 49 F3
Ramshill Av PLF/KEOS FY6 25 H2
Ranaldsway LEYL PR25 82 B4
Rangeway Av BPOOLS FY4 38 C1
Ranglet Rd BBR PR5 81 E2
Rangletts Av CHLY/EC PR7 93 F4
Ranglit Av FUL/RIB PR2 57 G2
Rathlyn Av BPOOLE FY3 3 H1
Rathmell Cl BPOOLE FY3 * 29 H1
Ratten La KIRK/FR/WAR PR4 70 D3
Ravenglass Cl BPOOLS FY4 39 E1
KIRK/FR/WAR PR4 43 E1
Ravenhill Dr CHLY/EC PR7 93 F1
Raven's Cl BPOOLE FY3 29 H3
Raven St PRES PR1 60 C1
Ravenswood FUL/RIB PR2 61 E1
Ravenswood Av BPOOLE FY3 29 H3
Ravenwood Av BPOOLS FY4 38 D3
Rawcliffe Dr FUL/RIB PR2 58 A3
Rawcliffe Rd CHLY/EC PR7 93 F3
Rawcliffe St BPOOLS FY4 4 B7
Rawlinson La CHLY/EC PR7 97 H4
Rawlinson St
KIRK/FR/WAR PR4 42 D2
Rawstorne Cl
KIRK/FR/WAR PR4 54 A5
Rawstorne Crs
KIRK/FR/WAR PR4 71 F5
Rawstorne Rd PRES PR1 72 A1
Raybourne Av PLF/KEOS FY6 26 A4
Raymond Av BISP FY2 28 D2
Read's Av BPOOL FY1 2 E6
Reaney Av BPOOLS FY4 39 E1
Rectory Cl CHLY/EC PR7 93 F1
Rectory Rd BPOOLS FY4 5 H5
Red Bank Rd BISP FY2 24 B3
Redcar Av CLV/TH FY5 17 E4
FUL/RIB PR2 44 B4
Redcar Rd BPOOL FY1 28 B2
Red Cross St PRES PR1 6 C4
Rede Av FTWD FY7 10 C4
Redeswood Av CLV/TH FY5 20 D4
Redhill KIRK/FR/WAR PR4 70 D5
Redhill Gv CHLYE PR6 89 H4
Red House La CHLY/EC PR7 90 A4
Red La CHLY/EC PR7 90 D4
Red Marsh Dr CLV/TH FY5 18 A5
Redmayne St PRES PR1 60 D3
Redsands Dr FUL/RIB PR2 46 D3
Redstart Pl CLV/TH FY5 21 F3
Redvers Ter BPOOL FY1 28 B2
Redwing Av CLV/TH FY5 17 F5
Redwing Dr CHLY/EC PR7 92 D3
Redwood Av LEYL PR25 82 D4
Redwood Cl BPOOLS FY4 38 C4
Redwood Dr CHLY/EC PR7 93 H4
Redwood Gdns CLV/TH FY5 22 C2
Reedfield BBR PR5 81 F5
Reedfield Pl BBR PR5 80 C2
Reedy Acre Pl LSTA FY8 64 A2
Reeveswood CHLY/EC PR7 90 A4
Regal Av BPOOLS FY4 39 E2
Regency Av BBR PR5 80 A1
Regency Cl KIRK/FR/WAR PR4 42 C3
Regency Gdns BISP FY2 28 D1
Regent Av LSTA FY8 50 C5
Regent Ct FUL/RIB PR2 45 G3
Regent Dr FUL/RIB PR2 45 F4
Regent Gv FUL/RIB PR2 45 G3
Regent Pk FUL/RIB PR2 45 G2
Regent Rd BBR PR5 74 A2
BPOOL FY1 2 D5
CHLY/EC PR7 93 E3
LEYL PR25 * 83 E3
Regent Rd East BPOOL FY1 2 D5
Regents Ter PLF/KEOS FY6 26 C4
Regent St CHLY/EC PR7 96 B4
PRES PR1 7 F6
Regentsway BBR PR5 80 B1
Regents Wy CHLY/EC PR7 88 A5
Reiver Rd CROS/BRETH PR26 82 B1
Renshaw Dr BBR PR5 74 B4
Renwick Av BPOOLS FY4 32 D5
Repton Av BPOOL FY1 28 C1
Reservoir Rd CLV/TH FY5 22 A1
Reta Dr CLV/TH FY5 21 G1
Rhoden Rd CROS/BRETH PR26 82 B3
Rhodesway BBR PR5 75 H4
Rhuddlan Gdns CLV/TH FY5 22 B2
Rhyl St FTWD FY7 11 H1
Ribble Av KIRK/FR/WAR PR4 54 A5
Ribble Bank PRES PR1 58 D5
Ribble Bank St PRES PR1 6 C4
Ribble Cl KIRK/FR/WAR PR4 54 A5
PRES PR1 72 D2
Ribble Ct FUL/RIB PR2 * 59 E2
PRES PR1 6 B6
Ribble Crs BBR PR5 * 60 C5
KIRK/FR/WAR PR4 43 F3
Ribble Rd BPOOL FY1 2 D7
FTWD FY7 11 F2
LEYL PR25 82 C4
Ribblesdale Cl BPOOLS FY4 33 G5
KIRK/FR/WAR PR4 42 D2
Ribblesdale Pl CHLY/EC PR7 93 E3
PRES PR1 7 F6
Ribble St LSTA FY8 48 D5
PRES PR1 6 D4
Ribbleton Av FUL/RIB PR2 60 D1
Ribbleton Hall Dr FUL/RIB PR2 47 F5
Ribbleton La PRES PR1 60 C2
Ribbleton Pl PRES PR1 7 K2
Ribbleton St PRES PR1 7 J2
Ribble View Cl
KIRK/FR/WAR PR4 53 H5
Ribble Wy KIRK/FR/WAR PR4 69 F4
Ribby Av KIRK/FR/WAR PR4 42 A4
KIRK/FR/WAR PR4 42 D3
Ribby Pl BPOOLS FY4 33 H4
FUL/RIB PR2 58 B2
Ribby Rd KIRK/FR/WAR PR4 42 A4
Ribchester Av BPOOLE FY3 33 H4
Ribchester Rd LSTA FY8 65 E2
Rice Gv BPOOL FY1 28 D2
Richardson Cl
KIRK/FR/WAR PR4 54 C5
Richardson St BPOOL FY1 2 C7
Richard's St KIRK/FR/WAR PR4 42 D2
Richards Wy CLV/TH FY5 21 F3
LSTA FY8 49 E1
Richmond Av CLV/TH FY5 21 E2
Richmond Ct CHLY/EC PR7 93 F4
CROS/BRETH PR26 82 A3
Richmond Rd BPOOL FY1 2 C1
CHLY/EC PR7 90 B3
CHLYE PR6 93 H4
LSTA FY8 49 E5
Richmond St PRES PR1 7 K4
Ridgeford Gdns FUL/RIB PR2 45 F3
Ridgemont FUL/RIB PR2 45 E2
Ridge Rd CHLYE PR6 93 H3
Ridge Wy PRES PR1 72 D2
Ridgeway Dr CLV/TH FY5 22 B4
The Ridgeway FTWD FY7 10 D3
Ridgwood Av BPOOLE FY3 3 H4
The Ridings CHLYE PR6 89 F1
Riding St PRES PR1 * 7 F1
Ridley Rd FUL/RIB PR2 59 E1
Ridley St BPOOLE FY3 3 G4
Rigby Cl KIRK/FR/WAR PR4 54 C5
Rigby Rd BPOOL FY1 4 C2
Rigby St PRES PR1 60 C2
Rigby Wk CHLY/EC PR7 * 93 F2
Riley Av LSTA FY8 62 C2
Riley Cl LEYL PR25 83 F4
Rimington Pl LSTA FY8 49 H5
Ring Dyke Wy LSTA FY8 64 B2
Rington Av PLF/KEOS FY6 25 H1
Ringway CHLY/EC PR7 92 D3
CLV/TH FY5 17 E5
Ring Wy PRES PR1 7 H2
Ringwood Cl LSTA FY8 63 H3
Ringwood Rd PRES PR1 60 C1
Ripley Dr LSTA FY8 49 H5
Ripon Cl CLV/TH FY5 17 E4
Ripon Rd BPOOL FY1 3 F7
LSTA FY8 63 G1
Ripon St PRES PR1 59 G1
Ripon Ter PRES PR1 61 F2
Rishton St BPOOL FY1 2 C7
Ritherham Av CLV/TH FY5 20 D1
River Hts BBR PR5 79 H1
River Pde PRES PR1 6 B7
River Rd CLV/TH FY5 18 B5
Riversedge Rd LEYL PR25 82 B4
Riversgate FTWD FY7 11 F2
Riverside BBR PR5 80 B2
PRES PR1 72 D1
Riverside Av
CROS/BRETH PR26 78 D5
Riverside Cl CROS/BRETH PR26 78 D5
Riverside Dr PLF/KEOS FY6 23 F2
Riverside Rd PRES PR1 72 D1
Riversleigh Av BPOOL FY1 28 C1
LSTA FY8 63 H3
River St PRES PR1 6 C4
Riversway BPOOLE FY3 29 F4
FUL/RIB PR2 57 G3
PLF/KEOS FY6 26 C2
Riverway Cl BBR PR5 79 H1
Rivington Av BISP FY2 24 C2
Rivington Cl PLF/KEOS FY6 26 B4
Rivington Rd CHLYE PR6 93 H1
Rixton Gv CLV/TH FY5 17 H5
Roberts St CHLY/EC PR7 93 F3
Robin Cl CHLY/EC PR7 96 A2
Robin Hey CROS/BRETH PR26 82 A3
Robins Cl PLF/KEOS FY6 25 G3
Robins La BISP FY2 25 F1
Robinson St FUL/RIB PR2 45 F5
Robin St PRES PR1 60 D2
Robson Wy BPOOLE FY3 25 G5
Rochester Av CLV/TH FY5 17 F5
Rochford Av CLV/TH FY5 21 E3
Rockburgh Crs
KIRK/FR/WAR PR4 76 B4
Rockingham Rd BISP FY2 24 D4
Rock St CLV/TH FY5 17 H5
Rock Villa Rd CHLYE PR6 * 85 F4
Rockville Av CLV/TH FY5 21 E4
Rodney Av LSTA FY8 49 E2
Rodney St PRES PR1 6 E2
Rodwell Wk BPOOLE FY3 29 F2
Roebuck St FUL/RIB PR2 59 E1
Roehampton Cl CLV/TH FY5 21 G2
Roe Hey Dr CHLY/EC PR7 96 C3
Rogerley Cl LSTA FY8 64 B2
Roman Rd PRES PR1 7 K5
Roman Wy CLV/TH FY5 21 F3
KIRK/FR/WAR PR4 43 G4
Romford Rd PRES PR1 60 C1
Romney Av BPOOLS FY4 5 F6
FTWD FY7 11 E3
Ronaldsway PRES PR1 46 D5
Rookery Cl CHLY/EC PR7 92 D4
PRES PR1 72 D4
Rookery Dr PRES PR1 73 E4
Rook St PRES PR1 60 B1
Rookwood CHLY/EC PR7 90 A4
Rookwood Av CHLY/EC PR7 89 F5
CLV/TH FY5 20 D4
Rosary Av BPOOLS FY4 5 J5
Roscoe Av CLV/TH FY5 22 B2
Roseacre BPOOLS FY4 38 C3
Roseacre Pl FUL/RIB PR2 58 A2
LSTA FY8 49 H3
Rose Av BPOOL FY1 5 F3
FUL/RIB PR2 45 E5
Rosebank FUL/RIB PR2 57 G2
Rosebank Av BPOOLS FY4 38 C3
Roseberry Av
KIRK/FR/WAR PR4 44 A3
Rosebery Av BPOOLS FY4 38 B2
LSTA FY8 63 E2
Rose Cl LEYL PR25 84 B2
Rose Ct FTWD FY7 * 11 F4
Rosedale Av BPOOLE FY3 33 G3
Rosedene Cl KIRK/FR/WAR PR4 44 A3
Rosefinch Wy BPOOLE FY3 33 H3
Rose Fold CLV/TH FY5 17 G5
PRES PR1 72 C2
Rose La PRES PR1 46 C5
Rose Lea FUL/RIB PR2 46 D2
Roselyn Av BPOOLS FY4 38 C3
Rosemary Av BPOOLS FY4 38 C3
CLV/TH FY5 21 F1
Rosemary Ct PRES PR1 72 B4
Rosemeade Av BBR PR5 79 G1
Rosemede Av BPOOLE FY3 33 F3
Rosemount Av PLF/KEOS FY6 13 E1
Rose St LEYL PR25 83 G1
PRES PR1 7 H4
Rose Ter FUL/RIB PR2 58 D2
Roseway BPOOLS FY4 38 C3
FUL/RIB PR2 58 C2
LSTA FY8 63 E1
PLF/KEOS FY6 26 A4
Rosewood KIRK/FR/WAR PR4 44 A3
Rosewood Av BBR PR5 75 F3
Rosewood Cl CHLY/EC PR7 93 G4
CLV/TH FY5 22 B3
LSTA FY8 63 H2
Rosewood Dr BBR PR5 75 E3
Rosklyn Rd CHLYE PR6 93 H3
Rossall Cl BBR PR5 75 H2
FTWD FY7 16 D1
Rossall Ct CLV/TH FY5 * 16 C4
FTWD FY7 * 11 E3
Rossall Dr FUL/RIB PR2 45 E4
Rossall Gdns CLV/TH FY5 16 D5
Rossall Ga FTWD FY7 16 C1
Rossall Grange La FTWD FY7 10 D3
Rossall La FTWD FY7 16 D3
Rossall Rd BPOOLE FY3 3 G1
CHLYE PR6 93 H1
CLV/TH FY5 16 D5
FUL/RIB PR2 45 E4
LSTA FY8 63 G2
Rossall St FUL/RIB PR2 59 E2
Rossendale Av North
CLV/TH FY5 21 H2
Rossendale Av South
CLV/TH FY5 21 H3
Rossendale Rd LSTA FY8 49 G4
Rossett Av BPOOLS FY4 34 A4
Rossington Av BISP FY2 25 E2
Rosslyn Av PLF/KEOS FY6 8 A5
Rosslyn Crs PLF/KEOS FY6 13 E1
Rosslyn Crs East
PLF/KEOS FY6 13 F1
Rostrevor Cl
CROS/BRETH PR26 82 A3
Rothay Av FTWD FY7 10 D4
Rothbury Pl LSTA FY8 64 D2
Rotherwick Av CHLY/EC PR7 93 E3
Rothwell Ct LEYL PR25 83 F2
Rothwell Crs FUL/RIB PR2 47 F4
Rothwell Dr FTWD FY7 10 D3
Rough Hey Pl FUL/RIB PR2 47 H1
Rough Hey Rd FUL/RIB PR2 47 H1
Rough Heys La BPOOLS FY4 39 E1
Rough Lea Rd CLV/TH FY5 20 C2
Round Acre BBR PR5 73 F5
Roundhay BPOOLS FY4 33 F5
Round Meadow
CROS/BRETH PR26 82 B3
Roundway FTWD FY7 16 C1
Roundway Down FUL/RIB PR2 45 E1
Round Wd PRES PR1 58 D4
Rowan Av FUL/RIB PR2 47 G4
Rowan Cl PRES PR1 72 A3
Rowan Cft CHLYE PR6 84 D3
Rowangate FUL/RIB PR2 46 C1
Rowan Gv CHLYE PR6 89 F4
The Rowans PLF/KEOS FY6 25 G5
Rowberrow Cl FUL/RIB PR2 46 D2
Rowland Cl CLV/TH FY5 21 F2
Rowland La CLV/TH FY5 21 F2
Rowntree Av FTWD FY7 11 F3
Roworth Cl BBR PR5 74 B3
Rowsley Rd LSTA FY8 48 D4
Rowton Heath FUL/RIB PR2 45 E1
Roxburgh Rd BPOOLS FY4 39 G2
Royal Av BPOOLE FY3 5 K3
FUL/RIB PR2 45 G2
KIRK/FR/WAR PR4 43 F4
LEYL PR25 82 D5
Royal Bank Rd BPOOLE FY3 5 J2
Royal Pl LSTA FY8 50 A3
Royal Troon Ct
KIRK/FR/WAR PR4 * 43 E4
Royalty Av KIRK/FR/WAR PR4 77 H1
Royalty Gdns
KIRK/FR/WAR PR4 77 H1
Royalty La KIRK/FR/WAR PR4 77 H1
Royds St LSTA FY8 62 B1
Roylen Av PLF/KEOS FY6 25 H2
Royle Rd CHLY/EC PR7 93 E2
Royles Ct CLV/TH FY5 21 H2
Royle St BPOOL FY1 4 B5
Royston Rd PLF/KEOS FY6 26 D2
Royton Dr CHLYE PR6 89 F2
Rudyard Pl BPOOLE FY3 * 29 F3
LSTA FY8 49 E3
Rufford Rd LSTA FY8 63 F1
Rufus St PRES PR1 60 C1
Rugby St BPOOLS FY4 5 F6
Runcorn Av BISP FY2 25 F5
Rundle Rd FUL/RIB PR2 45 F5
Runnell Vls BPOOLS FY4 * 39 G1
Runnymede Av CLV/TH FY5 20 D2
The Runriggs CLV/TH FY5 21 H3
Runshaw Hall La CHLY/EC PR7 87 F3
Runshaw La CHLY/EC PR7 86 D4
CHLY/EC PR7 87 F2
Rushy Hey BBR PR5 79 F1
Ruskin Av BPOOL FY1 4 C4
CLV/TH FY5 21 G1
LEYL PR25 83 F2
Ruskin Rd KIRK/FR/WAR PR4 54 B5
Ruskin St PRES PR1 7 K6
Rusland Av BPOOLS FY4 34 B4
Rusland Dr BBR PR5 75 H2
Russell Av CLV/TH FY5 20 D4
LEYL PR25 83 H4
PRES PR1 61 G3
Russell Sq CHLYE PR6 93 G1
Russell Sq West CHLYE PR6 93 G1
Rutherford Pl BPOOLS FY4 38 B4
Ruthin Dr CLV/TH FY5 22 B2
Rutland Av BBR PR5 * 74 A3
CLV/TH FY5 21 E1
FTWD FY7 11 E3
KIRK/FR/WAR PR4 54 C4
PLF/KEOS FY6 26 A4
Rutland Ct LSTA FY8 63 G1
Rutland Rd LSTA FY8 63 G1
Rutland St PRES PR1 60 C3
Ryburn Av BPOOLS FY4 5 H5
Rydal Av BBR PR5 74 A5
BPOOL FY1 4 E1
CLV/TH FY5 21 H3
FTWD FY7 11 E2
KIRK/FR/WAR PR4 54 A5
PLF/KEOS FY6 26 B4
PRES PR1 72 B3
Rydal Cl FUL/RIB PR2 46 C4
Rydal Pl CHLY/EC PR7 93 F4
Rydal Rd LSTA FY8 49 E3
PLF/KEOS FY6 23 G2
PRES PR1 60 D1
Ryddingwood PRES PR1 58 D5
Ryden Av CLV/TH FY5 20 D1
LEYL PR25 83 H3
Ryding Cl CROS/BRETH PR26 82 D1
Ryecroft Av PLF/KEOS FY6 23 G3
Ryefield Av PRES PR1 72 C4
Ryeheys Rd LSTA FY8 48 D3
Ryelands Crs FUL/RIB PR2 58 A3
Rye St PRES PR1 60 A2
Ryland Av PLF/KEOS FY6 26 A4
Rylands Rd CHLY/EC PR7 93 E3
Ryldon Pl BPOOLS FY4 33 G3
Ryscar Wy BISP FY2 25 F1
Ryson Av BPOOLS FY4 5 K5

S

Sabden Pl LSTA FY8 50 A4
Sackville St BPOOLS FY4 38 C1
CHLYE PR6 93 H3
Sadlers Rw LSTA FY8 50 B4
Saer Cl FTWD FY7 10 D3
Sagar Dr KIRK/FR/WAR PR4 54 A5
Sagar St CHLY/EC PR7 90 B4
Sage Cl BISP FY2 25 F4
Sage Ct PRES PR1 72 B4
Sage La PRES PR1 46 B5
St Aidans Pk BBR PR5 74 B4
St Alban's Pl CHLY/EC PR7 93 G5
St Alban's Rd BPOOL FY1 3 F7
LSTA FY8 49 F4
St Ambrose Ter LEYL PR25 * 83 G2
St Andrew's Av CLV/TH FY5 20 D2
FUL/RIB PR2 58 C1

St Andrews Cl CHLY/EC PR7 .....88 A3
  LEYL PR25 .....83 F4
St Andrew's Ct CLV/TH FY5 .....20 C1
St Andrew's Rd PRES PR1 * 60 A1
St Andrew's Rd North
  LSTA FY8 .....48 D4
St Andrew's Rd South
  LSTA FY8 .....49 E5
St Andrews Wy LEYL PR25 .....83 F4
Saint Annes Rd CHLYE PR6 .....4 E6
St Anne's Rd LSTA FY8 .....49 E4
St Anne's Rd East LSTA FY8 .....49 E4
St Anne's Rd West LSTA FY8 .....48 D5
St Anne's Rd PRES PR1 .....60 A1
St Anthony's Cl FUL/RIB PR2 .....45 G4
St Anthony's Crs FUL/RIB PR2 .....45 G4
St Anthony's Dr FUL/RIB PR2 .....45 H4
St Anthony's Pl BPOOL FY1 .....2 E1
  KIRK/FR/WAR PR4 .....43 E4
St Anthony's Rd PRES PR1 * 60 A1
St Austin's Pl PRES PR1 .....7 H5
St Austin's Rd PRES PR1 .....7 H5
St Barnabas' Pl PRES PR1 .....7 H1
St Bede's Av BPOOLS FY4 .....4 B6
St Bernard Av BPOOLE FY3 .....29 F3
St Bernard's Rd
  .....12 C1
St Catherine's Cl BPOOLE FY3 .....29 H1
St Catherines Cl LEYL PR25 .....83 H2
St Catherine's Dr FUL/RIB PR2 .....45 G4
St Catherines Wy BBR PR5 .....79 H2
St Chads Cl PLF/KEOS FY6 .....26 B5
St Chad's Rd BPOOL FY1 .....4 B4
St Christines Av LEYL PR25 .....79 H5
St Christopher's Rd
  PRES PR1 * 60 A1
St Clares Av FUL/RIB PR2 .....46 A2
St Clement's Av BPOOLE FY3 .....3 J4
  LEYL PR25 .....83 H1
St Cuthbert's Cl FUL/RIB PR2 .....45 F5
  BBR PR5 .....64 B3
St Cuthbert' Rd BBR PR5 .....75 F5
  PRES PR1 .....60 A1
St David's Av CLV/TH FY5 .....20 D2
St David's Gv LSTA FY8 .....49 E5
St David's Rd LEYL PR25 .....83 H2
  PRES PR1 .....60 A1
St David's Rd North LSTA FY8 .....48 D5
St David's Rd South LSTA FY8 .....49 E5
St Edmund's Rd BPOOLS FY4 .....5 J5
St Francis Cl FUL/RIB PR2 .....45 H4
St George Ct BPOOL FY1 .....3 F2
St George's Av CLV/TH FY5 .....20 D3
St George's La CLV/TH FY5 * 20 D2
St Georges Pk
  KIRK/FR/WAR PR4 .....42 C2
St George's Rd BPOOLS FY4 .....38 C2
  LSTA FY8 .....48 D5
  PRES PR1 .....59 H1
St George's Sq LSTA FY8 .....48 D4
St George's St CHLY/EC PR7 .....93 F3
St Gerrard's Rd BBR PR5 .....75 F5
St Gregory Rd PRES PR1 .....60 B1
St Gregory's Pl CHLY/EC PR7 .....93 F5
St Helen's Rd CHLYE PR6 .....85 F3
St Heliers Rd BPOOL FY1 .....4 D4
St Hilda's Cl CHLY/EC PR7 .....97 F1
St Hilda's Rd LSTA FY8 .....49 E5
St Ignatius' Sq PRES PR1 .....7 G2
St Ives Av BPOOL FY1 * 5 G2
  KIRK/FR/WAR PR4 .....54 A5
St Ives Crs FUL/RIB PR2 .....44 C4
St James Cl BBR PR5 .....79 G1
St James Rd BPOOLS FY4 .....38 C2
St James's Pl CHLYE PR6 .....93 H3
St James's Rd PRES PR1 .....59 H1
St John Av FTWD FY7 .....10 D4
St John's Av CLV/TH FY5 .....22 B5
  GAR/LONG PR3 .....15 E1
  KIRK/FR/WAR PR4 .....
  PLF/KEOS FY6 .....26 C2
St Johns Cl CHLYE PR6 .....85 E5
St John's Gn LEYL PR25 .....82 D3
St John's Pl PRES PR1 .....7 G4
St John's Rd BBR PR5 .....74 A1
St John's St LSTA FY8 .....64 D3
St Josephs Cl BPOOLE FY3 .....3 J4
St Josephs Pl CHLYE PR6 .....93 G1
St Joseph's Ter PRES PR1 * 60 C2
St Jude's La PRES PR1 .....74 A5
  LEYL PR25 .....79 H5
St Leonard's Rd BPOOLS FY4 .....33 F3
St Leonard's Rd East LSTA FY8 .....49 E5
St Leonard's Rd West
  .....48 D4
St Louis Av BPOOLE FY3 .....3 K1
St Luke's Dr ...
St Luke's Rd BPOOLS FY4 .....5 G5
St Margarets Cl FUL/RIB PR2 .....44 C4
St Margaret's Rd LEYL PR25 .....83 H2
St Mark's Pl BPOOLE FY3 .....29 E2
St Mark's Pl East PRES PR1 .....6 A2
St Mark's Pl West PRES PR1 * 6 A2
St Mark's Rd PRES PR1 .....6 A2
St Marlow Av LEYL PR25 * 83 H1
St Martins Cl FUL/RIB PR2 .....25 H2
St Martin's Ct CLV/TH FY5 .....21 F2
St Martin's Rd BPOOLS FY4 .....38 C2
  PRES PR1 .....60 A1
St Mary's Av BBR PR5 .....74 A5
St Mary's Cl BBR PR5 .....74 A5
  PRES PR1 * 60 C3
St Marys Ct FTWD FY7 * 11 H2
  PRES PR1 .....7 K3
St Mary's Ga CHLY/EC PR7 .....87 H4
Saint Mary's Rd BBR PR5 .....74 B5
St Mary's St PRES PR1 .....7 J2
St Mary's St North PRES PR1 * 7 J2
St Michael's Cl CHLY/EC PR7 .....93 E1
  FUL/RIB PR2 .....45 F5

St Michaels Rd BISP FY2 .....25 E4
  KIRK/FR/WAR PR4 .....43 G3
  LEYL PR25 * 83 H1
St Monica's Wy BPOOLS FY4 .....34 B4
St Nicholas Rd BPOOLS FY4 .....39 G3
St Oswalds Cl PRES PR1 .....62 D2
St Patricks Ct LSTA FY8 * 49 F4
St Patrick's Rd North LSTA FY8 .....49 E5
St Patrick's Rd South LSTA FY8 .....49 F4
St Paul's Av LSTA FY8 .....65 E2
  PRES PR1 .....7 G1
St Pauls Cl CROS/BRETH PR26 .....79 E2
St Paul's Rd BPOOL FY1 .....28 B2
  PRES PR1 .....60 A1
St Paul's Sq PRES PR1 .....7 H2
St Peters Cl PRES PR1 .....60 A1
St Peter's Pl FTWD FY7 * 11 H1
St Peter's Sq PRES PR1 .....7 H1
St Peter's St CHLYE PR6 .....93 H1
  PRES PR1 .....60 A1
St Philip's Rd PRES PR1 .....60 A1
St Saviour's Cl BBR PR5 .....80 C2
St Stephen's Av BISP FY2 .....24 B5
St Stephens Rd
  KIRK/FR/WAR PR4 .....43 E4
  LSTA FY8 .....49 F5
  PRES PR1 .....59 H1
St Teresa's Av CLV/TH FY5 .....20 D5
St Theresa's Dr FUL/RIB PR2 .....45 E4
St Thomas Cl PLF/KEOS FY6 .....29 H1
St Thomas' Pl PRES PR1 * 6 E1
St Thomas Rd
  KIRK/FR/WAR PR4 .....43 E4
  LSTA FY8 .....49 F5
  PRES PR1 .....59 H1
St Thomas St PRES PR1 .....6 E1
St Thomas's Rd CHLY/EC PR7 .....93 F2
St Vincent Av BPOOL FY1 .....5 G2
St Vincents Rd FUL/RIB PR2 .....45 G3
St Walburga's Rd
  .....29 F2
St Walburge Av PRES PR1 .....6 E1
St Walburges Gdns
  FUL/RIB PR2 .....6 B2
St Wilfrid St PRES PR1 .....6 E4
Salcombe Av BISP FY2 .....25 E5
Salcombe Rd LSTA FY8 .....48 C2
Salisbury Av PLF/KEOS FY6 .....12 C1
Salisbury Rd BPOOL FY1 .....3 F7
  PRES PR1 .....6 B5
Salisbury St CHLY/EC PR7 * 93 G3
  PRES PR1 .....60 D2
Salmesbury Av BISP FY2 .....25 E5
Salmon St PRES PR1 .....60 C4
Salop Av BISP FY2 .....24 C5
Saltash Rd CLV/TH FY5 .....17 H4
Saltcotes Pl LSTA FY8 .....65 E2
Saltcotes Rd LSTA FY8 .....65 E2
Salter St PRES PR1 .....59 H2
Salthouse Av BPOOL FY1 .....4 D2
Salt Marsh Cl PLF/KEOS FY6 .....23 F3
Salt Marsh La PLF/KEOS FY6 .....23 F3
Salwick Av BISP FY2 .....24 D2
Salwick Pl FUL/RIB PR2 .....58 A2
  LSTA FY8 .....49 G3
Samuel St PRES PR1 .....6 D5
Sanderling Cl CLV/TH FY5 .....21 F5
  LSTA FY8 .....50 C4
Sandersons Wy KIRK/FR/WAR PR4 .....33 F5
Sandfield CLV/TH FY5 * 21 G2
Sandfield St LEYL PR25 .....83 E2
Sandgate BPOOLS FY4 .....38 D5
  CHLY/EC PR7 .....93 G5
  LSTA FY8 .....48 C4
Sandham St CHLYE PR6 .....93 G2
Sandhams Wy BPOOLS FY4 .....34 B4
Sandhills Av BPOOLS FY4 .....38 B5
Sandhurst Av BISP FY2 .....24 D3
  LSTA FY8 .....49 E4
Sandhurst Cl
  KIRK/FR/WAR PR4 .....42 D5
Sandicroft Cl PLF/KEOS FY6 .....23 G5
Sandicroft Pl PLF/KEOS FY6 .....13 F2
Sandicroft Rd BPOOL FY1 .....28 C1
Sandiways Cl CLV/TH FY5 .....22 A4
Sandon Pl BPOOLS FY4 .....38 C4
Sandown Cl KIRK/FR/WAR PR4 .....42 C3
Sandown Rd CLV/TH FY5 .....21 H3
Sandridge Av CHLY/EC PR7 .....93 E5
Sandridge Pl BPOOLS FY4 .....38 B4
Sandringham Av CLV/TH FY5 .....21 H3
  LEYL PR25 .....83 H3
Sandringham Park Dr
  .....
Sandringham Rd BBR PR5 .....74 A3
  CHLY/EC PR7 .....90 B5
  CHLY/EC PR7 .....93 E2
  LSTA FY8 .....62 D1
Sandringham Wy
  KIRK/FR/WAR PR4 .....44 A2
Sandsdale Av FUL/RIB PR2 .....46 C3
Sands Wy BPOOL FY1 .....4 C2
Sandwick Cl FUL/RIB PR2 .....45 G1
Sandy Cl CLV/TH FY5 .....20 C1
Sandycroft FUL/RIB PR2 .....61 F1
Sandyfields KIRK/FR/WAR PR4 .....44 A3
Sandyforth Av CLV/TH FY5 .....21 H1
Sandyforth La
  KIRK/FR/WAR PR4 .....44 C1
Sandygate La GAR/LONG PR3 .....36 A4
Sandy La BPOOLS FY4 .....39 G4
  CHLYE PR6 .....85 F1
  FTWD FY7 .....16 D2
  LEYL PR25 .....83 F4
  PLF/KEOS FY6 .....23 G3
  PLF/KEOS FY6 .....13 G3
Sandy Pl LSTA FY8 .....49 E5
Sandywell Av CLV/TH FY5 .....22 A1
Santon Cl KIRK/FR/WAR PR4 .....43 E1
Sarahs Fold PLF/KEOS FY6 .....19 G2
Saul St PRES PR1 .....7 F3
Saunders La
  KIRK/FR/WAR PR4 .....71 F5

Saunders Ms CHLY/EC PR7 .....97 F2
Savick Cl FUL/RIB PR2 .....57 H2
Savick Cl BBR PR5 .....80 C1
Savick Rd FUL/RIB PR2 .....45 F4
Savick Wy FUL/RIB PR2 .....45 H4
Saville Av PLF/KEOS FY6 .....25 H1
Saville Rd BPOOL FY1 .....4 A5
Saville St CHLY/EC PR7 .....93 F5
Savoy St PRES PR1 .....6 D4
Sawley Av BPOOLS FY4 .....38 D3
  PRES PR1 .....50 A5
Sawley Crs FUL/RIB PR2 .....47 F5
Sawthorpe Wk PLF/KEOS FY6 .....25 G4
Saxby Gv BPOOLS FY4 .....33 F4
Saxon Cl CLV/TH FY5 .....21 H4
Saxon Hey FUL/RIB PR2 .....45 E5
Scafell Rd LSTA FY8 .....49 G1
Scale Hall La
  KIRK/FR/WAR PR4 .....55 G1
Scarborough Rd LSTA FY8 .....49 G3
Scarlet St CHLYE PR6 .....93 H3
Scarlett Dr KIRK/FR/WAR PR4 .....71 F5
Scarsdale Av BPOOLS FY4 .....38 C3
Scarfell Rd CHLY/EC PR7 .....93 E5
Sceptre Wy BBR PR5 .....81 E5
Schieswig St PRES PR1 .....7 H2
Schleswig Wy LEYL PR25 .....82 B5
Schofield Av BPOOLE FY3 .....29 H5
Scholars Gn FUL/RIB PR2 .....57 G2
School Brow CHLYE PR6 .....85 E5
School Fld BBR PR5 .....81 H4
School La BBR PR5 .....74 C4
  BBR PR5 .....79 E2
  CHLY/EC PR7 .....88 A4
  KIRK/FR/WAR PR4 .....43 F5
  KIRK/FR/WAR PR4 .....54 A4
  KIRK/FR/WAR PR4 .....55 F1
  KIRK/FR/WAR PR4 .....76 B2
  LEYL PR25 .....83 E2
  LSTA FY8 .....64 B5
  PLF/KEOS FY6 .....13 F5
School Rd BPOOLS FY4 .....5 G6
  CLV/TH FY5 .....22 A4
School St BBR PR5 .....74 C3
  KIRK/FR/WAR PR4 .....76 A4
  LEYL PR25 .....83 G2
  PRES PR1 .....6 C4
Scorton Av BPOOLE FY3 .....3 K1
Scotforth Rd PRES PR1 .....60 C5
Scotswood Av BPOOLS FY4 .....38 D2
Scott Cl BPOOLS FY4 .....5 K7
Scott Ms BPOOLS FY4 .....33 F5
Scott's Wd FUL/RIB PR2 .....45 E2
Scudamore Crs BPOOLS FY4 .....5 H6
Seabank Rd FTWD FY7 .....11 G1
Seabourne Av BPOOLS FY4 .....38 B1
Seabrook Dr LSTA FY8 .....49 G4
Seacrest Av BPOOL FY1 .....28 C2
Seafield Rd BPOOL FY1 .....28 B2
  LSTA FY8 .....49 F5
Seasiders Wy BPOOL FY1 .....4 C1
Seaside Wy BPOOL FY1 .....4 C4
Seathwaite Av BPOOLS FY4 .....34 A4
Seaton Av CLV/TH FY5 .....17 E5
Seaton Crs LSTA FY8 .....48 C3
Seattle Av BISP FY2 .....25 E5
Sea Vw KIRK/FR/WAR PR4 .....76 A4
Seaview Wy FTWD FY7 .....11 H2
Second Av BPOOLS FY4 .....38 C1
  KIRK/FR/WAR PR4 .....
  PLF/KEOS FY6 .....13 G5
Sedberg Av BPOOLS FY4 .....5 K4
Sedberg St FUL/RIB PR2 .....45 F5
Sedgeley Ms
  KIRK/FR/WAR PR4 .....54 A5
Sedgfield Cl BPOOLS FY4 .....39 F2
Sedgley Av KIRK/FR/WAR PR4 .....54 A5
Sedgwick St PRES PR1 .....7 G1
Sedwell Cl LSTA FY8 .....49 G3
Seedlee Rd BBR PR5 .....80 D3
Seed St BPOOL FY1 .....2 B5
  PRES PR1 .....6 E5
Sefton Av PLF/KEOS FY6 .....30 B1
Sefton Rd BBR PR5 .....74 A3
  LSTA FY8 .....49 F5
Segar St KIRK/FR/WAR PR4 .....42 D2
Selborne St PRES PR1 .....7 H7
Selbourne Rd BPOOL FY1 .....3 F2
Selby Av BPOOLS FY4 .....38 D5
  CLV/TH FY5 .....17 F4
Selby Rd KIRK/FR/WAR PR4 .....54 A5
Selby St PRES PR1 .....59 F2
Selkirk Dr BBR PR5 .....74 A4
Sellers St PRES PR1 .....60 C2
Senior Av BPOOLS FY4 .....33 F4
Sephton Av BBR PR5 .....79 F1
Sephton St BBR PR5 .....80 C1
Sergeant St BBR PR5 .....80 C1
The Serpentine LSTA FY8 .....64 B3
Settle Pl LSTA FY8 .....50 A4
Seven Acres BBR PR5 .....81 F4
Sevenoaks CHLY/EC PR7 .....97 F1
Sevenoaks Dr CLV/TH FY5 .....21 F4
Seven Sands
  KIRK/FR/WAR PR4 .....70 A5
Seven Stars Rd
  CROS/BRETH PR26 .....82 B2
Seventh Av BPOOLS FY4 .....38 C1
Severn Av LSTA FY8 .....49 H4
Severn Dr BBR PR5 .....74 A4
Severn Hl FUL/RIB PR2 .....36 B5
Severn Rd BPOOLS FY4 .....38 B1
Seymour Cl PRES PR1 .....59 F1
Seymour Rd BPOOL FY1 .....4 D4
  PRES PR1 .....
  LSTA FY8 .....63 G1
Seymour St CHLYE PR6 .....93 G3
  FTWD FY7 .....11 F2
Shackleton Rd
  KIRK/FR/WAR PR4 .....54 B1
Shady La BBR PR5 .....80 B5
Shaftesbury Av BISP FY2 .....24 C5
  BPOOLE FY3 .....29 H4
  CLV/TH FY5 .....16 C4
  KIRK/FR/WAR PR4 .....77 G1
Skipton Cl BBR PR5 .....74 B4

PRES PR1 .....58 D5
Shaftesbury Cl LSTA FY8 .....63 G1
Shaftesbury Pl CHLY/EC PR7 .....93 E2
Shakespeare Rd FTWD FY7 .....11 E2
  PRES PR1 .....60 D2
Shakespeare Ter CHLYE PR6 .....93 G3
Shalbourn Rd LSTA FY8 .....62 D2
Shalgrove Fld FUL/RIB PR2 .....45 E1
Shannon St BPOOL FY1 .....4 B1
Shap Ct FTWD FY7 .....10 D5
Shard La PLF/KEOS FY6 .....23 F4
Shard Rd PLF/KEOS FY6 .....23 F4
Sharman Av LSTA FY8 .....49 F2
Sharman Rd LSTA FY8 .....49 F2
Sharoe Green La FUL/RIB PR2 .....45 G1
Sharoe Green Pk FUL/RIB PR2 .....46 A3
Sharoe Mount Av FUL/RIB PR2 .....45 H1
Sharow Gv BPOOLS FY4 .....5 F3
Sharratts Pth CHLY/EC PR7 .....96 C1
Shawbrook Cl CHLY/EC PR7 .....87 H2
Shaw Brook Rd LEYL PR25 .....86 D1
Shaw Brow CHLYE PR6 .....85 E5
Shaw Hill Dr CHLYE PR6 .....89 E1
Shaw Hill St CHLYE PR6 .....89 E1
Shaw Hill St CHLY/EC PR7 .....93 F3
Shaw Rd BPOOL FY1 .....4 B6
Shaw's La GAR/LONG PR3 .....14 C3
Shaw St PRES PR1 .....7 G1
The Shay CLV/TH FY5 .....21 F5
Sheep Hill Brow CHLYE PR6 .....86 C2
Sheep Hill La CHLYE PR6 .....84 D1
Sheephill La KIRK/FR/WAR PR4 .....77 G2
Sheffield Dr FUL/RIB PR2 .....57 H1
Sheldon Ct PRES PR1 * 59 H2
Shelley Cl CHLY/EC PR7 .....96 C5
Shelley Dr CHLY/EC PR7 .....90 C5
Shelley Gv CLV/TH FY5 .....20 D4
Shelley Ms FUL/RIB PR2 .....59 E2
Shelley Rd FUL/RIB PR2 .....59 E2
Shelly Road Ml FUL/RIB PR2 * 59 E2
Shenstone Rd BPOOLE FY3 .....3 J1
Shepherd Rd LSTA FY8 .....49 G4
Shepherd Rd North LSTA FY8 .....49 G5
Shepherd St LSTA FY8 .....64 C5
  PRES PR1 .....7 H4
Shepherds Wy CHLY/EC PR7 .....93 G2
Sheppard St BPOOL FY1 .....2 C5
Sheraton Pk FUL/RIB PR2 .....44 C4
Sherborne Cl PLF/KEOS FY6 .....26 A2
Sherbourne Crs PRES PR1 .....46 B5
Sherbourne St BPOOL FY1 .....28 B2
  PLF/KEOS FY6 .....23 G2
Sherbourne St CHLYE PR6 .....93 G5
Sherburne Av
  KIRK/FR/WAR PR4 .....42 D3
Sherburn Rd PRES PR1 .....72 D5
Sherdley Rd BBR PR5 .....79 G2
Sheringham Av CLV/TH FY5 .....24 D1
Sheringham Wy PLF/KEOS FY6 .....26 C4
Sherwood Av BPOOLE FY3 .....29 E2
Sherwood Ct BPOOLE FY3 * 29 E2
Sherwood Pl CHLYE PR6 .....93 G2
  CLV/TH FY5 .....21 F3
Sherwood Rd LSTA FY8 .....50 A5
Sherwood Wy FUL/RIB PR2 .....46 A2
Shetland Rd BPOOL FY1 .....4 E4
Shipley Cl BPOOLE FY3 .....3 H1
Shipley Rd LSTA FY8 .....49 H4
Shire Bank Crs FUL/RIB PR2 .....45 G2
Shirley Crs BISP FY2 .....24 D1
Shirley Hts PLF/KEOS FY6 .....26 B5
Shirley La KIRK/FR/WAR PR4 .....70 B5
Shop La BBR PR5 .....75 J5
Shore Gn CLV/TH FY5 .....21 F1
Shore Rd CLV/TH FY5 .....20 C4
Shortridge Rd BPOOLS FY4 .....5 K7
Shrewsbury Cl
  KIRK/FR/WAR PR4 .....43 G3
Shrewsbury Dr CLV/TH FY5 .....21 G2
Shuttleworth Rd PRES PR1 .....59 H1
Shuttling Fields La BBR PR5 .....75 F3
Sibbering Brow Preston Rd
  CHLY/EC PR7 .....91 H5
Siding Rd FTWD FY7 .....11 G3
Sidmouth Rd LSTA FY8 .....48 C3
Sidney Av BISP FY2 .....25 E5
Silsden Cl BPOOLE FY3 .....29 H1
Silverdale BISP FY2 .....25 E1
Silverdale Av FTWD FY7 .....10 C5
Silverdale Cl BBR PR5 .....75 H2
  CHLY/EC PR7 .....93 H5
Silverdale Dr FUL/RIB PR2 .....46 D3
Silverdale Rd CHLYE PR6 .....93 H5
  LSTA FY8 .....50 A4
Silversmiths Rw LSTA FY8 .....50 A4
Silver St KIRK/FR/WAR PR4 .....56 B2
  PRES PR1 .....6 C4
Silverwood Av BPOOLS FY4 .....4 E7
Silverwood Cl FUL/RIB PR2 .....63 H2
Silvester Rd CHLY/EC PR7 .....93 F4
Silvia Wy FUL/RIB PR2 .....11 E2
Simmons Av BBR PR5 .....73 G3
Simpson St BPOOLS FY4 .....32 B5
  PRES PR1 * 6 A3
Singleton Cl BPOOLS FY4 .....45 H1
Singleton Av LSTA FY8 .....49 H4
Singleton Cl FUL/RIB PR2 .....45 H1
Singleton Rw PRES PR1 .....6 E2
Singleton St BPOOL FY1 .....4 B1
Sion Cl FUL/RIB PR2 .....47 F4
Sir Frank Whittle Wy LSTA FY8 .....38 D4
Six Acre La KIRK/FR/WAR PR4 .....76 D5
Sixfields CLV/TH FY5 .....21 F5
Sixth Av BPOOLS FY4 .....38 C1
Skeffington Rd PRES PR1 .....60 C2
Skelwith Rd BPOOLE FY3 .....33 H5
Skiddaw Rd BPOOLS FY4 .....5 K7
Skip La KIRK/FR/WAR PR4 .....70 C3
Skippool Av PLF/KEOS FY6 .....26 C1
Skippool Br PLF/KEOS FY6 .....26 C2
Skippool Rd CLV/TH FY5 .....22 C5
Skipton Av PLF/KEOS FY6 .....26 A2
Skipton Rd PRES PR1 .....74 B4

BPOOLS FY4 .....33 F4
Skipton Crs FUL/RIB PR2 .....47 E3
Skipton Rd LSTA FY8 .....49 H5
Slade St PRES PR1 .....6 C4
Slaidburn Pl FUL/RIB PR2 .....61 G1
Slaidburn Rd FUL/RIB PR2 .....61 F1
Slater La CROS/BRETH PR26 .....82 A4
Slater Rd FUL/RIB PR2 .....20 C2
Slinger Rd CLV/TH FY5 .....20 C2
Smalley Cft PRES PR1 .....73 E3
Smallwood Hey Rd
  GAR/LONG PR3 .....14 D1
Smith Cl FUL/RIB PR2 .....93 H1
Smith Rd CLV/TH FY5 .....20 D2
Smith St BBR PR5 .....80 C1
  CHLY/EC PR7 .....85 G4
  CHLYE PR6 .....85 F4
  KIRK/FR/WAR PR4 .....42 D3
Smithy Brow WGNNW/ST WN6 .....94 B5
Smithy Cl PLF/KEOS FY6 .....19 F2
Smithy La BPOOLE FY3 .....30 B4
  CHLYE PR6 .....81 H3
  LSTA FY8 .....50 A5
  PLF/KEOS FY6 .....19 F2
Smithy Ms BPOOL FY1 .....2 D1
Smithy St BBR PR5 .....80 B1
Snipe Cl BPOOLE FY3 .....29 H4
  CLV/TH FY5 .....21 F5
Snipewood CHLY/EC PR7 .....90 A4
Snowdon Cl BPOOL FY1 .....5 G1
Snowdon Rd LSTA FY8 .....49 G1
Snowdrop Cl LEYL PR25 .....84 B2
Snow Hl PRES PR1 .....7 F2
Snowshill Crs CLV/TH FY5 .....21 F5
Sod Hall La KIRK/FR/WAR PR4 .....77 H3
Sollam's Cl BBR PR5 .....74 C4
Solway Cl BISP FY2 .....24 C1
  PRES PR1 .....72 D5
Somerset Av BPOOL FY1 .....5 G1
  CHLY/EC PR7 .....93 F1
Somerset Ct BPOOL FY1 .....5 G1
Somerset Pl FUL/RIB PR2 .....44 D1
Somerset Rd LEYL PR25 .....83 G2
  PRES PR1 .....60 A2
Sorrel Cl CLV/TH FY5 .....17 F4
  PLF/KEOS FY6 .....8 A5
Sorrel Ct PRES PR1 .....72 B4
South Av CHLY/EC PR7 .....93 F4
  CLV/TH FY5 .....16 C5
  KIRK/FR/WAR PR4 .....77 G1
Southbank Av BPOOLS FY4 .....39 G1
Southbourne Av
  PLF/KEOS FY6 .....26 A5
Southbourne Rd BPOOLE FY3 .....33 F3
Southbrook Rd LEYL PR25 .....82 D3
South Cliff St PRES PR1 .....6 C6
Southdown Dr CLV/TH FY5 .....22 C3
Southdowns Rd CHLY/EC PR7 .....93 G5
South Dr FUL/RIB PR2 .....36 D5
South End PRES PR1 .....72 D1
Southern Av PRES PR1 .....7 K6
Southern Pde PRES PR1 .....7 K6
Southey Cl FUL/RIB PR2 .....45 H1
Southfield Dr BPOOLE FY3 .....30 A2
  KIRK/FR/WAR PR4 .....77 G2
Southfleet Pl FTWD FY7 .....11 E5
Southfleet Pl FTWD FY7 * 11 E5
Southfold Pl LSTA FY8 .....49 H4
Southgate FTWD FY7 .....16 D1
  FUL/RIB PR2 .....59 H2
  PRES PR1 .....59 H2
Southgates CHLY/EC PR7 .....90 A5
South Gv FUL/RIB PR2 .....56 D5
South Hey LSTA FY8 .....50 A5
South Holme LSTA FY8 .....64 C2
South King St BPOOL FY1 .....2 D5
Southlands KIRK/FR/WAR PR4 .....43 E4
Southlands Av BBR PR5 .....73 G5
Southlands Dr
  CROS/BRETH PR26 .....82 B5
South Lawn BPOOL FY1 .....5 J4
South Meadow La PRES PR1 .....6 C7
South Meadow St PRES PR1 .....7 J5
South Moss Rd LSTA FY8 .....50 A4
South Pde CLV/TH FY5 .....21 E5
South Pk FUL/RIB PR2 .....64 A2
South Park Dr BPOOLE FY3 .....5 K3
Southport Ter CHLYE PR6 .....93 H5
South Prom LSTA FY8 .....62 B3
South Ribble St BBR PR5 .....60 C5
  CLV/TH FY5 .....22 B2
Southside CHLY/EC PR7 .....87 H4
South Sq BPOOLS FY4 .....5 H5
South Strd FTWD FY7 .....16 C4
South Strd FTWD FY7 .....16 D2
South St CLV/TH FY5 .....65 E2
South Vw BBR PR5 * 79 F2
  KIRK/FR/WAR PR4 .....43 E4
South View Ter LEYL PR25 .....83 H3
South Warton St LSTA FY8 .....64 D3
Southsum FTWD FY7 .....10 D5
Southwell Cl FUL/RIB PR2 .....61 F1
Southwood Av FTWD FY7 .....11 E3
Southwood Cl LSTA FY8 .....64 C3
Southworth Av BPOOLS FY4 .....39 E1
Southworth Wy CLV/TH FY5 .....16 C5
Sowerby Av BPOOLS FY4 .....5 H6
Sower Carr La PLF/KEOS FY6 .....19 H5
Spa Rd PRES PR1 .....6 B3
Spa St PRES PR1 .....7 J3
Speedwell Cl CLV/TH FY5 .....17 F4
Spencer Ct BPOOL FY1 .....2 E1
Spendmore La CHLY/EC PR7 .....96 A5
Spen Pl BPOOLS FY4 .....5 J4
Spey Cl LEYL PR25 .....82 D4
Speyside BPOOLS FY4 .....38 B2
Spinnaker Cl BBR PR5 .....80 D2
Spinney Brow FUL/RIB PR2 .....46 C1
Spinning Jenny Cl KIRK/FR/WAR PR4 .....89 E1
  KIRK/FR/WAR PR4 .....77 G1
The Spinney CHLYE PR6 .....89 F5
  CLV/TH FY5 .....21 F5

PLF/KEOS FY6 ....26 C3
PRES PR1 ....71 G3
Spires Gv KIRK/FR/WAR PR4 ....44 A3
Spring Bank PRES PR1 ....6 C5
Springbank Av CLV/TH FY5 ......22 A2
Springbrook Av CLV/TH FY5 .....24 E4
Spring Crs CHLYE PR6 ....89 H1
Springcroft LEYL PR25 ....83 H1
Springfield
  KIRK/FR/WAR PR4 ....42 C3
Springfield Dr CLV/TH FY5 ....17 H5
Springfield Rd BPOOL FY1 ....2 B3
  CHLY/EC PR7 * 93 F2
  CHLY/EC PR7 ....96 B5
  LEYL PR25 ....82 C5
  LSTA FY8 ....49 E5
Springfield Rd North
  CHLY/EC PR7 ....96 B4
Springfield St PRES PR1 ....59 G2
Spring Gdns KIRK/FR/WAR PR4 ..54 B5
  LEYL PR25 ....83 E4
  LSTA FY8 ....49 F2
  PRES PR1 ....7 F5
Spring Hi KIRK/FR/WAR PR4 ......54 D4
Spring Meadow LEYL PR25 ....84 B2
Spring Ms CHLYE PR6 ....89 C5
Springsands CI FUL/RIB PR2 * 47 E3
Springs Rd CHLYE PR6 ....89 G5
Spring St LEYL PR25 ....83 G3
Springwood CI BBR PR5 ....3 G4
Springwood Dr CHLYE PR6 ....93 H5
Spruce CI FUL/RIB PR2 ....46 C1
The Square BPOOLE FY3 ....33 G3
  CLV/TH FY5 ....16 D4
  LEYL PR25 ....83 G2
Squires CI BBR PR5 ....43 F2
Squires Gate La LSTA FY8 ....38 B4
Squire's Gate Rd FUL/RIB PR2 ...45 E5
Squires Rd PRES PR1 ....59 E5
Squires Wd FUL/RIB PR2 ....46 D2
Squirrel Fold FUL/RIB PR2 ....61 F1
Squirrel's Cha PRES PR1 ....7 F4
  KIRK/FR/WAR PR4 ....56 B2
Stable CI KIRK/FR/WAR PR4 ....43 E2
Stable Yd GAR/LONG PR3 ....15 G1
Stack Cft CHLYE PR6 ....84 D2
Stadium Av BPOOLS FY4 ....38 D5
Stafford Av PLF/KEOS FY6 ....30 B1
Stafford Rd PRES PR1 ....60 A2
Stainforth Av BISP FY2 ....25 E2
Staining Av FUL/RIB PR2 ....58 B5
Staining Old Rd BPOOLE FY3 .....30 B5
Staining RI BPOOLE FY3 ....29 H5
Staining Rd West BPOOLE FY3 ...30 B5
Stakepool Dr GAR/LONG PR3 .....15 G1
Stamford Av BPOOLS FY4 ....38 D1
Stamford Ct LSTA FY8 * 48 D3
Stamford Dr CHLYE PR6 ....89 F2
Stanah Gdns CLV/TH FY5 ....22 C2
Stanah Rd CLV/TH FY5 ....22 C2
Standish St CHLY/EC PR7 ....93 F3
Stanhope Rd BPOOL FY1 ....28 C2
Stanhope St PRES PR1 ....59 F1
Stanifield CI LEYL PR25 ....83 G1
Stanifield La BBR PR5 ....83 G2
  LEYL PR25 ....83 G2
Stanley Av CLV/TH FY5 ....20 D2
  KIRK/FR/WAR PR4 ....71 E4
  LEYL PR25 ....79 H5
  PLF/KEOS FY6 ....25 E5
Stanley Ct KIRK/FR/WAR PR4 .....43 F4
Stanley Cft KIRK/FR/WAR PR4 ...36 A2
Stanleyfield CI PRES PR1 ....7 H1
Stanleyfield Rd PRES PR1 ....7 H1
Stanley Fold BBR PR5 ....79 E1
Stanley Ga FTWD FY7 ....10 D5
Stanley Gv PRES PR1 ....6 D5
Stanley Park Ct BPOOLE FY3 .....33 F2
Stanley PI CHLY/EC PR7 ....93 F2
  PRES PR1 ....6 D5
Stanley Rd BPOOL FY1 ....2 D6
  FTWD FY7 ....11 F5
  KIRK/FR/WAR PR4 ....79 H5
  LEYL PR25 ....79 H5
  LSTA FY8 ....63 G3
  PRES PR1 ....7 J5
Stanley Ter PRES PR1 ....7 H1
Stanmore Av BPOOLS FY4 ....39 E2
Stanning CI LEYL PR25 ....82 D4
Stansfield CI BPOOL FY1 ....4 D5
Stansford Ct PRES PR1 ....72 C2
Stansted Rd CHLY/EC PR7 ....92 D5
Starbeck Av BPOOLS FY4 ....5 F7
Starfield CI LSTA FY8 ....64 B2
Starkie St LEYL PR25 ....83 G3
  PRES PR1 ....7 F5
Starr Ga BPOOLS FY4 ....38 B4
Starrgate Dr FUL/RIB PR2 ....58 A2
Startley Nook
  KIRK/FR/WAR PR4 ....78 A3
States Rd LSTA FY8 ....49 H5
Station Rd BBR PR5 ....80 B1
  CHLY/EC PR7 ....96 C4
  CLV/TH FY5 ....17 H5
  FTWD FY7 ....11 G2
  KIRK/FR/WAR PR4 ....42 D2
  KIRK/FR/WAR PR4 ....77 G1
  LSTA FY8 ....64 C3
  PLF/KEOS FY6 ....26 C5
Station Sq LSTA FY8 ....31 G2
Station Ter BPOOLS FY4 ....32 B5
Staveley Av FTWD FY7 ....10 D4
Staveley PI FUL/RIB PR2 ....58 A1
Staynall La PLF/KEOS FY6 ....19 F5
Steeley La CHLYE PR6 ....93 G3
Steeple Vw FUL/RIB PR2 ....6 A2
Steeton Rd BPOOLE FY3 ....28 B5
Stefano Rd PRES PR1 ....60 C3
Stephendale Av BBR PR5 ....81 E1
Stephenson St CHLYE PR6 ....93 H5

Stephen St LSTA FY8 ....49 E4
Stevenson Av LEYL PR25 ....83 H1
Stewart St PRES PR1 ....6 B5
Stiles Av KIRK/FR/WAR PR4 ....70 D5
Stirling Ct CHLYE PR6 ....93 H5
Stirling St CHLYE PR6 * 5 H3
  LEYL PR25 ....83 H3
Stockdale Crs BBR PR5 ....80 C2
Stockdove Wy CLV/TH FY5 ....20 D1
Stockdove Wd CLV/TH FY5 ....21 E1
Stocks La CHLY/EC PR7 ....94 D2
  PLF/KEOS FY6 ....26 D3
Stocks Rd FUL/RIB PR2 ....59 E2
Stocks St PRES PR1 ....6 D2
Stockydale Rd FUL/RIB PR2 ....39 G1
Stoke Av BPOOL FY1 ....5 G4
Stokes Hall Av LEYL PR25 ....83 F4
Stonebridge Cl BBR PR5 ....79 H1
Stonechat CI BPOOL FY1 ....29 H4
Stonecroft Rd LEYL PR25 ....82 C5
Stonefield KIRK/FR/WAR PR4 ....76 A1
Stonefold Av
  KIRK/FR/WAR PR4 ....70 D5
Stonehouse Gn CHLYE PR6 ....85 E1
Stone Park Rd
  GAR/LONG PR3 ....36 B2
Stoney Rd CLV/TH FY5 ....21 E3
Stoney Butts FUL/RIB PR2 ....57 H5
Stoneygate CLV/TH FY5 ....21 F3
  PRES PR1 ....7 G4
Stoney Holt LEYL PR25 ....84 B5
Stoneyhurst Av CLV/TH FY5 ....22 B4
Stoney La BBR PR5 ....79 H5
  KIRK/FR/WAR PR4 ....67 G1
  PLF/KEOS FY6 ....23 G2
Stonycroft Av BPOOLS FY4 ....38 C3
Stony Croft Pl BPOOLS FY4 * 38 C3
Stony Hill Av BPOOLS FY4 ....5 H6
Stonyhurst CHLY/EC PR7 ....97 F1
Stopford Av BISP FY2 ....25 E5
Stork CI CLV/TH FY5 ....21 F3
Stour Ldg FUL/RIB PR2 ....45 E2
Strand Rd PRES PR1 ....6 A2
Strand St West FUL/RIB PR2 * ...59 E5
The Strand BPOOL FY1 ....2 B4
  FTWD FY7 ....16 C1
Stratfield PI LEYL PR25 ....83 G3
Stratford Dr FUL/RIB PR2 ....45 F4
Stratford Rd BPOOL FY1 ....5 H3
Stratford Rd CHLYE PR6 ....93 G2
  LSTA FY8 ....49 H5
Strathdale BPOOLS FY4 ....39 F1
Strathmore Gv CHLY/EC PR7 .....93 E3
Strathmore Rd FUL/RIB PR2 ......45 G4
Strathyre CI BISP FY2 ....25 F2
Street Gv LSTA FY8 ....49 F4
Stretton Av BPOOLS FY4 ....5 J7
Strickland's La PLF/KEOS FY6 ...19 H5
  PRES PR1 ....72 C2
Strike La KIRK/FR/WAR PR4 ....54 B3
Stronsay PI BISP FY2 ....25 F1
Strutt St PRES PR1 ....60 B2
Stryands KIRK/FR/WAR PR4 ....70 D5
Stuart CI FUL/RIB PR2 ....47 E5
Stuart Rd CLV/TH FY5 ....22 A2
  FUL/RIB PR2 ....47 E5
Studfold CLV/TH FY5 ....89 E5
Studholme Av PRES PR1 ....72 D4
Studholme CI PRES PR1 ....72 D4
Studholme Crs PRES PR1 ....72 D5
Stump La CHLYE PR6 ....93 G2
Sturminster Cl PRES PR1 ....72 A1
Styan St FTWD FY7 ....11 G2
Suffolk Rd BPOOLE FY3 ....33 G3
  PRES PR1 ....60 A2
Sulby Dr FUL/RIB PR2 ....47 F3
Sulby Gv FUL/RIB PR2 ....47 F3
Summerfield LEYL PR25 ....83 E1
Summerfield CI PRES PR1 ....73 F4
Summerfields LSTA FY8 ....48 C3
Summerville BPOOLS FY4 ....38 C2
Summerville Av BPOOLE FY3 .....30 B5
Summerwood CI BISP FY2 ....24 D5
Summit Dr KIRK/FR/WAR PR4 ....54 C5
Sumner St LEYL PR25 ....83 F3
Sumpter Cft PRES PR1 ....72 D4
Sunbury Av PRES PR1 ....72 D5
Sunderland Av CLV/TH FY5 ....17 E5
  PLF/KEOS FY6 ....23 H2
Sunfield Cl BPOOLS FY4 ....39 G1
Sunningdale GAR/LONG PR3 ......36 A2
Sunningdale Av FUL/RIB PR2 .....33 G3
  PRES PR1 ....16 D2
Sunningdale CI
  KIRK/FR/WAR PR4 ....43 E4
Sunningdale Crs LSTA FY8 ....49 G5
Sunningdale Dr CLV/TH FY5 ....22 B4
Sunny Bank KIRK/FR/WAR PR4 ..42 D3
Sunny Bank Av BISP FY2 ....24 C5
Sunny Brow CHLY/EC PR7 ....96 D3
Sunnyhurst Av FUL/RIB PR2 ....38 D2
Sunnyside Av
  KIRK/FR/WAR PR4 ....53 F5
Sunnyside Cl
  KIRK/FR/WAR PR4 ....54 B4
Surgeon's Ct PRES PR1 ....6 E4
Surrey St PRES PR1 ....60 C3
Sussex Rd BPOOLS FY4 ....3 H2
Sussex St PRES PR1 ....60 A2
Sutcliffe St CHLY/EC PR7 ....93 G3
Sutherland Rd BPOOL FY1 ....28 C5
Sutton Dr FUL/RIB PR2 ....57 H5
Sutton Pl BPOOL FY1 ....2 E7
Swainson St BPOOL FY1 ....64 A3
  LSTA FY8 ....64 A3
Swallow Av PRES PR1 ....72 D2
Swallow Dr CLV/TH FY5 ....17 G5
Swallow St CHLYE PR6 ....85 F5
Swallowfields
  KIRK/FR/WAR PR4 ....44 A4
Swanage Av BPOOLS FY4 ....38 B2
Swan Dr CLV/TH FY5 ....21 F3

Swansea St FUL/RIB PR2 ....59 E2
Swansey La CHLYE PR6 ....85 E3
Swan St PRES PR1 ....7 K2
Swarbrick CI FUL/RIB PR2 ....3 F1
Swarbrick St
  KIRK/FR/WAR PR4 ....43 E4
Swift CI BPOOLE FY3 ....33 H5
Swill Brook La PRES PR1 ....60 C5
Swindon Av BPOOLS FY4 ....5 H5
Swords Cross CI CHLY/EC PR7 ...97 G2
Sycamore Av BPOOLS FY4 * 39 F5
  CHLY/EC PR7 ....88 A4
Sycamore CI FUL/RIB PR2 ....46 C2
Sycamore CI CHLY/EC PR7 ....93 G5
Sycamore Dr PRES PR1 ....72 D3
Sycamore Rd CHLYE PR6 ....89 E1
  PRES PR1 ....61 G1
Sydney St LSTA FY8 ....49 F5
Syke Hi PRES PR1 ....7 H5
Syke St PRES PR1 ....7 G5
Sylvancroft FUL/RIB PR2 ....44 C3
Sylvan Gv BBR PR5 ....74 D4
Symonds Rd FUL/RIB PR2 ....45 G5

T

Tag Cft FUL/RIB PR2 ....44 B3
Tag Farm Ct FUL/RIB PR2 ....44 B3
Tag La FUL/RIB PR2 ....44 B2
Talbot Dr CHLY/EC PR7 ....88 B5
Talbot Rd BPOOL FY1 ....2 C3
  BPOOLE FY3 ....3 F1
  LEYL PR25 ....82 D2
  LSTA FY8 ....64 D1
  PRES PR1 ....6 E3
Talbot Rw CHLY/EC PR7 * 92 A1
Talbot Sq BPOOL FY1 ....2 C4
Talbot St CLV/TH FY5 ....93 H1
  FUL/RIB PR2 ....45 F5
  PRES PR1 ....6 D3
Talbot Ter LSTA FY8 ....64 C3
Tamar CI LEYL PR25 ....83 G5
Tamar St PRES PR1 ....61 E3
Tanglewood FUL/RIB PR2 ....46 B5
Tanners Wy LSTA FY8 ....50 B4
Tansley Av CHLY/EC PR7 ....96 A4
Tanterton Hall Rd
  FUL/RIB PR2 ....44 B2
Tanyard CI CHLY/EC PR7 ....96 A4
Tarnbrick Av
  KIRK/FR/WAR PR4 ....54 C4
Tarnbrook Dr BPOOLE FY3 ....29 C3
Tarn CI PRES PR1 ....71 G2
Tarn Ct FTWD FY7 ....10 D5
Tarn Hows CI CHLY/EC PR7 * 93 E5
Tarn Rd CLV/TH FY5 ....22 B4
Tarnway Av CLV/TH FY5 ....21 H5
Tarradale KIRK/FR/WAR PR4 ....70 A5
Tarragon Dr BISP FY2 ....24 D5
Tatham Ct FTWD FY7 ....10 C5
Taunton St BPOOLS FY4 ....5 F6
  PRES PR1 ....60 D2
Taybank Av BPOOLS FY4 ....38 D1
Taylors CI PLF/KEOS FY6 ....26 A2
Taylor St CHLY/EC PR7 ....93 E5
  PRES PR1 ....7 F5
Taymouth Rd BPOOLS FY4 ....39 G2
Tay St PRES PR1 ....6 B7
Teal Ct FUL/RIB PR2 ....33 H5
Taywood Rd CLV/TH FY5 ....17 G5
Teal CI CLV/TH FY5 ....17 G5
  PRES PR1 ....82 C5
Teal La LSTA FY8 ....50 C5
Tebay Av CLV/TH FY5 ....16 D5
  KIRK/FR/WAR PR4 ....48 C5
Teesdale Av BISP FY2 ....28 D2
Tees St PRES PR1 ....60 C1
Teil Gn FUL/RIB PR2 ....46 A3
Temperance St CHLYE PR6 ....93 H2
Temple Ct PRES PR1 * 7 F5
Temple St BPOOL FY1 ....2 B5
Temple Wy CHLYE PR6 ....89 G4
Tenby Rd PRES PR1 ....60 C5
Tennyson Av CHLY/EC PR7 ....93 F4
  CLV/TH FY5 ....21 G1
Tennyson Gdns
  KIRK/FR/WAR PR4 ....53 F5
Tennyson Mill Ct PRES PR1 ....60 D2
Tennyson PI BBR PR5 ....74 A4
Tennyson Rd BPOOLE FY3 ....29 F3
  FTWD FY7 ....11 G2
  PRES PR1 ....60 D2
Tensing Av BISP FY2 ....24 D2
Tenterfield St PRES PR1 ....7 F3
Terrace Rd BPOOLS FY4 ....5 J5
Terrace St PRES PR1 ....60 C2
Teven St BBR PR5 ....74 B5
Teviot Av FTWD FY7 ....10 D5
Tewkesbury Av BPOOLS FY4 ......38 D3
Tewkesbury Dr LSTA FY8 ....65 E1
Thames Rd BPOOLS FY4 ....5 J6
Theatre St PRES PR1 ....6 E5
Third Av BPOOLS FY4 ....38 C1
  PLF/KEOS FY6 ....26 C5
Thirlmere Av FUL/RIB PR2 ....45 H4
  PLF/KEOS FY6 ....25 H3
Thirlmere CI KIRK/FR/WAR PR4 ..32 C5
Thirlmere Rd BPOOLS FY4 ....5 J7
  CHLY/EC PR7 ....92 A1
  PRES PR1 ....61 F2
Thirsk Av CLV/TH FY5 ....49 H4
Thirsk Gv BPOOL FY1 ....49 H4
Thistle CI CHLYE PR6 ....93 H2
  CLV/TH FY5 ....17 F4
Thistlecroft FUL/RIB PR2 ....44 C3
Thistleton Rd FUL/RIB PR2 ....58 A2
Thomas St PRES PR1 ....6 E3
Thompson St
  KIRK/FR/WAR PR4 ....42 D2

PRES PR1 ....60 D1
Thornbank BPOOLE FY3 ....29 H3
Thornberry CI FTWD FY7 ....5 F2
Thornevcroft Cl
  PLF/KEOS FY6 ....25 H2
Thorncliffe Av FUL/RIB PR2 ....47 F5
Thorngate PRES PR1 ....72 A2
Thorngate CI PRES PR1 ....72 A2
Thorn Gv BPOOL FY1 ....5 H5
Thornhill Av FUL/RIB PR2 ....13 E1
Thornhill CI BPOOLS FY4 ....39 F3
Thornhill Rd CHLYE PR6 ....89 G5
  LEYL PR25 ....82 B4
Thornleigh CI CLV/TH FY5 ....21 G2
Thornley PI FUL/RIB PR2 ....47 G5
Thornley Rd FUL/RIB PR2 ....47 G5
Thornpark Dr FUL/RIB PR2 ....57 H5
Thorn St PRES PR1 ....60 C1
Thornton Av FUL/RIB PR2 ....44 D4
  LSTA FY8 ....49 H5
Thornton Dr BBR PR5 ....75 H5
  CROS/BRETH PK26 ....75 D5
Thornton Ga CLV/TH FY5 ....16 C5
Thornton Ms CLV/TH FY5 * 22 C5
Thorntrees Av FUL/RIB PR2 ....57 H2
Thornway Av CLV/TH FY5 ....22 B4
Thornwood CI LSTA FY8 ....65 E2
Thorpe CI PRES PR1 ....59 H2
Threefields FUL/RIB PR2 ....44 C3
Three Nooks BBR PR5 ....81 F4
Threlfall CHLY/EC PR7 ....88 C5
Threlfall Rd BPOOL FY1 ....5 F5
Thropps La KIRK/FR/WAR PR4 ...76 B3
Throstle Wy CLV/TH FY5 ....21 F3
Thurnham Rd FUL/RIB PR2 ....58 A3
Thursby Av BPOOLS FY4 ....38 D2
Thursfield Av BPOOLS FY4 ....5 J7
Thurston Rd LEYL PR25 ....83 F3
Thyme CI BISP FY2 ....25 F4
Tiber St PRES PR1 ....7 F5
Tinkerfield CI PRES PR1 ....45 G1
Tinniswood CI FUL/RIB PR2 ....58 D2
Tintern Av CHLY/EC PR7 ....93 G5
Titan Wy CROS/BRETH PK26 ......82 A3
Tithebarn Ga PLF/KEOS FY6 ......26 B3
Tithe Barn La CHLY/EC PR7 ....87 E3
Tithebarn Pl PLF/KEOS FY6 ....26 B3
Tithebarn St PLF/KEOS FY6 ....26 A3
  PRES PR1 ....7 G4
Tiverton CI FUL/RIB PR2 ....33 H5
Todd La North BBR PR5 ....75 H5
Todd La South BBR PR5 ....79 H1
Todmorden St FUL/RIB PR2 ....48 C3
Tollgate PRES PR1 ....72 D2
Tolsey Dr KIRK/FR/WAR PR4 ......71 E4
Tom Benson Wy FUL/RIB PR2 ....44 B1
Tomlinson Rd FUL/RIB PR2 ....59 E1
  LEYL PR25 ....83 E2
Tongues La GAR/LONG PR3 ....8 C5
Tootell St CHLY/EC PR7 ....93 E4
Topaz Wy CHLYE PR6 ....93 H4
Topping St BPOOL FY1 ....2 C3
Toronto Av BISP FY2 ....25 E4
  FTWD FY7 ....10 D4
Torquay Av BPOOLS FY4 ....33 G3
Torside Gv PLF/KEOS FY6 ....25 H4
Torsway Av BPOOLE FY3 ....29 G1
Tosses CI FUL/KEOS FY6 ....3 K2
Towbreck Gdns PLF/KEOS FY6 ...30 C2
Tower CI CLV/TH FY5 ....17 G5
Tower Gn FUL/RIB PR2 ....45 H1
Tower La FUL/RIB PR2 ....37 F5
Tower St BPOOL FY1 ....2 C5
Tower Vw BISP FY2 ....24 D5
  PRES PR1 ....6 B7
Town Brow CHLYE PR6 ....84 C2
Town End CLV/TH FY5 * 21 G2
Townfield CI
  KIRK/FR/WAR PR4 ....76 A2
Towngate CHLY/EC PR7 ....90 A2
  LEYL PR25 ....83 F4
Town La CHLY/EC PR7 ....94 B4
  CHLY/EC PR7 ....95 G5
  CHLYE PR6 ....85 F5
Townlea CI PRES PR1 ....71 H3
Townley Av BPOOLS FY4 ....54 C4
Townley La PRES PR1 ....71 E2
Townley St CHLYE PR6 ....93 G3
Townsway BBR PR5 ....79 H1
Trafalgar CI FUL/RIB PR2 ....45 F5
Trafalgar Rd BPOOL FY1 ....4 B5
Trafalgar St CHLY/EC PR7 ....93 F1
Tramway La BBR PR5 ....81 E3
Tranmere Rd BPOOLS FY4 ....5 F4
Tranmoor KIRK/FR/WAR PR4 ......76 A3
Travers PI FUL/RIB PR2 ....45 E2
Trawden Crs FUL/RIB PR2 ....47 E4
Trefoil CI CLV/TH FY5 ....17 G4
Trent Rd BPOOLS FY4 ....38 B1
Trent St LSTA FY8 ....65 E3
Tretower Wy CLV/TH FY5 ....22 B2
The Triangle FUL/RIB PR2 ....49 H4
Trinity CI KIRK/FR/WAR PR4 ......54 C4
Trinity Fold PRES PR1 * 7 F4
Trinity Gdns CLV/TH FY5 ....21 G1
Trinity Pl PRES PR1 * 7 F3
Trinity Rd CHLY/EC PR7 * 93 E5
Tristan Av KIRK/FR/WAR PR4 .....76 B4
Troon Av CLV/TH FY5 ....22 B4
Troon CI CHLY/EC PR7 ....88 A5
Troon Ct PRES PR1 ....58 C5
Troughton Crs BPOOLS FY4 ....5 J6
Troutbeck Av FTWD FY7 ....10 D4
Troutbeck Crs BPOOLS FY4 ....34 B5
Troutbeck PI FUL/RIB PR2 ....47 F4
Troutbeck Rd CHLY/EC PR7 ....89 E5
  LSTA FY8 ....48 D2
Trout St PRES PR1 ....7 K5
Trower St PRES PR1 ....7 K6
Trunnah Gdns CLV/TH FY5 ....21 H1
Trunnah Rd CLV/TH FY5 ....21 H1

Truro PI PRES PR1 ....60 D2
Truro St BPOOLS FY4 ....5 F7
Tudor Av FUL/RIB PR2 ....57 G1
  PRES PR1 ....61 F3
Tudor CI CLV/TH FY5 ....25 G3
Tudor Cft BBR PR5 ....79 H2
Tudor Dr KIRK/FR/WAR PR4 ......49 H5
Tudor PI BPOOLS FY4 ....33 G3
Tudor Rd BPOOLS FY4 ....48 D5
Tuer St PRES PR1 ....83 E2
Tulketh Av FUL/RIB PR2 ....58 D2
Tulketh Brow FUL/RIB PR2 ....59 E2
Tulketh Crs FUL/RIB PR2 ....59 E2
Tulketh Rd FUL/RIB PR2 ....58 D2
Tunbridge Dr PRES PR1 ....60 B5
Tunley Holme BBR PR5 ....81 E4
The Turbary FUL/RIB PR2 ....45 E5
Turks Head Yd CLV/TH FY5 ....22 B4
Turnberry Av BPOOLS FY4 ....5 J7
Turnberry CI
  KIRK/FR/WAR PR4 ....43 E4
Turnbury CI CHLY/EC PR7 ....88 A3
Turner Av FUL/RIB PR2 ....79 F3
Turner St PRES PR1 ....7 F1
Turnfield FUL/RIB PR2 ....44 B2
The Turnpike FUL/RIB PR2 ....45 F2
Turnstone BPOOLE FY3 ....29 H4
Turpin Green La LEYL PR25 ....83 G5
Turton Dr CHLYE PR6 ....93 H1
Tuson CI PRES PR1 ....6 C2
Tuxbury Dr CLV/TH FY5 ....22 B4
Tuxford Rd LSTA FY8 ....50 A5
Tweed St LSTA FY8 ....64 D1
Twickenham PI LSTA FY8 ....50 B5
Two Acre La PRES PR1 * 72 B5
Tydesley Rd BPOOL FY1 ....4 A3
Tyne Av BPOOLE FY3 ....3 G6
Tyne CI CLV/TH FY5 ....17 E4
Tynedale Rd BPOOLE FY3 ....29 G1
Tyne St BBR PR5 ....74 C5
  PRES PR1 ....6 B7
Tyrone Av BISP FY2 ....24 D5

U

Ullswater Av CLV/TH FY5 ....21 H2
  FTWD FY7 ....16 D1
Ullswater CI PLF/KEOS FY6 ....23 G5
Ullswater Rd BPOOLS FY4 ....32 C5
  CHLY/EC PR7 ....93 E4
  PRES PR1 ....60 C4
Ulverston Crs LSTA FY8 ....50 A4
Underbank Rd CLV/TH FY5 ....22 C3
Under Wd FUL/RIB PR2 ....45 E5
Union Pas
  KIRK/FR/WAR PR4 * 43 E3
Union St CHLY/EC PR7 ....93 F2
  BBR PR5 ....85 F4
  PRES PR1 ....6 E3
Unsworth Av PLF/KEOS FY6 ....13 E2
Uplands Cha FUL/RIB PR2 ....44 C3
Upper Lune St FTWD FY7 ....11 H1
Upper Westby St LSTA FY8 ....64 B3
Upwood CI BISP FY2 ....25 E2

V

Valentia Rd BISP FY2 ....24 D4
Valentines La
  KIRK/FR/WAR PR4 ....44 A4
Valentines Meadow
  KIRK/FR/WAR PR4 ....44 A4
Vale Royal KIRK/FR/WAR PR4 .....43 G5
The Vale FUL/RIB PR2 ....45 H5
Valeway Av CLV/TH FY5 ....72 C1
Valley Rd CLV/TH FY5 ....93 H5
  FUL/RIB PR2 ....46 A4
Valley View Rd BBR PR5 ....75 F5
Vance Rd BPOOL FY1 ....2 B3
Varley St PRES PR1 ....60 A1
Ventnor Pl FUL/RIB PR2 ....44 C4
Ventnor Rd BPOOLS FY4 ....38 B2
  CHLY/EC PR7 ....93 E4
Venture Rd FTWD FY7 ....17 G3
Vermont Gv CLV/TH FY5 ....21 E4
Vernon Av BPOOLS FY4 ....5 J1
Vernon Rd LSTA FY8 ....49 E2
Vernon St PRES PR1 ....59 H2
Vevey St LEYL PR25 ....83 G3
Vicarage Av CLV/TH FY5 ....20 D2
Vicarage CI CHLY/EC PR7 ....88 A4
  FUL/RIB PR2 ....49 H4
  LSTA FY8 ....49 F4
Vicarage La BPOOLS FY4 ....5 J5
  CHLY/EC PR7 ....97 H3
Vicarage Rd PLF/KEOS FY6 ....26 B4
Vicarage St CHLYE PR6 ....95 G3
Vicarsfields Rd LEYL PR25 ....83 F5
Victoria Gdns CLV/TH FY5 ....16 B3
Victoria Pde CLV/TH FY5 ....58 D2
Victoria Park Av FUL/RIB PR2 ....57 H2
Victoria Quay FUL/RIB PR2 ....58 C4
Victoria Rd BBR PR5 ....69 H5
  FUL/RIB PR2 ....45 H5
  KIRK/FR/WAR PR4 ....58 A3
  LSTA FY8 ....62 C1
  PLF/KEOS FY6 ....26 C5
Victoria Rd East CLV/TH FY5 .....21 G3
Victoria Rd West CLV/TH FY5 .....20 C2
Victoria St BBR PR5 ....79 G1
  BPOOL FY1 ....2 B5
  CHLY/EC PR7 ....93 F2
  FTWD FY7 ....11 H1

LSTA FY8 64 D3
PRES PR1 6 D1
Victoria Ter CHLYE PR6 93 G1
Victory Rd BPOOL FY1 2 E2
Victrex Rd CLV/TH FY5 18 B5
Village Ct PLF/KEOS FY6 * 26 B4
Village Cft CHLY/EC PR7 87 H4
Village Dr FUL/RIB PR2 61 F1
Village Green La FUL/RIB PR2 44 B2
Village Wks PLF/KEOS FY6 * 26 B4
Village Wy BISP FY2 24 D2
The Villas KIRK/FR/WAR PR4 44 A3
Villiers Ct PRES PR1 59 G1
Villiers St PRES PR1 59 G1
The Vinery KIRK/FR/WAR PR4 77 G1
Vine St CHLY/EC PR7 93 F1
PRES PR1 6 B3
Vulcan Rd KIRK/FR/WAR PR4 54 B2

W

Waddington Rd FUL/RIB PR2 61 G1
LSTA FY8 50 A5
Wades Cft KIRK/FR/WAR PR4 54 C5
Wadham Rd PRES PR1 7 J6
Wakefield Rd BISP FY2 25 E3
Waldon St PRES PR1 60 D2
Walesby Pl LSTA FY8 63 G1
Walgarth Dr CHLY/EC PR7 92 D3
Walkdale KIRK/FR/WAR PR4 71 E4
Walker La FUL/RIB PR2 44 D2
Walker Pl PRES PR1 7 J4
Walkers Hl BPOOLS FY4 39 G1
Walker St BPOOL FY1 2 B3
PRES PR1 7 F2
Walker Wy CLV/TH FY5 17 H5
The Walled Gdn CHLYE PR6 89 E1
Wallend Rd FUL/RIB PR2 57 H4
Waller Av BISP FY2 24 C2
Walletts Rd CHLY/EC PR7 93 E4
Wall St BPOOL FY1 2 D1
Walmer Gn KIRK/FR/WAR PR4 76 A4
Walmer Rd LSTA FY8 49 F3
Walmsley St FTWD FY7 11 G2
Walney Pl BPOOLE FY3 29 G3
Walnut Cl PRES PR1 72 A3
Walpole Av BPOOLS FY4 38 B3
Walter Av LSTA FY8 49 G1
Waltham Av BPOOLS FY4 38 D3
Walton Av PRES PR1 72 A3
Walton Gn BBR PR5 73 H2
Walton's Pde PRES PR1 6 D5
Walton Summit Rd BBR PR5 80 D3
Walton Vw PRES PR1 60 D3
Walverden Av BPOOLS FY4 5 F7
Wansbeck Av FTWD FY7 10 D4
Wanstead Crs BPOOLS FY4 5 H6
Wanstead St PRES PR1 61 E3
Warbreck Dr BISP FY2 24 C3
Warbreck Hill Rd BISP FY2 28 D1
Warbury St PRES PR1 61 E2
Ward Av CLV/TH FY5 20 D1
Wardle Ct CHLYE PR6 89 F1
Wardle Dr CLV/TH FY5 21 F1
Wardley's La PLF/KEOS FY6 19 E5
Ward's End PRES PR1 7 G4
Ward St BBR PR5 79 G2
BPOOL FY1 4 C5
CHLYE PR6 93 H3
KIRK/FR/WAR PR4 43 E3
Wareham Rd BPOOLE FY3 29 F1
Waring Dr CLV/TH FY5 21 G1
The Warings CHLY/EC PR7 94 C1
Warley Rd BPOOL FY1 28 B2
Warner Rd PRES PR1 60 D2
Warren Av North FTWD FY7 11 F2
Warren Av South FTWD FY7 11 F2
Warren Dr CLV/TH FY5 20 D4
Warren Gv CLV/TH FY5 21 E4
Warrenhurst Rd FTWD FY7 11 G2
Warren St FTWD FY7 11 H2
The Warren FUL/RIB PR2 46 D2
Warton Pl CHLY/EC PR7 92 D2
Warton St LSTA FY8 64 D3
PRES PR1 * 6 C7
Warwick Av CLV/TH FY5 17 E5
Warwick Cl FUL/RIB PR2 45 G4
Warwick Pl BPOOLE FY3 29 H2
Warwick Rd BBR PR5 74 A2
BPOOLE FY3 3 F2
CHLY/EC PR7 90 B3
LEYL PR25 82 D5
LSTA FY8 49 F5
Warwick St PRES PR1 6 E2
Wasdale Cl LEYL PR25 87 G1
Wasdale Rd BPOOLS FY4 33 G5
Washington Av BISP FY2 25 E5
Washington Ct BISP FY2 25 E5
Washington La CHLY/EC PR7 88 C5
Waterdale BISP FY2 25 E2
Waterfoot Av BPOOLE FY3 3 H3
Waterford Cl FUL/RIB PR2 46 C3
Waterhead Crs CLV/TH FY5 24 C1
Watering Pool La BBR PR5 73 G5
Water La FUL/RIB PR2 59 E3
PRES PR1 6 A1
Waterleat Gld PLF/KEOS FY6 30 C2
Waterloo Rd BPOOL FY1 5 H5
FUL/RIB PR2 58 D1
Waterloo St CHLY/EC PR7 93 G1
Waterloo Ter FUL/RIB PR2 59 E2
Water's Edge FUL/RIB PR2 44 B5
Waterside BISP FY2 24 D5
Waters Reach LSTA FY8 * 63 G3
Water St BBR PR5 74 B4
CHLY/EC PR7 93 G1
Watery La FUL/RIB PR2 58 D3
PRES PR1 60 D3
Watkin La BBR PR5 79 G2
Watkin Rd CHLYE PR6 85 E4
Watling Street Rd
FUL/RIB PR2 45 G5
Watson Ct BPOOLS FY4 38 D1
Watson Rd BPOOLS FY4 38 C1
Waverley Av BPOOL FY1 28 C2
FTWD FY7 10 D3
Waverley Dr
KIRK/FR/WAR PR4 77 G2
Waverley Gdns FUL/RIB PR2 61 E1
Waverley Rd PRES PR1 60 D2
Waxy La KIRK/FR/WAR PR4 54 C4
Way Ga CLV/TH FY5 16 D4
Wayman Rd BPOOLE FY3 3 G3
Wayside PLF/KEOS FY6 12 B1
Weavers Cl LSTA FY8 50 B4
Webster Av BPOOLS FY4 39 E1
Webster St FUL/RIB PR2 59 E2
Weeton Av BPOOLS FY4 39 E3
CLV/TH FY5 20 D1
LSTA FY8 49 G3
Weeton Pl FUL/RIB PR2 58 A2
Weeton Rd KIRK/FR/WAR PR4 42 C1
Weirden Cl PRES PR1 72 B5
Welbeck Av BPOOLS FY4 5 J6
FTWD FY7 11 F2
Welburn Wk CLV/TH FY5 22 B2
Weld Av CHLY/EC PR7 93 F5
Weldbank La CHLY/EC PR7 93 F5
Weldbank St CHLY/EC PR7 93 F5
Welland Cl BISP FY2 25 E3
Wellfield KIRK/FR/WAR PR4 70 A5
Wellfield Av LEYL PR25 83 E3
Wellfield Rd BBR PR5 79 F2
PRES PR1 6 B3
Wellington Av LEYL PR25 83 G4
Wellington Pl BBR PR5 74 A4
Wellington Rd BPOOL FY1 4 B4
FUL/RIB PR2 58 D2
Wellington St CHLY/EC PR7 93 F1
KIRK/FR/WAR PR4 42 D3
LSTA FY8 65 E2
PRES PR1 6 A2
Wellogate Gdns BPOOLS FY4 38 D2
Well Orch BBR PR5 81 E4
Wellow Pl LSTA FY8 63 G1
Wells Cl CLV/TH FY5 21 G2
Wells Fold Cl CHLYE PR6 85 F3
Wells St PRES PR1 60 D2
Welsby Rd LEYL PR25 82 D4
Welwyn Pl CLV/TH FY5 20 D3
Wembley Av BPOOLE FY3 29 E2
PLF/KEOS FY6 26 C4
PRES PR1 72 A1
Wembley Rd CLV/TH FY5 17 H5
Wendover Rd PLF/KEOS FY6 25 G1
Wensley Av FTWD FY7 11 E5
Wensleydale Av BPOOLE FY3 29 G3
Wensleydale Cl CLV/TH FY5 22 B4
Wensley Pl FUL/RIB PR2 46 D4
Wentworth Av FTWD FY7 16 D2
Wentworth Cl PRES PR1 58 C5
Wentworth Dr CHLY/EC PR7 88 A3
CLV/TH FY5 22 A4
GAR/LONG PR3 36 B2
Wentworth Ms LSTA FY8 49 G5
Werneth Cl PRES PR1 73 E5
Wesham Hall Rd
KIRK/FR/WAR PR4 43 E2
Wesley Ms BPOOLS FY4 39 G1
Wesley St BBR PR5 80 C1
West Av FUL/RIB PR2 44 C2
West Bank CHLY/EC PR7 93 F2
Westbank Av BPOOLS FY4 39 G1
West Bank Av LSTA FY8 63 H3
West Beach LSTA FY8 64 A4
Westbourne Av BPOOL FY1 4 D5
Westbourne Rd CHLY/EC PR7 93 E4
CLV/TH FY5 16 C4
PLF/KEOS FY6 12 B1
Westbrook Crs FUL/RIB PR2 44 C4
Westbury Cl CLV/TH FY5 20 C5
Westby Av BPOOLS FY4 39 E3
Westby Pl FUL/RIB PR2 58 B2
Westby Rd LSTA FY8 49 E3
Westby St LSTA FY8 64 B3
Westby Wy PLF/KEOS FY6 26 B5
West Cliff PRES PR1 6 C6
West Cliffe LSTA FY8 64 D3
Westcliffe Dr BPOOLE FY3 29 E2
West Cliff Ter PRES PR1 6 D6
West Ct CLV/TH FY5 16 C4
West Crs GAR/LONG PR3 36 B2
LSTA FY8 49 E5
West Dr CLV/TH FY5 20 D1
KIRK/FR/WAR PR4 42 C1
LEYL PR25 84 A1
West End PRES PR1 58 C5
Westend Av CHLY/EC PR7 96 A4
West End La
KIRK/FR/WAR PR4 52 D5
Westerlong FUL/RIB PR2 57 H2
Western Dr LEYL PR25 82 C3
Westfield BBR PR5 79 F1
Westfield Av BPOOLE FY3 29 F1
BPOOLE FY3 29 H3
FTWD FY7 11 E4
Westfield Dr BBR PR5 75 G5
FUL/RIB PR2 46 D4
KIRK/FR/WAR PR4 66 D1
LEYL PR25 82 C3
Westfield Rd BPOOL FY1 5 F4
West Ga FTWD FY7 10 D2
Westgate FUL/RIB PR2 45 F3
LEYL PR25 83 E4
Westgate Rd LSTA FY8 38 C4
Westhead Wk FTWD FY7 11 E4
Westlands CROS/BRETH PR26 82 B5
Westlands Ct CLV/TH FY5 21 H4
Westleigh Rd FUL/RIB PR2 58 B2
West Meadow FUL/RIB PR2 44 A5
Westminster Pl
KIRK/FR/WAR PR4 71 E5
Westminster Rd BPOOL FY1 28 C2
CHLY/EC PR7 93 F3
Westmorland Av BPOOL FY1 4 E2
BPOOL FY1 5 F1
CLV/TH FY5 16 D5
Westmorland Cl PRES PR1 72 A2
West Moss La LSTA FY8 50 B2
Weston Pl BPOOL FY1 4 E5
Weston St FUL/RIB PR2 6 B2
West Paddock LEYL PR25 82 D4
West Park Av FUL/RIB PR2 58 B1
West Park Dr BPOOLE FY3 3 J6
West Park La FUL/RIB PR2 58 C1
West Rd CLV/TH FY5 18 A5
FUL/RIB PR2 45 H5
Westside BPOOLS FY4 33 F5
West Sq KIRK/FR/WAR PR4 76 B1
West Strd PRES PR1 6 A2
West St BPOOL FY1 2 B4
CHLY/EC PR7 93 F3
West Vw BBR PR5 80 B2
BPOOL FY1 4 D1
KIRK/FR/WAR PR4 42 D1
KIRK/FR/WAR PR4 76 B1
PRES PR1 60 C1
West View Av BPOOL FY1 4 C4
West View Ter FUL/RIB PR2 59 E3
West Wy CHLY/EC PR7 88 D5
FTWD FY7 16 C2
Westway FUL/RIB PR2 46 A4
KIRK/FR/WAR PR4 53 H5
Westwell Gv BPOOL FY1 2 D6
Westwell Rd CHLYE PR6 93 G1
Westwood Av BPOOLE FY3 3 H6
FTWD FY7 11 E3
PLF/KEOS FY6 26 C4
Westwood Ms LSTA FY8 64 B3
Westwood Rd BBR PR5 81 F5
LEYL PR25 83 F2
LSTA FY8 64 B3
Wetherall St FUL/RIB PR2 59 F2
Wetherby Av BPOOLS FY4 38 B3
Weymouth Rd BPOOLE FY3 33 F2
Whalley Crs BPOOLE FY3 30 C5
Whalley La BPOOLS FY4 33 G5
Whalley Pl LSTA FY8 49 H5
Whalley Rd CHLY/EC PR7 94 C1
Whalley St BBR PR5 74 C4
CHLY/EC PR7 * 93 F3
Wham Hey KIRK/FR/WAR PR4 77 H2
Wham La KIRK/FR/WAR PR4 76 D5
KIRK/FR/WAR PR4 77 H2
Wharfedale BPOOLS FY4 39 F1
Wharfedale Av CLV/TH FY5 21 G1
FUL/RIB PR2 47 E3
Wharfedale Cl LEYL PR25 87 F1
Wharfedale Ct PLF/KEOS FY6 * 26 A4
Wharf St LSTA FY8 64 D3
Wharton Av CLV/TH FY5 22 B3
Wheatfield Cl CLV/TH FY5 21 F5
Wheatlands Crs BPOOLE FY3 34 A3
Wheel La GAR/LONG PR3 9 G5
Wheelton La LEYL PR25 83 F2
Whernside BPOOLS FY4 39 F1
Whernside Crs FUL/RIB PR2 46 D3
Whernside Wy LEYL PR25 83 H3
Whimberry Cl CHLYE PR6 93 H2
Whimbrel Dr CLV/TH FY5 17 G5
Whinfield Av CHLYE PR6 93 G1
FTWD FY7 11 E4
Whinfield La FUL/RIB PR2 58 B3
Whinfield Pl FUL/RIB PR2 58 B3
Whinney Heys Rd BPOOLE FY3 29 H5
Whinny La CHLY/EC PR7 88 B4
PLF/KEOS FY6 12 C2
Whinpark Av BPOOLE FY3 29 G4
Whinsands Cl FUL/RIB PR2 46 D3
Whitby Av FUL/RIB PR2 44 B3
Whitby Pl FUL/RIB PR2 44 B4
Whitby Rd LSTA FY8 49 G3
Whitebeam Cl CLV/TH FY5 17 F4
PRES PR1 72 A3
White Carr La CLV/TH FY5 21 F5
Whitecotes Dr LSTA FY8 65 E2
Whitecrest Av CLV/TH FY5 17 F5
Whitefield Meadow BBR PR5 74 C4
Whitefield Rd PRES PR1 71 H2
Whitefield Rd East PRES PR1 71 H2
Whitefield Rd West PRES PR1 71 H2
Whitefriar Cl FUL/RIB PR2 44 C3
Whitegate Dr BPOOLE FY3 3 G6
BPOOLE FY3 5 H2
White Gate Fold
CHLY/EC PR7 96 B2
Whitehead Cl BPOOLE FY3 30 B5
Whitehill Rd BPOOLS FY4 40 B3
Whiteholme Dr
PLF/KEOS FY6 25 H1
Whiteholme Pl FUL/RIB PR2 58 A2
Whiteholme Rd BISP FY2 21 F5
CLV/TH FY5 25 E1
Whitelees Wy PLF/KEOS FY6 26 B4
White Meadow FUL/RIB PR2 44 A5
Whitemoss Av BPOOLE FY3 29 H3
Whitendale Dr BBR PR5 80 C2
Whiteside St BPOOL FY1 2 D2
Whiteside Wy CLV/TH FY5 20 D1
Whitethorn Cl CHLYE PR6 84 D2
Whitethorne Ms CLV/TH FY5 21 H4
Whitethorn Ms LSTA FY8 49 G1
Whitethorn Sq FUL/RIB PR2 57 H2
Whitewood Cl LSTA FY8 63 H2
Whitley Av BPOOLE FY3 3 G4
CLV/TH FY5 17 E4
Whitmore Dr FUL/RIB PR2 61 G1
Whitmore Gv FUL/RIB PR2 61 G1
Whitmore Pl FUL/RIB PR2 61 F1
Whittaker Av BPOOLE FY3 3 G1
Whittam Av BPOOLS FY4 5 J5
Whittam Rd CHLY/EC PR7 93 E5
Whittle Pk CHLYE PR6 85 E2
Whitwell Av BPOOLS FY4 38 C3
Whitworth Ct
KIRK/FR/WAR PR4 * 43 E4
Whitworth Dr CHLY/EC PR7 92 D4
Whitworth St
KIRK/FR/WAR PR4 42 D2
Wholesome La
KIRK/FR/WAR PR4 77 F3
Wicklow Av LSTA FY8 65 F1
Widgeon Cl CLV/TH FY5 17 F5
Wigan Rd CHLY/EC PR7 87 H4
LEYL PR25 84 A1
Wigeon Rw LSTA FY8 50 C4
Wignall St PRES PR1 * 60 C2
Wigton Av LEYL PR25 82 C5
Wilbraham St PRES PR1 60 C2
Wilderswood Cl CHLYE PR6 85 F2
Wilding's La LSTA FY8 49 H3
Wild La BPOOLS FY4 40 B4
Wildman St BPOOLE FY3 3 G1
PRES PR1 59 G1
Wildoaks Dr CLV/TH FY5 22 B4
Wilford St BPOOLE FY3 29 E3
Wilkinson Av BPOOLE FY3 3 H7
Wilkinson St BBR PR5 79 G1
Wilkinson Wy PLF/KEOS FY6 12 D1
William Henry St PRES PR1 60 C3
Williams La FUL/RIB PR2 46 C1
William St BBR PR5 * 79 F1
BPOOLE FY3 29 E3
William Young Cl PRES PR1 * 60 C1
Willoughby Av CLV/TH FY5 20 D2
Willowbank Av BPOOLS FY4 39 E3
Willowbank Ct
PLF/KEOS FY6 * 25 H2
Willow Cl BBR PR5 75 H5
BBR PR5 79 F1
CLV/TH FY5 22 B3
KIRK/FR/WAR PR4 67 F1
PRES PR1 71 H2
Willow Coppice FUL/RIB PR2 44 A5
Willow Crs FUL/RIB PR2 60 D1
KIRK/FR/WAR PR4 * 67 F1
LEYL PR25 84 A1
Willowcroft Dr PLF/KEOS FY6 23 F3
Willow-dale CLV/TH FY5 22 B3
Willowdene CLV/TH FY5 21 E3
Willow Dr CHLY/EC PR7 96 A2
KIRK/FR/WAR PR4 42 A4
KIRK/FR/WAR PR4 67 F1
PLF/KEOS FY6 30 B2
Willow Fld CHLYE PR6 85 F1
Willow Gn FUL/RIB PR2 58 C3
Willow Gv BPOOLE FY3 29 G1
PLF/KEOS FY6 23 F2
Willow Grove Pk
PLF/KEOS FY6 * 13 E1
Willowmead Pk LSTA FY8 52 B1
Willow Rd CHLYE PR6 89 H5
Willows Av CLV/TH FY5 21 E3
LSTA FY8 63 H3
Willows La
KIRK/FR/WAR PR4 42 D3
The Willows CHLY/EC PR7 97 E1
Willow St FTWD FY7 11 G2
Willow Ter BPOOLE FY3 * 30 A4
Willow Tree Av GAR/LONG PR3 36 C2
Willow Tree Crs LEYL PR25 82 C3
Willow Wy KIRK/FR/WAR PR4 77 G2
Willshaw Rd BISP FY2 28 B1
Wilmar Rd LEYL PR25 83 H2
Wilmot Rd FUL/RIB PR2 47 E5
Wilson Sq CLV/TH FY5 20 C5
Wilton Gv PRES PR1 71 H2
Wilton Pde BPOOL FY1 28 B3
Wilton Pl LEYL PR25 * 83 G3
Wilvere Dr CLV/TH FY5 20 C4
Wimbledon Av CLV/TH FY5 24 D1
Wimbourne Pl BPOOLS FY4 38 A2
Winchcombe Rd CLV/TH FY5 21 E5
Winchester Av BPOOLS FY4 5 F6
CHLY/EC PR7 97 H2
Winchester Dr PLF/KEOS FY6 25 G1
Winckley Rd PRES PR1 6 B7
Winckley Sq PRES PR1 7 F5
Windermere Av FTWD FY7 16 D1
LEYL PR25 83 F1
Windermere Rd BPOOLS FY4 32 B5
CHLYE PR6 * 93 H3
FUL/RIB PR2 46 C4
PRES PR1 61 F2
Windermere Sq LSTA FY8 49 F1
Windflower Dr LEYL PR25 84 B2
Windle Cl BPOOLS FY4 38 B4
Windmill Av
KIRK/FR/WAR PR4 43 F4
Windmill Cl BPOOLE FY3 30 C5
Windmill Pl BPOOLS FY4 39 F2
Windmill Vw
KIRK/FR/WAR PR4 43 E2
Windsor Av BPOOLS FY4 32 B5
CLV/TH FY5 21 H2
FUL/RIB PR2 44 D5
KIRK/FR/WAR PR4 71 H5
PRES PR1 72 B3
Windsor Cl CHLY/EC PR7 93 E3
LEYL PR25 82 C5
Windsor Ct PLF/KEOS FY6 26 C4
Windsor Dr FUL/RIB PR2 45 F2
Windsor Rd BBR PR5 74 A3
BPOOLE FY3 29 H3
CHLY/EC PR7 90 B3
CHLY/EC PR7 93 E3
LSTA FY8 62 D1
Windsor Ter FTWD FY7 11 H1
Winery La BBR PR5 73 H1
Wingate Av CLV/TH FY5 20 D5
Wingate Pl CLV/TH FY5 20 D4
Wingates PRES PR1 72 B3
Wingrove Rd FTWD FY7 11 F4
Winifred St BPOOL FY1 2 B6
Winmarleigh Rd FUL/RIB PR2 58 D2
Winnipeg Pl BISP FY2 25 E4
Winscar Wk PLF/KEOS FY6 25 H4
Winsford Crs CLV/TH FY5 20 C4
Winslow Av PLF/KEOS FY6 25 H2
Winslow Cl PRES PR1 72 D4
Winsor Av LEYL PR25 83 G4
Winstanley Gv BPOOL FY1 2 D4
Winster Cl BBR PR5 75 H2
Winster Pl BPOOLS FY4 34 B4
Winston Av CLV/TH FY5 21 F2
LSTA FY8 49 H5
Winton Av BPOOLS FY4 33 G4
FUL/RIB PR2 45 H2
Winton Rd BPOOLS FY4 33 G3
Withington La CHLY/EC PR7 94 D3
Withnell Gv CHLYE PR6 93 H1
Withnell Rd BPOOLS FY4 32 B5
Withy Grove Cl BBR PR5 74 C5
Withy Grove Crs BBR PR5 74 C5
Withy Grove Rd BBR PR5 74 C5
Withy Pde FUL/RIB PR2 45 G4
Withy Trees Av BBR PR5 74 C5
Withy Trees Cl BBR PR5 74 C5
Witton Av FTWD FY7 11 E5
Witton Gv FTWD FY7 11 E5
Witton St PRES PR1 7 K3
Woburn Gn LEYL PR25 83 G3
Woburn Rd BPOOL FY1 28 C3
Wolseley Cl LEYL PR25 83 F4
Wolseley Pl PRES PR1 * 7 G5
Wolseley Rd PRES PR1 72 D1
Wolseley Ter PRES PR1 6 C7
Wolsey Cl CLV/TH FY5 21 E1
Wolsley Rd BPOOL FY1 4 C6
FTWD FY7 11 F2
Wolverton Av BISP FY2 24 B5
Woodacre Rd FUL/RIB PR2 61 G1
Wood Bank PRES PR1 72 B3
Woodcock Cl CLV/TH FY5 17 G4
Woodcock Fold CHLY/EC PR7 90 B3
Woodcroft Cl PRES PR1 72 B4
Wood End PRES PR1 72 B4
Wood End Rd CHLYE PR6 84 D1
Woodfall CHLY/EC PR7 89 E5
Woodfield BBR PR5 81 F3
Woodfield Av BPOOL FY1 4 B4
Woodfield Rd BPOOL FY1 4 B4
CHLY/EC PR7 93 F1
CLV/TH FY5 22 B3
Woodford Copse CHLY/EC PR7 92 C3
Wood Gn KIRK/FR/WAR PR4 43 F1
LEYL PR25 82 D2
Wood Green Dr CLV/TH FY5 21 F4
Woodhall Crs BBR PR5 75 H2
Woodhall Gdns PLF/KEOS FY6 23 G2
Woodhart La CHLY/EC PR7 90 B5
Woodhouse Rd CLV/TH FY5 22 C4
Woodland Av CLV/TH FY5 21 H2
Woodland Cl PLF/KEOS FY6 23 H2
Woodland Crs PLF/KEOS FY6 8 A5
Woodland Dr PLF/KEOS FY6 30 C1
Woodland Gv BPOOLE FY3 3 H7
PRES PR1 72 A1
Woodlands Av BBR PR5 74 D4
FUL/RIB PR2 61 E1
KIRK/FR/WAR PR4 42 D3
PRES PR1 72 C3
Woodlands Dr FUL/RIB PR2 36 D5
KIRK/FR/WAR PR4 43 F1
KIRK/FR/WAR PR4 66 B1
LEYL PR25 83 E4
Woodlands Meadow
CHLY/EC PR7 97 F2
Woodlands Rd LSTA FY8 63 G2
The Woodlands FUL/RIB PR2 58 A2
Woodlands Wy
KIRK/FR/WAR PR4 76 A1
Wood La CHLY/EC PR7 94 D1
Woodlark Dr CHLY/EC PR7 92 C5
Woodlea Rd LEYL PR25 83 E4
Woodley Av CLV/TH FY5 22 B3
Woodmancote CHLY/EC PR7 89 E5
Wood Park Rd BPOOL FY1 5 G5
Woodplumpton La
GAR/LONG PR3 36 B3
Woodplumpton Rd
FUL/RIB PR2 44 D5
FUL/RIB PR2 59 E1
Woodridge Av CLV/TH FY5 20 C4
Woodruff Cl CLV/TH FY5 17 F4
Woods Gn PRES PR1 72 D1
Woodside CHLY/EC PR7 87 H4
CHLY/EC PR7 97 H1
LEYL PR25 79 H5
Woodside Av CHLYE PR6 85 E3
FUL/RIB PR2 45 G4
FUL/RIB PR2 47 E5
KIRK/FR/WAR PR4 77 G2
Woodside Dr BPOOLE FY3 29 G5
Woodstock Av CLV/TH FY5 22 A4
Woodstock Cl BBR PR5 79 H1
Woodstock Gdns BPOOLS FY4 38 B1
Wood St BPOOL FY1 2 C4
FTWD FY7 17 E1
LSTA FY8 49 E5
PLF/KEOS FY6 26 D5
Woodvale Rd BBR PR5 * 81 E5
Wood View La PLF/KEOS FY6 19 G2
Woodville Rd CHLY/EC PR7 * 93 F2
PRES PR1 72 C4
Woodville Rd West PRES PR1 72 B4
Woodville St LEYL PR25 83 G1
Woodville Ter LSTA FY8 64 A3
Woodway FUL/RIB PR2 45 E4
Wookey Cl FUL/RIB PR2 46 D2
Woolman Rd BPOOL FY1 2 E7
Worcester Av LEYL PR25 83 G4
Worcester Pl CHLY/EC PR7 97 H2
Worcester Rd BPOOLE FY3 33 F2
Worden Cl LEYL PR25 83 E5
Worden La LEYL PR25 83 F5
Worden Rd FUL/RIB PR2 45 F5
Wordsworth Av BPOOLE FY3 33 H3
CLV/TH FY5 21 F2
KIRK/FR/WAR PR4 53 G5
LSTA FY8 65 E2
Wordsworth Pl BBR PR5 74 A4
Wordsworth Ter CHLYE PR6 89 G5
Worsley Av BPOOLS FY4 38 C1
Worsley Cl PLF/KEOS FY6 12 B1
Worsley Rd LSTA FY8 63 F1
Worthing Rd FUL/RIB PR2 44 C4
Worthington Rd BPOOLS FY4 39 G4
Worthy St CHLYE PR6 93 H3
Wray Crs KIRK/FR/WAR PR4 42 A4
Wray Gv CLV/TH FY5 20 D4
Wraywood Ct FTWD FY7 10 C5

Wren Av PRES PR1 ....72 D1
Wren Cl CLV/TH FY5 ....22 B4
PLF/KEOS FY6 ....25 G3
Wren Gv BPOOLE FY3 ....5 J5
Wrennalls La CHLY/EC PR7 ....90 A5
Wren St PRES PR1 ....60 B2
Wrights Fold LEYL PR25 ....83 H4
Wright St CHLYE PR6 ....93 H2
KIRK/FR/WAR PR4 * 42 D2
Wroxton Cl CLV/TH FY5 ....21 F5
Wychnor Fold KIRK/FR/WAR PR4 ...44 D1
Wycombe Av BPOOLS FY4 ....38 B2
Wykeham Rd LSTA FY8 ....4 A6
Wyndene CHLY/EC PR7 ....92 C1
Wyndene Gv
KIRK/FR/WAR PR4 ....54 B5
Wyndham Gdns BPOOLS FY4 ....38 D2

Wynfield BBR PR5 ....74 C4
Wynnwood Av BPOOL FY1 ....28 C1
Wyre Av KIRK/FR/WAR PR4 ....43 F3
Wyre Ct FTWD FY7 * ....
Wyredale Rd LSTA FY8 ....48 C5
Wyrefields PLF/KEOS FY6 ....27 E4
Wyre Gv BPOOL FY1 ....5 J5
Wyre Rd CLV/TH FY5 ....26 D1
Wyresdale Av BISP FY2 ....24 D3
PLF/KEOS FY6 ....26 A4
Wyresdale Crs FUL/RIB PR2 ....46 D4
Wyresdale Dr LEYL PR25 ....87 G1
Wyresdale Pk
FUL/RIB PR2 ....33 F2
Wyresdale Rd PLF/KEOS FY6 ......12 B1
Wyreside Dr PLF/KEOS FY6 ....5 H2
Wyre St FTWD FY7 ....11 F3

FUL/RIB PR2 ....59 E2
KIRK/FR/WAR PR4 ....42 D2
Wyvern Wy PLF/KEOS FY6 ....25 H2

Yarrow Ga CHLY/EC PR7 ....93 H4
Yarrow Pl LEYL PR25 ....82 C4
Yarrow Rd CHLYE PR6 ....93 H4
Yates St BPOOL FY1 ....82 C4
CHLY/EC PR7 ....93 E5
Yeadon Gv CHLY/EC PR7 ....92 D3
Yeadon Wy BPOOLS FY4 ....4 D7

Yew Ct FTWD FY7 ....10 C5
Yew Gn KIRK/FR/WAR PR4 ....43 F1
Yewlands Av BBR PR5 ....74 C5
CHLY/EC PR7 ....95 E2
FUL/RIB PR2 ....45 G2
Yewlands Crs FUL/RIB PR2 ....45 G2
Yewlands Dr FUL/RIB PR2 ....45 G2
LEYL PR25 ....83 E5
Yew Tree Av CHLY/EC PR7 ....87 H3
Yewtree Av FUL/RIB PR2 ....47 G3
Yewtree Cl CHLY/EC PR7 ....97 F2
Yewtree Gv BPOOLS FY4 ....79 F2
Yew Tree Rd BPOOLE FY3 ....29 G1
Yew Tree Vls CHLY/EC PR7 * 95 G2
York Av CLV/TH FY5 ....20 D2
FTWD FY7 ....11 E3

FUL/RIB PR2 ....45 G4
LEYL PR25 ....82 D5
York Dr KIRK/FR/WAR PR4 ....54 B1
York Rd BISP FY2 ....24 B3
LSTA FY8 ....62 C1
Yorkshire St BPOOL FY1 ....4 B1
York St BPOOL FY1 ....93 G3
CHLY/EC PR7 ....
Young Av LEYL PR25 ....83 H3

Zetland St PRES PR1 ....7 K5

Index – featured places

Abbey Road Clinic
BPOOLE FY4 ....38 C2
Ackhurst Business Park
CHLY/EC PR7 ....92 C2
Ackhurst Park Industrial Estate
CHLY/EC PR7 ....92 B2
Airport Terminal
LSTA FY8 ....38 C4
Albany High School
CHLYE PR6 ....93 H5
All Hallows C High School
PRES PR1 ....71 H3
All Saints CE Primary School
PRES PR1 ....93 E5
All Seasons Leisure Centre
CHLY/EC PR7 ....93 G1
AMF Bowling
BPOOL FY1 ....4 D2
AMS Trading Estate
KIRK/FR/WAR PR4 ....77 E2
Anchorsholme Primary School
CLV/TH FY5 ....21 E4
Ansdell Primary School
LSTA FY8 ....63 F1
Aqueduct Street Industrial
Estate FUL/RIB PR2 ....6 A1
Archbishop Temple High School
FUL/RIB PR2 ....45 H3
The Arena (Blackpool Pleasure
Beach)
BPOOLS FY4 ....38 B1
Arnold Junior School
BPOOLS FY4 ....38 C1
Arnold Medical Centre
BPOOLS FY4 ....38 B1
Arnold School
BPOOLS FY4 ....38 B1
Arts Centre
LEYL PR25 ....87 E1
Ashbridge Independent School
KIRK/FR/WAR PR4 ....71 G4
Ashton Health Centre
FUL/RIB PR2 ....58 C2
Ashton & Lea Golf Club
KIRK/FR/WAR PR4 ....57 G1
Ashton on Ribble High School
FUL/RIB PR2 ....58 B1
Astley Hall Museum &
Art Gallery CHLY/EC PR7 ....92 D1
Astley Park School
CHLY/EC PR7 ....93 E2
Back Lane Caravan Park
KIRK/FR/WAR PR4 ....66 B2
Baines Endowed
Primary School CLV/TH FY5 .....22 A4
Baines School
PLF/KEOS FY6 ....30 D1
Balshaw Lane Primary School
CHLY/EC PR7 ....92 B1
Balshaws CE High School
LEYL PR25 ....83 G5
Bamber Bridge Clinic
BBR PR5 ....74 C4
Bamber Bridge FC
BBR PR5 ....80 A1
Bamber Bridge (Withy Park)
Leisure Centre BBR PR5 ....74 C4
Bank View Industrial Estate
PLF/KEOS FY6 ....23 G3
Bates Swimming Pool
PLF/KEOS FY6 ....23 G2
Beach Patrol HQ
BPOOL FY1 ....2 B1
Bedford Hotel
LSTA FY8 ....49 E5
Beech Tree School
BBR PR5 ....80 D5
Beehive Industrial Estate
BPOOLS FY4 ....33 H5
Belgrave Madison Hotel
BISP FY2 ....24 B2
The Bennett House School
CHLYE PR6 ....93 H1
The Best Western
Glendower Hotel LSTA FY8 ....48 C5
Birchwood Medical Centre
FUL/RIB PR2 ....58 D1
Bispham Endowed CE Primary
School
BISP FY2 ....24 D3
Bispham High School &
Arts College BISP FY2 ....24 D5
Blackpool Airport
LSTA FY8 ....38 D5
Blackpool Baines Endowed CE
Primary
School 5 K6
Blackpool Business Park
BPOOLS FY4 ....39 E3
Blackpool Crematorium
(Carleton) BPOOLE FY3 ....25 F4

Blackpool CC
BPOOLE FY3 ....3 J6
Blackpool FC (Bloomfield Road)
BPOOL FY1 ....4 D3
Blackpool & Fleetwood
Tramway BISP FY2 ....28 B1
Blackpool & Fylde College
(Central Blackpool Campus)
BPOOL FY1 ....2 E7
Blackpool North Shore
Golf Club BISP FY2 ....24 C5
Blackpool Pleasure Beach
BPOOLS FY4 ....38 B1
Blackpool RFC
CLV/TH FY5 ....20 D5
Blackpool Sixth Form College
BPOOLE FY3 ....25 G5
Blackpool & The Fylde College
BISP FY2 ....25 E1
Blackpool Tower
BPOOL FY1 ....2 A5
Blackpool Welfare Clinic
BPOOLE FY3 ....29 F3
Blackpool Zoo Park
BPOOLE FY3 ....29 G5
Blessed Sacrament RC
Primary School
BPOOLE FY3 ....47 F5
Bloomfield Medical Centre
BPOOL FY1 ....4 E5
Boundary Primary School
BPOOLE FY3 ....29 G3
The Breck Primary School
PLF/KEOS FY6 ....26 D2
Brinde Gregson Lane
Primary School BBR PR5 ....75 H5
Brindle St Josephs RC
Primary School BBR PR5 ....75 H5
Broadoak Primary School
PRES PR1 ....72 B4
Broadoaks Centre
LEYL PR25 ....87 E1
Brockholes Wood
Primary School PRES PR1 ....61 G2
Brookfield Primary School
FUL/RIB PR2 ....47 E5
Brookfield School
PLF/KEOS FY6 ....26 D2
Broughton Business &
Enterprise College
GAR/LONG PR3 ....36 B3
Broughton CE Primary School
GAR/LONG PR3 ....36 C4
Broughton Park Private
Hospital GAR/LONG PR3 ....36 D4
Brownedge St Marys RC
High School BBR PR5 ....74 C5
Brynsing with Warton St Pauls
School KIRK/FR/WAR PR4 ....66 C1
Buckshaw Primary School
CHLY/EC PR7 ....88 D5
BUPA Fylde Coast Hospital
BPOOLE FY3 ....29 F5
Burn Hall Industrial Estate
FTWD FY7 ....17 G3
Burn Naze Primary School
CLV/TH FY5 ....21 H1
Camelot Theme Park
CHLY/EC PR7 ....95 F1
Cardinal Allen Catholic
High School FTWD FY7 ....17 E1
Cardinal Newman College
PRES PR1 ....7 J5
Carleton Cemetery
PLF/KEOS FY6 ....25 F3
Carleton Green Primary School
PLF/KEOS FY6 ....25 H1
Carleton St Hildas CE Primary
School PLF/KEOS FY6 ....25 H2
Carlton Hotel
BPOOL FY1 ....2 B1
Carousel Hotel
BPOOLS FY4 ....38 A3
Carr Head Primary School
PLF/KEOS FY6 ....26 C5
Carr Hill High School
KIRK/FR/WAR PR4 ....43 F4
Central Bus Station
PRES PR1 ....7 G3
Central Pier
BPOOL FY1 ....4 A1
Centurion Industrial Estate
CROS/BRETH PR26 ....79 G5
Chadwick Hotel
LSTA FY8 ....62 C2
Chandlers Business Park
CROS/BRETH PR26 ....82 D2
Chapel Lane Business Park
CHLY/EC PR7 ....96 C5
Charnley Fold Industrial Estate
BBR PR5 ....74 B3

Charnock Richard Golf Club
CHLY/EC PR7 ....95 G1
Charter Theatre
PRES PR1 ....7 G4
Chaucer Primary School
FTWD FY7 ....11 F2
Chorley AFC
CHLY/EC PR7 ....93 F4
Chorley Business & Technology
Centre
CHLY/EC PR7 ....88 B3
Chorley CC
CHLY/EC PR7 ....93 F3
Chorley North Business Park
CHLYE PR6 ....89 G4
Chorley North Industrial Park
CHLYE PR6 ....89 G5
Chorley Retail Park
CHLY/EC PR7 ....93 F3
Chorley & South Ribble District
General Hospital
CHLY/EC PR7 ....89 F4
Chorley West Business Park
CHLY/EC PR7 ....92 C2
Christchurch Charnock Richard
CE Primary School
CHLY/EC PR7 ....96 A1
Christ the King Catholic
High School PRES PR1 ....7 J7
Christ the King RC
Primary School
BPOOLE FY3 ....29 G3
Claremont Hotel
FUL/RIB PR2 ....58 D1
Claremont Primary School
BPOOL FY1 ....28 C2
Clayton Brook Primary School
BBR PR5 ....81 E4
Clayton Green Business Park
BBR PR5 ....81 E5
Clayton Green Sports Centre
BBR PR5 ....80 D5
Clayton le Woods CE
Primary School CHLYE PR6 ....84 D2
Cleveleys Health Centre
CLV/TH FY5 ....20 D2
Clifton Arms Hotel
LSTA FY8 ....64 B3
Clifton Primary School
LSTA FY8 ....50 A5
Clifton Retail Park
BPOOLS FY4 ....34 B5
Cocker Trading Estate
BPOOL FY1 ....2 D1
Collegiate High School
BPOOLS FY4 ....29 G1
Common Bank Employment
Area CHLY/EC PR7 ....92 C3
Common Bank Industrial
Estate CHLY/EC PR7 ....92 C3
Cop Lane CE Primary School
PRES PR1 ....72 B2
Copper Works Wood
CHLY/EC PR7 ....92 C3
The Coppice School
CHLYE PR6 ....74 D5
Coppull Community
Leisure Centre CHLY/EC PR7 ....96 B5
Coppull Parish CE Primary
School CHLY/EC PR7 ....96 C4
Coppull Primary School
CHLY/EC PR7 ....96 A4
Copse View Business Park
FTWD FY7 ....11 F4
Coral Island
BPOOL FY1 ....2 B6
Corpus Christi RC High School
FUL/RIB PR2 ....45 G4
Couge Green Primary School
BBR PR5 ....75 H2
Cowling Brow Industrial
Estate
CHLYE PR6 ....93 H4
Crossley House
Industrial Estate PRES PR1 ....73 E2
Crown Stage & Theatre
CROS/BRETH PR26 ....82 B1
Cuerden Church Infant School
BBR PR5 ....80 C2
Cuerden Church School
BBR PR5 ....80 C1
Cuerden Valley Country Park
CHLY/EC PR7 ....84 C1
Deepdale County J & I School
PRES PR1 ....60 B1
Deepdale Shopping Park
PRES PR1 ....46 C5
Dental Health Centre
PRES PR1 ....46 B5
De Vere Herons' Reach Hotel
BPOOLE FY3 ....33 H1

Devonshire Infant School
BPOOLE FY3 ....3 F2
Devonshire Junior School
BPOOLE FY3 ....29 F3
Devonshire Road Hospital
BPOOLE FY3 ....3 F2
Dewhurst Industrial Estate
PRES PR1 ....6 B1
Docklands Medical Centre
FUL/RIB PR2 ....59 E2
Duke Street Primary School
CHLY/EC PR7 ....93 F4
Dunkirk Hall Industrial Estate
CROS/BRETH PR26 ....82 B4
Duxbury Jubilee Park Golf Club
CHLY/EC PR7 ....97 G2
Duxbury Park Golf Club
CHLY/EC PR7 ....97 G1
Dyslexia North West
LSTA FY8 ....48 D5
East Chorley Business Centre
CHLYE PR6 ....93 G2
Eastham Hall Caravan Site
LSTA FY8 ....51 H4
Eccleston Primary School
CHLY/EC PR7 ....90 A4
Eldon Primary School
PRES PR1 ....59 G1
Elms School
PRES PR1 ....46 A5
Emmanuel Christian School
PLF/KEOS FY6 ....30 A2
English Martyrs RC
Primary School PRES PR1 ....59 G2
Euxton CE Primary School
CHLY/EC PR7 ....87 H5
Euxton Hall Hospital
CHLY/EC PR7 ....91 H1
Euxton St Marys RC Primary
School CHLY/EC PR7 ....87 H4
Fairhaven Golf Club
LSTA FY8 ....63 H2
Farington Business Park
CROS/BRETH PR26 ....83 F2
Farington Primary School
LEYL PR25 ....83 G1
Ferry Terminal
FTWD FY7 ....11 H2
Fishergate Shopping Centre
PRES PR1 ....6 E5
Fishwick Hall Golf Club
PRES PR1 ....61 F3
Fishwick Primary School
PRES PR1 ....61 E3
Flakefleet Primary School
FTWD FY7 ....11 E4
Fleetwood Charles Sear
Community Primary School
FTWD FY7 ....10 C3
Fleetwood CC
FTWD FY7 ....17 E1
Fleetwood FC
FTWD FY7 ....17 E1
Fleetwood Golf Club
FTWD FY7 ....10 D5
Fleetwood Health Centre
FTWD FY7 ....11 H2
Fleetwood High School
FTWD FY7 ....10 D5
Fleetwood Hospital
FTWD FY7 ....11 H1
Fleetwood Leisure Centre &
Swimming Pool
FTWD FY7 ....11 G1
Fleetwood Museum
FTWD FY7 ....12 A1
Fleetwoods Charity CE Primary
School PLF/KEOS FY6 ....13 F3
The Forward Industrial Estate
LEYL PR25 ....82 D2
Fox Industrial Estate
BISP FY2 ....29 E1
Freckleton CC
KIRK/FR/WAR PR4 ....54 B5
Freckleton CE Primary School
KIRK/FR/WAR PR4 ....54 C4
Freeport Fleetwood
Outlet Village FTWD FY7 ....11 G3
Frenchwood Community
Primary School PRES PR1 ....7 J6
Fulwood & Cadley
Primary School
FUL/RIB PR2 ....45 F4
Fulwood Hall Hospital
FUL/RIB PR2 ....46 B2
Fulwood High School
FUL/RIB PR2 ....45 F3
Fulwood Leisure Centre
FUL/RIB PR2 ....45 F3
Fylde CC
PLF/KEOS FY6 ....26 C2

Fylde RFC
LSTA FY8 ....63 G1
Fylde Road Industrial Estate
PRES PR1 ....6 B1
Gillibrand Primary School
CHLY/EC PR7 ....93 E4
Glades Clinic
PRES PR1 ....61 F1
The Grand Hotel
PRES PR1 ....62 B1
Grand Theatre
BPOOL FY1 ....2 C5
Grange Park Health Centre
BPOOLE FY3 ....29 G2
Grange Primary School
BPOOLE FY3 ....47 F4
Great Arley School
CLV/TH FY5 ....21 H1
Great Arley Swimming Pool
CLV/TH FY5 ....21 H1
Greenlands Primary School
FUL/RIB PR2 ....47 E5
Grove Park Industrial Estate
CHLY/EC PR7 ....90 B5
Guild Community Healthcare
PRES PR1 ....44 C2
Guild Trading Estate
PRES PR1 ....7 K1
Hambleton Health Centre
PLF/KEOS FY6 ....23 F2
Hambleton Primary School
PLF/KEOS FY6 ....23 H2
Harbour Trading Estate
FTWD FY7 ....11 F4
Harris Museum & Art Gallery
PRES PR1 ....7 G4
Harrison Trading Estate
PRES PR1 ....60 C2
Harris Primary School
FUL/RIB PR2 ....44 D1
Haslemere Industrial Estate
LEYL PR25 ....83 E2
Hawes Side Clinic
BPOOLS FY4 ....39 E1
Hawes Side Primary School
BPOOLS FY4 ....39 E1
Headlands Hotel
BPOOLS FY4 ....38 A2
Heskin FC
CHLY/EC PR7 ....94 C2
Heskin Pembertons CE Primary
School
CHLY/EC PR7 ....94 D3
Heyhouse Endowed CE
Infant School LSTA FY8 ....49 F4
Heyhouse Endowed CE
Junior School LSTA FY8 ....49 F3
Higher Walton CE
Primary School BBR PR5 ....75 F3
Highfield Industrial Estate
CHLYE PR6 ....89 F5
Highfield Primary School
CHLYE PR6 ....93 G2
Highfield Priory School
FUL/RIB PR2 ....47 F3
Highfurlong School
BPOOLE FY3 ....25 G5
HM Prison
KIRK/FR/WAR PR4 ....43 E5
Hodgson High School Technical
College PLF/KEOS FY6 ....26 C4
Holme Slack CP School
PRES PR1 ....46 C5
Holy Cross RC High School
CHLY/EC PR7 ....97 F1
Holy Family RC Primary School
BPOOL FY1 ....28 C2
FUL/RIB PR2 ....44 B4
KIRK/FR/WAR PR4 ....53 C5
Hoohill Industrial Estate
BPOOLE FY3 ....29 G2
Hotel Ibis
GAR/LONG PR3 ....36 D4
Hotel Sheraton
BISP FY2 ....24 B5
Houndshill Shopping Centre
BPOOL FY1 ....2 B5
Howick CE Primary School
KIRK/FR/WAR PR4 ....71 G3
Hutton Grammar School
KIRK/FR/WAR PR4 ....71 E4
The Imperial Hotel
BPOOL FY1 ....28 B3
Industrial Centre for the
Blind & Disabled
BPOOLS FY4 ....33 H4
Ingol Golf Club
FUL/RIB PR2 ....44 D2
Ingol Pool House County School
FUL/RIB PR2 ....44 C2

Ingol Primary School
FUL/RIB PR2 ....44 B4
Italian Gardens
BPOOLE FY5 ....3 K6
Jubilee Trading Estate
CLV/TH FY5 ....6 C1
Kaymar Industrial Estate
PRES PR1 ....60 C4
Kellets Trading Estate
PRES PR1 ....72 D2
Kennington Primary School
BISP FY2 ....46 A4
Kincraig Primary School
BISP FY2 ....25 F1
King Edward & Queen Mary
Pre-Preparatory School
LSTA FY8 ....62 D2
Kingsfold Medical Centre
PRES PR1 ....72 B3
Kingsfold Primary School
PRES PR1 ....72 C4
Kirkham Baths
KIRK/FR/WAR PR4 ....43 E3
Kirkham Grammar School
KIRK/FR/WAR PR4 ....42 C3
Kirkham Health Centre
KIRK/FR/WAR PR4 ....43 E3
Kirkham Museum
KIRK/FR/WAR PR4 ....43 E3
Kirkham Trading Park
KIRK/FR/WAR PR4 ....43 F4
Kirkham & Wesham
Primary School
KIRK/FR/WAR PR4 ....42 D3
Kneps Farm Holiday Park
CLV/TH FY5 ....22 C2
Knott End Golf Club
PLF/KEOS FY6 ....12 A1
Lancashire College
CHLYE/EC PR7 ....92 D2
Lancashire College
of Agriculture
KIRK/FR/WAR PR4 ....71 G3
Lancashire County
Museum Service *PRES* PR1 ....7 J5
Lancashire Enterprise Business
Park *CROS/BRETH* PR26 ....79 E4
Lancashire Records Office
PRES PR1 ....6 C4
Lancaster Lane Primary School
LEYL PR25 ....84 A3
Lane Ends Trading Estate
FUL/RIB PR2 ....59 E1
Langdale School
BISP FY2 ....28 C1
Larkholme Primary School
FTWD FY7 ....16 D1
Laton Cemetery
BPOOLE FY3 ....29 E3
Layton Medical Centre
BPOOLE FY3 ....29 F3
Layton Primary School
BPOOLE FY3 ....29 F2
Lea Community Primary School
FUL/RIB PR2 ....57 H2
Lea St Mary RC Primary School
KIRK/FR/WAR PR4 ....56 D1
Lever House Primary School
LEYL PR25 ....83 H1
Leyland Golf Club
LEYL PR25 ....84 A4
Leyland Leisure Centre
LEYL PR25 ....85 E4
Leyland Methodist J & I School
LEYL PR25 ....85 G3
Library & Grundy Art Gallery
PRES PR1 ....2 C3
Lido Pool
BPOOLE FY4 ....4 C6
Lidun Park Industrial Estate
LSTA FY8 ....65 F1
Lifeboat Museum
LSTA FY8 ....64 D4
Light Industrial Estate
KIRK/FR/WAR PR4 ....76 A4
Lindum Hotel
LSTA FY8 ....62 B1
Lisieux Hall Hospital
PRES PR1 ....84 D4
Little Hoole Primary School
KIRK/FR/WAR PR4 ....76 B4
Little Theatre
CHLYE/EC PR7 ....93 F2
Longsands Community
Primary School *FUL/RIB* PR2 ....46 D3
Longton County Primary
School *KIRK/FR/WAR* PR4 ....76 B1
Longton Health Centre
KIRK/FR/WAR PR4 ....70 B5
Lostock Hall Community
High School *BBR* PR5 ....73 H5
Lostock Hall Primary School
BBR PR5 ....73 G5
Louis Tussauds Waxworks
BPOOL FY1 ....2 B7
Lytham CE Primary School
LSTA FY8 ....64 C2
Lytham Community YMCA
Sports Centre *LSTA* FY8 ....64 D2
Lytham CC
LSTA FY8 ....64 A3
Lytham Green Drive Golf Club
LSTA FY8 ....64 C1
Lytham Hall Park
Primary School *LSTA* FY8 ....64 A3
Lytham Hospital
LSTA FY8 ....65 E3
Lytham Posey Bowl
LSTA FY8 ....64 C3
Lytham St Anne's High
Technology College
LSTA FY8 ....63 F1
Lytham St Anne's Sports &
Leisure Centre *LSTA* FY8 ....63 G1
Lytham Windmill
LSTA FY8 ....64 D3

Madisons New Leisure Centre
KIRK/FR/WAR PR4 ....56 A2
Manchester Mill
Industrial Estate *PRES* PR1 ....60 C3
Manor Beach Primary School
CLV/TH FY5 ....20 C1
Manor House Hotel
KIRK/FR/WAR PR4 ....42 C4
Manor Road Primary School
CHLYE PR6 ....85 E2
Marine Business Centre
LSTA FY8 ....65 F2
Marine Hall
FTWD FY7 ....11 C1
Marine Industrial Centre
LSTA FY8 ....65 F2
Market Walk Shopping Centre
CHLYE/EC PR7 ....93 H2
Marsh Mill Museum
CLV/TH FY5 ....21 G2
Marton Medical Centre
BPOOLE FY3 ....5 J3
Marton Mere Holiday Village
BPOOLE FY3 ....34 A2
Marton Primary School
BPOOLE FY4 ....39 F1
Matrix Park Business Area
CHLYE/EC PR7 ....84 A5
Mayfield Primary School
CHLYE PR6 ....49 E3
Mayfield School
CHLYE/EC PR7 ....93 F5
Medlar with Wesham CE
Primary School
KIRK/FR/WAR PR4 ....42 D2
Mereside Primary School
BPOOLS FY4 ....33 H4
Metropolitan Business Park
BPOOLE FY3 ....33 H3
Middleforth CE Primary School
PRES PR1 ....72 C3
Millfield High School
CLV/TH FY5 ....22 A5
Model Village
BPOOLS FY4 ....33 F1
Montgomery High School
BISP FY2 ....24 D2
Moorbrook School
FUL/RIB PR2 ....45 G5
Moorfield School
PRES PR1 ....46 A5
Moor Hey School
BBR PR5 ....73 F5
Moor Nook Primary School
FUL/RIB PR2 ....47 G5
Moor Park High School
BISP FY2 ....60 A1
Moor Park Industrial Estate
BISP FY2 ....25 F5
Moor Park Infant School
BISP FY2 ....25 E4
Moor Park Junior School
BISP FY2 ....25 E4
Moor Park Swimming Pool
BISP FY2 ....24 D3
Moss Side Industrial Estate
CROS/BRETH PR26 ....82 B1
Moss Side School
CROS/BRETH PR26 ....82 B2
Muslim Girls Secondary School
PRES PR1 ....7 K1
National Football Museum
PRES PR1 ....60 B1
The Natural Health Centre
PRES PR1 ....7 H2
Natural Therapy Clinic
BPOOLE FY3 ....29 F3
Naze Lane Industrial Estate
KIRK/FR/WAR PR4 ....67 G1
New Cemetery
BPOOLS FY4 ....4 E2
New Longton CE Primary
School *KIRK/FR/WAR* PR4 ....77 G2
New Mill Industrial Estate
BBR PR5 ....80 C2
Newton Bluecoat CE Primary
School
KIRK/FR/WAR PR4 ....55 G1
Norbreck Primary School
CLV/TH FY5 ....20 D4
Northbrook Primary School
LEYL PR25 ....83 E3
Northfold CP School
CLV/TH FY5 ....17 E5
North Pier
BPOOL FY1 ....2 A4
Novotel
BBR PR5 ....80 C3
Odeon Cinema
BPOOL FY1 ....4 D1
Old Brewery Trading Estate
PRES PR1 ....6 B3
Old Mill Industrial Estate
PRES PR1 ....74 A5
Otters Leisure Pool
GAR/LONG PR3 ....36 D3
Our Lady of the Assumption
RC Primary School
BPOOLS FY4 ....39 F3
Our Lady & St Edwards RC
Primary School
GAR/LONG PR3 ....36 C5
Our Lady & St Gerards RC
Primary School *BBR* PR5 ....79 F1
Our Ladys RC High School
FUL/RIB PR2 ....45 E3
Over Wyre Medical Centre
PLF/KEOS FY6 ....12 D1
Over Wyre Sports Centre
PLF/KEOS FY6 ....13 E1
Oxford Medical Centre
BPOOLS FY4 ....38 C3
Oxhey Trading Estate
PRES PR1 ....59 F1
Palatine High School
BPOOLS FY4 ....4 E7

Park Cemetery
LSTA FY8 ....50 C5
Park Crematorium
LSTA FY8 ....50 D4
Parker Street Industrial Estate
FUL/RIB PR2 ....59 F2
Park Hall Hotel
CHLYE/EC PR7 ....95 F1
Park Hall Leisure Centre
CHLYE/EC PR7 ....95 F1
Parklands High School
CHLYE/EC PR7 ....92 D2
Park School
BISP FY2 ....3 H7
Pear Tree School
KIRK/FR/WAR PR4 ....43 E3
Penwortham CC
PRES PR1 ....72 D2
Penwortham Girls High School
PRES PR1 ....72 B1
Penwortham Golf Club
PRES PR1 ....58 D4
Penwortham Holme
Recreation Centre *PRES* PR1 ....6 A7
Penwortham Primary School
PRES PR1 ....71 H1
Penwortham Sports Club
PRES PR1 ....72 D2
Phoenix Sporting &
Leisure Centre *CLV/TH* FY5 ....21 E5
Pines Hotel
CHLYE PR6 ....85 E1
Playhouse Theatre
PRES PR1 ....6 E3
Pleasure Island
LSTA FY8 ....62 B1
Post Graduate Medical Centre
BPOOLS FY4 ....45 H4
Poulton Le Fylde Golf Club
PLF/KEOS FY6 ....26 B2
Poulton St Chads CE Primary
School *PLF/KEOS* FY6 ....26 B4
Poulton Swimming &
Fitness Centre
PLF/KEOS FY6 ....26 C2
Preesall Mill Industrial Estate
PLF/KEOS FY6 ....13 F4
Premier Travel Inn
BBR PR5 ....80 A2
BISP FY2 ....24 D2
BPOOLE FY3 ....4 D7
BPOOLS FY4 ....40 C2
CHLYE PR6 ....89 H2
CHLYE PR6 ....93 H5
LSTA FY8 ....38 C4
LSTA FY8 ....49 E1
Premier Travel Inn Preston East
FUL/RIB PR2 ....47 F2
Premier Travel Inn Preston West
KIRK/FR/WAR PR4 ....56 D3
Preston Bowl
PRES PR1 ....59 F1
Preston CC
PRES PR1 ....72 D1
Preston College
FUL/RIB PR2 ....46 A3
Preston Golf Club
FUL/RIB PR2 ....45 F4
Preston Grasshoppers RFC
KIRK/FR/WAR PR4 ....36 A5
Preston Marriott Hotel
GAR/LONG PR3 ....36 C3
Preston North End FC
(Deepdale) *PRES* PR1 ....60 D1
Preston Sports Arena
KIRK/FR/WAR PR4 ....44 A5
Preston Sports Club
PRES PR1 ....6 D7
Primrose Hill Primary School
CHLYE/EC PR7 ....87 G3
The Priory Pool
PRES PR1 ....71 G1
Priory Technology College
PRES PR1 ....71 H1
Progress Business Park
KIRK/FR/WAR PR4 ....43 E4
Progress School
BBR PR5 ....81 E3
Queens Drive Primary School
FUL/RIB PR2 ....45 F3
Queens Retail Park
PRES PR1 ....7 J5
Queensway Industrial Estate
LSTA FY8 ....49 G1
Red Marsh School
CLV/TH FY5 ....21 H1
The Red Rose School
LSTA FY8 ....48 D5
Red Scar Industrial Estate
FUL/RIB PR2 ....48 D5
Revoe Primary Community
School *BPOOL* FY1 ....4 E2
Ribbleton Avenue County
Infant School *PRES* PR1 ....60 C1
Ribbleton Avenue Methodist
Junior School *PRES* PR1 ....60 D1
Ribbleton Hall High School
FUL/RIB PR2 ....47 F5
Ribbleton Hospital
FUL/RIB PR2 ....61 F1
Ribbleton Lane Trading Estate
PRES PR1 ....7 J2
Ribble Village Health Centre
FUL/RIB PR2 ....61 E1
Ripleys Believe It or
Not Museum *BPOOLS* FY4 ....38 A1
Riverside Medical Centre
PRES PR1 ....74 A1
Rock FM Radio Station
PRES PR1 ....7 H2
The Roebuck Primary School
FUL/RIB PR2 ....59 F1
Roseacre Primary School
BPOOLS FY4 ....38 C3
Rose Gardens
BPOOLE FY3 ....3 J5

Rossall Hospital
FTWD FY7 ....16 C1
Rossall Junior School
FTWD FY7 ....16 C3
Rossall School
FTWD FY7 ....16 C3
Royal Cross Primary School
FUL/RIB PR2 ....58 A2
Royal Lytham & St Anne's
Golf Club *LSTA* FY8 ....49 G5
Royal Preston Hospital
FUL/RIB PR2 ....45 H2
Royles Brook Primary School
CLV/TH FY5 ....21 G2
The Ryan Medical Centre
BBR PR5 ....74 B5
Sacred Heart Catholic
Primary School
FUL/RIB PR2 ....59 E2
Sacred Heart Catholic School
CLV/TH FY5 ....21 H1
Sacred Heart RC
Primary School *CHLYE* PR6 ....93 H5
St Aidans CE
Technology College
PLF/KEOS FY6 ....13 E3
St Aidans Primary School
BBR PR5 ....74 C5
St Andrews CE Infant School
LEYL PR25 ....83 E4
St Andrews CE Primary School
BBR PR5 ....58 D2
St Andrews RC Primary School
KIRK/FR/WAR PR4 ....44 A2
St Annes Catholic
Primary School *LEYL* PR25 ....82 C4
St Annes College
Grammar School
LSTA FY8 ....62 B1
St Anne's CC
LSTA FY8 ....62 B1
St Anne's Old Links Golf Club
LSTA FY8 ....49 E2
St Anne's Pier
LSTA FY8 ....48 D2
St Anne's Swimming Pool
LSTA FY8 ....48 D5
St Anthonys RC Primary School
FUL/RIB PR2 ....62 A1
St Augustines RC Primary School
PRES PR1 ....7 H5
St Bedes Catholic High School
CHLYE PR6 ....64 D2
St Bedes RC Primary School
BBR PR5 ....81 E5
St Bernadettes Catholic School
BISP FY2 ....24 D2
St Bernards Catholic
Primary School
FUL/RIB PR2 ....57 G2
St Catherines RC Primary School
LEYL PR25 ....83 H2
St Clares RC Primary School
FUL/RIB PR2 ....45 H2
St Cuthberts RC Primary School
PRES PR1 ....58 D5
St Fillans Medical Centre
PRES PR1 ....58 D5
St Georges CE High School
BPOOLS FY4 ....33 G4
St Georges CE Primary School
KIRK/FR/WAR PR4 ....93 H5
St Georges Shopping Centre
PRES PR1 ....7 F4
St Gregorys Catholic Primary
School *CHLYE/EC* PR7 ....93 F5
St Gregorys RC Primary School
BBR PR5 ....46 B5
St Ignatius RC Primary School
PRES PR1 ....7 F1
St James CE Primary School
CHLYE PR6 ....93 H3
St Johns Catholic Primary
School *PLF/KEOS* FY6 ....26 C2
St Johns CE Primary School
BPOOL FY1 ....2 D5
St John's Market
BPOOL FY1 ....2 D4
St Johns Shopping Centre
PRES PR1 ....7 G3
St John Vianney Catholic
Primary School *BPOOLE* FY3 ....5 J4
St Josephs Catholic
Primary School *CHLYE* PR6 ....89 G5
St Josephs CE Primary School
PRES PR1 ....60 C2
St Josephs RC Primary School
KIRK/FR/WAR PR4 ....42 D1
St Kentigerns RC
Primary School
BPOOLE FY3 ....3 G4
St Leonards CE Primary School
BBR PR5 ....73 H2
St Maria Goretti RC
Primary School
FUL/RIB PR2 ....47 F3
St Mary Magdalen RC
Primary School *PRES* PR1 ....72 D2
St Marys Catholic College
BPOOLE FY3 ....29 E3
St Marys Catholic
Technical College
PRES PR1 ....82 D3
St Marys CE Primary School
CHLYE/EC PR7 ....90 B4
St Marys Medical Centre
PRES PR1 ....72 A1
St Marys Primary School
BBR PR5 ....83 E3
St Marys RC Primary School
CHLYE/EC PR7 ....92 D5
FTWD FY7 ....11 D1
St Matthews CE Primary School
PRES PR1 ....60 D3
St Michaels CE High School
CHLYE/EC PR7 ....89 F5

St Michaels Primary School
KIRK/FR/WAR PR4 ....43 F3
St Nicholas CE Primary School
BPOOLS FY4 ....39 G4
St Oswalds RC Primary School
CHLY/EC PR7 ....95 H5
St Patricks RC Primary School
KIRK/FR/WAR PR4 ....76 D1
St Pauls CE Primary School
CROS/BRETH PR26 ....79 E2
St Pauls CE School
LSTA FY8 ....53 F5
St Pauls Medical Centre
BBR PR5 ....28 B5
St Peters CE Primary School
CHLYE PR6 ....89 H5
FUL/RIB PR2 ....45 H1
St Peters RC Primary School
LEYL PR25 ....64 D1
St Pius X Preparatory School
FUL/RIB PR2 ....45 G5
St Teresas Catholic
Primary School *CLV/TH* FY5 ....20 D2
St Teresas RC Primary School
PRES PR1 ....61 E3
St Thomas CE Primary School
LSTA FY8 ....49 F5
St Williams Catholic
Primary School
GAR/LONG PR3 ....15 G1
St Wulstans & St Edmunds
Catholic Primary School
FTWD FY7 ....11 E3
Sandcastle Leisure Centre
BPOOLS FY4 ....32 A5
Sandy Lane Clinic
LEYL PR25 ....83 F4
Savick Primary School
FUL/RIB PR2 ....58 A1
Sawmill Industrial Estate
FUL/RIB PR2 ....3 F5
Sealife Centre
BPOOL FY1 ....2 B7
Selby Industrial Estate
KIRK/FR/WAR PR4 ....42 D2
Shakespeare Primary School
FTWD FY7 ....11 E2
Sharoe Green Hospital
FUL/RIB PR2 ....45 H4
Sherburn School
PRES PR1 ....46 A5
Sherwood Primary School
PRES PR1 ....46 A1
Southlands High School
CHLY/EC PR7 ....92 D5
South Pier
BPOOLS FY4 ....4 A7
South Ribble Industrial Estate
BBR PR5 ....73 H1
South Ribble Museum &
Exhibition Centre
LEYL PR25 ....83 F4
South Ribble Tennis Centre
BBR PR5 ....80 A2
South Shore Hospital
BPOOLS FY4 ....38 C3
South Shore Library
BPOOLS FY4 ....4 C5
Spen Farm Business Park
BPOOLS FY4 ....34 A5
Springfield Industrial Estate
PRES PR1 ....59 G2
Squires Gate Industrial Estate
BPOOLS FY4 ....37 H5
SS Marys & Benedicts RC
Primary School *BBR* PR5 ....74 B5
Staining CE Primary School
BPOOLE FY3 ....30 B5
Stanah Country Park
CLV/TH FY5 ....22 D2
Stanah Primary School
CLV/TH FY5 ....22 B3
Stanley County Infant School
BPOOLE FY3 ....33 H3
Stanley Junior School
BPOOLE FY3 ....33 H3
Stanley Park Athletics Arena
BPOOLE FY3 ....3 K7
Stanley Park Municipal
Golf Course *BPOOLE* FY3 ....3 J5
Stanley Park Sports Arena
BPOOLE FY3 ....3 J7
Starkie Industrial Estate
PRES PR1 ....59 F1
Stonehouse School
LEYL PR25 ....83 E2
Strike Lane Primary School
KIRK/FR/WAR PR4 ....54 B5
Sunnybank Industrial Estate
PLF/KEOS FY6 ....23 H5
Superbowl
BPOOL FY1 ....2 B5
Sycamore Trading Estate
BPOOLS FY4 ....39 F4
Talbot Road Industrial Centre
CROS/BRETH PR26 ....82 C2
Tardygate Trading Estate
BBR PR5 ....79 F1
Taylors Industrial Estate
GAR/LONG PR3 ....15 G1
Thames Primary School
BPOOLS FY4 ....38 B3
Thornton Cleveleys CC
CLV/TH FY5 ....26 D1
Thornton-Cleveleys RUFC
CLV/TH FY5 ....21 G2
The Worlds Business Centre
LSTA FY8 ....65 E2
The Tickled Trout Hotel
BBR PR5 ....61 H2
Tower World
BPOOL FY1 ....2 B5
Towngate Healthcare Clinic
LEYL PR25 ....83 F4